PEOPLE AND PRODUCTS

By examining the interface between consumer behavior and new product development, *People and Products: Consumer Behavior and Product Design* demonstrates the ways in which consumers contribute to product design, enhance product utility, and determine brand identity.

With increased connectedness and advances in technology, consumers and marketers are more closely connected than ever before. Yet consumer behavior texts often overlook the application of the subject to product design, testing, and success. This is the first book to explore this interface in detail, exploring such issues as:

- the attributes and qualities that consumers demand from products and services, and social and cultural forces to be aware of;
- design and form and how they facilitate product usage;
- technological developments and the ways they have changed how consumers interact with products;
- product disposal and sustainability;
- emerging and future trends in consumer behavior and product development and design.

This exciting volume is relevant to anyone interested in marketing, consumer behavior, product development, technology, engineering, design, and brand management.

Allan J. Kimmel is Professor of Marketing at ESCP Europe in Paris, France. He holds MA and PhD degrees in social psychology from Temple University, USA. He has published extensively in the fields of consumer behavior and marketing, including articles in the *Journal of Consumer Psychology*, *Psychology & Marketing*, *Business Horizons*, *Journal of Marketing Communications*, and *European Advances in Consumer Research*.

Kimmel introduces a key strategic alliance for the 21st century: consumer research plus product design. He builds a convincing case for this partnership through a delightful mix of intriguing examples, broad scholarship, and engaging insights.

Russell Belk, *York University Distinguished Research Professor and Kraft Foods Canada Chair in Marketing*

At last, a book that lives up to its promised title, *People and Products: Consumer Behavior and Product Design*, and delivers on it. Today, people drive products, brands and markets more than ever before and it is important that Marketing takes this more seriously. Yet, Marketing can still be, and often is, a "one way" street" guised as a "two way" approach. This book draws upon examples to describe each element of the title and the ways these interact. I also like the personalized, often 1st person narrative. This is a refreshing and educative read of modern-day Marketing.

Philip Kitchen, *Research Professor in Marketing, ESC Rennes School of Business, France*

PEOPLE AND PRODUCTS

Consumer behavior and product design

Allan J. Kimmel

Routledge
Taylor & Francis Group

LONDON AND NEW YORK

First published 2015
by Routledge
2 Park Square, Milton Park, Abingdon, Oxon OX14 4RN

and by Routledge
711 Third Avenue, New York, NY 10017

Routledge is an imprint of the Taylor & Francis Group, an informa business

British Library Cataloging in Publication Data
A catalogue record for this book is available from the British Library

Library of Congress Cataloging in Publication Data
Kimmel, Allan J.
People and products: consumer behavior and product design/Allan J.
Kimmel.—First Edition.
pages cm
Includes bibliographical references and index.
1. Consumer behavior. 2. New products. I. Title.
HF5415.32.K56 2015
658.8'342—dc23
2014034747

ISBN: 978-1-138-81224-6 (hbk)
ISBN: 978-1-138-81225-3 (pbk)
ISBN: 978-1-315-74891-7 (ebk)

Typeset in Bembo Std by
Swales & Willis Ltd, Exeter, Devon, UK

CONTENTS

ILLUSTRATIONS

Figures

Tables

PREFACE

As consumers, we are surrounded by a steadily increasing array of things. In industrialized societies, there seems to be more of everything—products, brands, services, companies, retail settings, websites, and advertising. In a world that is rich in objects, the choices are endless, for better or for worse. I'm not the first to point out that the world was not always like this. In order to avoid the obvious cliché, I won't say that things were a lot tougher back when I was a middle-class child coming of age during the 1950s (a constant refrain of my parents' generation), but I will say that, in retrospect, the marketplace was a lot simpler and less cluttered. Nonetheless, people seemed pretty content with what they had. I don't remember anyone saying, "If only there were more brands," or "Why aren't there more things for me to spend my money on?," or "When is the next version of my telephone going to be launched?" The possibility that color was on the horizon for television, and perhaps even a remote control, was enough to fuel wild speculation about how advancing technology was soon going to make our lives better. In the meantime, we toted our transistor radios to the beach, honed our skills at the hula hoop, practiced writing with our typewriters, and spun our 45 r.p.m. vinyl records on our hi-fidelity record players.

Fast-forwarding to my years as a graduate student during the 1970s, I shake my head in amazement that I was able to complete my Ph.D. dissertation without owning a personal computer, having access to the Internet, or being able to use more sophisticated statistical tools than the rudimentary computer punch cards I had to tote over to the basement of the converted church/computer lab on the Temple University campus for analyses that were available the next day. The only real connection we had in those last years leading up to the digital revolution was a library card. But that is the way things got done for generations of doctorates that preceded me—and, with the exception of my contemporaries, without the punch cards. These sorts of observations help us recognize that people seem to have an uncanny ability to get by with what they have.

Needless to say, things are a lot different today. For the contemporary teen, the Internet has always existed, devices have always been portable, mobile phones have always been pervasive, and technology is always evolving. Consumers in general now must tolerate only a short wait for something new and improved to come along that is tastier, healthier, quicker-acting, stronger, cheaper, or longer-lasting than whatever preceded it. More jaded by the narratives devised by advertisers, people rely on their everyday experience with products, or the advice and recommendations of other consumers, to determine the relevance and utility of the things they buy and use. Experience leads to preferences and expectations and, over time, loyalties form and consumer–product relationships evolve. Products now, more than ever, play a central role in consumers' lives. That said, it seems that people rarely stop to think about their relationships with the things that they cannot do without, how products have altered their lives, what life would be like without the many offerings in the consumer marketplace, why products are designed the way they are, and how simple alterations in design could significantly influence satisfaction with the objects that are acquired and used. For marketers, consumer researchers, product manufacturers, and designers, however, these sorts of considerations provide the grist for their work.

Understanding and managing the complex relationship between consumers and products pose fundamental challenges for professionals who service the contemporary consumer. This book was written in the spirit of those challenges. There are some terrific textbooks on consumer behavior in the academic literature, but what often struck me about their content is how much of the focus is placed on consumers, and how little is discussed about the actual things that people consume and the role of product design in the consumption process. Overall, little attention has been devoted to the dynamic relationship between consumers and the functional and design elements of consumer goods and services. This book is intended to fill that gap through a consideration of product form and function from a consumer perspective, within the context of an evolving marketplace in which the centrality of the product designer is diminishing in the face of consumer participation, content creation, and sharing.

I want to thank Amy Laurens, Commissioning Editor for Marketing Books at Routledge, for her unbridled support for this book and her enthusiasm for what I promised to accomplish in writing it; Editorial Assistant Nicola Cupit, for her diligence in guiding the project to production; Pierre LeJoyeux for serving as a sounding board and sometime counterpoint for some of the ideas explained within; and, as always, my wife, Marie-Ange, for her devotion, inspiration, and patience.

Allan J. Kimmel
Paris, France

1

PEOPLE AND PRODUCTS IN AN EVOLVING MARKETPLACE

By the end of this chapter, you will:

- appreciate the centrality of possessions in everyday life;
- understand the role of product possessions in creating a self-identity;
- gain insight into the nature of materialism, material and virtual possession attachments, and consumer/brand relationships;
- recognize the role of material artifacts from cultural and historical perspectives.

In contemporary times, the buying and having of material goods, along with a growing array of services, have become as central to people's sense of being as family and career. "I shop, therefore I am, and I am what I consume" may well be the defining dictum of modern woman and man. Since the dawn of the Industrial Revolution, commercial selling and buying behavior have represented activities that essentially define successive generations, as fully interwoven within the fabric of industrialized nations as technological, scientific, social, and political developments. Whether it be the clothes we wear, the homes and communities where we reside, the types of pets we own, or the color of the earbud headset through which we privately listen to our preferred musicians as we wend our way through public settings, our consumption choices are inseparable from who we are to ourselves and to others.

Individuals and societies are inevitably shaped—and in some cases, transformed—by the products and services they create and utilize. Consider, for example, mid-twentieth-century scenes of families huddled around radios and televisions, images that are as firmly etched in our collective memories as Norman Rockwell paintings, illustrating how these early forms of broadcast media brought intimacy to the consumption of information and entertainment as unified experience within the family unit. Fast forward to the early years of the current millennium (the so-called "marketing 2.0 era") to recognize how the widespread adoption and use of electronic and mobile devices have rendered "intimacy" to the level of absurdity, as the Internet and its social networking offspring enable countless multitudes to connect through public revelations of personal thoughts and behaviors in 140 characters or less. We now nestle in front of the television in the bosom of our family while plugged into social networks, a phenomenon that has come to be referred to as "connected cocooning."[1] We choose our friends and lovers on the basis of the books they read, the music they listen to, the celebrities they idolize, their preferences in foods and restaurants, and their Facebook "likes." "We just didn't have much in common anymore" could sound the death knell of a relationship on grounds of incompatibility as much in the sense of "He's a Mac, she's a PC" as due to a divergence in lifestyles and values.

Consumers and products: Can there be one without the other?

The expression "iPod, therefore I am" signifies that in the contemporary era people and products have begun to merge, both literally and figuratively, and that it is nearly impossible to think of one without the other. This singularity between people and products suggests both the positive and dark sides of consumption (see Box 1.1).

BOX 1.1 THE SINGULARITY IS NEAR

Renowned inventor and futurist Ray Kurzweil envisions a remarkable future—one in which the rapidly expanding rate of technological change will have profound transformative effects on human life, enabling people to transcend their biological limitations and amplify their intelligence and creativity. This staggering vision reflects what Kurzweil refers to as the "singularity," a shortened version of the term "technological singularity" that originally referred to the arrival of machine superintelligence, beyond which our ability to predict the future breaks down. For Kurzweil, singularity refers to a penultimate evolutionary epoch that will follow the merging of human technology with human intelligence.

Kurzweil's predictions are based on the premise that technological change is exponential rather than linear (a point that we examine in greater detail in subsequent chapters), as progress in any one area feeds upon itself as well as accelerating progress in other fields:

> what would 1,000 scientists, each 1,000 times more intelligent than human scientists today, and each operating 1,000 times faster that contemporary humans (because the information processing in their

primarily nonbiological brains is faster) accomplish? One chronological year would be like a millennium for them . . . an hour would result in a century of progress (in today's terms).[2]

As nonbiological intelligence eventually comes to predominate, the nature of human life will undergo radical alterations in terms of how people learn, play, wage war, and cope with aging and death. As elaborated in his best-selling 2006 book *The Singularity is Near*, the predicted union of human and machine presents both opportunities and threats to the human race:

> In this new world, there will be no clear distinction between human and machine, real reality and virtual reality. We will be able to assume different bodies and take on a range of personae at will. In practical terms, human aging and illness will be reversed; pollution will be stopped; world hunger and poverty will be solved. Nanotechnology will make it possible to create virtually any physical product using inexpensive information processes and will ultimately turn even death into a soluble problem.[3]

The social and philosophical ramifications of these changes would be profound and, according to Kurzweil's detractors, the threats they pose are considerable. Others, however, view Kurzweil's ideas as a radically optimistic view of the future course of human development.

If it is true that we are what we consume, then it is not a stretch to say that consumption is central to what it means to be human. Further insight into what it means to be a consumer can be gleaned through a simple exercise by reflecting on what it is that one typically consumes during a typical day. Part of the answer, of course, is readily apparent through a consideration of the basic sustenance required to live—food, water, air, protection from the elements, and the like. In this sense, people consume to survive by striving to satisfy physiological (or "first-order"), unlearned needs. But we also regularly consume personal hygiene products like soap, toothpaste, hair shampoo, perfume; services such as electricity, heating, Internet service, mass transportation, and phone service; the ink and lead of writing implements we employ; ATM machines; electronic goods and services, including DVDs, online streams, radio and television; clothing; and health care items, such as headache remedies, birth control pills, cough syrup, massages, and the advice of doctors and pharmacists. We also consume various forms of entertainment, be it live (e.g., buskers on the street corner or in the subway; an opera performance or theater play; a football match) or recorded (a new *Star Trek* movie or Yo la Tengo CD).

Our brief exercise would not be complete without a recognition of the wealth of information and ideas we acquire and consume daily from the press, books, classroom lectures, podcasts, the Internet, computer tablet or smartphone, as well as the many intangibles we are apt to absorb only at an unconscious level, such as freedom and democracy, history, spiritual traditions, architecture, and art. As Richard Saul Wurman pointedly observed in his 1989 book *Information Anxiety*, "a weekday edition of *The New York Times* contains more information than the average person was likely to come across in a lifetime in seventeenth-century England,"[4] suggesting the dramatic expansion of information consumption in the contemporary era. These various forms of consumption satisfy needs that are less linked to basic survival than they are to more unlearned, psychological motives. In common parlance in the field of marketing, each of these listed objects of consumption, whether basic or learned, can be considered to be a *product*, defined as "anything that can be offered to a market that might satisfy a want or need"[5]—a definition that I have adopted for this book. This admittedly broad definition encompasses the full gamut of consumables, including physical goods (Panasonic microwave oven; Dyson vacuum cleaner), services (pizza delivery, tax preparation), persons (Beyoncé, David Beckham), places (Disneyland, the Paris Opera, Hawaii), organizations (Greenpeace, Médecins Sans Frontières), and ideas (safe sexual conduct, drinking and driving, religion).

The recognition of the broad array of consumption objects also helps us recognize the breadth of *consumer behavior*. At one time, this term was narrowly conceptualized as roughly synonymous with buying behavior. Marketers focused on the exchange process involving shoppers and retailers, with consumers paying to acquire desirable, needed goods and services typically produced by manufacturers and service providers and offered by third parties in stores or other business settings. As the complexity of consumer decision making took front and center among the concerns of consumer researchers and practitioners,[6] so too did the meaning of consumer behavior, which now encompasses the full range of the consumer decision-making process, beginning with the decision to consume (to spend or save, to have or not to have) and ending with product usage, disposition, and post-purchase reflections (e.g., "Am I satisfied with the purchase?"; "When shall I buy a new one?").

In a broader sense, consumer behavior also concerns processes related to having (or not having) and the ultimate state of being derived from the consumption process.[7] This is to say that a comprehensive understanding of consumer behavior requires a consideration of how the possession and use of consumption objects influences who we are, how we perceive ourselves and others, and how these objects impact the broader social and cultural worlds we inhabit in our various roles as citizens, parents, professionals, and so on. In the remainder of this chapter, I address these considerations with a focus on areas of consumer psychology (micro-level) and culture (macro-level) that are intricately linked to consumers' engagement with products, including a consideration of materialism, self-identity, consumer/brand relationships, and cultural artifacts.

Engagement in the material world: From "consumer" to "prosumer"

"Engagement" is a concept that is redefining contemporary marketing. From the marketer's perspective, the new challenges of greater consumer connectedness via social networking and online communities have harkened the call for marketing strategies that engage potential customers in collaborative relationships with compelling content and force a rethinking of the traditional means by which marketers attempted to communicate with and influence customer targets. The traditional "top-down" marketing paradigm (*business-to-consumer marketing*, or B-to-C) whereby consumers were content to select goods produced, distributed, and promoted by companies and advertisers which decided what customers needed and desired has been turned on its head in an amazingly short span of time. In its place are bottom-up, grass-roots approaches (*consumer-to-consumer marketing*, or C-to-C) that are shaping the business world in ways unimagined only a few decades ago. Consumers are increasingly taking control of the marketplace and are no longer merely passive participants in the wide array of activities that comprise the marketing enterprise. Whether it be the creation or modification of products, the establishment of prices, the availability of goods, or the ways in which company offerings are communicated, consumers have begun to take a more active role in each of the various marketing functions.

These developments have led some to call for a shift in nomenclature that replaces the term "consumer" with "prosumer," the latter of which is believed to better reflect how people have become more proactive and engaged in all facets of the consumption process. The prosuming notion—based on a combination of "producer" and "consumer"—dates back to pre-Internet 1980, when futurist Alvin Toffler envisioned a time when ordinary consumers would themselves become collaborative producers, actively improving or designing marketplace offerings.[8]

In Toffler's prescient vision, the production of goods and services within the marketplace, where people produce for trade or exchange ("Sector B"), would ultimately be displaced or substituted by those produced by ordinary people for themselves or for their families ("Sector A"). As an example, Toffler noted the Bradley GT kit, offered at the time by Bradley Automotive, which enabled customers to design their own luxury sports car using partly preassembled components, including a fiberglass body, Volkswagen chassis, electrical wires, and plug-in seats. The Bradley GT kit anticipated BMW's strategy prior to a new product launch of setting up an interactive website for users to design their own dream roadster. BMW automatically uploaded this information into a database and, based on data the company had already collected from loyal buyers, determined the most potentially profitable designs to put into production. This strategy was a precursor to BMW's Virtual Innovation Agency, an online collaboration between external innovation sources and developers from the BMW Group. BMW receives an average of 800 ideas, concepts, and patents annually from sources ranging from individual consumers to research institutes and other companies. The BMW Group directly puts into practice about 3% of the submissions in product design and service. This and other "crowd-sourcing" projects, such as those implemented by Dell, LEGO, and Starbucks, are discussed in greater detail in Chapter 5.

Just as the meaning of consumer behavior has broadened in recent decades, so too has our conceptualization of what it means to be a consumer. The changing nature of the modern consumer is depicted in Figure 1.1, as conceptualized by David Armano, social media blogger and managing director of Edelman Digital Chicago.[9]

In Armano's depiction, we see that consumers are no longer considered merely as customers or passive recipients of marketing content and offers, but as active and participative contributors to the marketing enterprise who actively create, produce, share, and monitor marketing-related content. As producers, an increasing number of consumers manufacture creative content (such as videos,

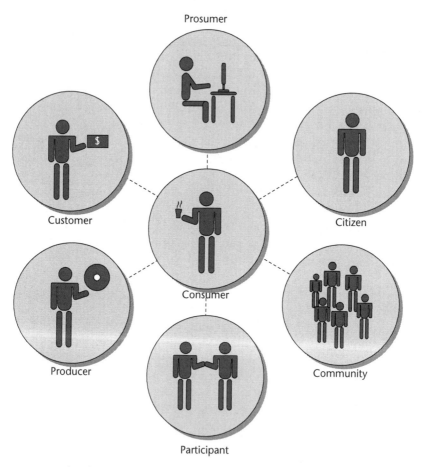

FIGURE 1.1 The changing faces of the twenty-first-century consumer

Source: David Armano.

photos, blogs) and content-creating and publishing tools. As 3-D printing technology evolves and acquires widespread usage (see Chapter 2), consumers will literally become product manufacturers. In an ideal sense, consumers participate in the marketing context as good citizens, pursuing environmentally friendly marketing policies and practices, and monitoring marketing practices involving unsafe or potentially harmful products, advertising to vulnerable groups, aggressive selling techniques, deceptive pricing, and so on. In turn, companies are increasingly pressured to provide efficient and reliable products, and to market them using transparent and socially responsible approaches.

The centrality of worldly possessions in everyday life

If our challenge is to fully understand the dynamics that underlie the relationships between people and products, a good starting point is to consider the central importance of product ownership and usage at the psychological and cultural levels, in terms of the ways products and brands are used by individuals to define and reinforce their own and others' self-identities, assist consumers in connecting with others who share similar preferences, and serve as cultural artifacts that help determine the pattern of life adopted by the members of a society.

How products determine identity

There are many aspects of human psychology that have a bearing on how and why people interact with products—two that stand out are self-identity and materialism. If you have ever lost or had an important possession stolen, you are doubtless aware of the intimate link between products and self-identity. The loss of a treasured possession can be a traumatic, unsettling experience for an individual, sometimes as profound a loss as that of a good friend or beloved pet. An obvious reason for this is that the lost possession may be irreplaceable. But from a psychological perspective, perhaps even more significant is the extent to which a person's self-concept is determined in part by what that person owns; in short, the loss of one or more possessions may be experienced as a partial loss of self, an idea that is elaborated on below in our consideration of the extended self-concept. The intimate relationship between products and the self goes beyond mere ownership—in fact, who we are to ourselves and others is a function of all the various marketing choices we make, be it the stores where we shop; the brands we prefer; or the products we own, use, and recommend to others.

At the heart of the relationship between products and one's personal identity is the self-concept, a psychological construction that can be understood as the sum total of beliefs and attitudes we each have about ourselves. The self-concept is at the heart of people's preoccupation with their self-identity, as implied by the question, "Who am I?," the answer to which is reflected in who one is to oneself and who one is with others. When a shopper opines, "I'd buy that miniskirt, but it's just not me," the comment belies how the self-concept plays a central role in how consumers behave in the marketplace—if not for miniskirts, certainly some other consumer product, whether it is a sports car, motorcycle jacket, a tattoo or nose piercing, or a conservative three-piece suit.

In the social and behavioral sciences, some of the early ideas about the self-concept were articulated by sociologists Charles Horton Cooley, George Herbert Mead, and Erving Goffman.[10] Cooley's "looking-glass self" (or "reflected appraisal") suggests that other people serve as a kind of mirror by which we can determine something about ourselves. Mead expanded this notion by suggesting that we come to know ourselves as a result of imagining what others think of us, and these perceptions are then incorporated into our self-concept. In this way, the appraisals received from others gradually mold the self-concept, especially when the feedback is received from credible, significant others in one's life. Applying the metaphor of a theatrical performance, and true to the Shakespearean assertion that "all the world's a stage," Goffman suggested that in public social contexts, the individual is like an actor, modifying his or her actions, appearance, and demeanor to manage impressions or to satisfy the expectations of his or her "audience." Thus, you may find that you are like a very different person in varying contexts or around certain kinds of people, even so far as using different products, brands, and services around your friends than you use around your family, or when accompanying a date to a fancy restaurant as opposed to going shopping with some close friends.

If it is true that "all the world is a stage," then just as actors strive to be liked and admired by their audiences, so too are people sensitive to the image they communicate to others with whom they interact in their everyday lives. Consider a situation in which a graduate student thinks twice about wearing his torn, but beloved, black leather jacket to a wine and cheese party attended by his professors. This sort of situation illustrates a typical concern about one's public image and the social appropriateness of engaging in specific consumption activities. In short, our self-image is shaped not only by how we currently think about ourselves (the *actual self*) and how we desire to perceive ourselves (the *desired self*), but also in part by our beliefs about how others see us (the *social self*). Thus, we often attempt to engage in behaviors that conform to the image that suits the situation, a personality trait known as "self-monitoring." High self-monitors are like social chameleons, better able than others to modify their behavior to fit the situation. In this light, we see that individual differences can play a significant role in terms of the impact of social forces on consumption and self-related behaviors.

As the foregoing discussion suggests, the self-concept is multidimensional and malleable over time. This implies that people can express their personality through actions that are consistent with their private view of themselves or by behaving in ways that bring them closer to their personal ideal. When actual and ideal self-images conflict, the individual must choose to behave more in accordance with the actual, ideal, or social self, a choice that will depend on various factors, including the public nature (i.e., visibility) of the action, the persons who will observe the behavior, and the importance of the action to one's self-image.[11] For example, returning to our previous example, the grad student may ultimately choose to wear his classical sports jacket instead of his torn leather jacket to the wine and cheese party because, despite his self-perception as something of a rebel, he ideally envisions himself in the future as a successful academic and regards his professors as role models in terms of conduct and appearance.

Product and self-congruence

Consumers' product choices and brand preferences often involve a comparison between self-concept and the perception of the product under consideration. To say that the miniskirt "isn't me" is the shopper's way of revealing that her image of the miniskirt (or a person wearing the miniskirt) does not conform to the way she currently perceives herself (or would like to be). Because consumers are motivated to act in accordance with their self-concept and convey a desired image to others, many consumption activities are based on a mental match between the consumer's self-concept and a product's image, attributes, or typical users of the focal product.[12]

Consumers select products, brands, and services that correspond to their self-image, a matching process that is more likely to occur when the choices under consideration relate to the self-concept, are publicly observable, and have distinct symbolic representations for consumers.[13] This comparison enables one to actively seek products and brands that serve to maintain or enhance one's self-concept, which then serves to reinforce the private self-concept or contribute to one's desired self-concept. It is difficult to say how conscious consumers are of this process—much of the influence of these kinds of psychological processes occurs automatically at an unconscious level (see Box 1.2).

BOX 1.2 BRAND PERSONALITIES "RUB OFF" ON CONSUMERS

Does a man who starts riding a Harley-Davidson begin to think of himself as more macho and rebellious? Does a female consumer feel more glamorous and sexy when she carries around a Victoria's Secret shopping bag? And what about a teen's beliefs about his own athleticism? Do they improve once he begins sporting a pair of Nike athletic shoes? According to contemporary ideas about *brand personality*—a level of subjective brand meaning whereby consumers come to associate various human qualities to brands—a brand's personality can indeed "rub off" on the consumers who use the brand.

In one of a series of experiments to investigate the influence of brand personality on self-perceptions,[14] researchers Ji Kyung Park and Deborah Roedder

(Continued)

(Continued)

John asked female shoppers in a commercial center to carry around either a Victoria's Secret shopping bag or a plain pink shopping bag for an hour during their shopping trip. The participants responded to various self-perception questions both before and after carrying one of the bags. When they rated themselves at the end of the hour on a list of personality traits, including ones associated with the Victoria's Secret brand (good-looking, feminine, and glamorous), it was discovered that shoppers who carried the Victoria's Secret bag perceived themselves as possessing more of the brand's traits than shoppers who carried the plain bag. Similarly, in a second experiment, MBA student participants perceived themselves as more intelligent, more of a leader, and harder-working (personality traits associated with MIT) after using an MIT pen than students using a plain plastic pen, a finding that persisted even after some participants were led to believe they had performed poorly on a math test.

Further scrutiny of the results, however, revealed that brand personality traits were more likely to "rub off" on persons classified as *entity theorists*— individuals who believe that their personal qualities are fixed and incapable of being improved through self-improvement efforts. Not believing there is anything they could do personally to improve their own personalities, they viewed the brands as providing a means to signal their positive qualities. By contrast, *incremental theorists*, people who believe that their personal qualities are more flexible and subject to improvement by personal efforts to better oneself, had greater faith in their own potential to improve their self-qualities and thus turned out to be less beholden to brands to do it for them.

Although the self-concept directs the consumer toward certain products and brands, once acquired, those items then may directly affect the personality structure of the consumer. In research focusing on the extent to which the self-concept is susceptible to situational influence, it was found that brands perceived as having certain personalities can act as situational stimuli that can influence assessments of different aspects of one's self-concept by transferring brand personality traits to consumer personality traits.[15] In the presence of brands that are perceived as sincere, for instance, consumers view themselves as more agreeable; similarly, brands thought of as competent influence consumers' level of sophistication. The impact of brand personality is stronger when the situational context in which the consumer and brand appear is consistent with the key association that the brand evokes, such as when using one's "competent" Sony laptop in the context of an academic conference.[16]

In the movie *Play It Again, Sam*, there is a scene in which the Woody Allen character frantically races around his apartment, placing half-opened intellectual books, a (purchased) track and field medal, and hip vinyl record albums on full display in an effort to impress his soon-to-arrive blind date, while admitting to a friend how the careful placement of objects and the appropriate background music (a cool jazz instrumental or a sophisticated classical opus?) can go a long way in creating a good impression. As written, this scene is right on the mark in terms of its recognition of how people make judgments about others based on their consumption choices—the clothes they wear, grooming habits, the color of the cars they drive, the books they read, and the music they listen to. People are able to make very accurate guesses about an individual's personality traits solely on the basis of having seen photographs of rooms in that person's home.[17] Some persons may define their rebellious and free-spirited self-image by owning a Harley-Davidson motorcycle, others exhibit their conscientious and caring nature by purchasing Body Shop products, and others demonstrate their environmental sensitivities by driving a Toyota Prius. When American consumers were asked for the main reason they purchased the Prius hybrid automobile, the most frequent response was "to make a statement about me," as reflected in one owner's admission, "I really want people to know that I care about the environment."[18]

Eating behavior provides another good example of the link between consumption choices, self-identity, and the creation of social images. Researchers have demonstrated that people form impressions of others based on what they eat (healthy food eaters are perceived as more attractive and more likable than eaters of non-healthy foods) and how much food they consume (overeaters are perceived as less attractive and less likeable than light eaters or dieters).[19] Moreover, these impressions seem to give rise to varying forms of treatment in the consumer marketplace. In one study, normal-weight graduate students were equipped with an "obesity prosthesis"—padded clothing that was designed to make them look fat—prior to their interacting with sales staff at a shopping mall.[20] According to observers who unobtrusively viewed the interactions, the sales clerks treated the "obese" customers more poorly than when the same students had shopped at the same mall a few days earlier without the obesity costume. As rated by the observers, the sales staff acted more unfriendly, did not smile, avoided eye contact, and ended the interactions prematurely when approached by the overweight shoppers. However, it was also observed that style mattered—obese shoppers who were dressed professionally were treated better than those who were casually dressed. A subsequent phase of the research had actual obese consumers complete questionnaires regarding their treatment when dealing with sales staff and the consequences of that treatment. When these consumers perceived that they were being discriminated against because of their weight, they claimed to spend less time and money in the store than they had intended to, and were less inclined to return.

Another interesting consideration related to the congruence between self and product pertains to the reparative nature of products when one's self-concept has been threatened or temporarily cast in doubt. When an important self-view is threatened—such as when a student's poor performance on a course evaluation runs counter to his belief that he is an intelligent person—confidence in that self-view will be shaken, motivating the individual to do something that could bolster the original self-view. One action that a consumer could take in such a situation is to choose products or brands that convey an appropriate personality. In the example, the purchase of a pen rather than a candy bar would be more likely to restore the student's belief in his intelligence. Consistent with this possibility, when investigators introduced subtle manipulations to temporarily shake research participants' faith in their personal self-confidence, this resulted in a propensity for the participants to choose products that bolstered their self-view.[21]

In another of the researchers' studies, they asked subjects to write about health-conscious behaviors using either their dominant or non-dominant hands. Next, some of the participants engaged in an activity that was designed to restore their confidence (writing an essay about the most important value in their lives). When then given a choice between a healthy snack (an apple) and an unhealthy snack (a candy bar), participants whose confidence had been shaken (by not using their dominant hand) but did not have the opportunity to reaffirm it with the essay were more likely to choose the healthy snack and thereby restore their confidence in their health-consciousness. Thus, it appears that just as consumers select products and brands that bring them closer to their ideal self, products and brands also can move consumers further from their undesired self-concept.

The extended self-concept: We are what we have

Take away a teenaged boy's cigarettes or a businessman's Porsche and either loss is likely to leave the male feeling at least somewhat emasculated. That is because the symbolic nature of such products contributes in no small way to these individuals' identities, bolstering their masculinity with self-confidence and enabling them to project an image of tough guy or successful professional. In fact, most of us become so attached to certain products or objects—anything from a favorite coffee mug to an acoustic guitar to one's pet—that when we lose these objects for whatever reason, it is as if we had lost a part of ourselves. Victims of burglaries, for instance, often report feelings not only of having had their privacy invaded, but also of being "violated" or "raped." The destruction of one's possessions via a natural disaster or some other catastrophe typically causes feelings of depression, alienation, and a diminished sense of self from which many people never fully recover. These examples pertain to the *extended self*, the dimension of the self-concept that is modified or created by the possessions one owns and uses.

The extended-self notion was introduced in the marketing literature by consumer behavior researcher Russell Belk, although the idea that possessions can contribute to the identity of the possessor dates back to early American psychologist William James' observation that people are the sum of their possessions:

> a man's Self is the sum total of all that he CAN call his, not only his body and his psychic powers, but his clothes and his house, his wife and children, his ancestors and friends, his reputation and works, his lands, and yacht and

bank-account . . . . If they wax and prosper, he feels triumphant; if they dwindle and die away, he feels cast down.[22]

In his influential 1988 paper "Possessions and the Extended Self," Belk similarly claimed that "we are what we have . . . [which] may be the most basic and powerful fact of consumer behavior."[23] The extended self is not limited to personal possessions (such as consumable and durable goods, home and property, and so on), but also includes one's body parts, personal space, significant others (lovers, children, friends), mementos, pets, and mobile devices. For many consumers, the smartphone has become such an integral element of their everyday lives that it is as if the product has begun to serve as an additional bodily appendage. (Unfortunately, the same can probably be said of the handgun amongst the American populace.) As a mass transit commuter, I have often marveled at the alacrity with which fingers sweep across mini-screens even as my fellow passengers' eyes are diverted elsewhere. As evidence of consumers' growing attachment to the mobile phone, a Pew Research Center study reported that 83% of millennials (i.e., those born after 1980) surveyed admitted to sleeping with their phone, followed by 68% of gen-Xers (born between the mid-1960s to 1980); on average, 57% of respondents from all generations studied made a similar admission.[24] In Ireland, there is a tradition of people being buried with some of their most treasured possessions alongside them in the coffin, and for many, that now includes their mobile phone.

The extended self is a concept that highlights how consumers can create themselves and allow themselves to be created by the products, services, and experiences they consume. Along these lines, it has been observed that for many Americans, the automobile represents an important part of one's extended self, with many owners meticulously cleaning, maintaining, and customizing this prized possession, including affixing bumper stickers to convey to others one's personal philosophy or political stance.[25] Through such actions, consumers can enhance their own self-worth via the personal and financial value of their vehicles, as suggested by writer and comedian Dan Berry's description of the "classic" car:

> A car becomes a classic not merely because of its age. A car earns the esteemed title of "classic" by its uncanny ability to define a generation by capturing people's hearts and compelling them to restore and resurrect these icons—no matter the cost or time involved.[26]

In some Western societies, the automobile has become a profoundly essential consumer product, transforming cities and linking owners to the world outside their homes. For a growing number of consumers, the mobile home represents a vehicle that operates as a "home away from home" when traveling or, more generally, as a response to housing crises.[27] The centrality of the car to the lives of individuals and societies is often a memorable theme in contemporary cinema, from the product's pioneering introduction (*The Magnificent Ambersons*) to James Bond's souped-up, lethal Aston Martin DB5 (*Goldfinger*) and the tough, militaristic Batmobile Tumbler (*Batman Begins*) (see Box 1.3).

BOX 1.3 THE CAR AND *BONNIE AND CLYDE*

In her astute critique of Arthur Penn's 1967 cinematic crime classic *Bonnie and Clyde*, Carolyn Geduld attributed a large part of the enormous appeal of the film to an ambivalent narrative that is built upon dramatic shifts in mood between the humorous aspects of the domestic comedy and the horrific violence of the Western and, at another level, between the clan and society ("the primitive, rurally-based tribe and the urban-centered society which evolved out of it").[28] Linking these diverse themes is the car, which is as much a key character in the film as the gang members (as family or clan) themselves:

> The car . . . is used not only to parody the horse and stagecoach of the Western, but also as the *container* which alienates the clan from society. In fact, it is only when the members of the gang leave the car, or open its door in Bonnie's case, that they are killed. Fundamentally, the car divides society into units of five or six people, and when it is in motion, there is no *verbal* means of communicating with the inhabitants—the cars of the Barrow gang have no radios, for instance. Thus they are far more effectively self-contained than in their motel rooms, where grocery boys can knock on the door. Because society's aim is to breach the small unit, the "law" tends to shoot at the car, at times, in preference to the gang itself, and thus, appropriately, one of the last shots in the film is a study of the bullet holes in the "dead" car.[29]

In her analysis, Geduld also discusses how glass, an important component of the automobile, signifies deeper levels of symbolic meaning in the film:

> In the film, the break-up of the clan is represented by the image of glass shattered. The opening shot of Bonnie's lips seen in a mirror is contrasted by the last shot of the car windows smashed by bullets. Significantly, glass is most often shattered by violence when the "law" confronts the gang—windows are broken, mirrors, windshields, and so forth. . . . Arthur Penn's obsessive shots of glass are also evident in his playful use of sunglasses. The Greek punishment for the breaker of taboos, blindness, is used in the film in the literal blinding of Blanche (who wears dark glasses) and in the figurative blinding of Clyde, who is wearing *shattered* sunglasses when he dies. . . . Blindness becomes the ultimate shattering of the fragile barrier between clan and society, a shattering which virtually means the death of the clan, and which began when their first victim was fatally blinded after being shot through a car window.[30]

Not unlike owners personalizing their cars through various idiosyncratic embellishments, employees often personalize their workspace by displaying possessions that they have brought from home. A study of the offices of 20 employees in a high-technology firm revealed various means by which expressions of the self in the workplace are evidenced by the objects one chooses to put on display.[31] For example, some work tools, such as one's personal laptop, Rolodex, special software, and phones, operate as "prosthetic possessions," which extend the self by expanding one's mental capacities and enhancing one's cognitive performance. Some employees perceive such objects as their "brains," which they "could not live without." Several photographs, posters, and paintings were on prominent display in the offices studied so as to evoke recollections of personal experiences (e.g., a photograph of a Halloween costume party at a former workplace) or to create and maintain a sense of the future (e.g., a poster of a luxurious "dream boat" that one employee aspired to purchase upon retirement). Decisions about which aspects of the self to reveal in the workplace reflect an ongoing negotiation between one's home and work boundaries, and personal possessions enable one to reconcile these competing spheres of identity.

As these examples demonstrate, most products that are associated with the extended self are distinct from the physical self, although there are exceptions, such as hairstyles and hair coloring, cosmetics, and tattoos and piercings. Other ways to alter both the extended self and the physical self include body building, exercise, diet, and plastic surgery. Tattoos, which have experienced a contemporary renaissance and are no longer restricted to enlisted men in the armed forces, criminals, and gang members, serve to convey private and symbolic meanings. A tattoo makes a statement about the wearer, as a person who is nonconforming and rebellious, and also can symbolize group membership, interests, relationships, and values.[32] In the current era, tattoos have proliferated to such an extent that they are more likely to represent a fashion statement, beauty embellishment, or work of art, perhaps totally devoid of any deeper signification than the personal taste of the consumer.

Tattoos, piercings, and other means of extending the self through products and services provide ways for consumers to satisfy their *need for uniqueness*, which refers to the extent to which an individual pursues differentness relative to others. The uniqueness need reflects the extent to which people strive to develop and enhance their personal and social identity through the acquisition, utilization, and disposition of consumer goods.[33] In essence, by surrounding oneself with particular products and brands, consumers are able to differentiate themselves from people who consume other products with (presumably) different meanings. Thus, it is not surprising that marketers have responded by offering customers the possibility of personalizing their purchases. For example, the websites of Nike and Converse offer a customization option to consumers, enabling shoppers to create their preferred pair of athletic shoes according to desired style, colors, and fit. Removable vinyl or silicon "skins" for portable devices like the mobile phone and mp3 player also allow buyers to personalize their product by adding some measure of difference that distinguishes it from others.

The extended self in the virtual world

Since the concept of the extended self was first discussed in the context of marketing, remarkable technological developments have come to pass, particularly in the digital world, and these developments have given rise to vast new possibilities for self-extension. Digital technologies, including the Internet, email, smartphones, social media, online games, virtual worlds, and digital photo sharing, have had dramatic effects on consumer behavior and implications for understanding of the self, the nature of possessions, and relationships with things in a digital world. The emerging dynamic between virtual self-construction online and self-construction in the physical world offline has become a key to defining the self in the digital age. In an update of his work on the extended self, Belk identified several changes with consequences for the digital extended self, one of which is *dematerialization*—the transformation of material objects, such as books, photos, data, greeting cards, and music into virtual ones (or, more precisely, digital ones and zeroes).[34]

As Belk points out, in the digital age, more and more possessions are disappearing before our very eyes. In many dwellings, CD, book, and photo album collections have begun to vanish from shelves as these possessions have migrated to mp3 players, tablet PCs, computers, and phones. In fact, the acquisition, storage, usage, and disposal of such possessions have been altered by new and continually evolving technologies, giving new meaning to what it means to interact with products. In one sense, we see that private ownership acts, such as acquiring and appreciating music or photos, have shifted to social practices, altering self-presentational behaviors in the process. As Belk observed:

> the ability to publish our playlists online can say a great deal more about us than opening the windows and cranking up our stereo . . . and we can judge others' personalities quite well based on the music that they listen to.[35]

Moreover, digital sharing has the capacity to reveal preferences and tastes, enable the building of communities comprised of like-minded individuals, expand involvement in the possessions, and spark additional information gathering via links to videos, reviews, and artist information.

There continues to be much debate as to whether virtual possessions enable the enhancement of the self to the same extent—or are as integral to the extended self—as material possessions in the physical world.[36] Apparently, this may depend on various factors, such as age, income, and culture. Younger individuals who were born into a digital world have been found to be more likely to regard virtual possessions as a part of their self-identity than older persons who spent more of their lifetime accumulating experiences and memories in a non-digital, material world.[37] Nonetheless, there is evidence that virtual possessions share a number of similarities with material goods in terms of consumer behavior, including motivations for their acquisition (e.g., to gain status and prestige, to increase attractiveness in the eyes of others, and to mark group identity) and degree of centrality to the self (e.g., attachment to the goods, reactions to their loss, and rituals that help singularize the goods).[38] The loss of digital possessions, such as one's inventory of possessions accrued in an online game like Second Life or Habbo Hotel, or a computer crash resulting in the loss of a digital music collection, can have devastating effects on consumers, especially when their acquisition was based on extensive amounts of time and effort. The fear of loss itself often results in a series of ritualistic, time-consuming curatorial practices, including backing up, archiving, and storing possessions.

Despite these similarities, it must be acknowledged that virtual possessions often come up short in terms of replicating the psychological and physical rewards proffered by material possessions. For example, because of their intangible nature, digital possessions in the virtual world are not capable of physical display, lack tactile and sensory characteristics, and are less capable of arousing the kinds of nostalgic and emotional associations that characterize beloved material possessions (see Box 1.4). As objects of extension, virtual possessions may be less effective than material possessions, or else may only extend the self within the virtual context, such as among other in-game players or with one's social network friends when they are online. However, within those virtual contexts, the impact of digital possessions can be profound.[39]

BOX 1.4 MATERIAL COLLECTIONS AS PERSONAL CHRONICLES

As a baby boomer born during the early 1950s and an avid music collector over his lifetime, the author has experienced mixed emotions as technologies for storing music have evolved from physical objects (45s, long-playing albums, compact discs) to intangible digital files. Unlike the transistor radio of an earlier era, which pioneered the portability of music outside the home, digital music files enable the customization of one's out-of-home listening experience across various mobile devices to the point of providing a personalized, ad-free soundtrack to one's life. Nonetheless, it was with great regret that I eventually sold my extensive vinyl record collection after years of keeping it in storage after I relocated abroad. Having evolved over several decades, the collection served as a veritable chronicle of my life,

(Continued)

(Continued)

reflecting my changing personal interests, tastes, history, and relationships perhaps more efficiently than had I been maintaining a biographical journal over the years.

As I looked over the albums for a last time prior to selling them to the owner of an independent music shop, I was struck by how many memories, sensations, and meanings they evoked, with specific details stimulated in my mind concerning their acquisition and listening occasions. I recalled past shopping experiences, apartments I had lived in, friends I had spent time with, girls I had dated, and so on, from a simple glance at an album cover, liner notes, and blemishes (such as the doodles my younger sister had inked onto the back cover of the first Beatles album). The trajectory of my musical tastes as the buyer and I flipped through the stacks, ranging across various genres—from folk and blues roots to acid rock to punk to avant-garde jazz to West African juju—revealed much about my personal history and personality, and on more than one occasion I received a knowing nod from the buyer, who intoned, "Of course you would have this one," after observing what had come before. Glancing over the playlists on my mp3 player or laptop, however, reveals a disparate, ever-changing music archive that evokes few if any of the associations and sensations that were derived from the physical counterpart.

Another disappearing material product—the postcard—similarly reveals how some objects in our everyday lives have the ability to serve as chronicles of self-identities, life stories, and relationships. In his *The New York Times* op-ed piece, contributor Joseph Distler rued the impending death of a communication medium that was so deeply linked to memories and emotions.[40] Distler recounted his daughters' shoe box collection of postcards and letters that he had diligently mailed to them during his extensive travels, each postcard carefully chosen to represent his most vivid experiences at the moment and bearing a special stamp of whatever country he happened to be visiting. Distler described the great joy taken later in randomly selecting a card from the collection and reading it out loud with his daughters:

> the cards bring back great memories for me, and inevitably my girls will ask me to tell stories about the trip I took—and I am transported back in time and as excited to talk of those moments as they seem to be listening to them.

Distler rued the fact that this form of communication was disappearing, recounting how a Spanish storekeeper, reflecting on racks of cards that were practically empty, commented that "No one sends postcards anymore. Everyone uses the Internet." Moreover, many post offices have begun to replace esoteric national stamps with generically applied rubber stamp markings:

I wonder, will those children who get e-mail feel the same excitement as mine will when they look back on those messages in years to come? Will they even have saved them? Will the joy of holding in your hand a small piece of your family history be lost? I fear they will be. Even letters that I wrote my girls are carefully put in an old wooden wine box. When we look together at those cards and letters and stamps we feel a great camaraderie, and I know that long after I am gone my kids will have those memories to perhaps pass on to their children and tell them stories of Grandpa and his travels. I certainly hope.

These examples are not meant to suggest that digital possessions within the virtual world are incapable of providing a sense of the past via associations with people and events in our lives. In fact, a wide range of digital devices and technologies now are available to provide access to expanded archives of autobiographical memory cues and factual information, not unlike the prosthetic possessions (e.g., computerized contact lists, calculators, and phones) that operate as technological extensions of the self in the workplace (see above).[41] Hard drives, USB keys, search engines, and cloud computing permit individuals to "outsource" their memory to the digital world and document, annotate, and share details of their lives through the use of digital photography, social media updating, blog archives, electronic calendars, and photo and video uploads.[42]

What your avatar says about you

If in the material world the self-identity question is "Who am I to myself and to others?" in the virtual world the Internet asks "Who are you, and what do you have to share?"[43] In fact, the virtual world offers individuals the opportunity to construct multiple identities and definitions of the self, including ownership of virtual goods and currency, in an environment characterized by anonymity and the lack of face-to-face interactions among participants. As the visual component of the Internet environment has broadened with the proliferation of photo and video sharing sites, virtual worlds, social media, online games, and the like, digital self-representations, or *avatars*, have become common, adding credence to the adage coined by Peter Steiner in his 1993 *New Yorker* cartoon, "On the Internet, nobody knows you're a dog."

According to recent estimates, more than 80% of Internet consumers and Fortune 500 companies have an avatar or presence in an online virtual community, including virtual worlds (e.g., *Second Life*) and social networks (e.g., Facebook). In contemporary usage, the term "avatar" is used to refer to "general graphic representations that are personified by means of computer technology."[44] Depending on the website, an avatar may take the form of a static picture or a dynamic cartoonish character, with facial and body characteristics and style of dress chosen by the real–life user. Internet users typically have some degree of choice as to the selection, modification, and accessorizing of a self-representational avatar, which can be constructed to represent one's ideal or aspirational selves, or as a canvas for experimentation of various alternative selves, as MIT psychoanalyst Shelly Turkle observed in interviews with participants of virtual games: "Online the plain represented themselves as glamorous, the old as young, the young as older. Those of modest means wore elaborate jewelry. In virtual space, the cripple walked without crutches, and the shy improved their chances as seducers."[45]

In the pre-digital era, new identities could be tested by changing one's hair style or color, growing facial hair, changing one's lipstick and eye coloring, buying new clothes or cars, and so on. Part of the great appeal of avatars for consumers in the digital era is derived from the physical invisibility that can be maintained within virtual space, which offers a relatively safe environment for self-experimentation. As suggested by Richard Allan Bartle, one of the creators of the first virtual world, MUD ("Multi-User Dungeon," 1998), avatars now facilitate this process online by "let[ting] you find out who you are by letting you be who you want to be,"[46] without the concomitant risks that would be evident in the physical world, providing a "looking glass" not only for others, but for ourselves. For example, the Ditto designer eyeglasses website invites each visitor to create a 3-D video of his or her face via their computer webcam to virtually try on glasses. In this way, online shoppers can "see" themselves in any pair of the site's growing collection of designer eyewear. Other emerging applications of avatars for product designers and consumers are beginning to emerge from research employing immersive virtual reality technology, which enables a user to feel present in a computer-generated environment through perceptive, cognitive, and functional immersion and interaction (see Box 1.5).

BOX 1.5 EMERGING RESEARCH ON VIRTUAL BODY EXPERIENCE

How would it be to have the body of a child again? Albeit an intriguing question from the layperson's perspective, imagine the implications from the point of view of a manufacturer or designer of children's goods and services. No longer a fascinating pipedream, researchers have begun to search for answers to this and similar body experience-type questions via the use of immersive virtual reality (iVR), which enables a user to feel present in a computer-generated environment.[47] As we choose our self-representations in virtual reality settings, our behaviors might be influenced accordingly. In other words, we don't only exert influence on our avatars—they also exert influence on us.

In an intriguing set of recent studies, Domma Banakou, Raphaela Groten, and Mel Slater from the Experimental Virtual Environments Lab for Neuroscience and Technology in Barcelona investigated the impact of immersion in a virtual child's body on the adult user's perception and behavior.[48] The researchers found that immersive virtual reality can create such a strong illusion of being inside the child's body that perception of the physical sizes of objects and their personal attributes are altered. The investigations were designed in such a way that one group of participants received an avatar of a 4-year-old's body, and a second group a scaled-down adult body that was the same size as the child body. The participants then viewed their virtual bodies from a first-person perspective in which the avatars moved in real time determined by the participants' movements. Both groups claimed to have experienced a sense of "ownership" over their virtual bodies, a phenomenon known as the "body-ownership illusion." As would be the case from a child's perspective, they overestimated the size of objects in the virtual environment, although the "children" participants did so to a greater degree and were far more likely to associate childlike attributes to objects than were the "small adult" participants. However, when the investigators disassociated participants' movements from their avatars, the sense of body ownership and perceptual differences disappeared.

Perhaps it is an exaggeration to say "we can go back again," to experience the world as we once had when we were young, but this type of iVR research has some intriguing implications. Altering bodily self-representation by having an adult "occupy" the body of a child does seem to have the effect of reproducing the experience of the world "as a child experiences it." This outcome has enormous potential for manufacturers and designers of products for children as well as adults. The ability to virtually put oneself in the shoes of potential customers could provide significant insight for the design of a wide range of products and services for various consumer groups. Immersion into the body of a virtual child can offer companies a better understanding of children's experiences and attitudes toward toys, furniture, clothing, and the like. Similarly, using disabled or obese virtual bodies could enhance the design of products and services to better conform to the needs and requirements of those special groups.

Just as people tend to form impressions of others based on their observable traits, so too may people form impressions of others based on the avatars they select or create. Canadian researchers Jean-François Bélisle and H. Onur Bodur wondered whether people choose to create virtual alter-egos that are fundamentally different from themselves, or whether avatars reflect the personality of their creators. Limiting their focus to avatar creation in Second Life, Bélisle and Bodur had avatar creators complete several personality inventories online to assess their personality traits.[49] In turn, perceivers—that is, consumers who were asked to observe avatars—completed questionnaires that assessed their impressions of the creators' perceived personality traits based on the appearance of the avatars. Visual clues as to the personality of the avatar creator were provided by the avatar's physical traits, including hair color and length, body shape, and style and type of clothing. The results revealed that, overall, the perceivers formed accurate personality impressions based on visual avatar cues. For example, attractive avatars with stylish hair and clothes were perceived as extroverted, which conformed to the personality measures obtained from the *Second Life* participants.

The close match between avatar and creator has strategic implications for companies interested in expanding to the virtual environment, in that avatars can assist in identifying the consumers behind their virtual representations. That is, avatars can be used as a proxy for actual consumer personality and lifestyles in a determination of targeting and segmentation strategy. Considering the various concerns about infringements of privacy rights among social network participants, the avatar approach clearly represents a more ethical approach to identifying online participants than other approaches considered to date.

Living in a material world

Whether people choose to admit it or not, and however ironic it may sound, material possessions arguably are fundamental to what it means to be human. Yet it is also true that people vary according to the extent to which material possessions are central to their lives. Some people are hoarders who obsessively acquire more and more worldly goods and find it next to impossible to throw anything away; others are collectors for whom one or more product category provides enduring fascination; and others choose to live austere lives with only the bare minimum when it comes to material possessions. These differences reflect a personality characteristic known as *consumer materialism*, which refers to the degree of importance a person attaches to worldly possessions. In short, although it cannot be denied that we are a shopping species, avidly amassing worldly possessions, it also is the case that consumers are not equally predisposed to acquiring and owning more and more things.

Materialistic consumers are the kinds of people who regard consumer goods as essential to their lives and identities, believing that happiness can be accrued from the possessions they own, whereas non-materialistic individuals tend to place greater value on experiences, with material possessions occupying a secondary role in their lives. The administration of standardized measures of materialism[50] has revealed that adult materialistic consumers seek lifestyles full of possessions; value acquiring and showing off their possessions; are more self-centered and selfish than others (based in part on research indicating an unwillingness to donate their body parts to science after death); are willing to spend large sums of money on publicly visible material goods, such as cars and houses, as opposed to transient experiences, such as eating in expensive restaurants; view possessions as a means of achieving personal happiness; and establish strong bonds with products to ease fears about their own mortality.

The lives of materialists revolve around the consumer goods that they either possess or desire, and they view worldly goods as the route to happiness and success. However, there is evidence that points to the tendency for high-materialistic consumers to derive inherently more pleasure from the state of anticipating and desiring a product than product ownership itself.[51] The expectation that greater happiness can be accrued from the owning of many possessions has not been borne out by research,[52] with evidence demonstrating that materialism is *negatively* related to fun and enjoyment; happiness; satisfaction with personal finances, career accomplishments, and standard of living; and satisfaction with family, friends, and life as a whole. In fact, materialism appears to have a negative effect on well-being, although apparently within limits. In two American studies—one a large-scale survey of adults and the other an experiment with students—materialism was found to result in greater stress and lower well-being when it conflicted with group-oriented values, such as family and religious values.[53] This does not bode well for consumers in developed nations where mixed messages and divergent pressures simultaneously emphasize material values and more collectivistic ones, such as family cohesion and religious fulfillment.

Given the growing participation of children in the consumer marketplace and marketers' heightened attention to them, marketing researcher Marvin Goldberg and his colleagues[54] assessed materialism in American "tweens"—the 27 million 9–14-year-old demographic that influences more than US$170 billion in annual sales of consumer goods. The research revealed that the tweens characterized by the highest levels of materialism behaved markedly different from their lower-scoring peers: they were more susceptible to advertising and most interested in new products; tended to shop more, save less, and have more purchase influence over their parents compared with lower-scoring tweens; were much more positive about their future financial well-being than their less materialistic counterparts; and performed somewhat more poorly in school than non-materialistic tweens. The materialistic tweens were more likely than others to have materialistic parents, which confirms, in part, the expectation that materialism is a value that is transmitted from parent to child.

Parents are not the only influences when it comes to the acquisition of materialistic values. In a study of 13–18-year-old Singapore students, imitation of celebrities and perceived peer influence proved to be the strongest predictors of materialism when compared with other marketing communication factors, such as response to marketing promotions and advertising viewing.[55] The finding that social factors hold greater sway in the acquisition of materialistic values in the children studied may have something to do with the fact that Singapore is a collectivistic country, where the emphasis is placed on family and work group goals above individual needs or desires. This suggests that advertising regulation may be less effective in discouraging materialistic consumption values than efforts to reduce children's desire to imitate media celebrities and their peers—at least in countries with high levels of collectivism.

Despite the strong influence of social factors on materialism, it goes without saying that television and the Internet also play a significant role in shaping the consumption knowledge, attitudes, and behaviors of children. It is through these channels that children are exposed to a constant onslaught of commercial and non-commercial messages about products and brands, along with indicators of cultural values and aspirations. The impact of mass-mediated content was demonstrated in a study that compared heavy (four hours or more per day) versus light (two hours or less per day) viewers of television.[56] Heavy viewers tended to overestimate the number of products and consumer-related activities associated with affluent life-styles, the message being that if you want to be successful in society, you must buy and own a lot of stuff. Other research has shown that greater attention devoted to television programming results in a higher level of materialistic values in viewers.[57]

Evidence also points to age differences in materialism, with materialism showing the greatest increase as children enter their adolescent years. In one study, children just entering adolescence (ages 12–13) exhibited the strongest materialistic tendencies: when asked to construct picture collages that reflected their answer to the question "What makes me happy?," their collages consisted of more material goods (e.g., money, computer games, brands) than non-material choices (e.g., friends, good grades, hobbies) when compared with the collages created by younger children (ages 8–9) and older adolescents (ages 16–18).[58] The researchers reasoned that happiness is an instrumental goal commonly associated with materialism. Materialistic tendencies apparently abate in later adolescence as attention is drawn to achievements (e.g., good grades and getting accepted by a good university) as a means to pursue happiness.

If parents and peers encourage materialism in young consumers by acting as materialistic role models, is it also possible that these influencers can discourage materialism? Apparently so. In one study, teenaged participants who had more supportive and accepting parents and peers in their lives were revealed to be less materialistic than participants with role models who were less supportive and accepting.[59] Thus, it appears that when parents and peers can provide sufficient levels of psychological support during the critical adolescent years, this reduces teenagers' need to embrace material goods as a substitute for boosting their self-worth and developing positive self-perceptions.

In terms of cultural differences, materialism can hardly be considered as a solely Western trait, limited to individualistically oriented cultures and periods of economic upturns. In fact, over the past century, materialism and the consumption of material goods for the sake of pleasure have spread to entire populations beyond the United States and Europe, not unlike the diffusion of a technological innovation. With globalization, the consumption patterns exhibited by more affluent parts of the world have carried over to less affluent regions, as tourism, immigration, and the export of popular culture and global mass media have served to fuel consumer expectations and desires. In 1996, Giiliz Ger and Russell Belk assessed average levels of materialism in 12 countries.[60] Their results, albeit limited to student samples, revealed the highest levels of materialism in Romania, followed in turn by the United States, New Zealand, Ukraine, Germany, and Turkey. These findings suggest that materialism "is neither unique to the West nor directly related to affluence, contrary to what has been assumed in prior treatments of the development of consumer culture."[61]

Material possession attachment and brand relationships

Our discussion of consumer materialism suggests a psychological underpinning that helps explain how and why people interact with their possessions. *Material possession attachment*, as defined by marketing professors Susan Schultz Kleine and Stacey Menzel Baker, refers to "a multi-faceted property of the relationship between a specific individual or group of individuals and a specific, material object that an individual has psychologically appropriated, decommodified, and singularized through person–object interaction."[62] To better understand the meaning of this complex concept, Kleine and Baker identified nine characteristics at the heart of attachment to material possessions:

1. Attachment forms with *specific material objects*, as opposed to product categories or brands, many of which are ordinary objects that have special meaning as a result of one's experience with them.
2. Attachment need only be based on *psychological appropriation*, or a sense that the object is "mine"—it does not have to be legally owned or physically possessed (e.g., regular diners taking possession of "their" table in a favorite restaurant; possessions that have been lost or destroyed).
3. Material possession attachment represents *a type of self-extension*, as discussed above, whereby individuals extend themselves into material objects and incorporate the objects as part of their self-identity.
4. Over time, a material object becomes a *decommodified, singular possession*; that is, attachment to a possession evolves as it comes to acquire symbolic, autobiographical meanings (such as a toy that a child regularly takes to bed).
5. Decommodification and singularity are based on a *personal history between the individual and the object*, the latter of which becomes increasingly difficult to replace or substitute, even with an exact replica (e.g., an athlete's baseball glove; see Box 1.6).
6. Attachment varies in *degree of strength*, with stronger attachment possessions more likely to reflect the self and more difficult to part with than weaker attachment possessions.
7. Attachment is a *multi-faceted* concept in the sense that possession objects are capable of varying in symbolic purposes and attachment to those objects is likely to be associated with various motivations linked to the private and public sides of the self.
8. The *emotional complexity* of attachment stems from the likelihood that possession objects bear personal, deeply emotional meanings, as opposed to merely functional ones.

9. The *dynamic nature* of attachment implies that the meaning of a possession and the intensity of attachment to it evolve over time as the personal history involving the person and the object develops and as the self-concept changes.

BOX 1.6 I LOVE MY BASEBALL GLOVE

For anyone who has played sports at the amateur or professional level or avidly followed a favorite team, it is stating the obvious to point out how certain objects acquire symbolic personal meanings and become irreplaceable. Part of this has to do with superstitions, as when a fan incorporates rituals with certain objects that the fan has associated with lucky outcomes in the hopes of assuring a victory, such as by sitting in a particular chair or only eating certain snacks while viewing a game. Similarly, fans and players alike "put on their rally caps," by turning their sports caps backwards on their heads to root on their team at a critical juncture in a game, and athletes will continue to wear the same unwashed piece of apparel, such as a pair of socks, in the hopes of prolonging a winning streak.

Beyond superstitious behavior, however, athletes' attachment to specific items of sporting equipment represents an excellent illustration of what Kleine and Baker refer to as the decommodification and singularization of material possessions, whereby people construct meanings for objects similar to how they construct meanings for other people as they come to know them over time. Certain possessions acquire their own unique personality—the "intuitive sum total of everything you know and feel about it"[63]—and, as we develop a personal history with them, they become irreplaceable. As a personal example, I can remember the baseball glove I used as a youth with great fondness, despite the many years that have passed since I last owned it, and the various possession rituals I engaged in over the years, such as how I used it, cleaned it, stored it (with thick rubber bands wrapped around it to keep it pliant), repeatedly banged my fist into the leather to create a deeper pocket, compared it with my friends' gloves, and so on. A published interview with former professional baseball player and current announcer for the San Francisco Giants Mike Krukow recounts a similar case of baseball glove attachment:

> Relaxing at home between spring-training assignments, Mike Krukow begins each morning with the essentials: a cup of coffee, the newspaper, Internet access and his baseball glove. As he pounds his fist into the pocket, things become clear in his mind. It could only get better if someone showed up to play catch. "But, Mike, you're a broadcaster," people say. "You haven't thrown a pitch in 24 years."
>
> They don't understand. The glove is Krukow's friend. It's a weathered and trusty companion, the Mizuno glove he used during his 20-win

season in 1986. Take away his car keys, his credit cards, maybe all the shirts from his closet—but do *not* mess with that glove. "It knows my hand," Krukow said. "It's like a member of my family. You can spit into that thing, throw it against the wall, and it always comes back for more. It forgives."

If a cherished glove ever became part of your life, you have a connection with Krukow and countless big-leaguers who play a little kid's game. It's the glove that reveals the innocence. Ask a ballplayer about the opposing team, a controversial incident or even his neighborhood, maybe he backs off a little. Mention the glove and you've gone straight to the heart.[64]

When these properties of material possession attachment are considered together, it does not require much of a leap in thinking to recognize how the attachments we develop with material objects bear certain similarities to the attachments that define the various relationships we maintain with people in our lives, from the superficial acquaintance to a best friend or intimate companion. This is not to suggest that people treat each other as possessions, however much that possibility may characterize some dysfunctional relationships. The point is that in the contemporary era, people develop attachments and lasting relationships with products and brands of the kind that previously was confined to fans of entertainment celebrities and professional athletes.

Despite their similarities, the bonds that people form with brands are not the same as the attachments they form with material possessions.[65] A material possession is something tangible, whereas a brand is more perceptual, reflecting the enduring mental image that describes the way the brand is perceived in the mind of the consumer. The differences between the two types of bonds are most evident with respect to singularity and irreplaceability. Certain attachment possessions, such as a treasured pair of Cartier earrings handed down from one's grandmother, are singularly irreplaceable—although the brand meaning is readily transferable to another pair of Cartier earrings, the personal meanings associated with the heirloom are not. From a marketing perspective, businesses encourage consumers to replace their products, while remaining loyal to their brands. In our example, a woman may appreciate her new replacement Cartier earrings, but nonetheless will probably continue to rue the loss of the original ones, which she cherishes and prefers to have instead.

Brand relationships do share certain similarities with material possession attachments, in that they involve self-extension, vary in strength, are multi-faceted, emotionally complex, dynamic, and may reflect a personal history between the consumer and the brand. Yet, according to some consumer researchers, brand relationships bear a stronger analogy to interpersonal bonds than material possession attachments. Starting with the assumption that consumers form relationships with brands not unlike the relationships they maintain with their human counterparts, consumer researcher Susan Fournier identified 15 types of meaningful human relationships, ranging from the superficial (e.g., arranged marriages, casual friendships) to the intimate (e.g., best friendships, committed partnerships).[66] Based on a small set of in-depth interviews with consumers, she found evidence of consumer relationships with brands that mirrored each human relationship type.

One of Fournier's respondents, Karen, discussed her Reebok running shoes in the following way: "I wear Reebok running shoes. Me and my Reeboks. They are beat up by now. Want to see them? Like a favorite pair of jeans, you know? You go through so much together." These comments reveal a commitment akin to a best friendship—a voluntary union based on reciprocity that endures so long as there is the continued provision of positive rewards. Karen's adoption of brands preferred by her ex-husband when they first married (e.g., Mop & Glo, Palmolive) is characteristic of an arranged marriage—that is, a non-voluntary union that is imposed by the preferences of another person. Accordingly, Karen's relationship with her Reeboks is stronger in that it is based on a higher level of emotional attachment or commitment than her relationship with her ex-husband's preferred brands.

Just as with interpersonal relationships, the dynamic nature of consumer relationships with brands is illustrated by a life cycle, with some bonds evolving over time (such as the casual use of a trial sample of a brand that evolves into a strong and loyal relationship) and others ultimately dissolving, sometimes abruptly (such as when a consumer decides to stop using a brand to which he or she had been loyal for many years after a bad experience). From her interviews, Fournier found evidence that brand relationships often dissolve because of some sort of environmental, partner-oriented, or dyadic/relational stress factor. Environmental stresses can lead to the break-up of a consumer/brand relationship when they are situationally imposed (e.g., a person moves to an area where the brand is not available) or due to the intrusion of alternatives (e.g., a more attractive or superior brand arrives on the scene). Partner-oriented stresses are either personally induced (e.g., a change in the consumer's lifestyle, needs, or values that render the product unacceptable) or managerially induced (e.g., a manufacturer decides to terminate or alter a product line). Finally, dissolution may occur as a result of dyadic/relational stresses when the partner (i.e., the brand) breaks certain unwritten relationship rules, such as a breach of trust, neglect, or a failure to live up to its promises. The following anecdote appeared in the "Metropolitan Diary" section of *The New York Times* (Oct. 2, 2006), a weekly column that publishes personal stories sent in by readers about life in New York City. It exemplifies how a person can quickly relinquish an attachment to a brand that breaches the trust of a loyal customer:

> Dear Diary: I'm so shaken. I had to break up with my coin laundry in Greenpoint, Brooklyn. We've been together five years, and I really thought

there was a trust between us. But when my white towels came out of the washer with rust brown stains, the owner (who has waved at me amiably since 2001) turned cold and suspicious. He wouldn't even give me a free cycle to try bleach. I think I was accused of bringing in stained towels and staging a scene—a suds con. I felt too human, a woman among urban machines. I ended it right there. I can never go back.

When products collide: How consumer goods influence each other

When trying to unravel some of the psychological forces that influence the people and products dynamic, we have to bear in mind that consumers do not acquire and use specific products in a vacuum. Especially in the modern era where multitasking rules (see Chapter 3), there are any number of ways that products influence each other within the same consumer use or shopping context.

Consumers like matching brands

"A friend of my friend is my friend." This commonly acknowledged adage seems to hold for brand relationships as well, at least in contexts in which different products are used jointly. A series of experiments carried out by researchers Ryan Rahinel and Joseph P. Redden revealed that when people consume certain products in tandem—such as nacho chips and salsa sauce—they enjoy the products more if the brands match.[67] So if you were to snack on, say, a bag of Tostitos nacho chips and Old El Paso salsa sauce while watching a televised football game, you probably would not enjoy the snack as much as had the chips and sauce brands matched (such as Tostitos chips and sauce or Old El Paso chips and sauce). Similarly, we might imagine that you would say your burger was tastier had the ketchup and pickles brands matched.

As to why matching brand labels lead to greater enjoyment, the researchers suggest that they encourage consumers to assume that the products were jointly tested and designed to go well together—that is, they were intentionally conceived to be used in tandem from the outset—which may or may not have been the actual case. Thus, although there is no universal answer to brand preference, it does appear that the brand that a consumer prefers most for a particular product depends on the brands of other products that are used at the same time. According to Rahinel and Redden, "A company that offers products that are consumed together will have an advantage over other rival brands that do not offer both individual products, since consumers will want to have matching brands."[68]

The transference of product properties

As a non-meat eater, I find myself sometimes mildly repulsed by having to place the products I have selected to purchase at the same spot on the checkout counter where I had seen the previous customer rest a package of raw liver or pork. Bear in mind that this revulsion occurs even though I am consciously aware that the various items concerned are safely wrapped in packaging. My reaction, which pertains to what marketers call "product contagion," may seem rather idiosyncratic or downright weird, but in fact it appears to be quite common. Contagion effects in consumer contexts demonstrate how perceived "contamination" by products, shoppers, or other forces can negatively affect behavior and attitudes. Consumer research has identified various products, such as feminine hygiene products (e.g., tampons), kitty litter, lard, anti-fungal goods, and gastrointestinal medications that have a certain "icky-ness" factor for consumers, which becomes manifest in the negative experience of disgust. Disgust has been conceptualized as a basic emotion involving a "revulsion at the prospect of (oral) incorporation of an offensive substance."[69] Although not limited to products orally ingested by the consumer, this definition highlights the strong link between certain products that come into contact with the body and feelings of disgust.

A series of experiments conducted by Andrea Morales and Gavin Fitzsimons demonstrated the strong influence of disgust in consumer contexts, revealing how consumers can be influenced by what they perceive as the transference of properties from one product to another. In various conditions, they exposed groups of university students to a shopping cart holding a variety of non-disgusting products (e.g., cookies or notebook paper), along with one product typically construed as disgusting (e.g., feminine napkins). In certain cases, the disgusting and non-disgusting products were arranged in such a way that they were placed near each other, whereas in others, the products actually were touching. The students then were asked to rate how likely they were to try or use the target (non-disgusting) product they had just seen in the cart, and to assess the quality of the target and non-target products (laundry detergent and breakfast cereal). One of the more compelling findings was that when a disgusting product touched a non-disgusting target product, evaluations of the target product and interest in trying or using it were lower than when the disgusting product was merely present but not touching. (Evaluations of other non-disgusting products in the shopping cart were unaffected by the presence of the disgusting product.)

These findings suggest that the product contagion effect does not occur simply as a function of consumers having associated the various products with each other, but rather that they come to believe that disgusting products actually contaminate and decrease the desirability of non-disgusting ones through physical contact. According to Morales and Fitzsimons, this consumer reaction is irrational, because the disgusting products included in their studies were both sterilized and wrapped in a closed and sealed package, and thus incapable of contaminating the target products. The impact of the contamination effect on consumer perceptions was apparent in a follow-up study in which the researchers placed a container of lard so that it was touching a package of rice cakes. This led research participants not only to rate the rice cakes as less appealing, but also as more fattening, as if the fattening characteristics of the lard had somehow been transferred over to the rice cakes. It also appears that the effects of product contamination are not fleeting; rather, their effects on consumer choice appear to persist over time. In one experiment, the student participants were not asked to report their evaluations of the various products until more than one hour had elapsed since they had viewed them in the shopping cart. Despite the delay, the ratings of the non-disgusting product (cookies) were still affected by having had contact with a disgusting one (sanitary napkins). Returning to the personal example at the beginning of this section, my reaction to placing my products at the checkout area where personally undesirable products previously resided suggests that perceived contamination can have an impact on consumers' attitudes even when direct contact is not evident.

To mitigate the possibility that shoppers will be affected by product contagion in the store, retailers can take steps to separate undesirable items from other products on store shelves and to provide grocery carts that have different compartments that allow for the separation of items prior to purchase. Because transparent packaging increases the likelihood of products being subject to contagion effects, manufacturers can instead block visualization through the use of opaque packaging. Similar kinds of approaches can be employed in other situations in which product contagion might impact consumers' reactions toward various products. For example, shoppers apparently are turned off by articles of clothing that they believe have been previously tried on, or simply touched, by other customers.[70] In this context, clothing retailers can discourage shoppers from trying on items in the store in lieu of instituting a more liberal product return policy.

Products and culture: The artifacts of everyday life

Having examined some of the psychological aspects of material possessions from the individual perspective, we now turn our attention to a consideration of products from a broader, societal viewpoint. Material goods have important meanings and functions for cultures and communities, even if those goods are intended for personal consumption. At the outset, however, it is useful to come to grips with the term "culture," which some writers have viewed as one of the most complicated words in any language because of its diverse meanings in different intellectual disciplines and varying uses in everyday speech. Sociologists typically view culture as the defining core of a society—"the essential character of its people that distinguishes it from other societies."[71] In essence, culture is akin to the "personality" of a society, in the sense that it represents the unique pattern of behavior and meaning shared and transmitted by societal members.

Just as human personality is made up of a unique combination of traits, demographic characteristics, lifestyles, and values, culture similarly is comprised of a mixture of elements that together determine its nature, including norms, traditions, rituals, meanings, knowledge, and meaningful symbols. Each of these components determine in part the pattern of life adopted by the members of a society that enables them to interpret, communicate, and interact together in mutually acceptable and understandable ways.[72] Although experts may differ as to the precise composition of the mixture of elements, most would agree that each element plays a critical role in determining the specific nature of the culture and its people.

Physical goods operate as a key ingredient of the cultural mix as *artifacts and material objects*, goods that carry special meaning for a culture's members, usually as a result of the role they play in *customs* (culturally acceptable patterns of basic and routinely occurring behaviors, such as the distribution of labor among family members or ceremonial practices) and *myths* (stories with symbolic elements that illustrate the shared values of a culture; e.g., the myth of Santa Claus reflects the value of materialism and conveys that children who engage in good behaviors are rewarded with gifts).

One of the key functions of material artifacts from a cultural perspective is evident in how they facilitate ritualistic behavior. *Rituals* are sets of interrelated patterns of actual behavior, but with symbolic overtones. Ritualistic behaviors are performed in a fixed sequence and are periodically repeated (e.g., baptisms, wedding ceremonies, gift-giving, father-and-son hunting and fishing trips, tailgating parties prior to sporting events, grooming rituals in preparation for a high school dance). Members of a brand community consisting of ardent fans of the Rolling Stones rock group, the Shidoobees, engage in a ritualistic pattern of behavior when the group goes on tour. They follow the group from city to city, meeting together before each concert in a local pub or bar, and singing along with the group's hits that they play on the jukebox as they ready themselves for the concert. In some cultures, individuals engage in the ritual of purchasing self-gifts to reward themselves for a personal achievement (see below).

Some common examples of material objects evident in the rituals of a culture (*ritualistic artifacts*) are birthday candles, wedding cakes, champagne, Easter eggs, greeting cards, retirement watches, and so on (see Table 1.1). In the early decades of the current millennium we have seen the rapid proliferation of digital artifacts in the form of online content (such as photos, videos, blogs, tags, and social bookmarks), which serve as the basis for online ritualistic behaviors that define the ways people engage with each other and with companies on social networks, community forums, and customer review websites.[73] In a broader sense, these digital artifacts serve as online content repositories that provide digital collective memories for families, communities, and societies—a function not unlike that served by traditional photo albums, journals, and home movies.[74]

Some of the most dynamic components of a culture are linked to changes in technology, as is seen in the example of computer technology having facilitated the spread of credit card use and legitimized the concept of credit in industrial societies.[75] Computer technology and credit cards underlie the dramatic recent growth in direct marketing, which permits marketers to communicate directly with or solicit an immediate response from individually identified customers and prospects. People are paying less and less often with cash these days, not only as a result of the widespread availability of credit cards, but also with emerging electronic applications, such as Square, which allow consumers to accept credit card payments from other

TABLE 1.1 Rituals and associated customs and material artifacts

Rituals	Customs	Material artifacts
Wedding ceremony (Jewish)	Breaking a glass and dancing the hora Veiling of the bride Decorating the newlyweds' car	Wedding cake Bridal gown Wedding rings Yarmulkes (skullcaps)
New Year's celebration (France)	Everyone kisses each other's cheeks at midnight Traditional feast for dinner or lunch Wearing of a cardboard crown by the person whose piece of cake includes a porcelain figure	Champagne Foie gras Galette des rois (traditional cake)
Senior high school prom (US)	Take pictures at home Drive to the dance in a limousine Stay out all night	Formal dress and tuxedo Flowers

Source: Adapted from W. D. Wells & D. Prensky (1996), *Consumer Behavior*. New York: John Wiley.

consumers via their portable devices. Additional options for completing transactions with business and non-business concerns, including e-cash (e.g., Bitcoins) and the "bumping" of portable devices, may forecast a not-too-distant future in which cash ultimately will disappear and become a collector's item, like stamps or rare coins.

Many of the meanings for everyday products are created by the culture in which one lives, and these meanings are transferred to consumers as a result of marketing efforts, such as advertising, that associate consumer goods with symbolic qualities. For example, during the 1980s, Calvin Klein designer jeans ads reinforced the value of "thinness" in some Western societies. The meanings and utilities of certain products also are defined in part by the historical era in which they appear. Even had the technology existed for the creation of bronzing creams and tanning beds—products that are now widely accepted for acquiring a healthy-looking tan—they likely would have failed dismally in an earlier era. In Western cultures during the nineteenth century, when apparel was meant to cover as much of the body as possible, a deep tan was associated with the working class—lower-income individuals who made their living by working outdoors. By the mid-twentieth century, more revealing clothing had begun to gain acceptability for fashion as well as comfort-related purposes; thus, the tanned look became a status symbol associated not with work, but with leisure. Tanning products and spas now proliferate, with a deep, full-body tan signifying health, beauty, and status.

Gift-giving: An example of ritualistic behavior

As a universal ritualistic behavior, gift-giving has clear ties to marketing. Primarily viewed as a form of economic exchange in which something of value is transferred from a giver to a receiver, the exchange may be carried out with or without the expectation of reciprocation. Like all rituals, the act of giving a gift is imbued with symbolic meaning, which often helps to define, reinforce, or evolve relationships. The ritual itself involves a pattern of behavior that includes searching for and selecting the most appropriate and best possible object; removing the price tag so that the object no longer appears merely as a commodity; adding a personal note, which further embellishes the meaning of the gift; deciding on the wrapping; and determining the most efficient and appropriate means of delivering it to the recipient.[76]

Within each culture, there are prescribed occasions and ceremonies for the giving of gifts, such as the celebration of birthdays, marriages, religious occasions (baptisms, bar mitzvahs), funerals, Valentine's Day, retirements, wedding anniversaries, births, Mother's Day, and so on. Gifts also are given as expressions of friendship, for example, when a close friend has achieved an important career goal or is in need of support and solicitude following a difficult period or event, such as a contentious divorce. It also happens that people commonly indulge themselves with self-gifts, which is a reflection of a decidedly self-orientated approach to purchase and consumption behavior. Like gifts given in friendship, self-gifts provide a means of rewarding oneself for personal accomplishments, may serve a therapeutic function during tough periods, or may simply be spurred by holiday situations. The phenomenon of such self-directed purchases has a long history, dating back to Swiss physician Paul Tournier's description of self-gifts as rewards or incentives for personal achievements, "consolation prizes for disappointments or upsets," and as means to celebrate holidays, such as one's birthday or Christmas.[77]

Consumer researchers David Mick and Michelle DeMoss shed considerable light on the self-gift phenomenon in their analysis of self-gift experiences in various contexts. Their research led them to define self-gifts as: "(1) personally symbolic self-communication through (2) special indulgences that tend to be (3) premeditated and (4) highly context bound."[78] Most importantly, authentic self-gifts thrive on the dimension of symbolic self-communication, which can be conceptualized, if only metaphorically, as a form of dialogue between our multiple selves. For example, your ideal self (which may be described in part as well-disciplined) may congratulate your actual self (sometimes lazy) for persevering on an important task, or, by contrast, your ideal self (compassionate) may console your real self (sometimes unlucky) when uncontrolled factors lead to an inability to achieve the task. Self-directed acquisitions provide the symbolic meanings for this self-dialogue to transpire. Mick and DeMoss' studies also revealed that self-gifts are premeditated; that is, they are active and intentional acquisitions, rather than impulsive ones. Finally, they found that self-gifts are highly context bound, which is why it is difficult to consider the giving of a gift to oneself outside the situation in which it took place. According to Mick and DeMoss, "the sociocultural environment is the principal arbitrator of what does and does not count as a potential gift-giving context."[79] Thus, a self-gift would be considered as motivated by a desire to reward oneself in the context of a personal accomplishment, to cheer up oneself during a holiday, to celebrate when one has earned some extra money, to console oneself after experiencing a personal defeat, and to relieve stress after suffering a particularly strenuous period at work.

It also appears that self-gifts may function as a form of compensation after buying gifts for others that threaten our own self-identity. Consumer researchers Morgan Ward and Susan Broniarczyk were curious as to what happens when we buy a gift for a close friend that is not necessarily the kind of gift we would want to receive ourselves, such as when a vegetarian buys a steak restaurant gift certificate for a friend.[80] In one of their studies intended to shed light on this question, the researchers set up a situation in which university students were asked to imagine giving a gift to a close friend that either had the emblem of their own school or a rival local school prominently emblazoned on the item. Participants giving the gift associated with the rival school exhibited obvious physical signs of discomfort during the study, and when offered either an expensive silver pen or a cheap plastic pen—the latter bearing their school's logo—as a gift for participating in the study, they were more likely to choose the cheaper plastic pen as a means of reaffirming their identities. The other participants who had not had their identities threatened during the study were more likely to choose the expensive gift.

Marketers often exploit the tendency for consumers' self-gift propensities in their advertising appeals and brand slogans. L'Oréal's slogan "Because I'm worth it" reminds the consumer that she merits L'Oréal products, McDonald's once informed customers of fast-food restaurants that "You deserve a break today," and Macy's department store included the tagline "to: me, from: me" in print ads for its "this one's for me" sales.

Products and collective identity

The case of gift-giving illustrates how material objects and artifacts can be seen as serving as agents that help shape individual self-identity (a focus on "me"; gifts as confirming or extending one's self-identity) and collective identity, or *communitas* (a shared sense of "we"; gift-giving as a ritualistic behavior that binds members of a community).[81] The role that material goods play in shaping collective identity is an important one because it demonstrates how possessions are associated with larger group meanings, providing self-continuity and self-definitional value to consumer groups, as explained by marketing professors Stacey Baker and Paul Hill:

> Through a sociocultural lens, we have come to understand that collective identity is negotiated through communication/interaction around symbolic consumption objects and activities. . . . For instance, we know that identity of a family may be linked to mundane or shared possessions, such as a table or home ..., and that these possessions are linked to larger

group meanings, as when Mormon pioneers used possessions to negotiate group identity and its continuity . . . . This sociocultural perspective helps us understand what personal consumption objects mean to collective identity and a sense of "we."[82]

Based on their analysis of material objects in the context of natural disaster recovery within a rural American town devastated by a tornado, Baker and Hill identified how object meanings within a community vary as objects move from the private to public realm (when goods are damaged), and from a situation of scarcity to abundance (when goods are donated). Consistent with the recognition that "groups find ways to protect and propagate what is valued and central for their survival," there was evidence that material goods served as agents of individualism and communitas. For example, in the immediate aftermath of the disaster, which led to the scattering of private possessions across the material landscape, people within the community came together for comfort and inspiration, sharing the scarce resources that were available. The tendency for private consumption items to transcend the individual by shifting within the domain of community life was evident in the following remarks from one of the victims:

> Their [mobile home] trailers were totally wiped out, and their possessions were everywhere . . . . Your entire life was on display, on pubic display . . . like pictures, these were private things . . . . People [were saying], "I had no idea how much a tornado exposed your entire life to the world." . . . There's nobody that I know of that was able, unless they moved in after the tornado, there's nobody that didn't see something . . . . Everyone had garbage that they had to clean up, and, you know, so we were all involved.

Later, once donations were disbursed through food banks, church services, and other charitable organizations, material resources became abundant; as a result, material goods began to move into the private sphere and people demonstrated a desire to make their own choices regarding the objects that would facilitate the reconstruction of their self-identities:

> Like I said, the people, the companies were so gracious up here that, we got about half a million dollars into this community out of people's pockets. . . . And I have no idea how many truckloads of furniture and clothing and VCRs and TVs and, I mean it was just unreal. I mean, you had about, you could go up there and if they didn't have what you wanted, you could wait a couple days.

The function of material goods in the context of natural disaster recovery is an interesting one given that the question "What to take when you only have minutes to decide?" when suddenly having to evacuate one's home during a cataclysmic

personal disaster—a house fire, a flood, and the like—has likely entered everyone's mind at one time or another. There is probably no other question that more
effectively reveals our most treasured possessions and the objects that are most
important to who we are and our personal history.

Revisiting history through objects

At the time of this writing, tracing history through objects had become a popular topic in contemporary culture, as exemplified by director of the British
Museum Neil McGregor's best-selling 2012 tome *A History of the World in 100
Objects* and the New York Historical Society's 2013 exhibition "The Civil War
in 50 Objects" (see Box 1.7). McGregor's book represents an ambitious effort to
explore past civilizations through the objects that defined them, ranging from
the stone chopping tool (1.8–2 million years old) and handaxe (1.2–1.4 million
years old) discovered at Tanzania's Olduvai gorge to the credit card in the United
Arab Emirates (2009) and the solar-powered lamp and charger in China (2010).
The book and its goal of using objects to recount the story of human history
recall a short-lived American TV game show, *The Object Is*, which challenged
contestants to identify the names of famous personalities, real or fictional, from
"object" clues.[83] If provided with the clue of a kite, for example, the person most
associated with that object might be Benjamin Franklin. If the clue was an apple,
the person could be Sir Isaac Newton or William Tell; however, if the second
clue was an arrow, the more obvious solution would be William Tell.

BOX 1.7 NEW YORK CITY IN 50 OBJECTS

Inspired by *A History of the World in 100 Objects*, and timed to coincide with
the New York Historical Society's Civil War exhibition (see text), *The New York
Times* correspondent Sam Roberts developed a list, "A History of New York
in 50 Objects," and then invited readers to contribute their own suggestions
as to the objects that they believed best represented New York City. There
was no shortage of replies, with more than 600 responses submitted to the
newspaper's website, suggesting not only New Yorkers' passion for their city,
but also the ease with which people can associate objects with places and
historical eras.

Roberts' original list was intended to include objects that not only evoked
New York, but which also told the city's story, such as a lottery wheel used to
draft citizens to fight in the Civil War, a crack vial from the 1980s to signify the
city's drug problems, and dust from September 11, 2001 to recall the terrorist
attacks on the World Trade Center. Another item that made Roberts' list was
the humble bagel from the early 1900s:

(Continued)

(Continued)

No other food is so associated with New York as the "Jewish English muffin," which spread from the Lower East Side in the early 20th century. "Pizza belongs to America now," Josh Ozersky, a food writer, said, "but the bagel was always the undisputed property of New York."[84]

Following on the heels of the bagel, food items represented the most frequently submitted objects received from readers, including pizza slices, egg creams (made with Fox's U-bet chocolate syrup), pastrami sandwiches, cheesecake from Junior's and Lindy's, Ebinger's Blackout Cake, Mello-Rolls and other ice cream treats, a pickle barrel, and hot dogs from Nathan's. Other offerings included a *Playbill* to represent New York's burgeoning theater district, a Stork Club ashtray, a bright red apple (to represent the city's nickname, "The Big Apple"), a brass doorknob (late 1800s), a 1976 *New Yorker* cover, wooden water tanks (late 1800s onward), one-time local politician Bella Abzug's hat, and the original city subway token.

Some of the suggestions received by readers revealed a rather liberal definition of "objects," with places (Grand Central Terminal, Kennedy Airport, Central Park), structures (the Statue of Liberty, the Empire State Building, the stainless steel Unisphere from the 1964 World's Fair), and people (former mayor Edward Koch) amply represented.

The New York Historical Society's Civil War exhibition included among its telling objects of that bloody period in American history slave shackles intended for children, a Confederate palmetto flag, a soldier's footlocker with belongings, a photography album, and artwork (e.g., a sculpture of Abraham Lincoln's hand).

Such material objects literally objectify the harsh realities of periods of history we likely would rather forget, but cannot. Whether or not they effectively define violent conflict is, of course, a subject open for debate, although it is hard to deny that things like a child slave's iron shackles exist as something more fundamental than tangible evidence keeping alive the memory of pivotal periods in human history—they also are revelatory of social, political, and cultural forces at play during the era, considered by some as justifications for wars in which they may have played a small part.

Perhaps it is not surprising that discussions of photographs figure so prominently in historians' works about war; as surviving artifacts themselves, photographs capture and preserve fleeting moments in history, but in many cases also provided some solace to the soldiers fighting the battles. A single snapshot can tell several stories, as evidenced by this description from Drew Gilpin Faust's vivid, heart-wrenching account of human loss suffered during the Civil War, *This Republic of Suffering: Death and the American Civil War:*

Descriptions of battle's aftermath often remark on the photographs found alongside soldiers' corpses. Just as this new technology was capable of bringing scenes from battlefield to home front, as in Brady's exhibition of Antietam dead in New York, more often the reverse occurred. A dead Yankee soldier at Gettysburg was found with an ambrotype of three children "tightly clasped in his hands." The ultimately successful effort to identify him created a sensation, with magazine and newspaper articles, poems, and songs celebrating the devoted father, who perished with his eyes and heart focused on eight-year-old Franklin, six-year-old Alice, and four-year-old Frederick.[85]

Faust also pointed out that as a new technology at the time, photographs provided a means by which the Civil War became "real" to those not fighting it:

> For the first time civilians directly confronted the reality of battlefield death rendered by the new art of photography. They found themselves transfixed by the paradoxically lifelike renderings of Antietam that Mathew Brady exhibited in his studio on Broadway. If Brady "has not brought bodies and lain them in our dooryards and along the streets, he has something very like it," wrote the *New York Times*.

Vietnam War veteran and author Tim O'Brien vividly recounted the story of war in his book *The Things They Carried* by focusing first and foremost on the objects coveted and carried (or "humped") by soldiers in the field; again, photographs were commonly noted:

> Almost everyone humped photographs. In his wallet, Lieutenant Cross carried two photographs of Martha. The first was a Kodacolor snapshot signed Love, though he knew better. . . . The second photograph had been clipped from the 1968 Mount Sebastian yearbook. It was an action shot—women's volleyball—and Martha was bent horizontal to the floor, reaching, the palms of her hands in sharp focus . . . . Whenever he looked at the photographs, he thought of new things he should've done.

Of course, most of the objects carried by soldiers consists of weapons and military gear, but O'Brien's chronicle also revealed some of the more mundane things that were taken to battle:

> What they carried was partly a function of rank, partly of field specialty. As a medic, Rat Kiley carried a canvas satchel filled with morphine and plasma and malaria tablets and surgical tape and comic books and all the things a medic must carry, including M&Ms for especially bad wounds. . . . Lee Strunk carried a slingshot; a weapon of last resort, he called it. . . . Kiowa carried his grandfather's feathered hatchet. . . . They carried all they could bear, and then some, including a silent awe for the terrible power of the

things they carried. . . . The things they carried were determined to some extent by superstition. Lieutenant Cross carried his good-luck pebble. Dave Jensen carried a rabbit's foot. Norman Bowker, otherwise a very gentle person, carried a thumb that had been presented to him as a gift . . . . [86]

The function of photographs as objects that recount human history and reveal cultural trends and concerns may be diminishing, as new technologies have begun to transform how and why people take photographs in the contemporary era. Apps for smartphones now encourage users to send real-time, temporary photos as a means of communicating where they are and what activity they are engaging in. At the time of this writing, this trend was exemplified by Snapchat, an app that allows a person to take a photo, send the image to a designated recipient, and control how long it is visible by the person who receives it, up to 10 seconds. After that, the picture disappears and cannot be seen again. This type of visual conversing is rapidly gaining popularity. Over 300 million images are shared daily on Facebook (equating to 100 billion photos per year), and WhatsApp (a messaging platform where people can share photos, videos, or audio notes), Vine (Twitter's 60-second video-sharing app), Flickr, and Instagram represent other thriving photo sharing options for consumers. The upshot, according to Harvard photography professor Robin Kelsey, is that "this is a watershed time where we are moving away from photography as a way of recording and storing a past moment" and are instead "turning photography into a communication medium."[87]

Time capsules: A civilization's gifts to the future

Perhaps nothing epitomizes the goods or information of a particular period better than a time capsule, a container specifically designated to do so. Narrowly defined as "deliberately sealed deposits of cultural relics and recorded knowledge that are intended for retrieval at a given future target date," time capsules are a more than 5,000-year-old cultural tradition, with origins identified in ancient Mesopotamian and Egyptian foundation deposits.[88] According to time capsule historian William E. Jarvis, early variations on time capsules consisted of deliberately indefinite deposits, with no fixed future date for opening, and were rooted in primal activities such as building project dedications or commemoration ceremonies. The modern target-dated variations, which are deliberately deposited for retrieval on specified dates, emerged during the second half of the nineteenth century as a means to communicate with future generations of archaeologists, anthropologists, and historians.

The first usage of the term "time capsules" has been traced back to G. Edward Pendray, who coined it during the 1938 New York World's Fair in connection with the ceremonial burial of the Westinghouse Time Capsule of Cupaloy (so named because of the copper, chromium, and silver alloy that made up the bullet-shaped sealed container), which was renamed "Time Capsule I" in 1964. However, the first modern time capsule is likely the "Century Safe" collection of artifacts curated by Mrs. Charles Diehm, which was officially sealed and buried in Philadelphia in

1879. In the contemporary era, time capsules have accompanied interstellar probes launched into deep space, such as the 1977 *Voyager 1* interplanetary mission.

As significant attempts to transfer cultural information into the future, time capsules tend to share certain characteristics, including deliberately chosen contents; an assemblage emphasizing long-term preservation; an intentional deposit with a predetermined retrieval or target date (usually fixed at a period between 100 and 10,000 years); and an association with earth-bound ceremonial events (with space launches representing a notable exception). From a present-day perspective, the contents of time capsules are unremarkable because they are intended to contain commonplace items indicative of the contemporary zeitgeist; in the future, however, it is assumed that the content will be deciphered as transparently meaningful artifacts and signs for understanding a vanished civilization. For example, the Cupaloy capsule, which was intended for retrieval 5,000 years after burial, included a number of everyday articles of common use (such as a woman's hat, fountain pens, a slide rule, and a set of alphabet blocks); representative textiles and materials; and a microfilm comprised of contemporary art, literature, and news events. As Jarvis points out, the contents of time capsules are in part revelatory of their depositors' vicarious anticipation of the target date's futurescape, given that they were selected with an eye to what would be informative to future generations and how their meanings might be understood:

> We seal these time capsules not so much to ward off ancient demons or fears. We do so to deliver a small measure of our lives to posterity, whether that is thought to be an imaginary time of shining peace and progress, or to an age as imperfect, confused and potentially lethal as our own. Still, we seal away some of the same things that the ancients did when they dedicated their major building complexes with cornerstones, images, special messages, coins and seeds. We sacrifice a little from our times in order to protect our cultural memory for the future.

In his final appraisal, based on a historical survey of 5,000 years' worth of time capsule experiences, Jarvis concludes that time capsules are capable of revealing a great deal about the civilization not only to future generations, but to the present one as well. Yet he also acknowledges the trivial, sideshow aspects of time capsule ceremonies as "historical carnivals of relics, oddities and mementos," an observation not lost in Robert N. Matuozzi's rather unceremonious description: "Time capsules are part of the ephemeral drollery of contemporary popular culture, here today, gone tomorrow, often reemerging after being lost, their collections of soggy and moldering remnants revealed, in the end, to be heaps of junk."[89]

Souvenirs (and mementos): Objects as memories

As a final example of the cultural aspects of material artifacts, we next turn our attention to souvenirs. *Souvenir* is the French term for memory and, in that sense, a souvenir may be thought of as a memory object—that is, an object acquired by an individual in large part because of the memories associated with it. In English, the term is roughly synonymous with memento, keepsake, memorabilia, and token of remembrance. Souvenirs typically are associated with tourism or other special experiences and represent a means not only to remember those experiences, but also to authenticate life events and to convey stories about them to others. The souvenir trade is a major source of income for a country's tourism industry, with estimates of nearly US$20 billion in souvenir store sales in the U.S. alone in recent years.[90]

In addition to serving as tangible symbols signifying travel experiences, in a broader sense souvenirs represent the identity and image of a culture's history, heritage, and geography.[91] Moreover, a souvenir can serve as a proud representation of one's cultural identity when one expatriates to another country, something that is evident among multinational cab drivers in cities like New York, where the cab's dashboard is likely to display items representative of the driver's cultural heritage.[92]

According to one traditional typology,[93] souvenirs can be classified into five distinct categories:

1. pictorial images (e.g., postcards, snapshots, books, and so on);
2. pieces-of-the-rock (i.e., things gathered or saved from the natural environment or taken from a built environment);
3. cultural icons (or "symbolic shorthand"; e.g., manufactured objects that are replicas or representations of the culture, such as a miniature Eiffel Tower or sombrero);
4. markers (i.e., souvenirs that in themselves have no reference to a particular place or event, but are inscribed with words that locate them in place and time, such as a generic T-shirt bearing the phrase "I ♥ New York");
5. local products (e.g., indigenous foods, food paraphernalia, liquor, local clothing, and local crafts).

In the broadest sense, souvenirs can be thought of as artifacts linked to any experience that the consumer hopes to authenticate and preserve in memory. The author can recall a friend who saved the ticket stubs for every visit she made to the cinema during a particular year, which she then attached to her refrigerator door. The stubs provided a way for her to recall the films she had seen, and effectively sparked one or more stories not only about the film attended, but also the experiences linked to the activity (including details about the cinema showing the film, the friends who accompanied her, the meal eaten before or after, and so on). A program or playbill is another type of souvenir that attests to the sporting event, concert, or theater play at which it was acquired. The value of souvenirs and the personal meanings with which they are associated can be enhanced by the souvenir recipient and, in the process, may elevate the souvenir to the status of collector's item, as when a baseball caught by a spectator is later autographed by the player who hit it into the stands.

According to environmental studies professor Beverly Gordon, items like the ticket stubs and baseball can be distinguished from traditional souvenirs and are more properly referred to as "mementos," which are individually saved or found objects that hold a deep personal meaning for the person who possesses them.[94] Souvenirs, by contrast, are commercially produced, universally recognized, and typically purchased objects that are of interest to product designers.

Based on interviews pertaining to memorable travel experiences, consumer researchers Lisa Love and Peter Sheldon found a relationship between degree of travel experience and the types of meanings travelers assigned to souvenirs. Experienced travelers were more likely to assign meanings to souvenirs through hedonic representation, focusing more abstractly on the relationships, events, or people associated with their travel experiences, whereas more naive travelers tended to assign meanings that served as representations of the travel destinations. One of the heavily traveled interviewees recounted details concerning a bouquet of paper flowers purchased at an open-air market during one of her many trips to Mexico by focusing on aesthetics and the impact on her senses stimulated by the travel experience, rather than by providing specific details about the paper flowers or Mexico:

> This was a typical Mexican market. Some of them can be very dirty, but there are certainly an assortment of sights and sounds and smells . . . . I immediately liked those paper flowers because they are so brightly colored, so I have several of them. . . . I just pick up what appeals to me, especially the colors, not necessarily what I do with the flowers, or how I display them.

Comments by a less experienced traveler demonstrate how the meanings assigned to souvenirs bought during his honeymoon emphasize the close association of the souvenirs with the destination context:

> When we went to Europe, we went to Abergavenny in Wales which is the used book capital of the world and we did buy a lot of books there. . . . There were sheep everywhere. We bought a wool blanket. We wanted woolen sweaters, "life-time" sweaters my wife calls them, but the wool from Welsh sheep aren't [sic] very good, especially for sweaters, and when they make sweaters, they're just plain ugly. So the blanket was the obvious choice.

Love and Sheldon's findings also revealed that the less experienced travelers were more likely to seek conspicuous authenticity in their souvenirs. For both types of travelers, the meanings assigned to souvenirs proved to be fluid, changing over time with respect to the experiences with which the object is linked.

Perhaps the most interesting aspect of a souvenir as memory object is how it concretizes or makes tangible an otherwise intangible experience; that is, although it is not possible to physically possess an experience—whether it be a trip to an exotic locale or a dinner at a Michelin-starred restaurant—it *is* possible nonetheless to take away some tangible signifier of the experience (e.g., a miniature Statue of Liberty or a pack of matches bearing the restaurant's inscription). As Gordon explained: "As an actual object, [the souvenir's] . . . physical presence helps locate, define, and freeze in time a fleeting, transitory experience, and brings back into ordinary experience something of the quality of an extraordinary experience."[95]

This aspect of souvenirs was elaborated further by Baker, Kleine, and Bowen:

> the function of a souvenir is to capture the essence of this extraordinary experience and bring sacred qualities of the tourist place back to the tourist's home. . . . Like the Star Trek transporter, the souvenir mentally beams the tourist from one location to another; it helps the tourist cross the boundary from the extraordinary back to the ordinary and vice versa. It is the re-entry fee into everyday life.[96]

From a marketing perspective, the concretization of intangibles is something of great significance to service providers like banks, hotels, restaurants, travel agencies, and hospitals, particularly in terms of satisfying marketing communication objectives. In this case, marketers are apt to turn to one or more variations of *identity marketing*, which involves the use of tangible promotional products bearing the company name and logo to create a visual identity and raise the awareness of the company and its intangible offerings. One common approach involves the distribution of branded merchandise, whereby the visual identity may be carried by the company's logos, stationery, brochures, business cards, and dress codes, as well as anything else that can be made available to consumers, such as coffee mugs, T-shirts, caps, pens and pencils, and wall calendars.

Conclusion

As examples of the material, physical "things" of everyday life, products offer functional and psychological value for their owners and users, and determine and convey much about the way of life within a cultural context. In line with the dramatic technological changes that we have witnessed in recent years, a case can be made that products have become more central to the way we live our lives than ever before—increasing comfort, convenience, access to information, and so on. At the same time, these developments have given rise to concerns about their potential adverse impacts on human psychology and interpersonal relationships. To wit, consumers are finding it increasingly difficult to do without. A reflection of this is seen in California, for example, where Digital Detox, a group dedicated to weaning technology-addicted people off their dependence on portable devices and social media, established Camp Grounded, an adults-only summer camp where people learn how to "disconnect to reconnect."[97] At Camp Grounded, phones, computers, tablets, and watches are prohibited.

Technological changes bring obvious changes not only in the nature of products, but also in how products are used, the impact that they have on our way of life, and the sorts of benefits that people seek or demand from them. Thus, our examination of the people and products dynamic will continue in Chapter 2 with a focus on technology and its impact on new product innovation, consumer behavior, and the consuming environment.

Further reading

Russell Belk's writings on the extended self, published in the *Journal of Consumer Research*, provide a fascinating, in-depth panorama of how consumer personalities and self-concepts are shaped, in part, by the products they used in both the physical and virtual worlds.

The signifying characteristics of material goods and artifacts within cultural and historical contexts are poignantly exemplified in the award-winning books about war, Tim O'Brien's *The Things They Carried* (Mariner Books, 2009) and Drew Gilpin Faust's *This Republic of Suffering: Death and the American Civil War* (Vintage, 2009).

The impact of technological change on human behavior and well-being is covered in the best-selling works by futurist and inventor Ray Kurzweil, including *The Age of Spiritual Machines* (Penguin, 2000) and *The Singularity is Near* (Penguin, 2006).

Notes

1 Reynolds, S. (2011). *Retromania: Pop culture's addiction to its past*. London: Faber and Faber.
2 Kurzweil, R. (2006). *The singularity is near*. New York: Penguin. pp. 24–25
3 Kurzweil, R. (2006), front flap.
4 Wurman, R. S. (1989). *Information Anxiety*. New York: Doubleday, p. 32.
5 Kotler, P. (2003). *Marketing management*, 11th ed. Upper Saddle River, NJ: Prentice Hall.
6 Kimmel, A. J. (2012). *Psychological foundations of marketing*. Hove, East Sussex, UK: Routledge.
7 Solomon, M. R., Bamossy, G., & Askegaard, S. (1999). *Consumer behavior: A European perspective*. Upper Saddle River, NJ: Prentice Hall.
8 Toffler, A. (1980). *The third wave*. New York: Bantam Books.
9 Armano, D. (2006). The many faces and interpretations of the consumer. Available: http://darmano.typepad.com/. Reproduced in Jaffe, J. (2007). *Join the conversation*. Hoboken, NJ: John Wiley & Sons, p. 45.
10 Cooley, C. H. (1964 [1902]). *Human nature and the social order*. New York: Schocken Books. Goffman, E. (1959). *The presentation of self in everyday life*. Garden City, NY: Doubleday. Mead, G. H. (1934). *Mind, self, and society*. Chicago: University of Chicago Press.
11 Wells, W. D. & Prensky, D. (1996). *Consumer behavior*. New York: John Wiley.

12 Belk, R. W. (1988). Possessions and the extended self. *Journal of Consumer Research, 15,* 139–168. Dolich, I. (1969). Congruence relationships between self-images and product brands. *Journal of Marketing Research, 6,* 80–84.

13 Onkvist, S. & Shaw, J. (1987). Self-concept and image congruence: Some research and managerial implications. *Journal of Consumer Marketing, 4,* 13–24. Sirgy, M. J. & Danes, J. E. (1982). Self-image/product-image congruence models: Testing selected models. In A. Mitchell (Ed.), *Advances in consumer research,* Vol. 9 (pp. 556–561). Ann Arbor, MI: Association for Consumer Research.

14 Fennis, B. M., Pruyn, A., & Maasland, M. (2005). Revisiting the malleable self: Brand effects on consumer self-perceptions of personality traits. *Advances in Consumer Research, 32,* 371–377.

15 Park, J. K. & John, D. R. (2010). Got to get you into my life: Do brand personalities rub off on consumers? *Journal of Consumer Research, 37,* 655–669.

16 Fennis, B. M. & Pruyn, A. (2007). You are what you wear: Brand personality influences on consumer impression formation. *Journal of Business Research, 60,* 634–639.

17 Nasar, J. L. (1989). Symbolic meanings of house styles. *Environment and Behavior, 21,* 235–257.

18 Maynard, M. (2007, July 4). Toyota hybrid makes a statement, and that sells. *The New York Times,* pp. A1, A11.

19 Buerkle, C. W. (2009). Metrosexuality can stuff it: Beef consumption as (heteromasculine) fortification. *Text and Performance Quarterly, 29,* 77–93. Mooney, K. M. & Lorenz, E. (1997). The effects of food and gender on interpersonal perceptions. *Sex Roles, 36,* 639–653. Pliner, P. & Chaiken, S. (1990). Eating, social motives, and self-presentation in women and men. *Journal of Experimental Social Psychology, 26,* 240–254. Sadalla, E. & Burroughs, J. (1981, October). Profiles in eating: Sexy vegetarians and other diet-based social stereotypes. *Psychology Today,* 51–57.

20 King, E. B., Shapiro, J., Hebl, M. R., Singletary, S., & Turner, S. (2006). The stigma of obesity in customer service: A mechanism of remediation and bottom-line consequences of interpersonal discrimination. *Journal of Applied Psychology, 91,* 579–593.

21 Gao, L., Wheeler, S. C., & Shiv, B. (2009). The "shaken self": Product choices as a means of restoring self-view confidence. *Journal of Consumer Research, 36,* 29–38.

22 James, W. (1890). *The principles of psychology,* Vol. 1. New York: Henry Holt, pp. 291–292.

23 Belk, R. W. (1988), p. 160.

24 Pew Research Center. (2010). *Millennials: A portrait of generation next. Confident. Connected. Open to change.* Available: http://www.pewsocialtrends.org/files/2010/10/millennials-confident-connected-open-to-change.pdf.

25 Banning, J. H. (1996). Bumper sticker ethnography: Another way to view the campus ecology. *The Campus Ecologist, 14,* 1–4.

26 Berry, D. (2010, April 13). The 12 most famous cars of film and television. *The Sixth Wall.* Available: http://blog.koldcast.tv/2010/koldcast-news/the-12-most-famous-cars-of-film-and-television/.

27 Wallis, A. D. (1997). *Wheel estate: The rise and decline of mobile homes.* Baltimore, MD: The Johns Hopkins University Press.

28 Tian, K. & Belk, R. W. (2005). Extended self and possessions in the workplace. *Journal of Consumer Research, 32,* 297–310.

29 Geduld, C. (1970). *Bonnie and Clyde:* Society vs. the clan. In J. Bellone (Ed.), *Renaissance of the film* (pp. 52–59). New York: Macmillan.

30 Geduld, C. (1970), pp. 56–57.

31 Geduld, C. (1970), pp. 57–58.

32 Velliquette, A. M., Murray, J. B., & Creyer, E. H. (1998). The tattoo renaissance. In J. W. Alba & J. W. Hutchinson (Eds.), *Advances in consumer research,* Vol. 25. (pp. 461–467). Provo, UT: Association for Consumer Research.

33 Tian, K., Bearden, W. O., & Hunter, G. L. (2001). Consumers' need for uniqueness: Scale development and validation. *Journal of Consumer Research, 28,* 50–66.

34 Belk, R. (2013). Extended self in a digital world. *Journal of Consumer Research, 40,* 477–500.
35 Belk, R. (2013), p. 479.
36 See, for example: Denegri-Knott, J. & Molesworth, M. (2010). Concepts and practices of digital virtual consumption. *Consumption Markets and Culture, 13* (2), 109–32. Lehdonvirta, V. (2012). A history of the digitalization of consumer culture. In M. Molesworth & J. Denegri-Knott (Eds.), *Digital virtual consumption* (pp. 11–28). London: Routledge.
37 Cushing, A. L. (2012). Possessions and self extension in digital environments: Implications for maintaining personal information. Unpublished PhD dissertation, University of North Carolina at Chapel Hill, School of Information and Library Science.
38 Belk, R. (2013).
39 Belk, R. (2013).
40 Belk, R. (2013).
41 Distler, J. (2013, June 20). Send me a postcard, drop me a line. *The New York Times.* Available: http://www.nytimes.com/2013/06/21/opinion/global/send-me-a-postcard-drop-me-a-line.html.
42 Baumgartner, H. (1992). Remembrance of things past: Music, autobiographical memory, and emotion. *Advances in Consumer Research, 19,* 613–620.
43 Belk, R. (2013).
44 Bélisle, J.-F. & Bodur, H. O. (2010). Avatars as information: Perception of consumers based on their avatars in virtual worlds. *Psychology & Marketing, 27,* 741–765 (p. 743).
45 Turkle, S. (2011). Alone together: Why we expect more from technology and less from each other. New York: Basic Books, p. 158.
46 Bartle, R. A. (2003). *Designing virtual worlds.* Berkeley, CA: New Riders.
47 Bélisle, J. F. & Bodur, H. O. (2010).
48 Kuntz, S. (2012). Immersive virtual reality. *SlideShare.* Available: http://www.slideshare.net/SebKuntz/immersive-virtual-reality.
49 Banakou, D., Groten, R., & Slater M. (2013). Illusory ownership of a virtual child body causes overestimation of object sizes and implicit attitude changes. *Proceedings of the National Academy of Sciences, 110* (31). Available: http://www.pnas.org/cgi/doi/10.1073/pnas.1306779110.
50 Richins, M. L. & Dawson, S. (1992). A consumer values orientation for materialism and its measurement: Scale development and validation. *Journal of Consumer Research, 19,* 303–316. Belk, R. W. (1984). Three scales to measure constructs related to materialism: Reliability, validity, and relationships to measures of happiness. In T. C. Kinnear (Ed.), *Advances in consumer research,* Vol. 11 (pp. 291–197). Provo, UT: Association for Consumer Research.
51 Richins, M. L. (2013). When wanting is better than having: Materialism, transformation expectations, and product-evoked emotions in the purchase process. *Journal of Consumer Research, 40,* 1–18.
52 Burroughs, J. E. & Rindfleisch, A. (2002). Materialism and well-being: A conflicting values perspective. *Journal of Consumer Research, 29,* 348–370.
53 Burroughs, J. E. & Rindfleisch, A. (2002).
54 Goldberg, M. E., Gorn, G. J., Peracchio, L. A., & Bamossy, G. (2003). Understanding materialism among youth. *Journal of Consumer Psychology, 13,* 278–288.
55 La Ferle, C. & Chan, K. (2008). Determinants for materialism among adolescents in Singapore. *Young Consumers: Insight and Ideas for Responsible Marketers, 9,* 201–214.
56 O'Guinn, T. C. & Shrum, L. J. (1997). The role of television in the construction of social reality. *Journal of Consumer Research, 23,* 278–294.
57 Shrum, L. J., Burroughs, J. E., & Rindfleisch, A. (2005). Television's cultivation of material values. *Journal of Consumer Research, 32,* 473–479.
58 Chaplin, L. N. & John, D. R. (2007). Growing up in a material world: Age differences in materialism in children and adolescents. *Journal of Consumer Research, 37,* 480–493.
59 Chaplin, L. N. & John, D. R. (2010). Interpersonal influences on adolescent materialism: A new look at the role of parents and peers. *Journal of Consumer Psychology, 20,* 176–184.

60 Ger, G. & Belk, R. W. (1996). Cross-cultural differences in materialism. *Journal of Economic Psychology, 17*, 55–77.
61 Ger, G. & Belk, R. W. (1996), p. 55.
62 Kleine, S. S. & Baker, S. M. (2004). An integrative review of material possession attachment. *Academy of Marketing Science Review, 2004, 1*. Available: http://www.amsreview.org/articles/kleine01-2004.pdf.
63 Kleine, S. S. & Baker, S. M. (2004), p. 3.
64 Jenkins, B. (2013, March 2). Glove love never dies, it just falls apart. *SFGate*. Available: http://www.sfgate.com/giants/jenkins/article/Glove-love-never-dies-it-just-falls-apart-4323880.php.
65 Kleine, S. S. & Baker, S. M. (2004).
66 Fournier, S. (1998). Consumers and their brands: Developing relationship theory in consumer research. *Journal of Consumer Research, 24*, 343–373.
67 Rahinel, R. & Redden, J. P. (2013). Brands as product coordinators: Matching brands make joint consumption experiences more enjoyable. *Journal of Consumer Research, 39*, 1,290–1,299.
68 Rahinel, R. & Redden, J. P. (2013), p. 1,298.
69 Rozin, P. & Fallon, A. E. (1987). A perspective on disgust. *Psychological Review, 94*, 23–41 (p. 23).
70 Argo, J., Dahl, D., & Morales, A. C. (2006). Consumer contamination: How consumers react to products touched by others. *Journal of Marketing, 70*, 81–94.
71 Wells, W. D. & Prensky, D. (1996), p. 100.
72 Rice, C. (1993). *Consumer behaviour: Behavioural aspects of marketing*. Oxford, UK: Butterworth Heinemann.
73 Toder-Alon, A., Brunel, F. F., & Fournier, S. (2014). Word-of-mouth rhetorics in social media talk. *Journal of Marketing Communications, 20*, 42–64.
74 Chalfen, R. (2002). Snapshots "r" us: The evidentiary problematic of home media. *Visual Studies, 17*, 141–149.
75 Wells, W. D. & Prensky, D. (1996).
76 Solomon, M. R., Bamossy, G., & Askegaard, S. (1999).
77 Tournier, P. (1966). *The meaning of gifts* (trans. J. S. Gilmour). Richmond, VA: John Knox.
78 Mick, D. G. & DeMoss, M. (1990). Self-gifts: Phenomenological insights from four contexts. *Journal of Consumer Research, 17*, 322–332, p. 328.
79 Mick, D. G. & DeMoss, M. (1990), p. 329.
80 Ward, M. K. & Broniarczyk, S. M. (2011). It's not me, it's you: How gift giving creates giver identity threat as a function of social closeness. *Journal of Consumer Research, 38*, 164–181.
81 Baker, S. M. & Hill, R. P. (2013). A community psychology of object meanings: Identity negotiation during disaster recovery. *Journal of Consumer Psychology, 23*, 275–287.
82 Baker, S. M. & Hill, R. P. (2013), p. 276.
83 Barron, J. (2013, July 22). Revisiting history through objects, and a long-gone game show. *The New York Times*. Available: http://cityroom.blogs.nytimes.com/2013/07/22/revisiting-history-through-objects-and-a-long-gone-game-show/.
84 Roberts, S. (2012, September 2). A history of New York in 50 objects. *The New York Times*. Available: http://www.nytimes.com/interactive/2012/09/02/nyregion/a-history-of-new-york-in-50-objects.html.
85 Faust, D. G. (2008). *This republic of suffering: Death and the American civil war*. New York: Vintage, p. 11.
86 O'Brien, T. (1990). *The things they carried*. London: Flamingo, pp. 5, 6, 7, 11.
87 Bilton, N. (2013, June 30). Disruptions: Social media images form a new language online. *The New York Times*. Available: http://bits.blogs.nytimes.com/2013/06/30/disruptions-social-media-images-form-a-new-language-online/.
88 Jarvis, W. E. (2003). *Time capsules: A cultural history*. Jefferson, NC: McFarland & Company, Inc. pp. 1–2.

89 Matuozzi, R. N. (2004). Time capsules: A cultural history (review). *Libraries & Culture, 39*, p. 241.

90 Statista. (2013). Gift, novelty, and souvenir store sales in the United States from 1992 to 2010 (in billion U.S. dollars). Available: http://www.statista.com/statistics/197723/annual-gift-and-souvenir-store-sales-in-the-us-since-1992/.

91 Love, L. L. & Sheldon, P. S. (1998). Souvenirs: Messengers of meaning. In J. W. Alba & J. W. Hutchinson (Eds.), *Advances in Consumer Research*, Vol. 25 (pp. 170–175). Provo, UT: Association for Consumer Research.

92 Boym, C. (2002). *Curious Boym: Design works*. Princeton, NJ: Princeton Architectural Press.

93 Gordon, B. (1986). The souvenir: Messenger of the extraordinary. *Journal of Popular Culture, 20*, 135–146.

94 Gordon, B. (1986).

95 Gordon, B. (1986), p. 135.

96 Baker, S. M., Kleine, S. S., & Bowen, H. E. (2006). On the symbolic meanings of souvenirs for children. *Research in Consumer Behavior, 10*, 213–252 (p. 214).

97 Haber, M. (2013, July 5). A trip to camp to break a tech addiction. Available: http://www.nytimes.com/2013/07/07/fashion/a-trip-to-camp-to-break-a-tech-addiction.html.

2

TECHNOLOGY AND INNOVATION IN EVERYDAY LIFE

By the end of this chapter, you will:

- understand the impact of evolving communication technologies, from typography to virtual reality;
- gain insight into some of technology's compelling effects on consumers;
- understand the nature of innovation and recognize some of the key elements underlying successful innovations;
- appreciate some of the consumer products that have had a dramatic impact on everyday life.

At the time of this writing, the following headlines typified some of the ongoing technological developments occurring circa early 2014:

Computerized homes finding mainstream market

3-D printing is moving closer to "plug-and-play" reality

Wearable tech still more geek than chic

Google sets its sights on robot brains

By the time this book goes to print, such stories are likely to be old news—that's how fast technology change occurs in the modern era. Technological developments, and the products and services they spawn, no longer pause or slow down to let ordinary consumers catch their breath. As technology rapidly evolves, lives and well-being are fundamentally altered, for good and bad. The marketing promise is that the quality and comfort of life will change for the better with technological advances that prove profitable for the firms that exploit them, but that is not always the case. The road to corporate profit is littered with the remains of products that never caught on with skeptical consumers who simply were not convinced that the offering had any value or offered any promise that would justify a change in purchase or usage behavior (see Box 2.1).

BOX 2.1 NEW PRODUCT FAILURES: A MARKETING INEVITABILITY

Innovation represents an essential strategy for a firm's efforts to gain competitive advantage.[1] According to the so-called "30% rule," nearly one-third of a company's sales come from products that are less than four years old (an objective ultimately modified by 3M in the company's efforts to achieve 10% of its sales from products in the market for only one year).[2] Nonetheless, despite the potential gains that can be accrued from successful innovation, the process of new product development and launch is costly, fraught with risk, and often results in failure. Although rates tend to vary across industries and firms, it is estimated that about 33% of new product launches turn out to be failures, and upwards of 50% fail commercially or are killed during the product testing phase (see Figure 2.2).[3]

Marketplace offerings that appear to offer no obvious benefits are likely to fail. For example, the 1990s ushered in a new color trend, with manufacturers emphasizing the lack of color in the design of various products. A variety of clear-colored products, or those with transparent exteriors, ranging from colas (PepsiCo's Crystal Pepsi and Coca-Cola's Tab Clear) and beers (Miller Brewing Company's Miller Clear) to laundry detergents (Purex Free & Clear) began to proliferate in the marketplace. Eliminating any hint of color is a means of conveying the purity and freshness of a product and, to conform to a growing sensitivity among consumers for health and environmental issues, is a way to suggest that a product is more natural, with fewer additives. The "clear" strategy turned out to be a short-lived fad. In fact, some clear products are actually less natural than their colored alternatives. For example, the brewing process for manufacturing a clear beer requires the addition of activated charcoal for absorbing the color—and, no doubt, some of the flavor. For a product like beer, a rich amber color is relied on by connoisseurs as a signal of quality. In the case of Crystal Pepsi, although the initial consumer response was favorable—perhaps due to curiosity associated with the novelty of the product—sales fell rapidly and the product was discontinued within one year. The clear cola was obviously different and distinctive (and readily communicable), but having no color quickly proved unimportant and irrelevant to the typical cola drinker. In short, the benefit—whatever that may have been—was not perceived by consumers.

(Continued)

(Continued)

Color may well have been a contributing factor in the failure of Heinz's Funky Fries, a line of frozen fried potatoes for kids which, in addition to their unique flavors (cinnamon, sour cream, and chocolate), were colored blue and dark green. Launched in mid-2002, the odd fries were discontinued in less than one year as a result of poor sales. Bearing the promotional message "Not what a potato is supposed to be," consumers found little familiarity with the offbeat offering. Blue may be one of the most popular colors for people, but have you noticed how few foods or beverages bear that color? In fact, researchers have found that blue is one of the least appetizing colors because the brain has learned to interpret dark colors as an indicator that something is unsafe to ingest. In their search for food, early foragers eschewed natural objects that were colored blue, black, or purple as likely to be spoiled or toxic. By contrast, red, green, and brown are among the most popular food colors, with red especially likely to stimulate the appetite. This may help explain why many restaurant decorating schemes and facades make heavy use of the color red.

The focus of this chapter falls squarely on innovation and the impact of technological advances on consumer behavior. Advances in digital technology and the emergence of innovative communication devices have transformed the consumer environment into one that has prompted trends towards multitasking, product sharing, co-creation, and so on. Technological developments can facilitate or pose threats to marketing efforts. For example, consumers are increasingly resorting to technology to screen out or otherwise prevent exposure to marketing messages, through the use of remote controls, online pop-up blockers, digital video recorders (DVRs), and the like.[4] With regard to the Internet, arguably one of the most transformative elements of modern life, psychologists are finding that the increasing time spent online is changing how people behave in society, interact with friends and family members, shop for and use material goods, use and learn from traditional media, and maintain social relationships. The role of technology in everyday life is a topic that could fill volumes in and of itself, but in this chapter, the need for brevity necessitates that only a small, albeit essential, part of the story can be told. Like many great stories, this one begins in ancient Mesopotamia.

Tracing the impact of technological change

If technology is understood as the application of scientific knowledge to improve the way things are done for practical purposes, then it could be said that the dawn of technology dates back to 550 BC with the development of a rudimentary postal service in ancient Persia.[5] Typically accredited by Greek historians Herodotus and Xenophon to the first king of the Achaemenids, Cyrus the Great, messengers on horseback carried letters and other documents from relay station to relay station, where the horse would be exchanged with a fresh one so that maximum delivery speeds could be maintained throughout the route.

Ironically, recent technological developments are posing threats to the very existence of modern postal systems around the world, as human behavior shifts from sending "hard copy" mail through the post, with its inherent time lag, to more instantaneous forms of virtual communication such as email, texting, and tweeting. Local postal services are cutting back services, including Saturday deliveries, and raising the prices of deliveries as operational costs continue to dwarf profitability—a trend that was given significant impetus with the growth of the Internet and its capacities for virtual forms of message delivery. For example, faced with losses totaling CAD$1 billion a year by 2020, in 2013 the Canadian postal system announced plans to phase out home delivery for five million households, replacing the service with community mailboxes and raising the cost of postage stamps by more than one-third.[6] The colloquialism "snail mail," used as early as 1942 to refer to the slow delivery of mail, entered widespread parlance by 1983 to contrast human-delivered mail with electronic mail, the latter of which appeared five years earlier.[7]

The telegraph: Disengaging transportation and communication

Another technological development that was especially crucial in connecting people who were increasingly separated by expanding borders was the telegraph, an invention that emerged when Samuel Finley Breese Morse figured out a way to put electricity to the service of communication. Dubbed "America's first true 'spaceman'" by communications professor Neil Postman,[8] Morse solved the problem that information could move only as fast as it could be carried by human beings, which, prior to the 1840s, was limited to the speed of a train, or about 35 miles per hour. Around the time of the telegraph's appearance, most countries around the world were composites of regions, with each conversing in their own ways on topics of local interest—continent-wide conversations were not possible. Postman adroitly summarized the significance of the telegraph in conquering the space problem when he observed that "the new idea was that transportation and communication could be disengaged from each other, that space was not an inevitable constraint on the movement of information."[9]

Despite Morse's boast that telegraphy would make "one neigbourhood of the whole country," not everyone was enthralled by the idea—an inevitable reaction to most dramatic innovations. Some critics considered the erection of telegraph poles across a country's landscape as akin to environmental pollution—a complaint later directed at outdoor advertising billboards[10]—whereas others feared that the telegraph would erode the quality of public discourse through the transmission of irrelevant, context-free information. Among the more vociferous critics was naturalist author Henry David Thoreau, who lamented that telegraphy would make relevance irrelevant:

> We are eager to tunnel under the Atlantic and bring the old world some weeks nearer to the new; but perchance the first news that will leak through into the broad flapping American ear will be that Princess Adelaide has the whooping cough.[11]

Summarizing the gist of such observations, Postman observed:

> telegraphy gave a form of legitimacy to the idea of context-free information; that is, to the idea that the value of information need not be tied to any function it might serve in social and political decision-making and action, but may attach merely to its novelty, interest, and curiosity. The telegraph made information into a commodity, a "thing" that could be bought and sold irrespective of its uses or meaning.[12]

Such points seem particularly prophetic in the current era that is seemingly inundated by celebrity journalism,[13] blogging, and tweeting, but the impact of the telegraph as a game-changing marketplace innovation cannot be denied. In contrast to previous reliance on typography, which introduced the newspaper as its core communication medium, the telegraph brought speed and distance—two critical elements of successful innovations—to the transmission of news and information. In the United States, for the remainder of the 1800s, the telegraph played a crucial role in social and commercial life and, like the postal service, served to advance national expansion. Returning briefly to the impact of the postal system, according to historian William Bergmann,[14] its national development enabled early settlers in the American West to stay in touch with their scattered families, assisted entrepreneurs in finding business opportunities, and facilitated commercial relationships between newly established Western merchants and wholesalers and factories on the east coast. The telegraph had similar consequences for the still fledgling nation, and quickly proved to be an even more efficient, inexpensive, and speedy means for connecting people and expanding the commercial sector. Eventually, two new inventions—the telephone and the radio—superseded the telegraph as more functional and convenient media for fulfilling communication needs.

From intimacy to fragmentation: Twentieth-century technological developments

The impact of late nineteenth-century to mid-twentieth-century technological innovations in telecommunications and mass media were far-reaching. One example of the influence of technology on marketing practices is apparent in advertising. Until around the turn of the twentieth century, advertisements were primarily text-driven, providing audiences with extensive product-related information, perhaps with an accompanying illustration of the product. Working from a rational model of the thinking processes of a typical consumer, early advertisers were inclined to provide as much of the details and information about a product as a customer might expect to obtain through an in-store interaction with a salesperson. Major advances in photographic technology and the emergence of radio during the early twentieth century had a significant effect on the ways advertisers addressed their audiences, enabling greater intimacy and attention-getting properties as a result of the addition of color, auditory, and other aspects.[15] The new media provided advertisers with greater opportunities to imbue advertisements with content reflecting emotional values like status, friendship, and sexuality and, in so doing, enabled brands to focus more on the development of relationships with consumers.

As mentioned in Chapter 1, the diffusion of radios in households during the early 1900s, followed by television sets, brought families together as the central loci for auditory and visual entertainment, news, and information consumption. Before the arrival of cable TV, the personal computer, and the Internet, it was fairly predictable that the majority of adult members of the population would be spending their evenings sitting next to their radios or TV sets, attending to a limited number of broadcasts. Today, of course, this is far from the case because the media options have expanded, thereby fragmenting the audience into a myriad of diverse media usage targets. Estimates are that in 1965, advertisers could reach 80% of Americans aged 18–49 years with ads run on the three major broadcast television networks. By 2004, they could only reach 31% through those same networks.[16] Today, an ad would have to be aired on 100 channels to reach 80% of adult Americans.[17] Primetime TV viewing hours may now be used to surf the Internet, read an e-magazine, trade SMS messages with friends, stream music on a portable handheld device, watch a movie on a portable DVD player, upload photos to a social networking site, and so on. Eric Schmitt of Forrester Research, Inc. effectively summarized this development when he stated that: "Monolithic blocks of eyeballs are gone. In their place is a perpetually shifting mosaic of audience microsegments that forces marketers to play an endless game of audience hide-and-seek" (see Box 2.2).[18]

BOX 2.2 THE MEDIA FRAGMENTATION FALLOUT FOR MARKETERS

Until recently, it would have been possible to introduce a new product or brand to 90% of the Australian population simply via a Sunday night "road block"—that is, by running an advertisement on the three major Australian TV networks at the same time during the airing of the Sunday night movie. Today, that is no longer possible now that the Internet and pay TV have emerged as significant new alternatives for media consumption.

As is the case in other industrialized nations, there has been a steady rise in Internet usage among Australians, where penetration rates now exceed 82% of the population (i.e., persons having used the Internet from any type

(Continued)

(Continued)

of device during the last 12 months). Mobile wireless devices represent the most prevalent Internet technology in Australia, accounting for half of all connections. The percentage of persons viewing commercial TV over the past seven days dropped from 75% in 1996 to 68% in 2003, compared with the viewing of pay TV during the past seven days, which rose from 5% in 1996 to nearly 20% in 2003. Nonetheless, as of early 2012, 98% of Australians were still watching TV in the home. The options for conventional viewing of video content in Australia have diversified, with significant percentages of Australians now streaming video on a PC or laptop (45%), watching digitally recorded playback TV (42%), and streaming video on a mobile phone (11%).[19]

Another consequence of new media choices in recent years is a decline in print circulation rates. According to a 2004 report on Australian media usage, newspaper and magazine readership figures remained fairly consistent over the period 1994–2003, with the percentage of people using either medium varying only slightly between 80% to 90%.[20] Since that time, however, Australian print circulation has shown steady declines, mirroring a global trend.[21] The survival of both newspapers and magazines is highly dependent on advertising revenues, and advertisers are apt to reduce their ad spending on those media outlets if they have reason to believe that readership rates are declining. Some newspaper publishers are quick to point out that daily circulation rates significantly understate actual newspaper readership now that we have entered a period when newspapers are increasingly read online. A *New York Times* analysis supported this view when figures were gathered for seven of the most widely read American newspapers, including *USA Today*, *The Wall Street Journal*, and *The Washington Post*. For each newspaper, average weekday circulation rates were significantly lower than Web-unique daily audiences in 2005. For example, the average weekday circulation figures for *The Washington Post* showed that 0.8 million people had purchased the newspaper, whereas the average daily readership of the newspaper online was pegged at 7.8 million. A similar trend appears to be occurring in Australia, where digital subscription rates for newspapers have grown by double- to triple-digit percentages for major publications, including *The Sydney Morning Herald* and *The Age*.[22] The fact that a growing number of readers are shifting from print to online publications represents an interesting opportunity for both newspapers and magazines, the latter in the form of e-zines.

Another study compared how newspaper readers are differentially reached by advertisers depending on the context in which the newspaper is read. A study conducted by the Asahi Shimbun Company compared the readership habits of Japanese businesspersons at home, while commuting, and at work. Overall, the results suggest that business professionals are more likely to read newspaper ads when the newspaper is read at home. More than half (50.8%) of business people who read the morning edition of a newspaper at home answered "I look at ads about interesting products or services," as opposed to 34.2% while commuting. More than one-fifth of the respondents who read the morning edition of a newspaper while commuting (21%) or at the office (20.4%) replied "I never look at ads," compared with only 9.1% at home.[23]

Publishers are holding out hope that technological innovations will revitalize the print industry. The creation of so-called *electronic paper*, which provides a high-quality electronic facsimile of ordinary paper, as exemplified by Amazon.com's Kindle, has facilitated the acquisition of thousands of online newspapers for portable device users. Another new technology on the horizon at the time of this writing is the online print-on-demand newsstand Meganews, a concept pioneered by Sweden AB in conjunction with the technology consultancy group Sweco and the industrial design firm LA+B.[24] Newsstand kiosk vending machines requiring less than 4 square meters of physical public space offer consumers a wide range of newspaper and magazine publications from around the world. Publishers store PDF files of their print offerings on a server, which can then be accessed by the newsstands. Using a touch screen, customers select the publication they want, pay with a debit or credit card and, within two minutes, their selection is printed and delivered as a high-quality print and image reproduction.

The Meganews concept offers a modern and efficient solution to problems for publishers that have traditionally been associated with the cost of producing and distributing copies of newspapers and magazines. Currently, print media must produce a surplus of copies because, without pinpointing where consumers will appear when they want to buy a copy of a publication, every copy produced will not be sold. Thus, publishers must supply outlets with too many copies, to avoid missing a sales opportunity. The result is that in some cases, 30–40% of copies are never sold. The newsstand innovation adjusts the consumer demand to a precise one-to-one ratio with what is produced, resulting in money savings by not producing something that will never be sold. The broader choice of distribution opportunities stands to benefit the publishing industry, consumers, and the environment, and enables niche magazine publishers to reach audiences they otherwise could not due to prohibitive distribution costs. Whether the newsstand kiosks and other technological advances will serve to reduce "digital shoplifting"[25]—the use of portable device cameras by shoppers to photograph magazine pages rather than make a purchase—remains to be seen.

Schmitt's description is indicative of the ongoing shift among marketers away from a broadcasting mentality to one that can properly be referred to as "narrowcasting"—attempting to reach the desired consumer segment, cluster, or niche, at the right time, through the appropriate media channels, with a message that is likely to strike a personal chord. As Procter & Gamble's (P&G's) chief marketing

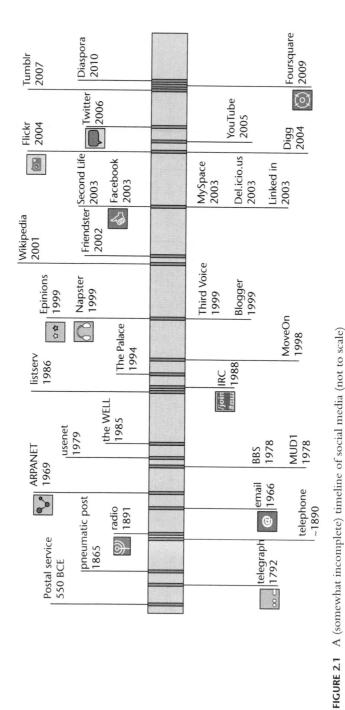

FIGURE 2.1 A (somewhat incomplete) timeline of social media (not to scale)

Source: idfive, 3600 Clipper Mill Road Suite 240, Baltimore, MD, 2014.

officer Jim Stengel noted during a 2004 advertising agencies conference: "We must accept the fact that there is no 'mass' in 'mass media' anymore and leverage more targeted approaches."[26]

Figure 2.1 provides a rudimentary chronology of the development of technology dating back to the Persian postal system (550 BC), revealing that a majority of the major technological developments up to the current era have occurred since 1969. Similarly, the website About.com's page for "The History of Communication" lists 35 landmark developments from 3500 BC (the Phoenician alphabet) to 1902 (Marconi's transmission of radio signals), followed by 32 developments thereafter up to the birth of the Internet in 1994.[27] Figure 2.1 illustrates how more than two-thirds of key communication milestones have occurred since the creation of Arpanet, the pioneering form of online networking that ultimately became the basis for the Internet. These chronologies add credence to Kurzweil's claim, discussed in Chapter 1, that the evolution of communication technology is exponential, not linear (see Box 1.1):

> The first technological steps—sharp edges, fire, the wheel—took tens of thousands of years. For people living in this era, there was little noticeable technological change in even a thousand years. By 1000 A.D., progress was much faster and a paradigm shift required only a century or two. In the nineteenth century, we saw more technological change than in the nine centuries preceding it. Then in the first twenty years of the twentieth century, we saw more advancement than in all of the nineteenth century. Now, paradigm shifts occur in only a few years time. The World Wide Web did not exist in anything like its present form just a few years ago; it didn't exist at all a decade ago. . . . [T]echnological progress in the twenty-first century will be equivalent to what would require (in the linear view) on the order of 200 centuries. . . . So the twenty-first century will see almost a thousand times greater technological change than its predecessor.[28]

New product innovation and keys to success

In the marketing context, "innovation" has always been a difficult term to define, largely because its meaning, like most questions of semantics, varies depending upon various considerations. Do we speak of innovation as a single event (i.e., *an* innovation), or does the term more appropriately refer to a process (i.e., the innovation process)? Do we view the meaning of innovation from the orientation of the firm (something newly produced or marketed by the company), the product (an original conception or new features inherent in an existing product that are likely to have an effect on consumers' established usage patterns), or the consumer (something perceived to be new by potential adopters)? Is the "newness" of an innovation determined by the extent of its difference from existing products and services, length of time on the market, or sales penetration level? How does one distinguish between an innovation and an invention?

Of course, the answers to each of these questions are relevant to our understanding of innovation and complicate the task of settling on a single definition of the term. One rather inclusive definition, offered by Myers and Marquis, reflects the varying nature of the innovation concept:

> Innovation is not a single action but a total process of interrelated subprocesses. It is not just the conception of a new idea, nor the invention of a new device, nor the development of a new market. The process is all these things acting in an integrated fashion.[29]

Although this definition dates back to 1969, its focus on integration is especially relevant nearly a half century later. In their fieldwork with Global 2000 companies (i.e., the world's biggest public firms, according to *Forbes*), Govinarajan and Desai concluded that successful companies are those that effectively integrate product innovation with business model, process, and service innovations. In other words, to achieve sustainable growth, it is important to broaden one's thinking beyond the notion that innovation is only about new products.[30] Without a dualistic mindset that incorporates acumen for conceiving and nurturing creative, valuable ideas as well as the facility to produce, market, and commercialize the conception, companies are likely to lose out to more astute competitors. As an example, Govinarajan and Desai point out how Sony had the product concept and engineering competence to create the first iPod equivalent, but lacked the organizational harmony that would have facilitated the idea's successful commercialization.

With these points in mind, new products expert Paul Trott defined innovation as "the management of all the activities involved in the process of idea generation, technology development, manufacturing and marketing of a new (or improved) product or manufacturing process or equipment."[31] In this sense, "innovation" is a global term that refers to the creation, modification, or renewal of more effective processes, products, or ways of doing things. An innovative business is one that is doing something that is new, different, smarter, or better, thereby resulting in a positive difference. The long-standing adage that "innovation is the lifeblood of the marketplace" continues to have resonance in the competitive contemporary business environment, where companies require new catalysts for growth and success in efforts to stay relevant, dynamic, and capable of adapting to rapid changes in the marketplace (see Box 2.3).

BOX 2.3 PATENTS: A ROADBLOCK TO INNOVATION?

Proprietary ownership and long-term protection of an invention is achieved via an application for a patent, which typically lasts for twenty years (or longer in the pharmaceutical industry). In many countries, the owner is required to demonstrate that the invention differs in some way from existing technology, involves an innovative advancement, and can be made or used in an industry. A patent gives the owner the exclusive right to commercially exploit a valuable idea and offers protection by preventing it from being commercially implemented by a business rival without penalty. Originally developed for mechanical inventions and new drug formulas, it has long been assumed that patent rules generate legal records of novel and useful ideas that help drive regional innovation and economic growth.[32] However, there are rising concerns that the existing patent rules that were crafted for a mechanical world are inadequate in the contemporary digital marketplace, where patents essentially grant ownership of concepts, as opposed to tangible creations.[33]

Initially, patent offices refused to grant patents for new computer software, equating such developments to ideas or laws of nature, like mathematical principles. In recent years, however, court cases have challenged this view, resulting in software patents involving algorithms or business methods that are rather vague and broad enough to theoretically give inventors ownership over more than a single invention, sometimes involving seemingly unrelated products developed by others.[34] This trend can be illustrated by comparing two inventions: the automobile and Siri, Apple's digital assistant for the iPhone. Regarding the former, a patent was issued to George B. Selden for a lightweight combustion gasoline engine for road vehicles in 1895. Some auto companies paid licensing fees on the patent, whereas others refused, including Henry Ford. Despite this point of contention, because Selden's patent applied to a mechanical invention, its application was straightforward and clear. The situation is different with a software patent for a digital invention like Siri, which is based more on abstract concepts than mechanics. As a result, Apple's 2011 patent could theoretically cover more than Siri, granting Apple ownership over the ability to search multiple databases on the Internet, hard drives, and other storage devices simultaneously.

The end result of the evolution of patenting from mechanical inventions to more conceptual ones is a dramatic increase in patent filings, leading to a morass of thousands of patents held by computing companies and a raft of patent infringement lawsuits. Today, nearly every major mobile computing company is involved in one or more expensive and time-consuming battles against the others over patents, while at the same time working hand-in-hand with attorneys to create larger portfolios of patents with which to pursue their cases.[35] Apple, for example, has filed lawsuits against HTC, Samsung, and Motorola Mobility (the latter now part of Google) over minor design aspects of smartphone technology. The impact of these legal fights could prove devastating for the future of technology innovation, with huge amounts of financial resources being redirected from research and development to patent-related spending.

As an example, consider the case of Michael Phillips, who spent decades developing software that gave computers the power to recognize human speech. Phillips co-founded a voice recognition company in 2006 and was

(Continued)

(Continued)

quickly approached by executives from Apple, Google, and other companies who proposed partnerships. However, in 2008, a larger company known as Nuance contacted Phillips and informed him that they held patents that could prevent Phillips' company from doing business in the voice recognition market. Phillips was given the choice of selling his firm to Nuance or risk being sued for patent infringement. Phillips refused to sell, resulting in a series of financially damaging lawsuits that ultimately gave him little choice but to capitulate and sell his company to Nuance. In the meantime, Apple and Google had transferred their partnerships to Nuance, and the money that Phillips' firm had set aside for research and development evaporated as a result of lawyer and court fees. Adding insult to injury, Phillips' technology had earlier been integrated into Siri, well before the digital system was applied by Apple as part of its iPhone technology.[36]

Before we turn to a consideration of specific types of innovations and the factors that underlie successful innovation, it is important to address the difference between innovation and invention, two concepts that are often confused. (In Chapter 4, we will consider another tricky distinction: that between invention and design.)

An *invention* is commonly understood to represent the conception of an idea—something that is first of its kind that has the potential to create a new market. In that sense, if a product is thought of as the output of innovation, than innovation is best regarded as the commercial and practical application of an invention into the economy. A simple equation clarifies the relationship between these various concepts:

innovation = theoretical conception + technical invention + commercial exploitation.[37]

Examples of successful landmark inventions include the automobile, computer, microwave oven, and videocassette recorder. An innovative company is not necessarily one that invents, but rather may be innovative in the sense of changing its business model and adapting to the competitive environment by delivering better products or services that were originally developed elsewhere.

Types of innovations

Various typologies have been suggested over the years to distinguish between different types of innovations. Given that our broad definition of innovation can encompass virtually any kind of organizational or managerial change, it is possible to classify innovations according to the nature of the change involved.[38] Thus, we can identify product innovations (the creation of some new marketplace offering, such as Amazon's Kindle e-book reader), process innovations (the development of a new manufacturing process, as exemplified by Apple's robotic laser manufacturing process for its iMac laptops[39]), organizational and management innovations (such as the recent "open innovation" movement with firms opening up their research and development processes to involve customers, suppliers, and other third parties in decision making and co-creation[40]), commercial/marketing innovations (such as mobile marketing, content marketing, and Big Data marketing strategies[41]), and service innovations (ranging from customer/service representative real-time interactive online chats to experiential marketing approaches[42]). Because our focus in this book is on consumers and products, much of the discussion that follows will pertain to product innovations, although it bears keeping in mind that it would be short-sighted to neglect the often hidden types of innovations that are inextricably tied to more tangible, technical developments.

Another long-standing means of differentiating innovations that is relevant to our interest in products from the consumer's perspective involves a continuum that reflects range of newness in terms of the innovation's effect on established consumption patterns. This conceptualization points to three categories of innovation, traditionally referred to as continuous, dynamically continuous, and discontinuous innovations.

Continuous (or "sustaining") *innovations* are marginal or incremental in nature, and represent the most common and least risky of new product developments. Such innovations are comprised of product alterations or variations on a theme (e.g., low-fat yogurt) as opposed to the development of a completely new product and, in this sense, they have the least disruptive influence on established consumer behaviors. Continuous innovations often serve a defensive function for firms in a competitive sense, as when a household cleanser is strengthened or paired with a particular scent in response to the introduction of a rival brand in the marketplace (see Box 2.4). Despite the fact that a company may have invested much time and financial resources to improving its existing products, continuous innovations may go unnoticed by consumers who are already familiar with similar modifications they have seen in the marketplace. Thus, such innovations must exceed the threshold of consumers' perceptual awareness (the so-called "just noticeable difference").[43]

BOX 2.4 INNOFLATION: TOO MANY NEW PRODUCTS?

An increasing number of products are entering the market over decreasing periods of time, a phenomenon referred to as "innoflation." According to various estimates, there are more than 48,000 different product references (so-called "stock-keeping units," or SKUs) in a typical hypermarket and more than nine million registered brand names—double the number of brands estimated in 1970. Some of the first brands to appear in the marketplace, such as Coca-Cola (1891), Gillette (1903), Vaseline (1899), Folger's (1850), and Hershey's Kisses (1923), have maintained their strong presence in the marketplace to this day, although their list of competitors has continued

(Continued)

(Continued)

to expand. For example, there are approximately a hundred different car brands, although each brand (e.g., Ford) incorporates any number of specific models and sub-brands (e.g., Ford Coupe, Ford Ranchero). Moreover, there are car accessory brands for products such as tires, mufflers, automotive oils, windshield wiper fluids, gasoline, and so on.

Also adding to the proliferation of consumer choices are the various extensions to product and brand lines. A *brand extension* (which may be seen as a dynamically continuous innovation from the firm's perspective, but not the consumer's) is the practice of using a brand name established in one product category (e.g., Calvin Klein fashion) to enter another product class (e.g., Calvin Klein eyewear, bedding and bath accessories, fragrances). An even more common practice is that of *line extensions* (akin to continuous innovations), whereby additional items are added within a product category under the same brand name (e.g., Coca-Cola Cherry, Coca-Cola Zero, Coca-Cola Vanilla). In fact, more than half of all new products introduced annually are line extensions, based on variations in the established product's flavor, size, nutrition content, color, additives, and so on.

An increasingly common business practice is for companies to add new offerings within an established product category using a different name, as when Toyota entered the executive luxury car segment with the Lexus brand in order to distinguish the luxury cars from Toyota's mass market offerings. This practice, known as *mutibranding*, is carried out for various reasons: to establish different features for different brands, to appeal to different buying motive segments, to have several identities within the same category, and to obtain more distributor space.

One variation of line extensions is the introduction of "me-too" imitative brands, a tactic employed by a market follower who avoids losing market share to a competitor by offering a product that mimics a competitor's new product innovation. Thus, when Amazon introduced its pioneering Kindle electronic book reader, the move was quickly followed by the appearance of competing "me-too" additions to the e-reader market, such as Barnes & Noble's Nook, Samsung's Papyrus, and the Sony Reader. *The New York Times* writer David Pogh aptly described the "me-too" phenomenon of companies predictably following on the heels of Apple, a company which prides itself on innovation:

> It's an old pattern by now. Phase 1: Apple introduces some new gadget. The bloggers and the industry tell us why it will fail. Phase 2: It goes on sale. The public goes nuts for it. Phase 3: Every company and its brother gets to work on a copycat. It happened with the iMac and the iPhone. Now the iPad is entering Phase 3. Apple sold 15 million iPads in nine months, so you can bet that 2011 will be the Year of the iPad Clone.[44]

At the other end of the spectrum from continuous innovations are *discontinuous (or "radical") innovations*—the introduction of new-to-the world products that give rise to brand new behavior patterns. Such products are disruptive in the sense that they render existing consumer habits obsolete and significantly reshape markets and competition. Some obvious examples include the Internet and mobile phone technology (which have had a major impact on how people communicate), the automobile and airplane (with their obvious effects on how we travel), and the iPod (which has altered the way we listen to and acquire music).

Falling between continuous and discontinuous innovations are *dynamically continuous (or "incremental") innovations*, which have clear effects on consumer patterns of behavior without significantly altering them. Discontinuous innovations may take the form of a new product (e.g., the tablet PC) or variations of existing offerings (e.g., electric toothbrushes, satellite television, mobile phones); in either case, consumers have enough familiarity and experience with related offerings that momentous changes in their behavior patterns are unnecessary.

In their discussion of new product innovations, marketing professors Schiffman and Kanuk observed how the introduction of the television, one of the most noteworthy discontinuous inventions of the twentieth century, itself spawned the development of each of the three types of innovations described above, including continuous innovations (remote control, flat screen, stereo sound, LED and plasma TVs, various cabinet styles), dynamically continuous innovations (color TV, portable pocket TV, cable-ready TV), and discontinuous innovations (videocassette recorder, video camera).[45] Of course, a more recent example of a significantly disruptive innovation is the personal computer, which has also given rise to a wide range of offspring products (and services) within each of the innovation categories, with varying behavioral consequences: laptops and tablet PCs, USB keys, pocket hard drives, printers, the computer mouse, the word processor, email, the Internet, basic text editor, markup language, search engines, wikis, instant messaging, social networking, microblogging, online content collaboration, virtual currency, massively multiplayer online games, among others.[46]

Keys to successful innovation

As described in Box 2.1, there are numerous examples of inventions that never progressed beyond the conception stage as commercial products or, when they did, died a quick death. However, there are far fewer new product failures than is often reported, because most firms follow a rigorous testing procedure before their commercial launch (see Figure 2.2). Weak products tend to be eliminated prior to entry into the market during the product testing phase. For example, the development process leading up to the launch of a new pharmaceutical drug typically will span a period of ten or more years, beginning with the discovery of an active chemical, and progressing through a preclinical period (during which the patent application is submitted and initial testing is carried out on microorganisms and animals), safety and efficacy trials (on human subjects), and final approval. In the US, a mere 10% of drugs that enter into preclinical testing ever

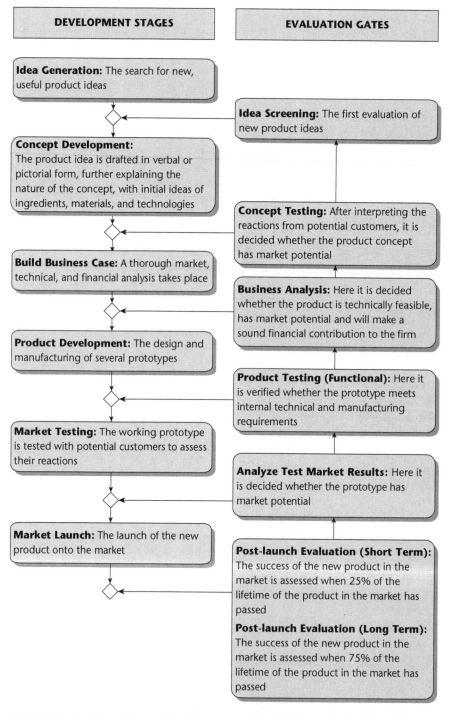

FIGURE 2.2 An illustrative model of the new product development (NPD) process

Source: Tzokas, N., Jan Hultink, E., & Hart, S. (2004). Navigating the new product development process. *Industrial Marketing Management, 33,* 619–626, p. 620.

progress to human clinical trials and, of those, only one in five is approved for human usage.[47]

Despite the deliberative care taken prior to launching a new product, when exuberant developers fail to consider the relevance or need of an innovation from the target consumer's perspective, self-serving blinders often lead to ill-fated product launches. One invention that must have looked good on paper was a lavatory cleaning product that fizzed and sparkled on contact with water, leaving the impression that it was a strong and active cleaning product. Preliminary market testing, however, revealed that the dramatic effect of the product in use aroused consumer fears about its safety and, combined with the technical research that revealed a short shelf life for the chemical mixture, the project was abandoned by the household cleaning products company that had developed it.[48]

Another invention, a computer accessory known as the CueCat Scanner, quickly flopped after its appearance in the marketplace, despite strong financial backing and high expectations from such investors as Coca-Cola, Young & Rubicam, and Radio Shack.[49] Released in 2000, the CueCat was a cat-shaped handheld barcode reader that connected to a computer by PS/2 keyboard port or USB. By scanning a barcode (or so-called "cue") on a product package or printed matter, such as a catalog, article, or advertisement, the user would be directed immediately to a Web page without the need to type the URL. Developed by the American firm Digital Convergence and sent out free to millions of consumers, the CueCat never caught on, investors lost US$185 million, and the product was subsequently dubbed one of the "25 Worst Tech Products of All Time" by *PC World* magazine and the "#1 worst invention of the '2000s' decade" by the gadget blog Gizmodo.[50]

The reason for CueCat's short-lived existence is perhaps readily apparent: consumers saw no real benefit or advantage to using the product, given that it is easier to type in a Web address than to have to bother with a cumbersome scanning device and the necessity to have whatever is being scanned in front of one's computer. As one critic facetiously pointed out: "You have to wonder about a business plan based on the notion that people want to interact with a soda can." The developers of the CueCat managed to convince corporate investors that the product would solve whatever problems they were experiencing in terms of driving traffic to their websites and generating click-through rates once they attracted visitors.[51] In reality, however, low website traffic is often attributed to more fundamental problems, such as the site's poor conception or design, along with lack of a good reason for people to visit the site in the first place. From the consumer perspective, there was no apparent problem that the CueCat promised to solve, nor did the device provide any added value.

By contrast, a more recent promotional development known as the Web Decoder has proven to be an effective means to gain Web traffic while at the same time providing something of interest and value to consumers. The Web Decoder provides a means for users to decode hidden images that are embedded in a variety of promotional elements, including labels, tags, coupons, postcards, and direct food contact materials. Users are directed to a specific website where, by passing the promotional material over their computer screen, a color cancellation process permits them to read the hidden message to determine if they have won a prize. The creators of Web Decoder have developed a variety of related proprietary engagement tools that work on print and mobile device marketing media and also offer the possibility for their corporate clients to collect consumer data and monitor behavior in unique and innovative ways.

These examples provide some preliminary insight into the factors related to the success of new product innovations. Before identifying these factors, it is first important to have some kind of idea as to what we mean by "success." Generally speaking, an initial criterion for the success of a new product innovation would be its commercial realization, but naturally the key is what happens once the new product is launched, which typically is gauged in financial terms, extent of market penetration, and long-term sustainability. One benchmark for a highly successful new product launch in the consumer packaged goods industry is that first-year sales should exceed US$50 million.[52] That figure may sound impressive, especially for firms that have much smaller aspirations, but the profits reaped from a first-year success may not be sustainable over the long term. Nonetheless, in their seminal paper "Success Factors in Product Innovation," Cooper and Kleinschmidt point out that a preoccupation with financial results leads one to miss other industry success parameters: a new product may have a major impact on its market, it may introduce a new technology to the industry, and it may open up a new window of opportunity to the firm.[53]

Based on an empirical case study investigation of the new product experiences of several firms, Cooper and Kleinschmidt concluded that the keys to new product success are that the product is uniquely superior, the firm possesses a strong market orientation that is global in nature, a sufficient amount of predevelopment work has been carried out, the product definition was clarified at an early stage, the project team was well organized, and the firm managed to leverage its core competencies. In short, success requires the appropriate management environment and marketing skills; careful pre-launch planning and testing; and a unique, superior product that will be perceived as desirable in the eyes of potential customers. Lack of preparation has been identified as one of the primary factors that can cause a new product to fail. In their assessment of failed product launches, Schneider and Hall concluded that "companies are so focused on designing and manufacturing new products that they postpone the hard work of getting ready to market them until too late in the game."[54] Another facet of poor preparation, apparent in the CueCat case, is a failure to adequately evaluate during the development phase whether the product is needed in the first place—an assessment that requires considerable consumer insight.

From the consumer perspective, the key prerequisite to new product acceptance is *relative advantage*: the extent to which the product is perceived to have an advantage over existing alternatives. The importance of relative advantage to success cannot be overstated. It is easy to assume that consumers will desire anything that is new, but such a presumption only somewhat accurately describes a small minority of people who are commonly referred to by marketers as *innovators* (see below). Consumers often respond negatively to change because, in their minds, change represents a threat to their current, well-established marketplace behaviors; that is, they are more comfortable with the familiar than they are with novelty and surprise. Consistent with this characterization, well-known brand consultant Jack Trout estimates that the typical American family repeatedly purchases, on average, the same 150 items, which together constitute up to 85% of their household needs.[55] However, if you can make it clear to consumers that they will benefit in some way—the product will save them time or money, it will make their lives easier, they will gain something desirable that they currently lack, and so on—a new product stands a much greater chance of being embraced.

Although I will have much more to say about relative advantage in Chapter 3, at this juncture there are two important assets that can be found at the heart of many successful game-changing innovations throughout history: an increase in speed and a reduction of distance. The examples at the beginning of this chapter regarding the modern technological advances of the telegraph and radio illustrate these advantages quite well. The emergence of the rail transport system during the mid-nineteenth century shrank countries dramatically, increasing the speed with which people could reach their destinations. People had to learn to ride on trains, which originally were noisy, uncomfortable, and unsafe, and which traveled at speeds far higher than people had understood to be possible.[56] Eventually, the advantages in terms of distance covered and time gained were undeniable (although the same cannot be said for some modern-era metropolitan bus systems).[57]

The rapidly evolving success of online shopping similarly owes much to the relative advantages of speed and distance. A descendant of earlier direct marketing approaches, such as catalog sales and television shopping channels, shopping on the Internet (itself facilitated by the proliferation and widespread acceptance of credit cards) enables customers to avoid transportation problems associated with brick-and-mortar stores; save time that would have been lost from traveling distance, parking, and waiting in lines; and overcome problems associated with shortage of retail help (see Box 2.5).

BOX 2.5 THE MINITEL: A FRENCH SUCCESS STORY

No doubt most French people born prior to the current millennium have fond memories of the Minitel, a France Telecom device dating back to the early 1970s that connected to telephone lines and provided online services during the era predating the Internet. Initially about the size of a toaster oven, the Minitel terminal, which was provided on loan for free to telephone subscribers, was limited to text-only services that initially enabled consumers to call up phone directories, with other pay services eventually added, such as online

(Continued)

(Continued)

mail-order shopping, airline and train ticket purchases, and weather and news updates. One of the more popular features of the device was the so-called "Minitel Rose," purported to be the world's first electronic adult chatroom, where people using pseudonyms could exchange seductive messages.

At its peak, it is estimated that about nine million French households had installed the Minitel terminal and, despite predictions of its rapid demise when personal computers and the Internet arrived, by October 2001, more French people were using the Minitel (about fifteen million) than the Internet (about twelve million).[58] Eventually, as the French gradually became enlightened about the advantages of the Internet relative to the rather primitive functions of the Minitel, the writing was on the wall for the innovative Internet precursor. However, it was not until June 2012 that the plug was finally pulled on the Minitel, a time when 900,000 of the devices were still in circulation.

There are a number of factors that explain why the French were so inclined to cling tenaciously to the Minitel. It was obvious to most that the Minitel provided important advantages over printed phone directories in terms of speed, simplicity, and up-to-date accuracy. Beyond such relative advantages, however, were two important keys to the long-running success for a majority of technology products: ease of use and security. In fact, a market survey conducted by Forrester Research of more than half a million Minitel users revealed that ease of use was rated as the most important feature of the device.[59] At a time when early users of the Internet were complaining of problems loading software, configuring modems, and the high cost of dial-up services, the relative simplicity of the Minitel was more than apparent. The Forrester survey also found that Minitel users had a higher level of trust in their service than Internet users reported for theirs. In retrospect, the success of the Minitel in France likely served as a significant obstacle to the diffusion of the Internet in France. Many loyal French Minitel users had to be independently convinced that purchasing a personal computer and connecting to the Internet could offer much more in the way of functions and services than their telephone terminals. It may not have happened overnight, but eventually the relative advantages of the Internet became abundantly clear.

In addition to relative advantage, four other new product characteristics are linked to consumer acceptance: compatibility, complexity, trialability, and observability.

Compatibility refers to the extent to which a new product is consistent with potential customers' lifestyles, values, beliefs, and behavioral practices; present needs; and past experiences. The greater the degree of consistency with these consumer characteristics and behaviors, the more likely the new product will be deemed acceptable to them and adopted. Although it was relatively easy for men to make the transition from permanent to disposable razors, marketers have encountered a far greater challenge in encouraging male personal care purchasers to make the conversion from bar soaps to liquid soaps and gels. Research by Procter & Gamble revealed that women purchased as much as 70% of the shower gel for men in their households, but that using body wash struck many male consumers as unmanly.

P&G's marketing solution for promoting its Old Spice line of shower gels for men was to develop an advertising campaign that appealed to female purchasers, but at the same time cast the product as decidedly masculine so as to lure men away from bar soap. P&G accomplished this tricky balance through the creation of the award-winning "Smell Like a Man, Man" campaign—a series of video ads featuring the ruggedly handsome American ex-football player and actor Isaiah Mustafa shirtless, delivering a quick monologue about how "anything is possible" if a man uses Old Spice. The filmed commercials became an Internet sensation on video-sharing websites like YouTube, striking a chord among both men and women. P&G followed up the campaign by uploading 187 one-minute comedic videos featuring Mustafa responding to social media comments, each of which effectively linked the brand to masculinity. The overall campaign resulted in a 300% increase of traffic to the Old Spice website and helped to propel the brand to the position of leading male body wash and deodorant brand in the US.[60]

In comparison, consider the likely compatibility problems associated with new products designed to eliminate some of the nuisances of everyday life, such as the Knee Defender, an inexpensive, small plastic device developed in 2003 by attorney Ira Goldman that prevents the airplane seat in front of the user from reclining. Although more than 1,000 of the devices were purchased during the first year of availability and they are still available for online purchase, it is unlikely that such a product would successfully gain widespread adoption because many people view it as incompatible with standards of interpersonal propriety and social conduct.[61] Given the already frayed nerves and tensions experienced by many airplane passengers, it is not surprising that the Knee Defender has been the target of much heated debate and criticism, and has been banned by some airlines.[62] Other new products, such as universal remote control devices that empower people to turn off television sets in public settings (e.g., TV B-Gone) or block mobile phone signals ("cell phone jammers"), are similarly likely to clash with interpersonal norms.

Complexity, or the degree to which a new product is perceived to be difficult to understand and use, represents another characteristic linked to the adoption of new product innovations. Jack Dorsey, the founder of the enormously popular microblogging social network Twitter and the mobile payments application Square, revealed the secret to his success when he commented, "My goal is to simplify complexity"—an idea we will return to in Chapter 3.[63] The key to understanding how complexity influences product acceptance lies in recognizing that complexity is in the eye of the beholder, a point that also applies to the other product attributes discussed in this section. Many consumers, for example, perceive the operation of some relatively simple new technological innovations, such as tablet PCs or digital microwave ovens, to be overly complex, but not others, such as driving a motor vehicle, the latter of which requires the coordination of a far greater set of cognitive and manual skills. A variety of consumer fears are linked to reluctance to accept certain high-tech products, including those of technical complexity, rapid obsolescence, social rejection, and physical harm (see Box 2.6). In Chapter 3, we will see that consumers are demanding products that are simple to use right out of the box (such as "plug-and-play" devices). However, it still is the case that many product manufacturers are wont to include numerous functions because it is often cheaper to install them on every device or machine in case they are desired by customers than to create modified, "edited" versions for different buyers.

BOX 2.6 PERCEIVED RISKS: BARRIERS TO NEW PRODUCT ADOPTION

Consumers approach most product purchase situations with a certain degree of trepidation, and this is nowhere truer than when the purchase involves something new to the marketplace. The sense of inquietude we experience leading up to our pulling the trigger on a new purchase emanates from a variety of perceived risks, where *risk* is defined in terms of the potential negative consequences perceived by a consumer in choosing a product or brand during a specific purchase occasion.[64] In essence, the greater the degree of uncertainty about a particular product, the less likely it will be adopted by the customer. This uncertainty may stem from a variety of sources, suggesting that there are different types of perceived risks:

- **Functional risk**—This type of uncertainty is based on concerns that the product under consideration will not live up to its promise or perform as expected or needed. Will the new movie streaming device for my television be able to access the channels I want to watch? Will the adaptor plug connect to my television?
- **Financial risk**—The concern here pertains to whether or not the price paid will be justified by the needs-satisfying properties of the purchase. Is the 3-D printer I'm thinking of buying worth the price they are asking for it? Will I be able to keep up with the monthly payments?
- **Physical risk**—This uncertainty involves fears that the product may prove harmful to the purchaser, other consumers, or the environment. Do electronic cigarettes really minimize harmful health effects? Will the microwave oven pose any risks to my baby or to the environment?
- **Social risk**—In this case, the consumer is concerned that the purchase will be unacceptable in the eyes of others, result in embarrassment among one's

peers or family members, or lead to ostracism from social groups. Will a new tattoo cause me any problems with my parents or boyfriend? Will my Google Glass purchase lead to any conflicts with my coworkers or neighbors?

- **Psychological risk**—This is the perception that the product under consideration may not prove to be a good match with the buyer's self-image. Is owning an electric car consistent with the way I see myself? Do I really deserve such a high-end tablet PC?
- **Aesthetic/design risk**—This uncertainty pertains to concerns about the stylistic and design merits of a purchase under consideration. Will the halogen lamp really fit in with the furnishing style of our living room? Will the Café Balão coffee maker fit well on our kitchen counter and be comfortable to pour?

Consumers may experience varying levels of one or more of these types of risk in any purchase situation, with the end result being that the purchase under consideration is likely to be delayed, reconsidered, or perhaps abandoned altogether. Certain conditions are predictors of higher levels of perceived risk, including inexperience with or limited knowledge about the product category, a bad or disappointing past experience, limited financial resources, low self-confidence, and a lack of clarity about one's buying goals. When these sorts of conditions are prevalent, consumers would be said to have "high involvement" with the product or purchase occasion, meaning that they would have a strong motivation to seek out and process product-related information. In fact, information seeking—consulting online reviews, reading company brochures, soliciting word of mouth from trustworthy persons, and the like—is an expected primary strategy for reducing uncertainty and perceptions of risk prior to an important purchase. Other risk-reduction strategies often employed by shoppers include buying from a reputable store or website; relying on the brand with the strongest image or one to which one is loyal; and reassurances, such as strong guarantees, warranties, and easy return options.

When a new product is capable of being used on an experimental, limited basis, it is said to possess the characteristic of *trialability*, which is another factor that enhances the likelihood of adoption. Who buys a new car without first taking it out for a test spin? When it comes to something that has not previously existed, the desire to try it out prior to adoption is quite compelling. Needless to say, some innovations are more readily trialable than others, such as a wide range of inexpensive items for which consumers can make a relatively low-risk trial purchase in small quantities (e.g., supermarket goods, personal hygiene items). In the digital world, there are many possibilities for computer and portable device users to download limited free-trial versions of software and applications, most of which can be easily uninstalled if they prove unsatisfactory.

Trialability is more difficult for other products, such as expensive, durable goods like refrigerators, portable computers, and solar energy systems. Among the solutions that have proven effective in overcoming consumer reticence in such cases is to offer leasing plans, with a subsequent option to purchase, in-store demonstrations, and the uploading of online videos showing the product in action and demonstrating how it functions. Many customers have taken to uploading videos to YouTube, blogs, and other websites to highlight the strengths and weaknesses of their new product purchases. One variation of this approach that has grown in popularity is the so-called "unboxing" video, which consists of the owner filming the unpacking of a new product—typically a high-tech item—and then uploading the video to a website, a practice that some have come to refer to as "geek porn."[65] When consumer questions such as "Does it come with a European adaptor plug?" are not readily answered by online service representatives, unpacking videos can provide invaluable information that can make or break a purchase decision.

Perfume manufacturers and retailers have found various means for exploiting trialability so as to stimulate the purchase of luxury brands, including the availability of tester bottles in perfume shops, the giving away of free sample vials of new fragrances with a purchase, and the relatively less expensive use of fragrance strips in magazines. Fragrance or scent strips, which have frequently accompanied print advertisements for perfumes since the early 1980s, are a direct descendant of "scratch-and-sniff" materials that have long been used to promote deodorants, shampoos, and other products. Based on a microencapsulation process developed during the mid-1960s, each strip contains nearly a quarter of a million tiny capsules of fragrance safely sealed in chemical bubbles that are released when a covering tab is broken. About 100,000 of the bubbles break during the initial trial, enabling the consumer to capture the scent, while the remainder provide fragrance for a few more rubs on the wrist.[66] In addition to providing a pre-purchase assessment of the product, testing strips also offer the relative advantage of time savings for consumers who are unable to fit a visit to a perfume shop into a busy schedule. The testing strip technology has been used in recent years within a range of industries, including tobacco, liquor, food and beverage, and luxury automobiles, the latter having used the aroma of fine leather to lure customers.

Another rising trend consistent with the trialability notion has been dubbed "tryvertising" by some marketing pundits—an approach that represents a real-life alternative to traditional advertising by providing consumers with opportunities to try out products before purchasing them.[67] One variation that originated in 2007 in Tokyo is Sample Lab, a members-only shopping space that exhibits new products for sampling and testing. For a modest fee, members can try out the products in the shop and take home up to five items per visit, with the requirement that they complete surveys about the products once they have tested them. Members are also encouraged to spread positive word of mouth about the products that they like. Since Sample Lab emerged on the scene, other sampling salons have opened in Japan, and the testing concept has begun to take root in other parts of the world. In addition to membership fees, revenue for such spaces comes from manufacturers who pay to have their products displayed, as well as from market research organizations that use the salon as a kind of final hurdle prior to launching a new product into the market.

Another key new product attribute linked to consumer acceptance is *observability* (or communicability), which pertains to the extent to which the product and its benefits are visible or can be readily described, perceived, or imagined by potential customers. Some products, by their very nature, are publicly visible to others, such as a new car, fashion item, eyewear, luggage, notebook computer, and the like. Observability clearly played an important role in the widespread adoption of Apple's iPod portable music player, introduced in 2001. Although the device itself was typically transported out of view in the user's pocket, the iconic white earbud headset was unmistakable, and explicitly distinguished the iPod from other brands. The more prevalent the dangling white headset wires became in public settings, the more likely they were to convey the popularity of the device, thereby reassuring potential adopters of the product's quality.

Intangible and privately used offerings are far less communicable, especially if their benefits or consequences are not immediately forthcoming, as would be the case with nutritional products, exercise equipment, and the energy-saving attributes of some appliances. Service marketers face a strong challenge in communicating the nature and benefits of the services they promote, which are extremely difficult to depict in formal advertising efforts. The introduction of the first public telephones during the late nineteenth century encountered significant challenges prior to garnering widespread acceptance. The idea of a device capable of transmitting the voice of a non-present individual was a completely new concept. Many people were of the belief that human speech was sacred and should not be carried by electricity, whereas others perceived Alexander Graham Bell's invention as a "magical box," which was somehow linked to the supernatural or witchcraft.[68] Within the business community, the prevailing belief was that the telephone offered no apparent advantages over the existing capabilities of the telegraph. To counter these reservations, Bell attempted to persuade people by holding numerous public demonstrations of his "magic box" until the device had "passed out of the realm of suspected witchcraft."[69] On the heels of Bell's demonstrations, telephone salesmen made a concerted effort to demonstrate the product's utility face-to-face with potential customers. Around the same time, there was an organized effort to install public telephones in conspicuous places, such as hotel lobbies, so that their usage was readily observable.

How innovations spread

If one considers the process by which new product or service innovations spread over time among the members of a social system, it becomes apparent that the diffusion follows a predictable course not unlike a normal distribution. What this means is that a predictable proportion of all ultimate adopters will acquire the product right away, and other adopters will follow in due course.[70]

People high in consumer innovativeness, so-called "innovators," represent the initial adopters of an innovation, and typically comprise a rather small percentage (roughly 2.5%) of all eventual adopters. In terms of adoption timing, innovators are followed by early adopters (approximately 13.5% of all those who ultimately adopt the new product)—persons who represent another important group to marketers because they often serve as role models who transmit advice and recommendations to others. Early adopters are followed, in turn, by the early majority (34%), the late majority (34%), and laggards (18%). The normal distribution that depicts the timing of adoption across these categories of consumers tends to coincide with the life cycle of the innovation itself; that is, by the time the late majority and laggards adopt the innovation, the product may be nearing the end of its successful run and about to be superseded by something new.

Consumer *innovativeness* refers to the degree to which consumers are open to new ideas and willing to try products, services, and brands soon after their introduction.[71] From a marketing standpoint, the identification and study of consumer innovators is important because their response is often crucial to the ultimate success of a new product or service. Generally speaking, innovators are relatively young, well-educated, and higher in financial well-being than others in their social group. They are not "typical" consumers; rather, they are dynamic and curious by nature, and are venturesome people who like to take risks. New product innovations tend to be highly priced when they first appear in the marketplace and, no matter how much product testing they may undergo prior to launch, are usually perceived as unproven by most consumers. Should innovators respond unfavorably, it is a bad sign that suggests the product is unlikely to succeed among the general consuming public. On the other hand, if innovators and, in turn, influentials, are observed by others to adopt an innovation, that innovation may well spread throughout the population.

Because it is an important trait to consider when launching new products, researchers have developed various self-report scales to measure consumer innovativeness, such as Goldsmith and Hofhacker's Domain-Specific Innovativeness (DSI) scale and Manning, Bearden, and Madden's Consumer Innovativeness Scale (CIS).[72] Using these sorts of measures, researchers have found that consumer innovativeness is related to various behaviors in addition to new product adoption, including novelty seeking, risk taking, information seeking, and online shopping.[73] Consumers who are high in variety seeking tend to possess some of the same characteristics that are associated with innovativeness, including open-mindedness, extroversion, creativity, and ability to deal with complex or ambiguous stimuli.[74] Finally, there is evidence that innovators and non-innovators tend to respond differently to promotional campaigns, with innovators more likely to react favorably to informative or factual advertising and to judge the merits of a new product according to personal standards. Non-innovators tend to be more responsive to marketing messages that depict the product being used within social contexts and to communications presented by a recognized and trusted expert or celebrity.[75]

Overcoming product launch failures

There are any number of factors that can undermine the success of a new product. As discussed above, lack of preparation and poor management on the part of the firm, and the development of new products that are not attuned to the needs of customers or that fail to offer any perceived technological superiority, are among the main problems leading to product launch failures. Based on their analyses of actual new product cases, Schneider and Hall point to five key flaws that are predictive of failure:

1.   the company cannot support fast growth;
2.   the product falls short of claims and gets heavily criticized shortly after it is launched;
3.   the new item exists in "product limbo"—that is, its benefits or unique selling proposition are unclear;
4.   the product defines a new category, which the company fails to support through substantial consumer education;
5.   the product is revolutionary, but there is no market for it.

Based on these critical missteps, Schneider and Hall derived, respectively, five basic lessons for firms:

1.   have a plan in place to quickly support the product if it takes off;
2.   delay your launch until the product is ready;
3.   test the product to make sure its differences can be identified and communicated to potential buyers;
4.   develop a strong educational campaign to assure that consumers can quickly grasp how to use the product;
5.   do not avoid the basic questions concerning who will buy the product and what represents a reasonable price.

The initial two flaws are largely matters of timing that often can be dealt with by postponing the launch and resolving any manufacturing and quality problems. The other flaws pertain more directly to the nature of the product itself, and overcoming them will require coordination across company departments, including product and brand management, sales, advertising, public relations, and Web management.

Obtaining feedback from potential customers is also essential to determine whether the product should be launched at all or presented in some modified form. In recent years, companies have increasingly enlisted the assistance of customers during the new product development process. The term *co-creation* has emerged to describe how firms and consumers can innovate together, and is considered in depth in Chapter 5.

How companies should engage in conversations with customers during the product development process is the focus of a recent investigation by Swedish researchers Gustafsson, Kristensson, and Witell, the results of which point out that the customer may not always be right.[76] According to the research findings, based on a survey of 334 managers who had previous experience with the new product innovation process, the utility of customer insight depends in part on the nature of the innovation under consideration. For incremental innovations that consist of minor improvements to products and services, it appears most advantageous for companies to engage customers in frequent two-way communication and to listen carefully to what they have to say. It is often the case that consumers know better than product managers what should be done to a product to increase its potential to satisfy, and how much they are willing to pay for that improvement.

For radical innovations, however, although it is important to communicate frequently with customers to gain better insight into what is important to them, customer proposals for entirely new products tend not be very useful, often leading to failure for companies that place too much credence in the recommendations. This is not to downplay the significant value that a meaningful and extensive dialogue with consumers can bring to the product development process: as long as consumers are given the right parameters for their active participation, customer input clearly should be added to the list of success factors for the development of new products.

The impact of technology on human life

There is little doubt that technology has long had profound effects on our daily lives, although clearly there are mixed perspectives on whether, how, and under what conditions these effects may contribute to human betterment or human detriment. This is a vast subject to tackle in a few pages in a book chapter, especially given that there are arguments replete with supporting evidence on both sides of the ledger. Even as developments in information technology historically were viewed as having a positive impact on bringing people together, informing and educating them more effectively, and reducing distances, those same advances also provided governments and militaries with greater power and means of control—a poignant point relative to contemporary concerns about how the Internet is increasingly employed by government agencies and businesses as a tool to track the private behaviors of ordinary citizens. Similarly, advances in medical technology, from genetic mapping and robotics for complex surgeries to the 3-D printing of human tissue and organs, have aroused ethical concerns about the morality of genetic determination, selective abortions based on neonatal biological markers, the consequences of prolonging life in the face of a growing scarcity of planetary resources, and so on. One can also add here the growing concerns about the potential for homemade creation of guns and other weapons via the 3-D printing process.[77]

Moreover, there are both generational and economic implications to bear in mind when it comes to evaluating the impact of technology. For contemporary teens born in industrialized countries, devices have always been portable, mobile phones have always existed, technology is always evolving at an exponential rate, and communicating online is something that has always been possible. For many contemporary youths, the idea of what the world was like prior to the Internet and mobile phones is no doubt a foreign one. There are also growing concerns that economically advantaged groups within a society—and on a broader scale, nations—have greater access to information technologies and communication tools, and the resources to use them, than disadvantaged people who lack such access and resources. If information is power, then this so-called "digital divide" stands to exacerbate the economic advantages of the former, to the detriment of the latter.

Simple innovations that changed our lives

Even the most apparently mundane advances in technology can have profound influences on everyday life. Imagine what your daily experiences would be like without such elegantly unpretentious modern inventions as Velcro, Post-it notes, zippers, light bulbs, escalators, staplers, paper clips, tape, and perforations. Perhaps no one has written more eloquently of such taken-for-granted creations than Nicholson Baker in his 1986 book *The Mezzanine*, in which an innovation like the perforation is elevated to the pantheon of our civilization's landmark advances:

> Perforation! Shout it out! The deliberate punctuated weakening of paper and cardboard so that it will tear along an intended path, leaving a row of fine-haired white pills or tuftlets on each new edge! It is a staggering conception, showing an age-transforming feel for the unique properties of pulped wood fiber. Yet do we have national holidays to celebrate its development? Are festschrift volumes published honoring the dead greats in the field? People watch the news every night like robots, thinking they are learning about their lives, never paying attention to the far more immediate developments that arrive unreported, on the zip-lock perforated top of the ice cream carton, in reply coupons bound in magazines and on the "Please Return This Portion" edging of bill stubs, on sheets of postage stamps . . . on paper towels, in rolls of plastic bags for produce at the supermarket . . . .[78]

It is easy to identify with Baker's bemused queries about why even highly educated persons have little if any idea about how the perforations on such products as the toilet paper roll are accomplished and who pioneered the idea.[79] It should not surprise us that innovations that have given rise to what on first glance appear to be simple products, like perforated paper, tape, Post-it notes, and Velcro, typically escape our everyday reflections, in part because their applications are so ubiquitous. Tape—whether the Scotch, duct, masking, or electrical variety—satisfies a range of versatile uses, including the binding of packages for mailing; the insulation of one's home to save energy costs; hanging of posters or photos for home or office decoration; repairing of torn paper, broken objects, and frayed electrical wires; and even played a role in the survival of the Apollo 13 astronauts.

It is unlikely that Swiss inventor George de Mestral could have foreseen in the early 1940s the numerous practical applications of Velcro when he created the fastening technology following years of contemplating how burrs stuck to his woolen socks and his dog's fur. Yet it is the rare day in which a person does not come into contact with Velcro—the name a combination of the French words *velour* (velvet) and *crochet* (hook)—in one form or another in a variety of contexts, including clothing, sportswear and equipment, office and medical equipment, and the aircraft and automotive industries.

Post-it notes represent another good example of high-tech minimalism that has become a vital part of everyday life, particularly in the workplace, where the sticky rectangles of colored, blank paper frequently serve as reminders, place-marks, and temporary labels. The product itself was serendipitously created following an unsuccessful effort by the 3M Company to develop a new super-sticky adhesive. Initial tests on the marketability of the slightly sticky temporary bookmarks that ultimately gave birth to Post-its proved futile, as no one could figure out how they could be used by consumers.[80] The answer emerged when 3M carried out a seeding trial in 1977 among a sample of opinion leaders within the office supplies industry: secretaries to senior management staff at US companies. The secretaries were sent boxes of Post-it notes from the company, and were invited to suggest possible uses for them. Before long, the Post-its started appearing on memos, drafts, desks, and correspondence, and eventually spread like wildfire across companies. This was all the evidence 3M needed to successfully launch the eventual multi-million-dollar brand. Today, we see the evolution of the original Post-its in various digital formats, including operating software widgets and document-saving tools like Evernote.

The rise of multitasking

Advances in digital technology and the emergence of innovative communication devices have transformed the consumer environment into one that has spawned a trend towards *multitasking*—a tendency for individuals to engage in multiple tasks at the same time. People are surfing the Internet while watching TV, chatting on their mobile phones while driving, and reading their emails on personal digital assistants (PDAs) during business meetings. A 2003 analysis by the Media Center at the American Press Institute and BIGresearch reported that 70% of consumers in general are apt to engage in media multitasking, and the Mobium Creative Group found that as many as 83% of business professionals do so as they carry out their work-related tasks.[81] More recently, a 2009 European study led by Microsoft

Advertising found that watching TV while surfing the Internet has become a mainstream activity, with 70% of Europeans reporting that they do so.[82]

On the surface, it may appear that simultaneous media use is a positive development for marketers who fear that new media are undercutting the potential to reach consumer targets through traditional channels. However, results from the Mobium Creative Group study suggest otherwise: it appears that rather than reinforcing consumer reach through multiple channels, media multitasking tends to dilute the impact of marketing messages. Fully 80% of business professionals surveyed claimed to pay more attention to one medium as opposed to others when they multitasked. Specifically, when asked about the last time they used media simultaneously, business professionals revealed that they paid the most attention to the Internet (41%), newspapers (20%), and television (18%), with all other media scoring 5% or less (i.e., trade journals, general business publications, radio, direct mail, and sales literature).

What these findings seem to suggest is that broad, multi-channel marketing campaigns not only exacerbate the growing problem of advertising clutter, but they also appear to be surprisingly ineffective at capturing consumer attention. For instance, if a target consumer group is comprised of television/personal computer multitaskers, an expensive television campaign may escape the attention of viewers whose heads are down during advertising breaks. Unless a media mix is strategically developed and carefully targeted, increased ad spending will continue to reap diminishing returns.

Technology's impact on human cognition

As often tends to be the case when there are rapid, significant advances in information and communication innovation, enthusiastic projections about their potential benefits for individuals and societies are inevitably tempered by dire prophesies about the wide range of harmful consequences that inevitably will be wrought by new technologies. In the current Web 2.0 era, one emerging issue that has been greeted with great trepidation by social commentators has to do with the impact of new technologies on the human brain. This issue was given impetus by a 2008 *Atlantic Magazine* article written by author Nicholas Carr, who asked, "Is Google making us stupid?"—a question that emerged in part from the following observations:

> Over the past few years I've had an uncomfortable sense that someone, or something, has been tinkering with my brain, remapping the neural circuitry, reprogramming the memory. My mind isn't going—so far as I can tell—but it's changing. I'm not thinking the way I used to think. I can feel it most strongly when I'm reading. Immersing myself in a book or a lengthy article used to be easy. My mind would get caught up in the narrative or the turns of the argument, and I'd spend hours strolling through long stretches of prose.

That's rarely the case anymore. Now my concentration often starts to drift after two or three pages. I get fidgety, lose the thread, begin looking for something else to do. I feel as if I'm always dragging my wayward brain back to the text. The deep reading that used to come naturally has become a struggle.[83]

Carr concluded that while computers may be providing us with formidable skills for information search, they also are reconfiguring the neural pathways in our brains, with the end result being that our abilities to comprehend and retain information—particularly in the form of written text—are becoming significantly impaired.

During the modern era, such concerns have predictably accompanied the emergence onto the scene of seductively powerful new technologies. More than fifty years ago, Marshall McLuhan tempered his now famous expression "The medium is the message" with warnings of the homogenizing and dehumanizing effects of mass media, particularly in response to the growing role of television in society. Neil Postman, whose ideas about the impact of telegraphy were discussed earlier in this chapter, similarly warned about the ill effects likely to befall a public increasingly seduced by television. In his view, once television overtook the printed word as the center of industrialized cultures, serious, in-depth public discourse began its descent into trivialization:

When a population becomes distracted by trivia, when a cultural life is redefined as a perpetual round of entertainment, when serious public conversation becomes a form of baby-talk, when, in short, a people become an audience and their public business a vaudeville act, then a nation finds itself at risk; culture-death is a clear possibility.[84]

Although Postman's predictions of the death of culture may have been greatly exaggerated, at the center of his arguments is a grim vision of a future in which people become addicted to technologies that reduce their critical thinking faculties, ultimately eroding their ability to think. It is hardly surprising that these points appear particularly relevant in the contemporary context, where the often obsessive use of digital devices and smartphones has become a central feature of everyday life.

The implications of the impact of our increasing reliance on the Internet—and, by extension, digital, portable technological devices—on the brain are as profound as Postman's warnings about television. As one reviewer pointedly inquired: "What are the consequences of new habits of mind that abandon sustained immersion and concentration for darting about, snagging bits of information?"[85] Returning to Carr's ideas, which he elaborated on in his best-seller *The Shallows: What the Internet is Doing to Our Brains*, the emergence of the Internet is causing the human brain to change. In his view, as people become more efficient at multitasking and searching for information, they become less creative in their thinking and ultimately lose their abilities to engage in a more contemplative, coherent, and critical mode of thought. Carr elaborated on the root of this ominous evolutionary trend in an interview with *The New York Times*:

> What changes our brains is, on the one hand, repetition and, on the other hand, neglect. That's why I believe the Net is having such far-reaching intellectual consequences. When we're online, we tend to perform the same physical and mental actions over and over again, at a high rate of speed and in a state of perpetual distractedness. The more we go through those motions, the more we train ourselves to be skimmers and scanners and surfers. But the Net provides no opportunity or encouragement for more placid, attentive thought. What we're losing, through neglect, is our capacity for contemplation, introspection, reflection — all those ways of thinking that require attentiveness and deep concentration.[86]

There is no question that these are compelling arguments, and it is likely that most avid Internet users could proffer any number of anecdotal observations in the way of supportive evidence. What Internet user would argue that attention span has not been affected as a result of having so much information at one's fingertips, available both instantaneously and simultaneously? Are we "evolving" into a race of super-multitaskers who lack the capacity for contemplation? Are we regressing to a preconscious state? These questions recall some of the ideas that appear in psychologist Julian Jaynes' 1976 book *The Origins of Consciousness in the Breakdown of the Bicameral Mind*.[87] Drawing on split-brain laboratory studies and archaeological evidence, Jaynes compellingly argued that ancient peoples, ranging from Mesopotamia to Peru, could not "think" as we do today (or at least prior to the Internet) and thus literally were not conscious. Lacking the ability to introspect, people experienced auditory hallucinations attributed to the voices of the gods, which told them what to do in novel or stressful situations. Humanity essentially had to learn consciousness as a result of catastrophe and cataclysm, as recently as 3,000 years ago. In this light, Carr's arguments about the effects of the Internet on human thought would suggest another compelling question: if ancient societies were *preconscious*, are we heading to a future in which humanity is, in essence, *post-conscious*?

In recent years, these questions have begun to be put to the test as the focus of research on the brain, which has evolved considerably since the days of the split-brain studies described by Jaynes. Researchers are now studying brain activity through the use of functional magnetic resonance imagery (fMRI), a scan that assesses changes in blood flow related to neural activity in the brain and is one of several new techniques that are being employed in studies of attention, emotion, and memory. Within the field of marketing, this work collectively falls under the label of "neuromarketing," a nascent field that attempts to link brain activity to consumer response, with the ultimate goal of shedding light on the larger question of how the consumer brain makes decisions.

Although still in the early stages, the results of preliminary brain activity research add some credence to concerns that excessive Internet use can physically alter the brain. One investigation employing fMRI scans assessed the brains of 14–21-year-old Chinese adolescents who were classified as suffering from Internet Addiction Disorder (IAD)—a condition involving excessive use of the computer to the point that it interferes with daily living, and which is now more commonly referred to as Problematic Internet Use (PIU) or Compulsive Internet Use (CIU).[88] Compared with non-addicted Internet users, multiple structural changes were apparent in both the white and gray matter of the IAD participants' brains, resulting in disruption to nerve fiber connections that link brain areas involved in emotions, decision-making, and self-control. Such changes in brain function are consistent with impaired individual psychological well-being, academic failure, and reduced work performance in adolescents. Moreover, it appears that excessive Internet use shares psychological and neural mechanisms with types of substance addiction and impulse control disorders, including alcoholism and excessive video game playing.

The results of an ongoing research project led by Gary Small, director of UCLA's Memory and Aging Research Center, add further support to the contention that heavy Internet usage results in brain alterations, but that these in fact may serve to *enhance* certain cognitive skills.[89] On the basis of fMRI analyses, Small and his team have identified a "brain gap" between young "digital natives"—persons born into a world of computers and digital devices who spend an average of eight-and-a-half hours a day exposed to digital technology—and older "digital immigrants" who were born before the emergence of new digital technologies and eventually adopted them later in life to a lesser extent than natives. Overall, the research reveals that for digital natives, heavier Internet exposure results in a rewiring of the brain's neural circuitry, leading to a heightening of multitasking skills, complex reasoning, and decision making. However, the researchers also concluded that the cognitive developments associated with immersion in tech-related activities entails a cost in "people skills," such as a reduction in emotional aptitudes like empathy. Although digital immigrants have had to embrace technology with their already-developed brain structure and function, it appears that the brain remains flexible in older persons and is highly trainable, such that simple tasks like searching on the Internet are capable of enhancing brain circuitry.

These representative studies are consistent in demonstrating that new technologies can indeed alter brain structure and functioning, but also point out how the impact on cognitive skills and other human capabilities is not necessarily negative, as many critics have contended. For example, although much psychological research has focused on the potential harms of video games related to aggression, addiction, and depression, the potential benefits of "gaming," which has become more complex, realistic, and social in nature, cannot be denied. A recent Dutch review of research on the positive effects of interactive video-game playing concluded that such activity has the potential to enhance learning, health, and social skills.[90] Several studies demonstrate that some gaming activities—particularly the playing of shooter games that are often violent—can strengthen cognitive skills related to spatial navigation (e.g., the player's capacity to think about objects in three dimensions), and can also lead to improvements in reasoning, creativity, memory, and perception. Games that are simple, easy to access, and quickly played, such as the popular *Angry Birds* video game application, can serve as effective tools for learning resilience in the face of failure, and can improve players' moods and reduce anxiety. Contrary to the stereotype that gaming promotes social isolation, the research also reveals that a majority of gamers play with a friend (more than 70%) and participate as members of virtual social communities in massive multiplayer games such as World of Warcraft and Farmville. Involvement in massive virtual communities encourages cooperation and promotes social decision-making skills related to how to lead a group and who can or cannot be trusted.

Technology's impact on social interaction

"I Forgot My Phone" is the title of an amusing and enormously popular two-minute video that first appeared on YouTube and other websites in September 2013, quickly garnering more than 15 million views. The video, which struck many viewers as more sad than funny, depicts a day in the life of a young woman who increasingly observes that the people around her are living their lives more through their portable devices than through direct experience with each other. In successive scenes, we see the woman ignored by her companions during lunch, at a concert, while bowling, at a birthday party and, finally, while in bed with her boyfriend, as these various individuals stare at their phones. The video poignantly echoes a refrain that has become all too common in recent years concerning the social and experiential downsides to societies grown addicted to technology and lives lived through computer and smartphone screens. In a broader sense, the argument is that technology—particularly of the mobile device variety—is undermining our capacity to be human and our ability to acknowledge the social world around us. Of course, it could be argued that despite the fact that people are spending an increasing amount of their waking hours texting, tweeting, checking their email, and chatting on their portable devices, they obviously are connecting with *someone*. Nonetheless, a legitimate corollary question to Carr's "Is Google making us stupid?" is the one that asks, "Does technology make us less social?" Ironically, much of the focus on the latter question has been placed on *social* media.

The oft-repeated argument, espoused by such well-known writers as Malcolm Gladwell in his article "Small Change: Why the Revolution Will Not be Tweeted" and blogger Mark W. Schaeffer in his online post "Is Social Media Creating a Generation of Cowards?," is that social media inhibit human interaction and have deleterious effects on real-life social relationships.[91] The idea that technology encourages a retreat from the social world despite the greater opportunities it offers for connectedness is not a new one. When *The New York Times* first reported on the telephone in 1876, even before Bell's invention had been introduced to the public, it warned: "The telephone, by bringing music and ministers into every home, will empty the concert-halls and the churches."[92] Today, similar concerns have been voiced about the socially isolating potential of the Internet and the ease of connection via smartphones and other portable technology.

On the research side, a widely cited mid-1990s study by psychologist Robert Kraut and his colleagues at Carnegie Mellon University found a variety of negative effects associated with Internet use on measures of social involvement and psychological well-being among a sample of American families.[93] Based on this evidence, the researchers concluded that Internet usage replaces close social interaction and thereby increases isolation. However, on closer scrutiny, other investigators identified some methodological flaws in the research. For example, the nature of the recruitment process led to the selection of research participants who were very likely to experience a decrease in social contacts and community involvement during the course of the study, even without Internet access. In a follow-up paper published four years later, Kraut's research team reported that the negative effects identified in their earlier study actually dissipated over time, and that another of their studies revealed a variety of positive effects of Internet use on communication, social involvement, and personal well-being, regardless of age.[94]

In her 2011 book *Alone Together: Why We Expect More from Technology and Less from Each Other*,[95] Professor Sherry Turkle of MIT examined the effects of technology use on human relationships amidst the increased predilection of people to forgo face-to-face contact. The book begins with the stark assertion that "technology proposes itself as the architect of our intimacies," suggesting that technology serves as a mechanism by which people can exert greater management over their interpersonal relationships. This empowerment is reflected in Turkle's interviews with adolescents who admitted a preference for texting rather than the more socially awkward and intrusive use of the telephone, and who claimed to test out ideas and expressions online in order to see how others would react. Those same teens admitted to experiencing high anxiety when they did not receive quick replies to their text messages.

What emerges from Turkle's analysis is a disconcerting yet complex portrait of the effects of technology on social interaction. At the same time that immersion in virtual space via mobile phones and Internet usage is resulting in various forms of human disconnectedness, increasing the frequency of interactions but reducing their quality and substantiveness, and altering social codes by diminishing the significance of real-life conversations and direct social experiences, there also are certain psychological benefits that cannot be ignored. Among the benefits are opportunities for self-exploration via non-threatening means of "trying out" different self-identities and social identities online. This notion was touched upon in Chapter 1 in my discussion of the ways that Internet users can create avatars as a means of experimenting with different identities. In his paper on the extended self in the virtual world, Russell Belk elaborated on the idea that the online environment provides a secure context for individuals to co-construct and reaffirm their sense of self through activities like posting photos, tagging, and sharing comments (see Box 2.7). For example, comments from participants in one's social network that are added to a "selfie" (a self-portrait photograph taken with a hand-held digital device and uploaded to the Internet) can play a role in shaping one's sense of self and provide a mechanism for the reception of reassuring, self-confirming feedback. This process of self-construction is reflected in the following passage from Jenna Drenton's study of online mobile photo sharing among 13 teenage girls:

> Giggling and chatter comes streaming through the dressing room door as three teenage girls stand inside, trying on dresses covered in rhinestones and beads. One of the girls pulls out her cellular phone and turns on the camera feature. Instinctively, the other two girls strike a pose alongside their camera-wielding friend as she snaps a digital photograph of their reflection in the dressing room mirror. With the touch of a button, the picture is uploaded from the girl's mobile phone to her Facebook profile. Almost simultaneously, her online friends begin posting comments: "Cute dress!" "Looks great—you should definitely get it!" Thus, a consumption experience that was once only privy to the girls physically inside of the dressing room is now displayed for public viewing and feedback on the World Wide Web.[97]

Box 2.7 SELF-ENHANCEMENT IN ONLINE CONVERSATIONS

Are people more adept at managing their social identities on the Internet or in real life? And if there is a difference, what are the implications in terms of the nature of what people talk about in the online and offline modalities? One recent investigation considered these sorts of questions in the context of research on a topic of increasing interest to marketers: word of mouth (WOM), the informal communications that take place among consumers concerning a marketing organization, product, or service.

Marketing researchers Berger and Iyengar compared the nature of WOM content transmitted through online channels of communication (such as email or posting online reviews) and offline channels (such as face-to-face or telephone).[96] Although there are several differences between online and offline WOM (e.g., offline WOM is characterized by higher trust levels; online WOM is apt to be

(Continued)

(Continued)

written and more likely to persist over time), one difference that has largely been neglected by researchers has to do their degree of synchronicity. Offline (oral) conversations tend to be synchronous, in that the participants in the exchange interact in real time, with little if any delay between one person's utterance and another's response. By contrast, online (written) conversations tend to be more asynchronous in nature, typically with various delays or breaks occurring during the exchange. For instance, in contrast to a phone conversation, when someone sends an email, there is likely to be a delay of several hours, or even days, before a response is forthcoming. (This is also true, albeit to a lesser extent, in terms of the break between responding to a text message or online chat.)

Berger and Iyengar reasoned that the inherent asynchrony of online exchanges allows participants to more carefully construct and refine their communications, as opposed to simply speaking spontaneously about whatever comes to mind. In essence, this means that asynchrony provides opportunities for people participating in WOM exchanges to engage in selective self-presentation, carefully choosing more interesting things to talk about. Based on a series of laboratory experiments, the researchers found strong support for their contention that the communication modality influences what is discussed by WOM conversation partners. When participants communicated using the written channel rather than the oral one, they mentioned more interesting products and brands (e.g., Apple's iPhone, Nike, and American Apparel) as opposed to not very interesting ones (e.g., toothpaste, toilet paper, and Kleenex) and, in so doing, were better able to enhance their self-identity.

These research findings help us better understand why young people—perhaps the age cohort most apt to be wrestling with self-identity issues—feel so comfortable interacting in the more anonymous online universe, which offers the possibility to put one's best foot forward through careful planning when interacting with others (impulsive Facebook or Twitter posts notwithstanding). Because of the greater spontaneity of face-to-face conversations, it is more difficult to plan what to say in advance, especially for chance encounters and unanticipated responses. For marketers, the research findings pose a challenge to their efforts to stimulate WOM through different channels, especially given the likelihood that certain kinds of products and brands may be more "talkable" online or offline. To generate more online WOM, it will be necessary to frame one's offerings in an interesting or surprising way, whereas the stimulation of offline WOM may necessitate making the offerings more salient or accessible in people's minds.

These ideas about online co-creation were put into practice by the Italian *prêt-à-porter* clothing company Diesel when the firm launched its ingenious Diesel Cam campaign in 2010 as a short-term effort to promote the brand via social media in Spain. Touch-screen systems were placed outside dressing rooms in Diesel's real-world stores, enabling shoppers to photograph themselves in outfits they were trying on, add a comment, and directly upload it to Facebook to share with and obtain feedback from their friends. Of course, nowadays, as evidenced in the excerpt above from Drenton's study, most digital devices provide the same sort of social photo-sharing functions as were employed by the Diesel Cam.

A recent research project carried out by the digital marketing resources and analytics company ExactTarget provides additional evidence that runs contrary to the suspicion that social media usage increases the likelihood of social isolation.[98] Data obtained on the basis of a series of focus groups, personal interviews, and questionnaires involving ExactTarget's subscribers, followers, and fans revealed that increased usage of social media among the participants directly corresponded to more face-to-face interactions, rather than fewer. Specifically, the study demonstrated that as Internet users became more active on Facebook and Twitter, they were also interacting with friends in real-life settings more often. For example, among participants who claimed to have increased their Facebook use, 27% said they were meeting more frequently with their friends in person, 60% said the frequency of their in-person meetings with friends were unchanged, and only 13% said the frequency of their meetings had declined. According to ExactTarget's principal researcher Jeff Rohrs, an important conclusion derived from the project is that:

> social media is not a zero sum game where an increase or decrease of activity in one channel only happens when there's a corresponding increase or decrease in activity in another channel. Far from making people less social in the physical world, social media seems to encourage more in-person contacts.[99]

Finally, it is important to bear in mind that like digital natives, older digital immigrants are also deriving various benefits from their growing involvement with new technologies. Elderly consumers have exhibited a high readiness to utilize computers, smartphones and other digital devices, especially for exchanging emails and photos and making online purchases. In senior centers and retirement homes, elderly residents are increasingly being trained to acquire rudimentary computer skills enabling them to connect with their family members on social networks like Facebook, where they can view photos and get regular updates on the activities and life experiences posted by their grandchildren.

Although to date the evidence suggests a relatively low level of participation among seniors in social networking activities via their mobile phones or computers, there has recently been a dramatic increase in social networking by persons aged 50 and over. A demographic analysis of online social network users in the US (conducted as part of the Pew Internet & American Life Project) revealed that the share of adults from that population with profiles on online social networking sites virtually doubled from 2009 to 2010; however, younger online adults were far more likely than their older counterparts to use social networks, with

86% of 18–29-year-olds doing so by 2010 compared with only 47% of Internet users aged 50–64 and 26% for those aged 64 and over.[100] By 2013, the percentage of persons over the age of 65 using social networks had increased to 43%, revealing that group as the fastest social media adopters in the US.[101]

Marketers are increasingly coming to grips with the realization that advancing age does not imply a disconnection from the marketplace or lack of involvement with new technologies. Studies of elderly consumers' online behavior have shown that seniors tend to perceive themselves as 15 to 20 years younger than their biological age; accordingly, their online purchasing does not tend to diverge much from younger segments, with some predictable exceptions (e.g., higher purchasing of medications and health care products and minimal buying of youth-oriented products, such as trendy fashion items).[102]

Conclusion

A famous quote, often attributed to science fiction writer and inventor Arthur C. Clarke, asserts that "no communication technology has ever disappeared, but instead becomes increasingly less important as the technological horizon widens." Perhaps an argument could be made that takes issue with the first part of the quote when we consider technologies that spawned products and services as far-reaching as the Betamax videocassette format and the telegraph, which today exist predominately in our collective memories. Nonetheless, as the technology horizon continues to expand, the notion that certain innovations not only diminish in importance, but also are transformed into something quite different is eminently clear, and the impact of these changes on people continues to unfold as a developing story.

In Chapter 1, I briefly touched upon one aspect of this developing story in the context of dematerialization—the tendency for more and more material objects to be transformed into virtual ones online. In his 2011 book *Retromania*, author Simon Reynolds reflected on the implications of such digital technology developments:

> When cultural data is dematerialised, our capacity to store, sort and access it is vastly increased and enhanced. The compression of text, images and audio means that issues of space and cost no longer deter us from keeping anything and everything that seems remotely interesting or amusing. Advances in user-friendly technology (the scanner, the domestic video recorder, the mobile-phone camera) make it irresistibly quick and convenient to share stuff: photographs, songs and mix tapes, excerpts from television, vintage magazines, book illustrations and covers, period graphics, you name it. And once it's up on the Web, a lot of it stays out there, for ever.

> We have available to us, as individuals, but also at the level of civilisation, immensely more "space" to fill with memorabilia, documentation, recordings, every kind of archival trace of our existence. And naturally, we are

busily filling that space, even as its capacity continues to balloon. Yet there is no evidence that we have significantly increased our ability to process or make good use of all that memory. . . . We've become so used to this convenient access that it is a struggle to recall that life wasn't always like this; that relatively recently, one lived most of the time in a cultural present tense, with the past confined to specific zones, trapped in particular objects and locations.[103]

Like it or not, digital technologies promise to continue to significantly alter our lives, our memories, and the material objects we use in everyday life. Two of the developments noted at the beginning of this chapter—3-D printing and smart home technology—more than hint at an unavoidable future that will be increasingly programmed and digital. As people have become dependent on now well-established innovations such as mobile devices to tell time, shoot photos, manage their agendas, carry out calculations, read books, and complete financial transactions, it is worth pondering the extent to which certain physical products will inevitably be rendered obsolete, such as wristwatches, cameras, wallets, pocket calculators, remote controls, Post-it notes, printed books, and money, with only their symbolic and nostalgic assets remaining. In the near future, one's reliable Timex watch may soon go the way of the dependable Minitel and the ludicrous Crystal Pepsi, remembered wistfully as bygone evidence of our technologically naïve recent past.

It is easy to view many of these developments with distress—perhaps another reflection of our predilection to view paradigmatic shifts in innovation as alarming. However, these concerns notwithstanding, the benefits of these inevitable changes cannot be neglected. The medical applications of 3-D printing for tissue repair and other relatively instantaneous treatments holds the promise of prolonging life, reducing health costs, and relieving much suffering. Likewise, advances in the "Internet of Things"—where everyday devices become "smart devices" that are equipped with sensors and connectivity so that they work together—promise to make our daily living easier and more convenient, enabling us to save time to pursue more self-actualizing, interpersonal, and creative goals. Not everyone will consider a bathroom cabinet that lets one know it's running low on toilet paper as an essential development of contemporary life, but rest assured that it is an inevitable one.

Further reading

There are several excellent books on many of the technology and innovation topics covered in this chapter. One standout that has aged well since its publication is Neil Postman's *Amusing Ourselves to Death* (Methuen, 1985), which evaluates the impact of technology in light of the diverse visions of the future proposed by George Orwell and Aldous Huxley. Although Postman's thin volume focuses primarily on the ways television has transformed thinking and culture, many of his ideas are pertinent to contemporary technological advances.

Two books brilliantly ruminate on the often taken-for-granted "things" of everyday life and the various ways in which they exert influence on the people who use them. James Gleick's focus in *Faster: The Acceleration of Just About Everything* (Pantheon, 1999) is on time-saving devices and strategies, whereas Nicholson Baker's *The Mezzanine* (Vintage, 1986) is a novel that centers on a central character's musings—triggered by a broken shoelace, of all things—about the mundane details of everyday life and the objects we regularly encounter in personal and work contexts.

Merritt Ierley's *Wondrous Contrivances* (Clarkson Potter, 2002) is an engaging analysis of the various ways people adjust to technological change so that the impact of innovations contribute to the betterment of humanity. Nicholas Carr's thought-provoking *The Shallows: What the Internet is Doing to Our Brains* (W. W. Norton, 2011) offers a darker perspective on the consequences of our increasing dependency on digital technology developments, whereas Catherine Steiner-Adair and Teresa Barker's *The Big Disconnect* (Yale University Press, 2013) offers an insightful perspective on strategies for coping with technological dependencies.

Academic papers summarizing research on innovation and the innovation process can be found in such journals as the *European Journal of Innovation Management*, *Economics of Innovation and New Technology*, *Industry and Innovation*, the *International Journal of Innovation Management*, and *Creativity and Innovation Management*.

Notes

1 Cravens, D. W. & Piercy, N. F. (2009). *Strategic Marketing*, 9th ed. New York: McGraw-Hill. Tzokas, N., Hultink, E. J., & Hart, S. (2004). Navigating the new product development process. *Industrial Marketing Management*, *33*, 619–626.
2 Trott, P. (2008). *Innovation management and new product development*, 4th ed. Harlow, Essex, UK: Prentice Hall/Financial Times.
3 Cooper, R. G., Edgett, S. J., & Kleinschmidt, E. J. (1998). *Portfolio management for new products*. Reading, MA: Addison-Wesley.
4 Kimmel, A. J. (2010). Connecting with consumers: Marketing for new marketplace realities. Oxford, UK: Oxford University Press.
5 It could be said that the first actual postal system predates that of Persia by nearly 2,000 years. During 2400 BC, Egyptian pharaohs used couriers to transmit their decrees across the territory in what, according to some, represented the first organized delivery system for written information. See Early history of postal systems. *Salt Lake Mailing & Printing Systems Blog*. Available: http://www.saltlakemailing.com/mailing/early-history-postal-systems/.
6 McKenna, B. (2013, December 11). *The Globe and Mail*. Available: http://www.theglobeandmail.com/report-on-business/canada-post-delivery/article15868531/.
7 "Snail mail." *Merriam Webster*. Available: http://www.merriam-webster.com/dictionary/snail%20mail.
8 Postman, N. (1985). *Amusing ourselves to death*. York, UK: Methuen, p. 66.
9 Postman, N. (1985), p. 65.
10 Dunlap, D. W. (2012, January 23). Advertising or not, billboards have a towering presence. *The New York Times*. Available: http://cityroom.blogs.nytimes.com/2012/01/23/advertising-or-not-billboards-have-a-towering-presence/.
11 Thoreau, H. D. (1957). *Walden*. Boston: Houghton Mifflin, p. 36.

12 Postman, N. (1985), pp. 66–67.
13 In 1959, author Norman Mailer lamented the "new electronic landscape of celebrity" in his book *Advertisements for Myself* (New York: Putnam).
14 Bergmann, W. H. (2008). Delivering a nation through the mail. *Ohio Valley History, 8* (3), 1–18.
15 Kimmel, A. J. (2013). *Psychological foundations of marketing.* Hove, East Sussex, UK: Routledge.
16 Bianco, A. (2004, July 12). The vanishing mass market. *BusinessWeek.* Available: http://www.businessweek.com/stories/2004-07-11/the-vanishing-mass-market.
17 Solomon, M. R., Marshall, G. W., & Stewart, E. W. (2011). *Marketing: Real people, real choices,* 7th ed. Upper Saddle River, NJ: Prentice Hall.
18 Schmitt, E. (2004). *Left brain marketing.* Cambridge, MA: Forrester Research. Available: http://web.asc.upenn.edu/courses/comm530/secure/Left%20Brain%20Marketing.pdf.
19 Levine, M. & Pownall, S. (2004). *Best practice information trends—what works?* Available: http://www.roymorgan.com/~/media/Files/Papers/2004/20041102.pdf. Australian Bureau of Statistics. (2013, August 10). Internet activity, Australia, June 2013. Available: http://www.abs.gov.au/ausstats/abs@.nsf/Products/8153.0~June+2013~Chapter~Type+of+access+connection?OpenDocument. *Australian multi-screen report.* (2012). Available: http://www.oztam.com.au/documents/other/australian%20multi%20screen%20report%20q1%202012_final.pdf.
20 Levine, M. & Pownall, S. (2004).
21 Christensen, N. (2013, November 8). ABCs: Newspapers show more double digit declines. *mUmBRELLA.* Available: http://mumbrella.com.au/abcs-newspapers-3-188553.
22 Christensen, N. (2013, November 8).
23 The Asahi Shimbun Company. (2011, March). *Businesspeople Survey, 2011.* Available: http://adv.asahi.com/english/index_image/media_info_2012.pdf.
24 Meganews—a new magazine publishing model? (2013, June 21). *Ricoh Europe Business Driver.* Available: http://ricoheuropebusinessdriver.wordpress.com/2013/06/21/meganews-a-new-magazine-publishing-model/.
25 New cellphones used in digital shoplifting. (2003, June 30). *IOLscitech.* Available: http://www.iol.co.za/scitech/technology/new-cellphones-used-in-digital-shoplifting-1.108972/.
26 Schmitt, E. (2004).
27 The history of communication. *About.com.* Available: http://inventors.about.com/library/inventors/bl_history_of_communication.htm.
28 Kurzweil, R. (2001, March 7). The law of accelerating returns. *Kurzweil Accelerating Intelligence.* Available: http://www.kurzweilai.net/the-law-of-accelerating-returns.
29 Myers, S. & Marquis, D. G. (1969). *Successful industrial innovation: A study of factors underlying innovation in selected firms.* Washington, DC: National Science Foundation, NSF 69-17.
30 Govindarajan, V. & Desai, J. (2013, September 26). Innovation isn't just about new products. *HBR Blog Network.* Available: http://blogs.hbr.org/2013/09/innovation-isnt-just-about-new-products/.
31 Trott, P. (2008).
32 Patenting and innovation in metropolitan America. (2013, February 1). *Brookings.* Available: http://www.brookings.edu/research/interactives/2013/metropatenting. Patents. (2013, November 23). *Australian Government IP Australia.* Available: http://www.ipaustralia.gov.au/get-the-right-ip/patents/types-of-patents/standard-patent/.
33 Duhigg, C. & Lohr, S. (2012, October 9). Innovation a casualty in tech patent wars. *International Herald Tribune,* pp. 14, 16.
34 Duhigg, C. & Lohr, S. (2012, October 9).
35 Black, M. (2013). Innovation and consumers as casualties of war in global technology patent battles. *Transnational Law & Contemporary Problems, 22,* 181–205.
36 Duhigg, C. & Lohr, S. (2012).
37 Trott, P. (2008), p. 14.

38 Trott, P. (2008).
39 Purcher, J. (2013, October 17). Apple reveals new laser manufacturing process for the iMac. *Patently Apple*. Available: http://www.patentlyapple.com/patently-apple/2013/10/apple-reveals-new-laser-manufacturing-process-for-the-imac.html.
40 Chesbrough, H. (2011, May/June). Management innovations for the future of innovation. *Ivey Business Journal*. Available: http://iveybusinessjournal.com/topics/innovation/management-innovations-for-the-future-of-innovation.
41 Betinger, K. (2013, December 17). Four marketing strategy trends for 2014. *Outmarket*. Available: https://www.outmarket.com/four-marketing-strategy-trends-for-2014/.
42 Voss, C. & Zomerdijk, L. (2007, June). Innovation in experiential services—an empirical view. In *DTI Occasional Paper No. 9: Innovation in Services* (pp. 97–134). Available: http://webarchive.nationalarchives.gov.uk/20070603164510/http://www.dti.gov.uk/files/file39965.pdf.
43 Kimmel, A. J. (2013).
44 Pogue, D. (2011, February 23). Before rush, one tablet stands out. *The New York Times*. Available: http://www.nytimes.com/2011/02/24/technology/personaltech/24pogue.html.
45 Schiffman, L. G. & Kanuk, L. L. (2009). *Consumer behavior*, 10th ed. Englewood Cliffs, NJ: Prentice Hall.
46 Communication through the ages. *Atlassian*. Available: https://www.atlassian.com/en/communication-through-the-ages-infographic.
47 California Biomedical Research Association. (2012). *Fact sheet: New drug development process*. Available: http://ca-biomed.org/pdf/media-kit/fact-sheets/cbradrugdevelop.pdf.
48 Trott, P. (2008).
49 Rosenberg, S. (2001, July 11). CueCatastrophe. *Salon*. Available: http://www.salon.com/2001/07/11/cue_cat/.
50 Tynan, D. (2006, May 26). The 25 worst tech products of all time. *PCWorld*. Available: http://www.pcworld.com/article/125772/worst_products_ever.html?page=8. Barrett, B. (2009, December 23). Worst gadgets gallery. *Gizmodo*. Available: http://gizmodo.com/5431759/worst-gadgets-gallery/.
51 Rosenberg, S. (2001, July 11).
52 Schneider, J. & Hall, J. (2011, April). Why most product launches fail. *Harvard Business Review*. Available: http://hbr.org/2011/04/why-most-product-launches-fail/ar/1.
53 Cooper, R. J. & Kleinschmidt, E. J. (1987). Success factors in product innovation. *Industrial Marketing Management, 16*, 215–223.
54 Schneider, J. & Hall, J. (2011, April).
55 Trout, J. (2014, March 3). Personal communication.
56 Ierley, M. (2002). Wondrous contrivances: Technology at the threshold. New York: Clarkson Potter.
57 Hess, A. (2012, July 10). Race, class, and the stigma of riding the bus in America. *The Atlantic Cities*. Available: http://www.theatlanticcities.com/commute/2012/07/race-class-and-stigma-riding-bus-america/2510/.
58 Schofield, H. (2012, June 27). Minitel: The rise and fall of the France-wide web. *BBC News Magazine*. Available: http://www.bbc.com/news/magazine-18610692.
59 Borzo, J. (2001, October 15). Past its prime. *The Wall Street Journal Europe*, pp. 1, 36.
60 Barker, M., Barker, D., Bormann, N., & Neher, K. (2008). *Social media marketing: A strategic approach*. Mason, OH: South-Western.
61 Higgins, M. (2012, March 28). Your knees, their seat: Discuss. *The New York Times*. Available: http://www.nytimes.com/2012/04/01/travel/your-knees-their-seat-discuss.html.
62 Hunter, J. A. (2009). *Anger in the air: Combating the air rage phenomenon*. Farnham, Surrey, UK: Ashgate.
63 "My goal is to simplify complexity."—Jack Dorsey on The Charlie Rose Show—Watch it ASAP! *JASONPOLLOCK.TV*. Available: http://jasonpollock.tv/2011/01/my-goal-is-to-simplify-complexity-jack-dorsey-on-the-charlie-rose-show-watch-it-asap/.

64 Rossiter, J. R., Percy, L., & Donovan, R. J. (1991). A better advertising planning grid. *Journal of Advertising Research, 31*, 11–21.

65 Unboxing: The new geek porn. (2009, January 14). *The Independent*. Available: http://www.independent.co.uk/life-style/gadgets-and-tech/features/unboxing-the-new-geek-porn-1333955.html.

66 Malcolm, A. H. (1988, March 27). Overpowering the scent market. *The New York Times*. Available: http://www.nytimes.com/1988/03/27/magazine/overpowering-the-scent-market.html.

67 "Trysumers." (2007, March). *trendwatching.com*. Available: http://trendwatching.com/trends/trysumers.htm.

68 Chen, H. & Crowston, K. (1997). Comparative diffusion of the telephone and the World Wide Web: An analysis of rates of adoption. *Proceedings of WebNet '97—World Conference of the WWW, Internet and Intranet*. Available: http://crowston.syr.edu/system/files/webnet97.html.

69 Brooks, J. (1976). *Telephone: The first hundred years*. New York: HarperCollins, p. 54.

70 Rogers, E. M. (2003). *Diffusion of innovations*, 5th ed. New York: Free Press.

71 Midgley, D. F. & Dowling, G. R. (1978). Innovativeness: The concept and its measurement. *Journal of Consumer Research, 4*, 229–242. Rogers, E. M. & Shoemaker, F. F. (1971). *Communication of innovations*. New York: The Free Press.

72 Goldsmith, R. E. & Hofhacker, C. (1991). Measuring consumer innovativeness. *Journal of the Academy of Marketing Science, 19*, 209–221. Manning, K. C., Bearden, W. O., & Madden, T. J. (1995). Consumer innovativeness and the adoption process. *Journal of Consumer Psychology, 4*, 329–345.

73 Hirunyawipada, T. & Paswan, A. K. (2006). Consumer innovativeness and perceived risk: Implications for high technology product adoption. *Journal of Consumer Marketing, 23/24*, 182–198. Dabholkar, P. A. & Bagozzi, R. P. (2002). An attitudinal model of technology-based self-service: Moderating effects of consumer traits and situational factors. *Journal of the Academy of Marketing Science, 30*, 184–201. Robertson, T. S., Zielinski, J. & Ward, S. (1984). *Consumer behavior*. Glenview, IL: Scott, Foresman. Manning, K. C., Bearden, W. O., & Madden, T. J. (1995). Consumer innovativeness and the adoption process. *Journal of Consumer Psychology, 4*, 329–345. Citrin, A.V., Sprott, D. E., Silverman, S. N., & Stem, D. E. (2000). Adoption of internet shopping: The role of consumer innovativeness. *Industrial Management & Data Systems, 100*, 294–300.

74 Hoyer, W. D. & Ridgway, N. M. (1984). Variety seeking as an explanation for exploratory purchase behavior: A theoretical model. In T. C. Kinnear (Ed.), *Advances in Consumer Research*, Vol. 11 (pp. 114–119). Provo, UT: Association for Consumer Research.

75 Baumgartner, H., Sujan, M., & Padgett, D. (1997). Patterns of affective reactions to advertisements: The integration of moment-to-moment responses into overall judgments. *Journal of Marketing Research, 34*, 219–232. Tomaseti, E., Sicilia, M., & Ruiz, S. (2004). The moderating effect of innate innovativeness on consumer response to symbolic and functional innovations. *Australian and New Zealand Marketing Academy Conference 2004*. Wellington, New Zealand.

76 Gustafsson, A., Kristensson, P., Witell, L. (2012). Customer co-creation in service innovation: A matter of communication? *Journal of Service Management, 23*, 311–327.

77 Bilton, N. (2012, October 7). Disruptions: With a 3-D printer, building a gun with the push of a button. *The New York Times*. Available: http://bits.blogs.nytimes.com/2012/10/07/with-a-3-d-printer-building-a-gun-at-home/.

78 Baker, N. (1986). *The mezzanine*. New York: Vintage, p. 74.

79 Perforations are created by a process using tiny needle punches accomplished via the use of rotary pinned perforation rollers. The identity of the creator of the perforation device, which dates back to the 1840s, remains a mystery. Todd, R. H., Allen, D. K., & Alting, L. (1994). *Manufacturing processes reference guide*. New York: Industrial Press.

80 Marsden, P. (2006). Seed to spread: How seeding trials ignite epidemics of demand. In J. Kirby & P. Marsden (Eds.), *Connected marketing: The viral, buzz and word of mouth revolution* (pp. 4–23). Oxford, UK: Butterworth-Heinemann.

81 Greenspan, R. (2004, April 2). Media multitaskers may miss messages. *ClickZ*. Available: http://www.clickz.com/clickz/news/1694502/media-multitaskers-may-miss-messages.

82 EIAA Mediascope Europe. (2009). EIAA media multi-tasking report. *SlideShare*. Available: http://www.slideshare.net/robertmattar/eiaa-media-multitasking-report.

83 Carr, N. (2008, July 1). Is Google making us stupid? *The Atlantic*. Available: http://www.theatlantic.com/magazine/archive/2008/07/is-google-making-us-stupid/306868/.

84 Postman, N. (1985). p. 161.

85 Seaman, D. (2010). Editorial review of Nicholas Carr's *The shallows: What the Internet is doing to our brains*. Available: http://www.amazon.com/Shallows-What-Internet-Doing-Brains/dp/0393072223.

86 Stray questions for: Nicholas Carr. (2010, June 4). *The New York Times*. Available: http://artsbeat.blogs.nytimes.com/2010/06/04/stray-questions-for-nicholas-carr/.

87 Jaynes, J. (1976). *The origins of consciousness in the breakdown of the bicameral mind*. Boston: Houghton Mifflin/Mariner Books.

88 Yuan, K. et al. (2011, June 3). Microstructure abnormalities in adolescents with Internet addiction disorder. *Plos One*. Available: http://www.plosone.org/article/info%3Adoi%2F10.1371%2Fjournal.pone.0020708.

89 Small, G. (2009). *iBrain: Surviving the technological alteration of the modern mind*. New York: Harper. Lin, J. (2008, October 15). Research shows that Internet is rewiring our brains. *UCLA Today*. Available: http://www.today.ucla.edu/portal/ut/081015_gary-small-ibrain.aspx.

90 Granic, I., Lobel, A., & Engels, R. (2014). The benefits of playing video games. *American Psychologist, 69*, 66–78.

91 Gladwell, M. (2010, October 4). Small change: Why the revolution will not be tweeted. *The New Yorker*. Available: http://www.newyorker.com/magazine/2010/10/04/small-change-3. Schaeffer, M. W. (2010, October 10). Is social media creating a generation of cowards? {*grow*}. Available: http://www.businessesgrow.com/2010/10/10/is-social-media-creating-a-generation-of-cowards/.

92 Bilton, N. (2014, March 16). Staying home, connected to the world. *The New York Times*. Available: http://bits.blogs.nytimes.com/2014/03/16/staying-home-connected-to-the-world/.

93 Kraut, R., Patterson, M., Lundmark, V., Kiesler, S., Mukopadhyay, T., & Scherlis, W. (1998). Internet paradox: A social technology that reduces social involvement and psychological well-being? *American Psychologist, 53*, 1,017–1,031.

94 Kraut, R., Kiesler, S., Boneva, B., Cummings, J., Hegelson, V., & Crawford, A. (2002). Internet paradox revisited. *Journal of Social Issues, 58*, 49–74.

95 Turkle, S. (2011). Alone together: Why we expect more from technology and less from each other. New York: Basic Books.

96 Berger, J. & Iyengar, R. (2013). Communication channels and word of mouth: How the medium shapes the message. *Journal of Consumer Research, 40*, 567–579.

97 Drenton, J. (2012). Snapshots of the self: Exploring the role of online mobile photo sharing in identity development among adolescent girls. In A. Close (Ed.), *Online consumer behavior: Theory and research in social media, advertising, and e-tail* (pp. 3–34). New York: Routledge, p. 3.

98 New research dispels interactive marketing myths. (2010, October 27). *Bloomberg*. Available: http://www.bloomberg.com/apps/news?pid=conewsstory&tkr=WC:US&sid=a2JzfvAZTA3Q.

99 New research dispels interactive marketing myths. (2010, October 27).

100 Brockman, J. (2010, August 27). Social networking surges for seniors. *npr*. Available: http://www.npr.org/templates/story/story.php?storyId=129475268.

101 Fox, Z. (2013, August 8). Seniors are fastest social media adopters in US. *Mashable*. Available: http://mashable.com/2013/08/08/senior-citizens-social-media/.

102 Bloch, M. (2005). Marketing to seniors on the web. *Taming the Beast.net*. Available: http://www.tamingthebeast.net/articles5/web-marketing-seniors.htm.

103 Reynolds, S. (2011). *Retromania: Pop culture's addiction to its past*. London: Faber and Faber, p. 56.

3

CONSUMER DEMANDS AND PRODUCT USABILITY

By the end of this chapter, you will:

- appreciate the nature and breadth of current and emerging consumer marketplace demands;
- become familiar with the concept of product usability and its essential role in the marketing process;
- gain insight into how product manufacturers and marketers can respond to consumer demands through product design;
- understand the role of product desirability in consumer preferences.

As consumers, we are demanding lot. We expect the things we buy, rent, borrow, or create to work and work well, to last a long time, to be easy to use and maintain, to make us feel good about our choices and skills, and to produce a range of additional emotional, psychological, and social satisfactions. However, it is rare to find consumers who do not have a love/hate relationship with many of the material (and virtual) goods that serve as fundamental elements of their daily lives—a relationship that, at times, could be said to border on the dysfunctional, not unlike a doomed romantic relationship. Products—can't live with them, can't live without them. When one's laptop is humming along swimmingly, performing the functions expected and required without a hitch, all is right with the world. You marvel at how lucky you are to be living in an era in which technological advances have produced such an amazing instrument, capable of performing an endless array of important functions at lightning speed. But in those situations where surfing the Internet slows to a crawl, the laptop's fan begins making a grinding noise worse than a dentist's drill, an unsaved document suddenly disappears from existence, strange and foreboding error messages keep appearing on the screen, or one keeps hitting the wrong key because of the ergonomically challenged design of the keyboard, the impulse is to grab the laptop and throw it out the window.

Yet we keep coming back. We buy a more expensive model next time, with even more functions and features, that can satisfy our ever-growing demands. We are confident that the manufacturer has worked out the problems that led to the unfortunate, premature demise of the previous acquisition, and we assure ourselves that we will profit from prior experience. We decide that this time, we really will install more reliable virus protection software, regularly scan for malware, avoid dicey websites and immediately delete suspicious emails, back up files, transport the device more carefully, and so on. In many cases, we merely delude ourselves into thinking that history won't repeat itself. And perhaps it doesn't. But then the microwave goes on the fritz.

In the constant fight against rapid obsolescence, technical problems, lack of satisfactory service support, and rising prices, it may seem that despite our periodic victories, products are winning the war. Yet most people would doubtless agree that we are far better off today than, say, a century ago when we did not have all the "stuff" that, at times, causes us so much grief. Despite the headaches and costs that often are associated with our participation in the marketplace of things, products have become critical not only to our survival, but also to our well-being, peace of mind, comfort, and happiness.

A primary focus of this chapter is to identify and examine the various elements that underlie both positive and negative consumer/product experiences. Consumer experience with products is a fascinating but daunting topic, complicated by a convergence of several powerful forces in the contemporary marketplace: rapid technological developments, changing consumer lifestyles, rising concerns about the health-related consequences of product usage, environmental and sustainability issues, social connectivity trends, and so on. The acquisition of goods and services is no longer based solely on their functional qualities, with little consideration of the design and style of the offerings or their social, symbolic, and ecological implications. Businesses are challenged more than ever to provide offerings that satisfy the evolving needs and demands of increasingly connected consumers. Relative to the product component of the 4 Ps classical marketing mix (product, place, price, and promotion), this requires the development of goods that effectively and efficiently fulfill the functions for which they were created, are aesthetically designed, environmentally friendly, and which convey the desired subjective meanings for varying consumer cultures and potential customers. To succeed in the contemporary business world, marketers and product developers must have a thorough understanding of their customers, and a large part of that insight pertains to what those customers want and need. At the outset, this concern brings us into the realms of consumer motivation and lifestyles—explanatory constructs that that help us identify the forces underlying consumer behavior.

Consumers in action: The concept of motivation

Derived from the Latin term *movere* ("to move"), motivation pertains to the processes that arouse a person to behave, the direction that behavior takes, as well as how behavior is sustained or maintained (see Figure 3.1). Motivated behavior, which typically stems from a psychological or physiological imbalance that moves a person to action, is goal-directed behavior—that is, it is not randomly selected, but chosen on the basis of learning (e.g., the outcomes of previous experiences) and cognitive processes (e.g., expectations of future outcomes).

To say that consumer behavior is goal-directed is not exactly a surprising revelation, but it is an important notion nonetheless, and one that is fundamental to our understanding of motivation. Psychologists Baumgartner and Pieters commented that "Proposing that consumer behavior is goal directed seems like arguing that water is wet"[1]—a statement that is underscored by Greek philosopher Aristotle's (384–322 BC) famous assertion centuries earlier that "Man is a goal seeking animal. His life only has meaning if he is reaching out and striving for his goals." Given the consumer-oriented societies of the contemporary era, Aristotle's comments could hardly be more appropriate. In fact, Aristotle further suggested that the final objective of goal-directed behavior is happiness.

Motivated behavior is directed toward certain end states or outcomes (typically referred to as "goal objects" or "incentives") that the individual anticipates will satisfy extant needs, reduce the inner state of tension, and thereby restore the system to a state of balance. The manifestation of a need that serves to direct us toward certain goals and away from others is typically referred to as a *want*, which is likely to be influenced by personal factors (e.g., past experience with brands),

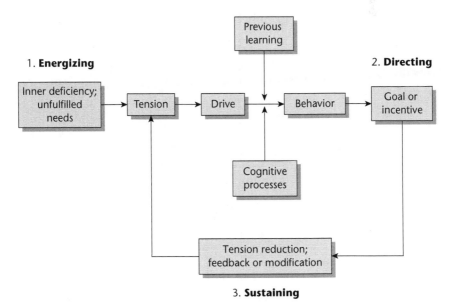

FIGURE 3.1   Model of the motivational process

Source: Kimmel, A. J. (2013). *Psychological Foundations of Marketing.* East Sussex, UK: Routledge, p. 24.

social factors (e.g., peer-group pressure), and cultural factors (e.g., normative beliefs about the appropriateness or desirability of certain products or services). In the case of a physiological imbalance such as hunger, for example, your choice of what, where, and how to eat are likely to be influenced to some extent by each of these factors.

Motivational conflicts

When we consider products as potentially need-satisfying goal objects, it often is the case that consumers find themselves in situations where they are torn between various goals or attempt to satisfy multiple needs simultaneously. Kurt Lewin was one of the first psychologists to suggest that goal objects exert pulling or pushing forces on an individual. As a fundamental aspect of his field theory of learning, Lewin proposed that each individual exists in a field of attracting or repelling forces, which he referred to as "valences."[2] The blending of these various forces creates a dynamic that is central to learning, compelling the individual to cope with the conflicting forces within the ongoing situation. Bringing these notions within the realm of consumer behavior, goal objects that attract consumers (so-called "positively valent" objects) reflect consumer wants (such as the desire to purchase a seductive perfume that will make the buyer more sexually attractive) and, in that sense, represent external manifestations of consumer needs. By contrast, undesired goal objects (so-called "negatively valent" objects) repel behavior, as would be the case when a consumer avoids a brand of soap that is thought to cause skin dryness.

A person's needs are strongly interrelated and, as a result, they can operate simultaneously on behavior. An expensive fur coat can satisfy certain practical or utilitarian needs (e.g., to be warm during the winter) as well as more emotional or experiential needs (e.g., the excitement associated with wearing the coat in public) and status needs (e.g., the personal satisfaction that comes from being envied by others), thereby mutually reinforcing a purchase. Thus, various needs might be satisfied through the acquisition and use of the same product, and different types of product benefits might appeal to different people, depending on their developmental and environmental circumstances.[3] If more than one force can act on an individual in a consistent fashion to enhance the likelihood of a particular action, divergent forces, by contrast, can place consumers in a state of conflict. For example, a motivational conflict would occur when the attracting forces of an expensive fur coat are opposed by the need to maintain one's budget or the desire to protect the rights of endangered animals. In such cases, a so-called "stable equilibrium" would prevail, in that both attracting and repelling forces would be in play to leave a consumer in a state of indecision. Attracted by the goal object (the fur coat), but experiencing increasing reticence when approaching it (e.g., the excessive price becomes more salient), the consumer would likely vacillate in the decision to obtain the product. This example highlights why it is that many people procrastinate when it comes to some purchases. Marketers can assist consumers in overcoming such "approach-avoidance" conflicts by designing appeals that emphasize the desirable aspects of the product while downplaying the negative (e.g., by offering a suitable financing arrangement for the purchase, allowing payment by credit card, offering rebates or a free gift if purchased by a certain date). Given the competitive environment for most product categories in today's marketplace, the approach/avoidance conflict is apt to be complicated by the pushing and pulling forces of other brand alternatives, each of which may possess varying positive and negative features.

Another type of motivational conflict can cause some palpable tension in consumers who find themselves deciding between more than one desirable alternative. Imagine a situation in which a teenager with a limited budget must decide between allocating limited purchasing resources to acquire either a new mp3 player or a smartphone. In the typical "approach/approach" conflict situation of this sort, we can expect that the indecisiveness and vacillation between alternatives will be short-lived because an unstable equilibrium prevails. That is, as the consumer makes a move toward accepting one alternative (say, the mp3 player), its positive attracting force will increase; conversely, the attracting force decreases as one moves away from a positively valent object (in this case, the smartphone).

The resolution of an approach/approach conflict can be facilitated through the provision of information that is useful for evaluating the alternatives (e.g., promotional literature, a salesperson's arguments, positive recommendations from other consumers); an attractive promotional offer; or by selecting an alternative that provides the achievement of both goals. In the latter case, our hypothetical consumer might decide to purchase a smartphone with an mp3 file player function. Although approach/approach conflicts typically result in a satisfying outcome—the consumer in our example ends up with either a valued new music player or a smartphone—such conflict resolutions often have a downside when the buyer experiences remorse at not having picked the other alternative, a state referred to as "buyer's remorse," or "post-decisional dissonance." Many marketing messages are designed specifically to make consumers aware of the needs that can be satisfied through the purchase or use of certain products or services, and in so doing, can help resolve motivational conflicts. Thus, an Ericsson advertisement heralded the GH388 cellphone as the one "made to match the needs of the international traveller," and a Barney's of New York advertisement claimed that the shopper "will have no difficulty finding anything you need" at the retail clothing store. An early advertisement for Pall Mall cigarettes suggested how consumers could overcome an approach/avoidance conflict by choosing the brand that offer smoothness and mild taste without the aversive "throat scratch."

The role of consumer lifestyles

Choices of goods and services, as well as responses to promotional campaigns, are intimately linked to consumer lifestyles: the distinctive or characteristic ways of living adopted by consumer segments or communities. Lifestyle can be viewed as a pattern of consumption that reflects a person's choices of how to spend time and money, and in that sense can be seen as functioning as an intermediary between who we are (i.e., lifestyle determinants, such as demographics, social class and culture, motives, and past experiences) and how and what we choose to consume.

When changes in lifestyles and demographics occur, marketers must rethink their business strategies. As the population ages, or as consumers become more concerned about health and fitness, decisions have to be made about whether to continue marketing within existing product categories, target different consumer segments, enter new markets, and so on. One recent example in Asia illustrates the dramatic impact changes in the consumer marketplace can have in terms of consumer preferences and behaviors. In the Indian marketplace, where more than 54% of the 1.21 billion population are estimated to be under the age of 25, a growing number of young consumers have adopted a *bindaas*, or free-spirited, Westernized lifestyle.[4] This is largely a function of the evolution of media access in India, where more than fifty private television channels have recently overtaken the state-run broadcaster Doordarshan, and a larger selection of international magazines than Indian ones appear at newsstands. During the past decade, bans on late-night shopping have been lifted, closing times for restaurants and bars have been extended, and late-night bus services and adequate electrical supplies have been assured. Fitness has become an important preoccupation among Indian youth, with health clubs supplied with up-to-date fitness equipment, saunas, and jacuzzis gaining in popularity to the point of having to turn away numerous affluent, young consumers. One reason for the rise of fitness as a central lifestyle concern is linked to the increasing numbers of Indians who have begun wearing Western clothing. As one fitness club owner explained: "It is easier to hide flab in the folds of a sari than in a micro-mini."

Another lifestyle story has unfolded over the past two decades in the consumption of music, a development that reflects evolving lifestyle choices brought on by advances in digital technology. As the technological format for recorded music has transitioned from analog (vinyl to cassette to compact disc) to digital (mp3, FLAC, and other file formats), this shift has begun to have significant influences on the acquisition, consumption, and appreciation of music. Although the purchasing of vinyl recordings has made something of a modest comeback in recent years—itself a consequence of some consumers' disenchantment with the dematerialization of music in its virtual manifestations—consumers have increasingly begun to spurn the purchasing and collecting of record albums and CDs, instead opting for digital versions of songs obtainable through online file downloads (iTunes, peer-to-peer) and music streaming websites (Spotify, Pandora, SoundCloud, Jango).

According to Simon Reynolds, the impact of such a shift is noteworthy, "robbing some of the romance and random epiphanies from record shopping in the real world of stores and music fairs," while eliminating some of the downsides, "such as the physical effort of finding the stuff, the problems with storage space and organising the collection."[5] Reynolds and others have argued that the relative ease and lack of financial outlay in acquiring music in its digital form has led to a corresponding reduction in music appreciation, where excessive quantity and availability have served to diminish attention to and immersion in the actual listening experience. As blogger Matthew Ingram observed about this trend: "I can't help thinking that if one really *listened* to one's records, one would have a lot *less* of them."[6] At the same time, the digital music format has led to an increase in consumer empowerment, enabling music aficionados to rearrange the order of album tracks to their liking, remove weaker tracks, and pause or skip ahead while listening to individual songs. Moreover, it has led to something of a resurgence in live music, which is more likely than the digital variety to involve undivided attention, uninterrupted listening, exclusivity, and a higher level of emotional attachment.

Consumers as active goal seekers

Consumers play an active role in selecting their goals, whereby products and services represent means by which they can satisfy their various needs. With the proliferation of products and brands in the contemporary marketplace, the constant battle for marketers is to ensure that their offerings are the ones that consumers want. But what *do* consumers want? That is, what are their priorities when seeking out products for the purpose of satisfying various needs? Although the simple answer is rather obvious—they want products that are *capable* of satisfying their needs—that explanation nonetheless is rather insufficient for gaining insight into the product-related forces that drive consumer motivation.

As a starting point, one way of capturing the various product requirements actively sought by consumers was suggested by Jon Wiley, lead designer for Google Search, who argued that product design can be thought of in terms of three factors: usability, utility, and desirability.[7] Although it is difficult to think of these three design essentials separately, given how they are intricately entwined and operate together in terms of their impact on consumers, in a general sense *usability* pertains to the effectiveness and ease of use of a product, *utility* focuses on the usefulness or need for the product, and *desirability* reflects the emotional allure of a product. Each of these design concepts is considered in detail below.

Product usability

"Usability" is a familiar term within the business community, where it is perhaps most commonly employed by tech and software industry professionals. Like many widely used terms, its specific meaning has become somewhat obscured, oversimplified, and differentially applied over the years, such that it now connotes different things to different people. The term was initially introduced during the early 1980s as a replacement for the expression "user-friendly," which by that time had acquired an array of undesirable, subjective connotations. However, it was not long before "usability" began to be similarly devalued as vague and subjective, likely a result of lack of clarity as to its meaning. In their attempt to answer the question "What is usability?," Bevan, Kirakowski, and Maissel identified three different perspectives from which definitions of usability have been derived, differing in terms of how usability should be measured:

1. the product-oriented view—a narrow view that holds that usability can be measured in terms of the product's ergonomic attributes (e.g., size, weight, user interfaces);
2. the user-oriented view—which focuses on the measurement of the mental effort and attitude of the product user;
3. the user performance view—which measures usability in terms of how the user interacts with the product, emphasizing either how easy the product is to use or whether it will be used in the real world.[8]

These views suggest that usability can be interpreted narrowly, focusing more on the product itself, or broadly, taking into account the product user and the usage situation. For example, software engineers tend to apply a narrow definition, suggesting that usability is something that can be built into a product, such as skills in interface design that complement such design objectives as functionality, efficiency, and reliability.[9] This view is relatively close to "ease of use," which arguably is the most common way the term is treated. A more general way of defining usability, which is the interpretation adopted here, takes into account the extent to which the product enables users to achieve their goals. This broader perspective maintains that usability not only depends on ease of use, but also quality of use, as reflected in GfK Consumer Experiences CEO David Karjicek's definition of usability as "the effectiveness, efficiency and satisfaction of using a particular device or service to achieve a certain goal."[10] This definition is consistent with product consultant Nigel Bevan's recognition that what sets usability apart from the rest of design considerations is its focus on human issues.[11] Thus, when one considers the usability of a product, it is necessary to think not only about ease of use, but also how and why people use the product.

Consistent with these defining elements, it is important to note that usability is in part determined by product attributes, the goal or task that the consumer has in mind, and the organizational and environmental contexts within which use of the product will take place. The relationship between these various factors is depicted in Bevan, Kiakowski, and Maissel's model of the determinants of usability (see Figure 3.2). The product attributes component of the model includes product elements that contribute to usability, such as the style and durability of the product design, the nature of the product's functionality, and other relevant properties related to efficiency, reliability, ease of use, convenience, and the like. Measures of attitudes, understanding and mental effort, and the user's performance with the product serve as criteria for determining whether the design of the product's attributes is successful in achieving usability. Diagnostic

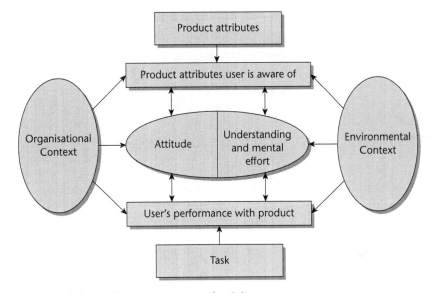

FIGURE 3.2 Model of the determinants of usability

Source: Bevan, N., Kirakowski, J. & Maissel, J. "What is Usability?" In H. J. Bullinger (Ed.), *Proceedings of the 4th International Conference on Human-Computer Interaction.* Copyright Elsevier (1991).

evaluation of these contributors to usability occurs within a particular context, delineated by the product usage situation.

In recent years, marketers have made a concerted effort to determine consumers' usability demands. A variety of methodologies have been employed to gain insight into consumer needs, including traditional approaches, such as surveys and questionnaires, as well as more innovative approaches like ethnographic case study research and lead user analysis.[12] For example, the *lead user method* collects information about needs and solutions from members of the target market (so-called "lead users") who are already experiencing problematic situations or a need for a specific innovation well in advance of the general marketplace.[13] (Some examples of the lead user method are described in Chapter 5.) Drawing from this broad array of research, as well as my own modest survey of a diverse group of millennials, some of the more compelling usability demands of consumers, and their implications for product development and design, are identified and discussed below (see Boxes 3.1 and 3.2).

BOX 3.1 WHAT DO MILLENNIALS REALLY WANT?

If there is one group that has most captured the attention of marketing practitioners and researchers in recent years, it is the generation of consumers

(Continued)

(Continued)

commonly referred to as *millennials* (also known as "Generation Y" and "Echo Boomers"). Millennials represent the first generation to have come of age in the new millennium, roughly acknowledged to have been born sometime between 1980 and 2000. As digital natives, millennials are avid participants in social networks and arguably represent the generation most engaged with the new technologies described in Chapter 2. When asked during a Pew Research Center study to identify what makes their generation unique, 24% of the millennial respondents pointed to their use of technology—this being by far the most frequent response to the open-ended question—compared with 12% of Generation X participants (i.e., those born between 1965 and 1980).[14]

Despite the emerging profile of the millennial generation, marketers have been somewhat frustrated in their efforts to tap the marketplace attitudes and preferences of millennials as consumers. Typical of this is the following conclusion derived from an investigation carried out by the marketing research firm Civic Science:

> When we looked at our first month's worth of data, we found almost NO contrast among brands. Not only do the Ms not dislike anything. They seem to think that "Love" is too strong of a feeling for a brand. Our 5-point scale quickly turned into a 3-or even 2-point scale. It seems that "Neutral" is about the most damning way these Ms can feel about anything.[15]

Perhaps part of the problem with these sorts of studies is that researchers are asking the wrong questions. For millennials, the terms "like" and "dislike" are no doubt largely devoid of meaning, with "liking" in recent years reduced to an emotion indelibly associated with a simple computer mouse click to indicate a relatively mild, detached nod to a brand on Facebook or a prerequisite to gaining access to a website for free online content. What would be more useful to know, by contrast, is what this group desires from the consumer marketplace and what is most important to them when they seek to obtain products and actually use them. This is something I attempted to do in a small-scale study, the results of which are summarized in Table 3.1.

The findings of my study in part suggest that millennials are not very different from other consumer groups in terms of their putting the highest priority on product efficiency. They demand products that are efficacious in fulfilling the functions for which they were created, are practical and convenient to use, and are likely to last a long time. However, added to the mix were indications that efficiency should not come at the expense of pleasure (in the sense of sensory, physical, and psychological satisfactions and comforts during the consumption process), with this demand ranking high in importance among respondents. By contrast, the respondents generally gave little importance to more social and moral priorities, such as the ethicality (in the sense of the product being associated with economic, political, or social virtues) and ecological/green benefits associated with products. These latter results may be construed as being consistent with characterizations of millennials as persons having higher levels of narcissism compared with members of previous generations.[16]

A recent promotional campaign launched by the Marriott hotel chain targeting young business travelers (including both Generation Xers and Generation Ys) provides a good indication of how millennials can be approached for meeting marketing objectives.[17] Starting from a portrayal of their targets as mobile global travelers who demand style and design, for whom technology is central to their lifestyle, and who seamlessly blend work and play, Marriott's "travel brilliantly" campaign was launched in mid-2013 with online commercials depicting stylish young travelers, portable devices in hand, taking full advantage of the work- and pleasure-oriented opportunities provided by Marriott. The ads were accompanied by the following voiceover narration:

> This is not a hotel. It's an idea that travel should be brilliant. The promise of spaces as expansive as your imagination. This is not business as usual, it's a new take on taking a meeting. A new way to inspire, create and, yes, dream. Because it's not only about where you're staying, it's about where you're going. Marriott, travel brilliantly.

The brand followed up the online commercials with digital and mobile advertising and by sponsoring a new travel page on the Fast Company website.

BOX 3.2 MILLENNIAL DEMANDS: RESEARCH RESULTS

In a relatively small-scale investigation of consumer demands, I surveyed 56 millennial students enrolled in master's programs at the ESCP Europe business school in Paris. A wide mix of nationalities was represented in the study sample, which was comprised of 31 Europeans (55.4%), 17 Asians (30.4%), 5 North Americans (8.9%), and 3 South Americans (5.4%), aged 19–30 (with an average age of 23.5). In part, the participants were asked to rate the importance of various product attributes or benefits. Specifically, they were asked: "When you search for or go shopping for various products or services, what is important to you and likely to influence your purchase decision?"

The results are summarized in Table 3.1. The various product and service "demands" are listed in the first column of values from highest to lowest average (mean) score on a scale ranging from 0 = not at all important to 10 = extremely important. The respondents were also asked to rank the various attributes or benefits from the most important to the least important. These

(Continued)

(Continued)

results are summarized in the remaining columns of the table. For example, for "efficacity (the product will fulfill the function for which it was created; it must work, and work well)," the average rating for the 56 respondents on the 10-point importance scale was 9.09; 32 (57.1%) of the respondents ranked efficacity as the most important product attribute; a total of 46 (82.1%) respondents ranked efficacity as either first, second, or third most important; and no one ranked efficacity as least important.

A primary demand in the contemporary marketplace is that products and services satisfactorily fulfill the functions for which they were created.[18] The value of usage has become essential, such that only products that are effective can hope to last in the marketplace, especially given the increasing choice of offerings available to consumers and economic constraints on purchasing power. In addition to the capacity to achieve a desired result (i.e., "efficacity"), however, there is a set of related demands that operate hand-in-hand in determining the customer's overall evaluation of and satisfaction with the need-satisfying properties of a product, including practicality (i.e., the product makes life simpler), durability (i.e., the product and its effects last a long time), convenience and simplicity (i.e., the product is easy to use), and multifunctionality (i.e., the product is designed to perform more than one function for the user) (see Figure 3.3). Collectively, these various demands might be said to reflect a product's usability or "efficiency" properties (i.e., overall effectiveness and satisfaction in using a good to achieve a particular goal).

TABLE 3.1 Millennial demands: research results

		Rank order frequencies (%)		
Product/service demands	*Mean scores*	*Most important**	*Top 3 ranks combined*	*Least important*
1. Efficacity	9.09	32 (57.1)	46 (82.1)	0
2. Durability	7.95	0	17 (30.4)	1 (1.8)
3. Convenience	7.77	4 (7.1)	23 (41.1)	1 (1.8)
4. Pleasure	7.68	8 (14.3)	20 (35.7)	4 (7.1)
5. Time-saving	7.14	0	6 (10.7)	2 (3.6)
6. Healthy	7.09	4 (7.1)	16 (28.6)	3 (5.4)
7. Portable/mobile	6.96	0	4 (7.1)	6 (10.7)
8. Practical/simple	6.57	4 (7.1)	24 (42.9)	0
9. Multifunctional	5.80	1 (1.8)	4 (7.1)	8 (14.3)
10. Ethical	5.14	1 (1.8)	2 (3.6)	16 (28.6)
11. Ecological/green	5.14	0	0	15 (26.8)

Note: *In response to an open-ended "other" option, one respondent noted "design" and another indicated "price/quality relationship" as most important.

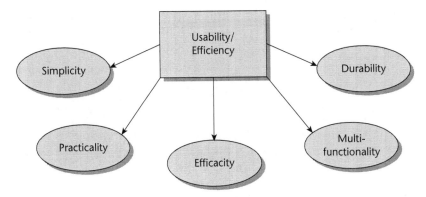

FIGURE 3.3 The usability/efficiency demand cluster

Efficacity and multifunctionality

"Efficacity" means that a product has the power to produce a desired, expected result. Products must work, and they must work well: the stain remover must completely remove the stains, the hair conditioner should condition the hair effectively; the cooking knife should effectively cut raw meat and slice vegetables; the computer should function as desired by its owner. Despite the fact that value of usage has become essential, the marketplace is hardly lacking in relatively useless gadgets, as noted in a *Complex Tech Newsletter* column written by Alex Bracetti:

> For every groundbreaking gadget to come along and revolutionize the consumer market—the Amazon Kindle, iPhone, and TiVo just to name a few—comes a handful of tech atrocities not even worth throwing inside Atari's infamous *E.T.* video game landfill. We're talking about devices that serve more as gimmicky novelties rather than high-quality goods. Ridiculous contraptions like air-conditioned sneakers, SMS chandeliers, electronic bubble wrap, and foot tanners.[19]

Readers may recall popular product novelties of earlier decades, some of which became instant, but short-lived fads, such as the pet rock (with or without walking leash and training manual), mood rings, chia pets, Newton's cradle office desk toys, and lava lamps (which have made something of a comeback in recent years). These sorts of useless products often strike a fancy with consumers because of their novelty value, or perhaps capture the interest of serious collectors, yet they serve no practical purposes and are unlikely to last once consumer curiosity dwindles. As British author Douglas Adams once famously opined: "we are stuck with technology when what we really want is just stuff that works."[20] Designer Victor Papanek had harsher words for his own profession when he spoke of the "tawdry idiocies" concocted by industrial designers:

> There are professions more harmful than industrial design, but only a few of them. . . . Never before in history have grown men sat down and seriously designed electric hairbrushes, rhinestone-covered file boxes, and mink carpeting for bathrooms, and then drawn up elaborate plans to make and sell these gadgets to millions of people.[21]

In contrast to products with no obvious uses or functions, marketers are increasingly responding to consumer demands by offering products that promise to provide high levels of efficacity, facilitating the satisfaction of consumer's goal-oriented demands in the carrying out of specific tasks. A representative listing of products that have garnered increasing marketplace success in recent decades, in part because of their abilities to efficiently fulfill useful functions for consumers, includes microwave ovens, wi-fi, e-book readers, smartphones, cloud computing, multimedia computers, laser printers, computer scanners, steam cleaners, scooters, and remote controls. Efficacity also is an essential selling point for fast-moving consumer goods, such as household cleaning products and inexpensive hygiene items. The French supermarket chain Super U promotes one of its private label bleach-free stain removers with the tagline, "Efficacity Assured." Two other Super U private label cleaning products stress their *multifunctional* properties: a "multi-purpose" cloth that eliminates dirt without the need for chemical products, and a "multi-stain" remover that is usable on most textiles (cotton, silk, etc.) and other materials (leather, etc.).

The previous examples suggest that in contrast to products with no obvious uses or functions, marketers are increasingly offering new products that serve more than one function. This is evident in multifunctional goods such as computer printers that offer the user the ability to print, scan, photocopy, and upload documents and photographs, and smartphones that enable consumers to make phone calls, take photos, listen to music, watch videos, easily connect to social networks, and surf the Internet (see Box 3.2). As mentioned in Chapter 2, the multifunctional nature of new tech innovations is rendering superfluous once-familiar objects like watches, cameras, printed books, and calculators, whose functions can be executed more efficiently (and with less damaging environmental effects) by the applications commonly found on smartphones and computers. The demise of the pocket calculator, as described by design critic Alice Rawsthorn, is typical:

> Today, the pocket calculator is a dying product, a casualty of digitization, which has been relegated to the role of a graphic icon on phone and computer screens rather than an object in its own right . . . . It is a victim of "Moore's Law," the theory that the number of transistors that can be squeezed on to a microchip will roughly double every two years, thereby increasing computing power at the same rate. In practical terms, this means that even tiny digital devices have become so powerful that they can fulfill the functions of numerous products.[22]

BOX 3.3 MALES, MASCULINITY, AND MULTITASKING

In the personal hygiene category, Nivea recently introduced Active3 for men, a 3-in-1 product that can be used as a body wash, hair shampoo, and shaving cream. Active3 facilitates the personal hygiene routine for men, providing the completion of multiple tasks through the use of a single product, and reflects the growing interest of men in body care products that traditionally fell within the domain of women's products. Marketers have come to recognize that the way a man cares for his body is demonstrative of the way he desires to be perceived as a man.[23] Thus, in recent years, formerly "feminine products" like fragrances, hair dyes, jewelry, and personal care products have begun to be marketed to male consumers. These products are often positioned as appealing to men who do not conform entirely to the masculine stereotype, but who embrace an ideal personality that includes such traits as romantic, tender, and playful, albeit accompanied by confidence and independence.[24]

In the realm of body care products, marketers have acknowledged the tendency of men to operate as multitaskers: sunscreens double as moisturizers, toners also function as conditioners, and several products promise an "age-defying" property in addition to their primary function, which appeals to men who are reluctant to purchase a separate wrinkle reverser. Commenting on these developments, Celeste Hilling, the founder and CEO of Skin Authority, emphasized that "Men are very utilitarian. When it comes to beauty routines, they are willing to do two steps, not eight, like a woman."[25]

Efficacity has become a key focus in the design of products for aging consumers. Marketers have come to grips with the realization that advancing age does not imply a disconnection from the marketplace or lack of involvement with new technologies. Many of the product usage and purchase patterns acquired during our youth, as well as company and brand loyalties, do in fact persist as we age. The senior consumer segment is growing faster than any other segment globally. Fully 12.7% of the 304.3 million people who comprised the US population in 2010 were aged 65 years or older, a percentage that is forecast to double by 2030, four times the growth rate of the 18–59 age group for the same period. In Europe, the growth of the senior market is even more pronounced: the median age of Europeans at the time of this writing was approaching 38 years, but predicted to rise to over 50 years by 2050. Similarly, across Asia, the number of people aged 65 and older is forecast to more than triple by 2050, a result of a 314% increase from 207 million in 2000 to 857 million by 2050.[26]

Acknowledging that many seniors suffer diminished skills and abilities, such as visual acuity and manual dexterity, firms have modified certain product offerings to improve their functional utility for older consumers—for example, by adding larger, more readable dials to automobile dashboards, equipping mobile phones with large keys and easier-to-read screens, and replacing door locks with ones that operate by fingerprint scans. Additionally, various high-tech innovations specifically designed for meeting the needs of elderly consumers have begun to appear in the market.[27] One such product is TabSafe, a medication management system that dispenses up to 13 different medications, which are inserted into a cartridge by a caregiver or pharmacy. The system includes a memory chip and other components that provide reminders and alerts, as well as data on compliance, inventory, and other health information, all of which are accessible from any Internet-capable device. Another new device, Telikin, is a simple and easy-to-use touch-screen computer that is intended to satisfy social networking needs for seniors via video chat, photo sharing, email, and other features. TV Ears is a wireless headset device that assists people with hearing loss to listen to their television clearly via a preset volume and tone, while others around them can set the television volume to their own preferred level.

In-store modifications for older shoppers also are becoming a common fixture in the retail sector. The Adeg Aktiv Markt 50+ supermarket chain, launched in Austria in 2003 specifically to cater to older customers, has met with such great success that it has become a model for other national markets. Each Aktiv Markt is designed with the needs of older shoppers in mind, including signage in large type, magnifying glasses available on store shelves, wide aisles, non-skid floors, plenty of places to sit, lower shelves with more accessible items, and wider parking spaces.[28] Similar changes have been introduced by the Lawson convenience store chain in Japan, a country in which 21% of the population are over the age of 65.[29]

Convenience, practicality, and simplicity

Twitter co-creator Jack Dorsey's guiding principle as an inventor, previously mentioned in Chapter 2, bears repeating in our discussion of the elements that contribute to product efficiency: "My goal is to simplify complexity."[30] Indeed, consumers desire efficacious products, but not if they are overly difficult or complicated to use. Consumers are increasingly demanding (and correspondingly respond to in terms of purchase behavior) products and services that add to their personal convenience (i.e., they make one's life easier and simpler) and are practical and simple to use (i.e., likely to be easy to employ to fulfill their functions, without unnecessary features). They are rejecting high-tech products and appliances that are difficult to program, cameras and smartphones with functions that will never be used, and foods that require long and complicated preparation (see Box 3.4).[31] Rather, people are progressively more attentive to anything that makes life simpler: products that are easy to use, plug-and-play, multifunctional, and compact and portable. It is true that at one time, consumers may have been easily impressed by the multiple functions, buttons, and dials on new product innovations, which were taken as a reflection of technological development and engineering advances. This is not unlike the early era of computing, when people interpreted the large size of computers as a sign of capability and power, and could not foresee a future in which incredibly powerful computers could be conveniently transported in one's backpack or embedded in the lens of a pair of eyeglasses. Because life in general has grown more complex, there has been a shift to simplicity and practicality, which are no longer viewed as defaults, but rather as virtues.

BOX 3.4 PRODUCT FUNCTIONS: WHEN MORE IS LESS

In Chapter 2, I suggested that from a strategic economies of scale perspective, it makes more sense for product manufacturers to include multiple functions on every device among their various offerings rather than to produce customized or "edited" versions for different buyers. The upshot is that even lower-cost, simplified models of products tend to have various functions that never will be used by purchasers. This tendency to load up products with spurious, non-essential features, however, runs counter to consumer preferences for simplicity and ease of use. Personally speaking, I don't think I've ever used more than a third of the functions on any of the digital cameras I have purchased. I recognize there are some interesting features that no doubt would be useful to know about and employ, and, if used correctly, would improve the quality of the photos I take. But I am generally happy with their quality already, so why bother trying to fathom the complicated user's manual to figure out how to use those other features and run the risk of messing with the camera's currently satisfactory performance? These reactions are probably not atypical among the general consuming public for a wide range of consumer products that are overburdened with difficult-to-use, esoteric functions.

One problem with added features is that many consumers simply equate too many "bells and whistles" with higher cost. Young car buyers, for example, have been wooed by car makers with environmentally friendly components and new technological accessories, such as those that provide convenient connectivity for mobile devices and dashboard features that recognize the presence of other vehicles and alert the driver when the speed limit has been exceeded. According to a recent survey of young American car buyers aged 18–34, however, four out of every five respondents claimed that cost remained their number one priority despite the attractiveness of the new features. According to one young buyer: "I have so many gadgets. Do I need another one in my car? No. Would it be nice to have? Yes."[32]

In many cases, the underlying problem related to overcomplicated design is that many innovations that promise to make life easier end up having the opposite effect due to the fact that the product was poorly conceived in the first place. This problem extends beyond the inclusion of multiple, superfluous product

(Continued)

(Continued)

features to other design-related cases, including sometimes inoperable products (computer routers, Bluetooth devices), websites that are nearly impossible to navigate, multiple layers of packaging, over-stylized objects, and unnecessary digital versions of things better left undigitized.[33] In a competitive sense, it is understandable that companies are forever attempting to distance their products from those of competitors by offering more of something: speed, performance, power, functions, and so on. And when implemented efficiently, businesses can indeed outdistance themselves from the competition and uniquely position their brands. But when the changes are merely specious and amount to nothing more than "shot-in-the-dark" stabs at differentiation or improvement, they often end up scaring away customers whose lives are already overcomplicated. In addition to running counter to the consumer desire for simplicity, the tendency to introduce poorly designed devices loaded up with needless features runs the risk of undermining their "clarity"—that is, the specific meaning, image, or perceived quality of the product in consumers' minds is blurred.

In contrast to the "all-in-one" or "more is better" approach, software designer John Maeda argues for "thoughtful reduction" as a key guiding principle for responsible design, maintaining that simplicity is now not only a good idea, but a necessity.[34] Unfortunately, according to Maeda, product designers are often prone to overcomplicate things out of habit, accepting— but not formally testing—the long-standing premise that adding "more" will make things better. One example that fails the thoughtful reduction principle, according to journalist and design commentator Alice Rawsthorn, is evident among the new lines of espresso machines, some of which are awkwardly styled, too large for the typical kitchen, and beset with clunky features that are extremely difficult to use.[35] On the other hand, certain digital devices, such as Apple's iPhone and iPad, stand as exemplars of clarity and simplicity, boasting user interfaces that can be operated easily and instinctively.

With regard to Apple, it cannot be denied that one early contributor to its success in the tech industry was the choice of the company's name, which helped demystify the personal computer for consumers who were fearful of the relatively unfamiliar product's perceived complexity. According to company co-founder Steve Jobs' explanation, he chose the name shortly after returning from a weekend in the country pruning apple trees on an organic farm. In his words, Apple "sounded fun, spirited and not too intimidating, plus, it would get us ahead of Atari in the phone book."[36]

The related demands for convenience, practicality, and simplicity are apparent in the obvious appeal of portable devices (netbooks, tablet PCs, smartphones), frozen foods, microwave ovens, central locking for cars, digital cameras, home shopping (e-commerce, catalogs, shopping TV networks), plug-and-play computing, electric grills, credit cards, home delivery of groceries and prepared meals, easy-opening and resealable product packages, and the euro (which eliminates the need for currency exchange when traveling throughout much of Europe). After relocating to France, I remember being surprised by the prevalence and success of frozen food shops throughout the country. Like most people, I viewed France—and still do—as a country at the pinnacle of culinary sophistication, and it seemed paradoxical that the discerning French would find something as pedestrian as frozen foods so appealing. Despite the stereotype of the French as perpetual vacationers rather than hard workers, many French spend long hours at work, not returning to their homes until the early hours of the evening. Thus, frozen foods—as well, it might be said, as fast food restaurant chains and carry-outs, which also have grown in popularity throughout France in recent years—provide a readily available, more convenient alternative to having to prepare a dinner from scratch. Another of my surprises during my early days in the French capital was the high quality of the dishes sold in the better-known frozen food store chains. One chain played on these notions in a popular advertising campaign, which showed a hostess being heartily complimented by her guests for her superb cooking, with the hostess taking special care not to reveal that the meal was composed from the chain's frozen foods dishes, the discarded packaging discreetly buried in the kitchen garbage bin.

The frozen food example is one in which product quality is not sacrificed for the sake of convenience, although in other cases, consumers may indeed opt for convenience over quality. Returning to the previous discussion of vinyl and compact discs giving way to mp3 files for casual music listening, it is well known among music technology specialists that the sonic richness of sound in the digital mp3 format is greatly diminished compared to its earlier counterparts. The process of creating mp3 files—part of which involves converting certain elements of the frequency spectrum from stereo to mono—results in thin-bodied textures and a greater flatness of sound (a point that is driving some audiophiles back to vinyl). Nonetheless, the greater convenience of mp3s in terms of acquisition, portability, and sharing appears to have trumped quality for most casual music listeners. As Simon Reynolds observed: "for many listeners, mp3s and music heard through computers and iPods is simply what recorded sound sounds like."[37] A similar case can be made for the enormous success of YouTube, which offers greatly enhanced access and quantity at the expense of image and sound quality.

The great appeal of digital devices is that they not only effectively fulfill their primary functions, but also add convenience because of their capacity to do other things. Developments in new digital technology have heralded the introduction of numerous new product innovations that highlight greater convenience and practicality. As I was writing this section, my Facebook feed for the Mashable tech and social media blog consisted of a post titled "9 Super Simple Apps That Will Make Your Life Easier," including Cal, a calendar for smartphones and tablets with integrated functions that practically combine one's contacts and social media accounts; Solar, a simple interface that provides the daily weather forecast; Pocket, an organizational tool that conveniently saves website links to be read later, even without a wi-fi connection; and RedLaser, which tracks bargains by reading barcodes scanned by consumers while they are shopping and then provides price comparisons from other stores in the area, making for quick and practical shopping.[38] Some firms are going even further to add convenience to the shopping experience. MasterCard, in collaboration with Condé Nast, the publisher of several popular magazines, developed an application called Shop-This, which provides digital magazine readers the opportunity to instantly buy items that are described in an article or displayed in an advertisement by tapping a shopping cart icon that appears on the page. The tagline promoting ShopThis promises that the "initiative makes it easier than ever to buy on a whim."[39]

The value of practicality and convenience has not escaped the attention of designers and design experts. As Alice Rawsthorn reminds us, "Finding new ways of making our lives more efficient or enjoyable, ideally both, has been one of design's roles throughout history."[40] This is often accomplished when designers translate leaps in technology into things that people find useful or that more practically solve common problems. Illustrative of this idea, Rawsthorn points to everyday innovations that successfully apply new technologies that add convenience, practicality, and simplicity to various activities, such as the planning of a journey. In one case, the New York Metropolitan Transit Authority (MTA) created the Weekender, a simple solution to a common frustration that often plagues weekend riders on the New York City subway—the unannounced closings or delays on subway lines. The Weekender is an interactive map that appears on the home page of the MTA's website, enabling visitors to click on the station where a planned journey is to embark from (or any station on the planned route) to receive updates on the travel situation and recommendations for a faster route. Elegantly simple, the Weekender is an example of the sort of interactive digital information systems that have begun to replace traditional maps and timetables. Similar approaches are now commonly used by other mass transportation systems and for commuters by car, who can check up-to-the-minute traffic conditions and estimated travel times without reliance on less efficient and unpredictable updates by radio or other traditional sources.

A decidedly low-tech innovation to facilitate commuting is Metro Cuffs, a Designhype innovation consisting of wearable stainless steel bracelets embossed with the main lines of several of the world's widely used metro systems. The product assists passengers in navigating subway lines in an easy and discreet way, simply by glancing at one's wrist—a significant improvement over having to struggle with the unfolding of paper maps. Another example, Crumple City maps, represents a modest example of how maps in general can stave off obsolescence at a time when people are increasingly relying on GPS apps on their mobile phones. Crumple City maps are aesthetically pleasing, light, and practical: they are waterproof, indestructible, easy and quick to unfold and, unlike the image that appears on a small screen of a digital device, they give a good sense of a city's overall geography, pointing out commonly visited points of interest.[41]

As the preceding discussion illustrates, new products that add convenience and simplify the lives of consumers are not all dependent on high-tech innovations. A good example that further drives home this point is the line of ShaveMate all-in-one razors that dispense shaving cream from the handle. The product was developed by inventor brothers Peter and Lewis Tomassetti in 1997 as a way to simplify the shaving process, which they believed was becoming increasingly complicated, by combining the shaving cream with the razor.[42] Upon learning that American soldiers in Iraq and Afghanistan were dry shaving, they approached the military in 2002, offering a rugged two-blade solution with the shaving cream, and quickly won an important repeat customer.

A somewhat different twist on the redesign of an everyday product is apparent in Heinz's modification of its ketchup packet, which was intended as an effort to overcome criticisms related to efficacity and practicality issues linked to traditional condiment packaging. Who hasn't experienced the typical inconveniences associated with traditional single-serving plastic packets of ketchup, mustard, and other condiments (so-called "blister packs")? Blister packs are difficult to open, especially if one is holding food in one hand; messy; imprecise and uneven in the amount of condiment that is applied to a sandwich; and there is often the impression that one is never quite getting all the content out of the packet. The new Heinz packaging was intended to fix these problems, and was guided by research revealing that three times as many consumers prefer dipping (chicken nuggets, fries, etc.) to squeezing.[43] Three times larger than the traditional ketchup packet, the redesigned package offers the user two usage options via a dual output system: a tear-off top through which the content can be squeezed, or a peel-off cover that allows the user to dip; in short, squeeze-and-spread or peel-and-dip. The result is that with the larger tub-like packet, the ketchup comes out of the top much more gradually, providing the user with greater control for more even spreading, and despite a somewhat inadequate amount of depth for dipping, the peel-and-dip option eliminates the need for users to build a mound of ketchup from several packets for their fries. Stylistically, the new packets are designed with a functional graphic that clearly illustrates how the two opening systems work. The new packet still has to be opened using both hands, thus remaining a focus for subsequent redesign efforts.

Durability

The fact that consumers demand products that are simple and practical to use does not imply that concerns about quality are necessarily diminished; in fact, a corresponding demand is that products be durable—that is, be dependable and last a long time. On average, durability ranked second to efficacity in terms of average level of importance for the millennials who responded to my consumer demands questionnaire (see Table 3.1). Few consumers feel obliged to frequently change relatively expensive durable products, such as their car, television, microwave oven, or washing machine, and tend to attribute a high degree of weight in their decision making to assurances of sturdiness, solidity, and reliability during the shopping process. As an example, the average age of passenger cars world-wide prior to a repurchase has gradually increased over the years, with estimates in European Union countries revealing an increase from 6.9 years in 1995 to 7.5 years in 2004 and 8.4 years in 2013.[44] In the US, the average age of a car reached 11.1 years by 2011.[45]

Perhaps made more salient as a result of persistent economic crises, consumers more than ever expect that good products are those that last a long time, as evidenced by the marketplace success of jeans, Timberland shoes, Duracell batteries, diesel automobiles, equipment with self-diagnostic systems (e.g., some photocopiers), anti-rust treatments for motor vehicles and home gates, software updates, antique furniture, after-sale service, warranties (i.e., assurances of quality that a product can be returned for repair, replacement, or refund), and guarantees (i.e., general assurances that a product can be returned if the buyer is unsatisfied). Another aspect of durability is the tendency for consumers to take great comfort in the presence of familiar products and brands that have been around for many years and seem to never change. In France, for example, products like the hazelnut chocolate spread Nutella (1944), the popular chocolate drink Banania (1912), and the La Vache Qui Rit (1921) line of cheeses represent familiar elements of French consumers' everyday universe and evoke childhood memories of early product usage and brand loyalties. In a time of rapid change, consumers appreciate some degree of consistency and familiarity.

The increasing consumer demand for long-lasting durable goods, of course, runs counter to the long-standing notion that the modern economic system requires consumers to regularly replace their acquired possessions with newly purchased goods. More than fifty years ago, in his book *The Waste Makers*, Vance Packard attacked the consumer goods industry for following a policy of planned obsolescence (i.e., the deliberate curtailing of the lifespan of consumer goods).[46] As described by professor of sustainable design and consumption Tim Cooper, this approach has culminated in "throwaway cultures," in which millions of prematurely obsolete consumer goods are discarded yearly, "technologically out-dated but not upgradable, faulty but irreparable. Often they have been designed for lifespans far shorter than those technically possible."[47] As he elaborated in his edited volume *Longer Lasting Products: Alternatives to the Throwaway Society*, the failure to produce and maintain longer-lasting products is both odd, yet utterly predictable:

> The odd thing is that it ought to be—most of the time, at least—in our own best interests to have things that last. Appliances that don't break down at crucial moments. Laptops and phones that don't need replacing every year. . . . The predictability stems from our implicit understanding that to keep an economy going we are required, almost obliged, to consume and throw away more and more stuff. The "throwaway society" is not so much about thoughtless plundering. It's not just a confluence of

carefree consumers with little or no concern for their own future or the future of the planet. It's a society locked into perverse consumption practices by its own ineluctable logic.[48]

In recent years, however, there have been indications that the "perverse consumption practices" described by Cooper have begun to change. Ecological concerns, prompted by growing interest in resource efficiency and demands for waste reduction, have begun to render planned obsolescence as untenable from a sustainability perspective. Along with consumer discontent over the planned obsolescence model, these developments have resulted in the implementation of more sustainable practices that expand product lifetimes. Governments are initiating efforts to move from recycling to waste prevention policies and are putting increased pressure on companies to produce longer-lasting goods—developments that are discussed in greater detail in Chapter 6.

Product utility

Attention to the usability demands that people have for the various goods they see before them in the consumer marketplace (Will it function correctly? Will it last? Will it be easy to use?) is often paid at the expense of considering whether there is any need for those goods in the first place. *Product utility* is a term that pertains to the usefulness of consumer offerings and the extent to which the right functionality is provided, which for marketers and manufacturers represent necessary prerequisites to product development and innovation. While it is true that no one needs a product that functions poorly or not at all, assuming that the product has the potential to satisfy a compelling need or purpose for consumers, there is always the possibility that its quality could be modified and improved. But if it serves no useful function at all, it makes no difference how well it performs.

As is the case in so many areas of marketing, consumer perception is at the heart of product utility issues, and a key challenge in the development and design of products is identifying what it is that consumers perceive to have utility. Some pundits underplay utility from the consumer's perspective, preferring instead to adopt an "if you build it, they will come" mentality, wryly expressed in social historian Daniel Boorstin's comment, "We are always ready—even eager—to discover, from the announcement of a new product, what we have all along wanted without really knowing it."[49] In an era in which consumers are better informed and more skeptical of business practices than ever before, such a mindset in marketing is shortsighted and underestimates the power and intelligence of the buyer. Successful innovations typically take a user-centered approach to product utility issues (see Chapter 2).

Just as our discussion of usability focused on various product properties and attributes expressed as consumer demands, it is possible to identify additional demands linked to product usefulness. Among the more compelling requirements that have become particularly apparent in recent decades are those for

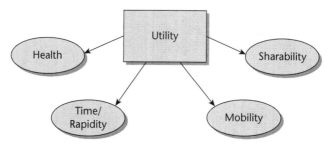

FIGURE 3.4 The utility demand cluster

products that are healthful, help us save time, and facilitate mobility and sharing (see Figure 3.4).

Health

A growing trend throughout much of the industrialized world is a tendency toward increased health consciousness, as evidenced by a significant rise in availability of and spending on health and safety products. In France, for example, the proportion of the household budget allocated to food steadily declined from 1970 (26%) to 2000 (16.5%), while spending on pharmaceuticals and other health-related products steadily rose during the same period (7.1% to 16.4%). Throughout Europe, mirroring other parts of the world, products such as red meat, tobacco, and alcohol have lost ground, as spending on low-calorie, light, diet products has shown clear gains.[50] Health and safety consciousness is reflected in the marketplace success of over-the-counter medicines, dental hygiene products, mineral water, fruit juices, active health dairy drink products, unsweetened natural breakfast cereals and granolas, bifidus and low-fat yogurts, electronic cigarettes, non-alcoholic beers, soya products, whole-grain breads, smoke detectors, breathalyzers, and condoms.

One of Danone's key profit drivers in Europe is Actimel (known as DanActive in other parts of the world), a probiotic dairy drink containing a special ferment that helps protect the body's natural defenses. Introduced in France in 1997, more than 1.5 billion bottles had been sold in the country by 2005.[51] In Ireland, the arrival of Actimel, also in 1997, revitalized a stagnant dairy market, where a small health segment was showing a mere 2% annual growth rate. The arrival of Actimel coincided with a 23% growth of the Irish dairy market and a 22% increase in the health market, where today Actimel is regularly consumed by about half of the Irish population. According to one analysis, "this impressive change shows that Danone Actimel struck a chord with its consumers, providing a solution to a previously unrecognized need."[52] Another success story for Danone in the health drink category is Activia, a bifidus yogurt that contains a non-harmful bacterium that aids in digestion. Modeled after a longstanding Japanese yogurt concept, Activia is marketed as a health food and is now available in more than seventy countries on five continents.[53]

In 2003, PepsiCo launched a new range of health-oriented chilled fruit juices under the Tropicana brand umbrella. Tropicana Essentials, which responds to consumers' expectations for health and pleasure-oriented products, has contributed 50% to Tropicana brand growth and has been successfully recruiting new consumers from outside the chilled category ever since.[54] At the time of this writing, the Essentials line was comprised of four product references, each of which addresses a specific consumer health need:

- Tropicana Essentials Multivitamins contributes to energy, with a recipe containing 12 vitamins.
- Tropicana Essentials Fibers contributes to internal comfort with fruit and vegetables rich in fibers, like pineapple and carrot.
- Tropicana Essentials Magnesium contributes to wellness through a sweet and savory recipe composed of banana, passion fruit, and pineapple.
- Tropicana Essentials Antioxydation contributes to the fight against cellular aging through a recipe rich in polyphenol that naturally exists in fruits.

Health consciousness is also reflected in an increased demand in other consumer categories, including body care products, sports articles, fitness centers and health clubs, and "green" products. For example, despite an ongoing recession, the UK health and fitness industry showed a total market value growth of 1.4% to £3.86 billion over the twelve-month period ending in March 2012, coinciding with an overall 3.4% rise in the number of fitness center members.[55] According to a recent International Health, Racquet & Sportsclub Association (IHRSA) health club report, participation in health clubs and gyms is rapidly becoming one of the largest sporting activities in the world. Leading the way in Europe, where a total of 44 million members frequent 48,000 clubs with revenue exceeding €25 billion, are Germany, which has the highest number of clubs (more than 7,500 facilities), and Norway, which claims the greatest membership penetration rate (nearly 16% of the total population).[56] In the US, the fitness center industry began to come into its own during the 1970s and 1980s as more and more Americans began to turn seriously to exercising activities, led by running and aerobics. Beginning in the early 2000s, the industry began to show enormous growth, with the number of fitness clubs increasing from 16,938 at the beginning of the decade to 29,636 by January 2008. By early 2008, there were more than 41 million Americans who held memberships in a health club, with 16 million attending the clubs more than 100 days a year.[57] From 2009 to early 2014, the gym, health, and fitness industry in the US has shown a 2.3% annual growth rate.[58]

The rise in health consciousness and its impact on marketing appeals is apparent in promotional messages that emphasize how products can enable users to take better care of their bodies and protect themselves from environmental threats. Actimel is not a pharmaceutical product, but Danone's advertising campaigns tend to stress the product's health benefits, with an appeal to taste demoted to secondary status. In recent years, major cosmetics companies, such as Estée Lauder and Helena Rubenstein, have launched campaigns focusing on how beauty creams and other skin care and makeup products hydrate the skin, protect it from the harmful rays of the sun, and slow down the aging process. Similar campaigns have begun to target men with non-traditional body care products, consistent with the trend discussed in Box 3.2. Advertisements for bottled mineral water, currently the fastest-growing beverage category, especially for single-service containers, emphasize the product's natural purity compared to drinking tap water. One French print ad for Volvic mineral water underlined this point by showing a beaker filled with a pink liquid and a straw, with the headline reading (translated into English): "Sodium benzoate, synthetic sweetener, dye 110 . . . you want some ice cubes? Volvic—there is nothing fresher than nature."

A number of emerging product lines and promotional campaigns focus on how parents can improve and protect the health and well-being of their children. A Carrefour print ad promoting the store's private label food products showed a young girl eating a dairy product, clad in a pair of pajamas that she had obviously outgrown, along with a headline reading: "When one eats healthfully, it is obviously seen." The ad's text explains how the multinational retailer is continuously working toward the development of healthy and balanced foods, which are identified in the chain's grand surface stores with a unique Carrefour health seal.

During the past decade, natural and organic products for babies have become more prevalent in the marketplace, usually priced much higher than traditional brands. This includes cotton clothing, bed mattresses, and blankets that are labeled "organic," "natural," "pure," or "eco-friendly."[59] Another example is the newly emergent premium baby skin care category, where companies like Bobbi Brown, Estée Lauder, and California Baby offer products for babies that emphasize all-natural and organic ingredients like almond and safflower oil, flower extracts, and aloe, and claim to be free from chemicals that can harm the skin. Sales data from the London-based market research firm Euromonitor reveal that sales of premium baby care products in the US increased 68% from 2005 to 2010, compared with a 16% rise in sales of total baby care. Companies can demand exorbitant prices for these sorts of products for babies because they are well aware that parents want to pamper their newborns and do what is best for them, as evidenced by one new mother who commented: "I am not necessarily into natural lines myself. But it was important for me to find pure and nontoxic products for my kids because I feel like their skin is so new." Another mother revealed: "I spend more on my kids than I do for myself. It's worth it to me to get something pure for them."[60] Once they reach their tweens (i.e., the 9–14-year-old demographic), children can take advantage of visits to health spas, where they have the opportunity to partake of hair styling, pedicures, facials, massages, and temporary tattoo offers. Many spas that cater to children offer workshops on hair and skin care, clothing choices, and proper nutrition and exercise. According to an IHRSA report, 824,000 children between the ages of 6 and 17 use personal trainers, which accounts for nearly 13% of all personal trainers' clients.

Some critics have legitimately questioned whether the "organic" and "natural" ingredients of baby care products really are better, or simply more expensive, and whether spas and personal trainers represent examples of conspicuous consumption that increase the likelihood that overindulged children will become materialistic adults.[61] But the point remains that the market is there for the asking for astute marketers—a function of changing consumer preferences and lifestyles, and contemporary trends that would have been unimaginable to previous generations.

In addition to a focus on individual health and safety, companies have begun to acknowledge that consumer choices are increasingly guided by ecological and "green" issues, and that health consciousness extends to more general concerns about the health of the planet. The "green consumer" is a person who is aware that the production, use, and disposal of products can have negative effects on the earth, its environment, and its inhabitants, and who consciously makes an effort to reduce those effects through his or her consumption behavior. Nine in ten consumers surveyed claim to exhibit green behaviors at least to some extent in their daily lives, including a willingness to pay a premium for products they know are made of ecologically friendly, organic materials; searching for information on alternative energy and green technologies; recycling; cooking with healthy recipes; and using natural remedies.[62] Product manufacturers and marketers have responded to this emerging trend by incorporating more energy-efficient elements in product design, utilizing environmentally safer production processes, and by positioning their offers so as to create a more environmentally friendly brand image. For example, Reckitt Benckiser in the UK, which sells Woolite and Lysol and other automatic dishwasher products, launched an ad campaign intended to appeal to consumers' environmental conscience by claiming that the use of dishwashers saves water and energy compared with washing dishes by hand; Ford introduced its Escape Hybrid with the tagline "I guess it is easy being green"; and Bosch promises buyers that "It pays to be green" by purchasing one of the company's environmentally friendly washing machines.

Time and rapidity

Although lifespans have significantly increased during the past century, with people today expected to live on average more than thirty years longer than those born in 1900, a common refrain in industrialized countries is that there is never enough time—an apparent paradox in light of the appearance of numerous products and services that help us save time (see Box 3.5). The consumer demand for marketplace offerings that provide time savings has never been stronger, as evidenced by a multitude of recent developments emphasizing rapidity: fast-food restaurants, ready-to-eat (or cook) foods, digital cameras (which avoid the delay required by photographic film development), one-hour eyeglasses assembly, high-speed commuter trains, motorbikes, instant lotteries, products with multiple functions, and the like. In his compelling book *Faster: The Acceleration of Just About Everything*, James Gleick points out that in the past, inventions like the cotton gin, automobile, and vacuum cleaner permitted people to work, travel, and clean faster, saving hours of time in the process.[63] Today, consumer goods are providing savings measured in milliseconds ("a millisecond here, a millisecond there"), as evidenced by quicker-heating coils in toasters and irons, telephones with speed dialing, answering machines with quick playback, flip-top (versus screw-top) product containers, laser printers, fast-reading electronic thermometers, texting (with its now common abbreviations), and Twitter (getting one's message across in 140 characters or less).

BOX 3.5 HOW PEOPLE SPEND TIME

I am probably not alone in saying that when it comes to precision as to how much time I spend in non-productive activities during the day, such as waiting online, searching for misplaced objects or documents that often are never found, being put on hold when trying to reach a company representative on the telephone, and so on, my response is: "I don't want to know." Yet some researchers have been inspired enough by the time usage question to study how much time people spend engaged in various everyday activities. One way of finding this out is simply by asking people to estimate how long they spend on an activity, although as James Gleick observed in his book *Faster*, this is at best an imperfect method, in part because of the fallibility of human memory, but also because people tend to think about a typical day that never occurs.[64] Gleick cites surveys that find strikingly diverse results to similar, but essentially different kinds of questions: for example, "How much time *do* you spend reading *each day*?" and "How much time *did* you spend reading *yesterday*?" As Gleick explains: "For reading and most other activities, *each day* is the unreal typical day and *yesterday* usually comes up short."

Another approach to the time estimation question, albeit a time-consuming one (however ironic that might be), is simply by observing and timing people in their natural habitats and then extrapolating the results to estimate time usage over the long term. From this approach, a variety of rough estimates of time consumption have emerged: people spend about six years of their lives eating, one year searching for misplaced objects (or about 16 minutes per day), four years doing housework, four years waiting online, six months sitting at traffic signals, four minutes per day having sex, and seven minutes per day caring for plants and pets. My personal favorite: by the age of 70, the average French person has spent a total of eight days saying "Bonjour!"

A quick Google search will reveal statistics for a wide range of other activities, including amount of time waiting, browsing, chatting, and surfing on the Internet; time spent visiting other people; time spent shopping; time spent filling out government forms; time spent commuting, and so on. These estimates change over time (e.g., the time spent visiting others face-to-face has declined over the years with the rise in usage of the Internet, telephone, and other portable devices, each of which saves travel time and expedites communication). Most time usage statistics vary cross-culturally, as well. For example, according to Neilsen's Global Television Audience Measurement statistics, the average daily time spent watching TV (in hours:minutes) ranges from 2:11 in Thailand to 5:39 in Serbia.[65]

A recent breakdown of American time usage derived from a detailed Bureau of Labor Statistics survey provides some interesting insight into how people differ in time usage depending on such basic human characteristics as age, gender, and education.[66] The results revealed that sleeping accounts for more than one-third of a typical American's (aged 15 years or older) average day, with women sleeping 11 minutes more per night than men. Women spend 29 more minutes cooking and clearing up per day than men. Men spend four minutes more a day eating and drinking, 10 minutes more exercising per day, and, on the days they work, men labor 47 minutes more than employed women. Although television accounts for the largest share of Americans' leisure time, individuals over the age of 25 who have not obtained a high school diploma spend two-thirds more time watching television than those who hold a bachelor's degree, and also spend four times as much time thinking and relaxing. Academic high achievers, by contrast, spend more time reading, exercising, and playing games on their computer for leisure.

From our present-day perspective, it is difficult to imagine an era when saving time was not a serious priority, yet Gleick reminds us that time-saving is a relatively modern notion in human history. Indeed, in the past, personal time management typically revolved around concerns about worthy ways to *spend* time, rather than ways to save it. According to Gleick: "Our culture has been transformed from one with time to fill and time to spare to one that views time as a thing to guard, hoard, and protect."[67] Today understood to mean reducing the time spent or required to do something, "time-saving" originally appeared in dictionaries about a century ago, and was commonly defined as "prompt," "expeditious," or "expedient." Accordingly, Gleick concluded that the earlier definitions have implications for the utility of time-saving devices in the contemporary context:

> In a slow world, a time-saving device made an unpleasant task—washing clothes, perhaps—pass faster. Now we live in a faster world. Our time has different layers. It might seem that to *save* time means to preserve it, spare it, free it from some activity that might otherwise have consumed it in the hot flames of busy-ness. Yet time-saving books are constantly admonishing people to do things. Some of the recommended time-savers replace

pleasant pastimes with less pleasant, for minutes or seconds. Some spare us a chore that was passing almost unnoticed in the background of our lives and replace it with a task that grabs more of our foreground attention. . . . Some of us say we want to save time when really we just want to *do more.*[68]

This passage perhaps gets at the root of the aforementioned paradox (losing time amidst new devices that help us save it) and suggests the role that technology plays in shaping our relationship to time. Technology offers us more choices (an obvious example being the proliferation of television channels made accessible by the introduction of cable, satellite, and online streaming), and people are compelled to take advantage of those choices, which means that they are filling their newly available free time with activities that would not have been apparent or readily accessible without the technology. For example, as I am typing this paragraph on my laptop, which offers significantly greater facility and speed compared to the typewriters I used when I was younger and, at the same time, provides direct Internet access to source material that in the past would have required a time-consuming trip to the library, I also find that the number of distractions—that is, time-wasters (or is it seducers?)—are endless. No doubt like most people, I find it difficult to resist periodically checking Google news updates and sports scores, reading emails, following my Twitter feed and a baseball game that is playing in the background, all of which can be accomplished by a few simple mouse clicks. This potentially self-destructive tendency to attend to other things when a single-minded focus on the task at hand would ultimately accomplish that task quicker (and perhaps better) is the result of what author Alex Soojung-Kim Pang refers to as "distraction addiction," the overwhelming imposition of digital devices in our everyday lives. It is easy to identify with the Silicon Valley engineer who observed: "Computers used to be part of my daily life. Now they're part of my daily *minute.*"[69] Interestingly, one view of addiction attributes its cause to an underlying unconscious motivation to simplify life and structure time or, in another sense, to avoid boredom and "kill" time.[70]

Despite these reservations linked to our complex relationship to time relative to the devices that have become a central part of daily living, it cannot be denied that from a usability standpoint, new marketplace innovations—many of which today are taken for granted—are directly related to time management, not only in the sense of providing means by which consumers can save time, but also to have greater control over it. Television programs that are inconvenient to watch during their scheduled time slots can be digitally recorded for viewing when it is more convenient. When listening to music on a CD player or portable device, the user can pause, rewind, or fast-forward content as desired, thereby eliminating any problems related to inattention or interruptions, or to facilitate leaping ahead to favorite songs or song fragments. An article on a website can be saved for reading at a more expeditious time through the use of an Internet application like Pocket (formerly Read It Later) or Evernote. Electronic agendas with reminder functions alert us to our appointments so that we don't forget them. And watches, clocks, and digital time-keepers let us know what time it is so that we can arrive at those appointments on time.

Mobility

Modern consumers understand that life increasingly implies the need for flexibility and adaptation in a geographic, intellectual, and psychological sense. This is reflected by the ascendance of nomadism, as seen in transportable products that can be consumed everywhere, including mobile phones, netbooks, tablet PCs, e-book readers, mp3 players, DVD viewers, wi-fi, Bluetooth, GPS and tracking apps like Foursquare, portable speakers, mini-bottles of mineral water, portable iceboxes and thermos bottles, rolling luggage, travel trailers and recreation vehicles, Square, Google Wallet, and Facebook mobile and messenger. According to a 2009 McKinsey survey of 2,500 American consumers, portability (i.e., being small and lightweight) ranked as the most important reason for purchasing a netbook among laptop users (53%), followed by affordability (31%), and ease of use (16%).[71]

In 2001, the Perrier Group of America launched a US$10 million three-year campaign to revitalize the brand in the US by increasing its appeal among "echo boomers" (consumers in their early twenties to early thirties). Recognizing that their key targets—young social drivers who follow the latest styles in fashion, food, and entertainment—are characterized by active, on-the-go lifestyles, one of the first decisions was to introduce a one-liter plastic bottle for its benchmark Perrier carbonated water brand. This was a clear departure from the brand's original marketing efforts to attract young professionals with its sophisticated glass bottle and upscale French cachet, but it was clear that adding a more portable plastic bottle, along with the new slogan, "Perfect anytime," would enable Perrier to capture greater success among younger consumers.

The appeal of mobile products has much to do with the changing nature of consumers' relationship to work, which in recent decades entails greater flexibility between home and work boundaries. In their research pertaining to the extended self in the workplace, previously discussed in Chapter 1, Tian and Belk observed that the contemporary postmodern workplace has led to a blurring between home and work spaces: "For example, as employees transport aspects of the self back and forth between the workplace and spaces external to it, the notion of home as a privileged place for privacy, leisure, and intimacy begins to dissolve."[72] In a more competitive, rapidly changing business environment, professional workers now are expected to conduct business and be reachable via email, text, mobile phone, and Internet technology for work-related purposes well beyond the strictures of the eight or so hours actually spent at their established place of business. I vividly recall being on a business trip to Israel around the time when mobile phones were beginning to diffuse in the marketplace, with my foreign associate frantically checking his pager, endlessly taking calls on his hands-free cell phone, and confessing to me that he wanted "to be reachable

24/7." This profile, which I viewed at the time as aberrant behavior and perhaps indicative of a Type A personality, today appears to be the norm, and for most professionals, mobility is an essential requirement.

Software designers are responding to these trends through efforts to create workplace software that can conform to the needs of users on the move. Major companies like Microsoft and Google have begun to assure that their offerings reflect a mobile work environment, where speed and ease of use are incorporated into software design for workers who are in nearly constant contact with each other. For example, Microsoft developed a mobile version of Microsoft Office, and Google Docs, which is now a component of Google's online storage service Drive, provides users with the ability to create and edit documents online while collaborating live with other users. Another major player is Quip, a start-up company that offers document-writing software focusing on mobile work, combining instant messaging with document creation, storage, and sharing, primarily for touch-screen devices.[73]

As suggested by sociologist Richard Sennett, the "traveling body" is experienced differently than the body confined in specific spaces and places—an idea that extends to the nature of the objects we take along with us on our journeys.[74] Not unlike the way Carolyn Geduld described the car as the container which alienates the clan from society (see Box 1.3), mobile products empower their users to create private spaces in public places, through a sort of self-containment that is constructed in various ways: by the texts people are responding to and games they are playing on their mobile phones and tablets, the magazines and books they are attending to on their e-readers, and the content they are processing as they surf the Internet on their portable devices—all utilized within the context of a personal soundtrack provided by the music streaming through their mp3 headsets. By creating such personal "bubbles" through the use of portable technology, people can take advantage of commuting time, for example, as an opportunity to stay in touch with friends, keep up with current events, and psychologically protect themselves from the frequent unpleasantries associated with public transport. According to Publicis Groupe executives Maurice Lévy and Dan O'Donoghue, the mobile phone has rapidly become the dominant means by which the world is being recreated by and for consumers: "Indeed, the Internet is a fascinating medium, but the mobile phone allows you to be the center of your universe."[75] From a product utility standpoint, the benefits of portability are clear; yet, in a broader sense, such developments can be seen as having important adverse consequences on individuals and groups, as suggested by the "I Forgot My Phone" video described in Chapter 2. That is, technology may be leading us along a path whose destination is inhabited by "pod people" who eschew direct interpersonal contact and experience the world around them only as it is consumed through their mobile devices. By the time evolving mobile technologies further proliferate (e.g., Google Glass, smart watches), it may very well be that any remnants of clear demarcations between public and private spaces, work and home places, and personal and public lives are relegated to one's distant memories.

Sharability

As products have become more portable, conforming to increasingly mobile lifestyles, they have facilitated the means by which consumers can connect with each other, at any time and from any place, taking advantage of the opportunities provided by widespread access to the Internet. In this context, consumers expect to be able to share information, recommendations, discoveries, and personal updates with others; thus, they respond enthusiastically to products that provide those possibilities, including several of the portable devices mentioned in the discussion of mobility above: smartphones, computers, tablet PCs, wi-fi, Bluetooth, Skype, along with other technological devices, software, and apps that provide immediate access to exchanges with friends, relatives, colleagues, and acquaintances. Content-sharing devices have rapidly become familiar fixtures of the technological landscape, beginning with the creation of floppy disks and evolving to higher-capacity compact discs, USB flash drives, cloud storage, and online file hosting services led by Dropbox, Let's Crate, Box, Hightail, and a long list of imitators. Sharability is not restricted to online activity; in fact, some of the earlier forms of consumer sharing predate the Internet, such as property sharing in its various forms: timesharing (an activity dating back to the early 1960s, whereby multiple parties retain the rights to a property and rotate usage throughout the year), apartment exchanges, and car-pooling (see Box 3.6).

BOX 3.6 TRANSUMING, SHARABILITY, AND THE AUTOMOTIVE INDUSTRY

Coined in 2003 by the global design and business consultancy Fitch, "transumers" is a term that was originally used to refer to "consumers in transition," in the sense of frequent travelers and the various novel and innovative shopping opportunities that have become increasingly prevalent at airports, train stations, and hotels catering to this consumer segment.[76] In recent years, the term has expanded beyond the travel context to refer to consumers who are driven by experiences instead of the "fixed" and predictable; by entertainment, discovery, fighting boredom, and increasingly living a transient lifestyle that is free from permanent ownership and possessions.[77]

Consistent with this profile, transumers are persons who are turning to transitory experiences as a means of liberating themselves from a lifestyle overwhelmed by the ownership of material goods—products that are rapidly out of date or obsolete, in need of maintenance and upgrades, and increasingly taking up large chunks of time, budgets, and physical space. This accounts for the growing appeal of leasing and rental opportunities over product purchasing, fractional ownership as opposed to sole ownership, and

(Continued)

(Continued)

the sharing of material goods and services. This trend is evident in a growing number of cities, such as Paris, where bicycle and car sharing programs have become enormously attractive to commuters who are tired of the problems of car ownership or having to ride often overcrowded mass transportation.

In an effort to circumvent a major threat to their survival as a result of consumer sharing programs, major auto makers and car rental companies have recently concluded that if you can't beat them, join them. Several companies have begun to launch new rental ventures in the hopes of holding on to current customers and attracting future ones. For example, in 2013, in response to a growing preference among young, urban dwellers for car sharing as opposed to car ownership, Daimler developed a partnership with the rental firm Europcar to create Car2Go and BMW joined forces with the car rental company Sixt to form DriveNow. These ventures take advantage of new technologies that add more flexibility and appeal to the car rental program. Cars are equipped with GPS and an Internet connection, which enable customers who want to rent a car to locate the one closest to them via their smartphones. By the end of 2013, Car2Go had expanded across Europe and North America with 9,500 cars and 500,000 customers in 25 cities. Reflecting on auto makers' embrace of the car sharing trend, BMW's mobility unit head Tony Douglas commented: "Our core business in the '70s was selling cars; in the '80s came the great innovation of leasing and financing. Now you can pay per use of a car. It's like the music industry. You used to have to buy an album, now you can pay per play." According to Daimler Mobility Services CEO Robert Henrich: "We just think it's the future, as simple as that. Young customers cannot imagine a life without smartphones anymore, and we need to be part of the smartphone world."[78]

The numbers add credence to the view that car sharing is the wave of the future: at the end of 2012, about 2.3 million drivers worldwide belonged to either a station-based car sharing service or one-way approach with no set home location, a figure expected to rise to 26 million by 2020.[79] At the time of this writing, in addition to Daimler and BMW, Volkswagen, Citroën, and Ford had also entered the car sharing arena. It is difficult to foresee whether the rise of car sharing will result in a decrease in vehicle sales for these players or, conversely, will attract new customers who had not originally thought about owning a car. Nonetheless, by responding to the sharing trend, the automotive and car rental companies can at least hope to avoid becoming irrelevant.

It is the social Web, including networks like Facebook and LinkedIn, that best serves to illustrate the profound power of technology in connecting consumers in the contemporary era. The social Web has been defined as "the online place where people with a common interest can gather to share thoughts, comments, and opinions."[80] Consumer sharing is most fully realized through social networks—primarily World Wide Web-based virtual spaces where people come together to share content, questions, and advice related to mutual interests. Such networks are manifest in various formats that facilitate interactions and connections between users, such as discussion groups, message boards and forums, file-sharing websites, and voice chat applications. Social network users are able to set up personal profiles and explore the interests and activities in other users' profiles, thus enabling the identification of persons with similar interests and the possibility of connecting with them. Photos, videos, and music have moved to the center of the field in terms of online content-sharing activity, accounting for the rise in popularity of photo sharing and peer-to-peer websites.

Leading in terms of Web traffic and influence among the many social network sites that have appeared on the scene over the past couple of decades are Facebook, Twitter, and Pinterest, which have attracted previously unheard of numbers of participants on the basis of their community-building and sharing-friendly nature. According to the Venture Capital-backed online sharing company Shareaholic, these three social network powers collectively accounted for 15.22% of overall referral traffic in September 2013, with Facebook having grown 58.81%, Pinterest 66.52%, and Twitter 54.12% since September 2012.[81] The worldwide embrace of social networks has been rapid and impressive, and recent analyses of Internet usage activity attest to their soaring popularity. In fact, there is evidence that social networks are driving Internet usage in the European Union: as the general online Internet audience has begun to plateau, social network audiences have steadily increased since the beginning of 2007.

Unlike traditional media, new technologies allow for bidirectional communication between consumers and marketers, thereby adding the variable of interactivity to the marketing communications mix. These developments have provided consumers with a greater degree of control over how they choose to receive information, what information they are willing to receive, the means by which they may gain direct access to marketing communication sources, and the outlets through which marketing messages are shared with other consumers. In the past, consumers kept their insights and preferences about the things they consume largely to themselves because they lacked adequate opportunities and means to interact with companies. With greater access to professional hardware, software, and online distribution channels allowing them to share content with companies, that situation has begun to change, and consumers are proving to be more than willing to accept the invitation to enter into a collaborative dialog with firms.

Blogs represent another means by which ordinary consumers can share their opinions and establish conversations with virtually anyone with similar interests, at virtually no cost. Blog content tends to have higher credibility than content disseminated through traditional broadcast outlets because blogs are typically perceived by readers as independent and unaffiliated, with blog authors (considered by some as "citizen journalists") expressing their honest viewpoints untarnished by any apparent ulterior motives. This latter point is one reason why company blogs are rapidly becoming a fixture of the corporate online landscape. Such blogs represent a key means by which companies can effectively communicate and engage with current and prospective customers, and posted blog content is less likely to be seen as a formal selling effort than if it were to appear through more traditional communication channels.

A variation of blogging that has become a burgeoning, albeit legally contentious, focus of sharing on the Internet is the creation of file-hosting and storage services, where ordinary consumers and obsessive collectors alike upload video, music, software, and book content for peer-to-peer exchange. This new blog-like network activity is sometimes referred to as *sharity*—a combination of "share," "charity," and "rarity," reflecting the online availability of rare and obscure content in addition to mainstream fare. According to Eric Lumbleau, creator of the music blog Mutant Sounds,[82] the motivation behind sharity is a form of "self-aggrandizing altruism . . . blog authors anointing themselves as gurus and presiding over their own little kingdom of cool." Musicologist Simon Reynolds similarly views the impetus behind sharity as a form of "competitive generosity," whereby the objective behind record collecting has shifted from "I want to have something that no one else has" to "I've just got hold of something no one else has got, so I'm immediately going to make it available to EVERYBODY."[83]

Product desirability

In addition to the more utilitarian considerations related to usability and utility of consumer goods, it would be remiss to neglect the significant role emotional factors play in the consumption process, and their implications for product design. Product desirability, or the emotional allure of a product, plays a key role in the motivation to acquire marketplace offerings and the resulting satisfaction that consumers derive from them (see Box 3.7). Researchers have found that even mundane product and service experiences entail high levels of emotional dynamics for consumers.[84] Aesthetical, more visceral elements related to product design, including color, scent, and tactile stimulation, are crucial in helping us understand the reasons why wine tastes better in fancy glasses; that the amount of food eaten, taste satisfaction levels, and amount of money consumers are willing to pay for food vary according to the types and colors of packaging and the dishes on which the food is served; that the emotional experience of an armchair is enhanced when a consumer interacts intensively with it; and that consumers are more likely to purchase an item in a store if they can first touch it.[85]

BOX 3.7 WHY ELEGANT THINGS MAKE US BUY MORE

Consumer research has uncovered an unusual finding: a buyer's seemingly innocent purchase of a luxury item can set off an unintended buying spree on the part of that individual. In a 2011 series of controlled experiments and field studies involving hundreds of shoppers, consumer psychologists Patrick and Hagtvedt found that when the purchase of a new item fails to fit in with one's existing possessions, consumers generally tend to regret the purchase and return it to the store.[86] There's nothing very surprising about that. However, when the mismatched purchase happens to involve a higher-end offering, such as an item from a designer product line or a luxury branded item, consumers experience less regret, but greater frustration. Rather than returning the designer item, people actively seek out ways to integrate the new purchase with their other possessions. One way to do that is to make a series of complementary purchases—that is, they purchase other items that closely match the initial one. This process, which the researchers dubbed "aesthetic incongruity resolution," may ultimately result in a far greater cumulative expenditure than the consumer had anticipated when the initial purchase was made.

To explain why elegant things make us buy more, it is essential to understand the role of emotions in determining whether a purchase will be returned or not. Aesthetical purchases imbued with unique design characteristics have intrinsic value and are therefore more difficult for the consumer to relinquish. So even though the purchase of an irresistible pair of designer shoes, for example, may prove to be totally at odds with one's current wardrobe, once the buyer returns home from the store and more carefully contemplates the implications of the purchase, it may not be very long before the buyer attempts to resolve the incongruity by subsequently purchasing a matching handbag, jewelry, and formal dress. A simple safeguard against potentially exceeding one's budget in this way is simply to think twice before a purchase, and to consider whether that special purchase matches what one already owns. If not, then buyer beware.

It is possible to glean at least three marketing implications from the findings of the incongruity resolution research. First, marketers of relatively inexpensive products with which aesthetic appeal is not typically associated might consider how unique design elements could be added to appeal to the aesthetic sensibilities of buyers. This is something that the makers of various household products, such as kitchen appliances, have already begun to do for the product design of such items as coffee makers, electric grills, and the like.[87] Second, the findings highlight the growing tendency for companies to target sales to individual consumers based on their previous purchases and current possessions. Evolving customer relationship management (CRM) technologies permit firms to carefully target product promotions based on detailed information about

(Continued)

(Continued)

consumers' previous purchases, to the point of tracking and even contributing to the development of their consumption environments. More practically, the common sales practice of suggesting various add-ons (e.g., a belt or tie) for a current purchase (e.g., a new suit) represents another way to increase sales while enhancing customer satisfaction with appropriately matched purchases.

The third implication derived from the incongruity resolution research is one that reflects marketers' ethical responsibilities toward the satisfaction of customer needs and the potential for shaping long-term loyalties. If shoppers end up spending beyond their means without a corresponding increase in satisfaction, neither the customer nor the seller are likely to be best served over the long term. This outcome could add to the rapidly spiraling mistrust consumers have for marketers and the marketing process.

In a more general sense, product desirability brings us within the realm of *customer experience*, a topic that has begun to receive much attention from marketers, which refers to a consumer's internal and subjective interpretations resulting from contact with a company or its offering.[88] Although more commonly discussed in the context of services, the creation of positive customer experiences is also significantly influenced by characteristics of product design, packaging, and brand. This point is evident in Simon Reynolds' observation regarding the digitization of music: "It was easier to develop an attachment to music when it was a thing."[89] Although I will have much more to say about design and consumer experience in Chapter 4, this section will focus on three consumer requirements that are relevant to product desirability: pleasure and comfort, sensory gratification, and engagement (see Figure 3.5).

Pleasure and comfort

Of increasing importance for consumers is that the products they use offer certain sensory, physical, or psychological satisfactions or comforts when they

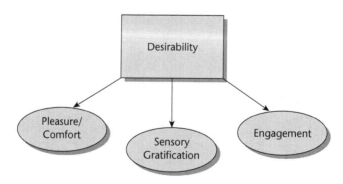

FIGURE 3.5 The desirability demand cluster

are consumed. This demand was especially evident in the results of my survey of millennials, which revealed that although these young consumers placed the highest level of importance on product efficiency, in their view efficiency should not come at the expense of the more pleasure-oriented aspects that can be derived from product usage (see Table 3.1). It is no surprise that consumers seek to obtain various pleasures and comforts from the products they buy and use. In part, this is a reaction to the many aspects of daily life that are difficult and frustrating, ranging from tensions relating to work, conflicts in interpersonal relationships, mass transit strikes, lack of courtesy on the part of others, lousy weather, and the like. For many, the "no pain, no gain" exercise trend of the 1980s, which gave rise to obsessive jogging, body building, and aerobics, has receded in recent years, replaced by health-oriented leisure-time activities that lead to stress reduction, longevity, and feeling better about oneself, including bicycling, dancing (salsa, tango), massage, and yoga.

A common consumer practice linked to pleasure is the tendency for people to indulge themselves with self-gifts, which is a reflection of a decidedly self-orientation in purchase and consumption behavior. Like gifts given in friendship, self-gifts provide a means of rewarding oneself for personal accomplishments, may serve a therapeutic function during tough periods, or may simply be spurred by holiday situations. As discussed in chapter 1, researchers have long been aware of the phenomenon of such self-directed purchases, dating back to Swiss physician Paul Tournier, who described self-gifts as rewards or incentives for personal achievements, "consolation prizes for disappointments or upsets," and as means to celebrate holidays, such as one's birthday or Christmas.[90] Consumer behavior investigators David Mick and Michelle DeMoss found support for Tournier's early ideas about self-gifts, their research revealing in part that self-gifts are premeditated—that is, they are active and intentional acquisitions, rather than impulsive ones. They also found that self-gifts are highly context-bound, which is why it is difficult to consider the giving of a gift to oneself outside the situation in which it took place. Thus, a self-gift would be considered as motivated by a desire to reward oneself in the context of a personal accomplishment, to cheer up oneself during a holiday, to celebrate when one has earned some extra money, to console oneself after experiencing a personal defeat, and to relieve stress after suffering a particularly strenuous period at work.

The search for pleasure and well-being is reflected by the appeal of various products that in one way or another contribute to physical comfort and an agreeable life, including seating for relaxation, comfortable bedding, temperature-controlled mattresses, insecticides, massage chairs and cushions, air conditioning, large-screen televisions, chocolates, alcohol, two- or three-star camping, comfortable clothing, cordless desktop keyboards with comfort grooves, automobile air bags, tranquilizers, and guarantees and after-sale service. The food and beverage categories represent obvious examples of products that are linked to pleasure and comfort. Despite the rise in health consciousness discussed earlier, researchers have found that consumers are more likely to associate "to eat well" with "to eat for pleasure" than is the case for "to eat for health" and "to eat intrinsically good and fresh food"—a tendency that unfortunately has contributed to a worldwide rise in obesity levels.[91] Nonetheless, food habits are evolving as a result of health campaigns, dietary injunctions, and the dissemination of medical standards and recommendations for healthy diets. Consumers are increasingly expecting that food products offer both pleasure as well as nutritional and curative benefits.

The association of food with pleasure and comfort is seen in the emergence of two nascent food trends: fooding and comfort dining. "Fooding" is a neologism coined in 1999 by the French food critic Alexandre Cammas on the basis of a contraction of the words "food" and "feeling."[92] As a reaction against tradition, rituals and boredom, fooding is a mixture of different gastronomic trends, such as world food, fusion food, easy eating, street food, and "bistronomie." Reflecting an appreciation of eating for pleasure, not unlike the underlying appeal associated with the craft beer movement in the US, fooding represents the art of cooking and eating for novelty, a craving for sincerity and fun, and an approach to eating as a leisure-time activity.

Comfort food, on the other hand, is a movement typically associated with tradition, nostalgia, and sentimentality. As the name suggests, the consumption of comfort food is viewed as an activity that comforts by serving as a means of relieving emotional stress and improving one's mood. Trying to nail down the specific foods that are considered to fall under the heading of "comfort" is more difficult than one might imagine, since what consumers tend to regard as falling within that category varies according to whether the food is considered to evoke feelings of familiarity and nostalgia at the cultural or individual level. Certain comfort foods tend to be associated with different countries: for example, shepherd's pie, fish and chips, and Yorkshire pudding in England; borscht, blini, and solyanka in Russia; apple pie, clam chowder, and hamburgers in the United States. Chicken soup is regarded as a comfort food across several countries, where it conjures up childhood memories as a meal served to a sick child for its curative effects.

A commonly held misconception is that comfort food is nutritionally unhealthy. Consumer psychologist Brian Wansink, who directs the Cornell University Food and Brand Lab, where he and his research team conduct experiments to uncover the psychological dynamics underlying dietary behaviors, found that many of the most popular comfort foods consumers mention are actually fairly healthy. In the US, 23% of Wansink's research participants identified potato chips as their favorite comfort food, but 40% named pasta, meats, soups, main dishes, casseroles, and the like as their favorite. What these individuals found appealing about such foods was described in Wansink's book *Mindless Eating*:

> These people not only wanted a great-for-the-moment taste of fat, salt, or sugar, they also wanted to tap in to the psychological comfort that these foods provided and the memories linked to them. Comfort foods are not

always indulgent. They are the foods that feed not only our body, but also our soul.[93]

Wansink also found gender differences in which foods men and women found personally comforting: females rated ice cream, chocolate, and cookies (all of which are sweets and snack foods) most highly, whereas for males, ice cream, soup, and pizza or pasta came out on top (with the exception of ice cream, these are hot foods and more meal-like offerings). Explaining these preferences, males claimed that when they ate such foods, they felt "spoiled," "pampered," or "waited on." By contrast, females associated such foods as reminding them of the work they or their mothers had to put in to produce them, unlike the snack-like foods they preferred, which do not require much effort to produce or clean up. Finally, the research findings countered another misconception about comfort foods, which holds that people are more likely to eat them when they are sad, depressed, bored, or lonely. When Wansink surveyed over 1,000 North American consumers, they reported that they were nearly twice as likely to seek out comfort foods when they were in a happy mood (86%) or wanted to celebrate or reward themselves (74%) than when they were feeling depressed (39%), bored (52%), or lonely (39%), consistent with the points discussed above concerning self-gifts.

Sensory gratification

From the consumer's perspective, product desirability is a subjective phenomenon that does not physically exist within the product itself, but instead is to a great extent a function of the relationship between product features and the consumer's senses. Before considering that relationship more closely, it is important to bear in mind that a large part of a product's perceived desirability is independent of the technical aspects that are essential to how the product performs. This point is astutely illustrated by an example provided by the French theorist Jean Baudrillard, in his book *The System of Objects* concerning an everyday product:

> the most "essential" and structural aspects of a coffee mill, and hence the most concretely objective things about it, are the electric motor, the electricity furnished by the power company, and the laws governing the production and transformation of energy; what is already less objective, because it depends on a particular person's need, is the mill's actual coffee-grinding function; and what is not objective in the slightest, and hence inessential, is whether it is green and rectangular or pink and trapezoid.[94]

Baudrillard's interest in this example lies outside the marketing arena, yet from a marketer's point of view, whether a coffee mill is "green and rectangular or pink and trapezoid" is essential for distinguishing the product from the competition and for enhancing its desirability when a customer is faced with deciding which coffee mill to choose from among the many on the market. In recent decades, certain basic realities concerning the consumer marketplace have become apparent: (1) brands have proliferated in nearly every product and service category; (2) the gap in quality between brands has converged; and (3) the leader's performance edge has never been smaller. In this context, the aesthetical features of a product (e.g., color, shape, texture), its packaging, and the way a product is displayed in the store, or how it appears within the context of the usage situation provide vital means for achieving differentiation, and can create brand images so that consumers can develop preferences and make purchase decisions.

Research has demonstrated that consumers often exaggerate the performance quality of a product under purchase consideration on the basis of its external appeal or observable features (e.g., a freshly painted used car). This so-called *heuristic bias* results when decision makers rely on cognitive shortcuts to make a choice and are misled by rules of thumb shaped by previous experience. Such an effect was demonstrated in research showing that consumers rate orange juice as sweeter the richer the orange coloring on the container; similarly, ground coffee packed in a yellow can is more likely to be perceived as weak, a blue can as mild, and a brown can as too strong.[95] Another example of how consumers are influenced by sensory factors pertains to food serving, where presentation is important—a point reflected in the French expression, "Nous goûtons d'abord avec nos yeux" ("We taste first with our eyes") and the Japanese notion "katachi no aji" ("the shape of the taste"). A study at the Cornell University Food and Brand Lab demonstrated the power of presentation by manipulating how a cafeteria presented its customers with a free brownie dusted with powdered sugar. Claiming that the brownie was based on a new recipe that the cafeteria was considering for its dessert menu, customers were served the brownie (identical in all other respects) either on a snow-white piece of china, a paper plate, or a paper napkin. Not only was the brownie rated as "excellent" when served on china (compared to "good" and "nothing special" for the other two servings, respectively), customers said they would be willing to pay an average of US$1.27 for the dessert served on china compared to US$0.76 on a paper plate and US$0.53 on a paper napkin.

In addition to product usability aspects, consumers require the aesthetical— that is, products must at the same time be efficient and attractive. According to Titterton and Fiorni, "today a winning product must be able to appeal not only to reason, and therefore to *what a product does, what it contains and how it works* [their emphasis], but also to the emotions and the senses."[96] As mentioned in Box 3.7, manufacturers are increasingly imbuing household and office products with aesthetical features that appeal to customers. Examples of marketplace offerings that conform to the desirability demand include perfumes, scented deodorants and soaps, touch-screens, music player and mobile phone skins, aesthetic surgery, customized sneakers, teeth whiteners, olfactory advertising, vibrating ring tones, landscape lighting, fresh-cut flowers and indoor plants, and luxury design and fashion items.

In a concerted effort to enhance the desirability aspect of product offerings, marketers have increasingly turned to *sensory marketing*, which utilizes tactics that attempt to forge emotional relationships with consumers by appealing to their five senses—sight, sound, smell, taste, and touch.[97] This approach is consistent with the recognition that consumers have moved into an era of *polysensualism*, whereby their experience of a product is shaped by the raw, unprocessed sensory information (e.g., light, color, texture, scent) received through multiple sensory channels. The raw information is perceived—that is, rendered meaningful—on the basis of innate human abilities, prior learning, and past experiences. A red object resting on a table might be perceived at a quick glance as a Coca-Cola soft drink, without any apparent indication of the brand name. Perceptual processes are critical to the marketing process because subjective experience has a profound impact on consumers' reactions to marketing phenomena (see Box 3.8). One development that stands out in recent years, and which will be explored in greater detail in Chapter 4, is that people have become more tactile-oriented, perhaps best exemplified by consumers' smooth transition from the traditional keyboard to touch-screen devices like ATM machines, mobile phones, mp3 players, tablets, and e-book readers.

BOX 3.8 IF IT SOUNDS AND FEELS GOOD, IT PROBABLY TASTES BETTER

Taste is a unique sense that incorporates sensory input not only from the tongue, but from other senses, particularly olfaction, or how the food smells. For example, wine connoisseurs rely heavily on three senses—taste, vision, and smell—when evaluating the quality of a wine. They assess the richness of the color of the wine in the glass, they carefully evaluate the bouquet by smelling the wine, and they taste the flavor of the wine by letting it linger for several seconds in the mouth. Less obviously, the taste of the wine may also be affected by nondiagnostic haptic (i.e., touch-related) cues provided by the serving container—that is, wine is perceived as better-tasting when it is served in an expensive crystal glass than a disposable plastic cup. (The touch qualities of the serving container are considered "nondiagnostic" because they do not provide input about an inherent quality of the product itself.)

The fact that taste is influenced by multiple sensory inputs means that it is a human sense that is suggestible and ambiguous. Accordingly, consumer researchers Elder and Krishna argue for a "top-down process" for taste perception, which suggests that external information provided about food is cognitively taken into account by the consumer to affect taste perception, as opposed to a "bottom-up" approach which posits that taste is influenced more automatically by the intrinsic aspects of the food.[98] Food advertising, for the

(Continued)

(Continued)

most part, tends to focus solely on the qualities of the product's taste (e.g., "long-lasting flavor"), while neglecting potentially influential information pertaining to other sensory modalities (e.g., "stimulate your senses"). In a series of laboratory studies, Elder and Krishna demonstrated that multisensory advertising for food can enhance perceptions of taste.[99] To test the expectation that advertisements mentioning multiple senses would have a more powerful impact on flavor than those only mentioning taste, the researchers randomly assigned participants to view ads that appealed to multiple senses or to taste alone. For example, in one experiment, a multiple-sense ad for potato chips emphasized "the rich barbeque smell" and "the delicious crunch texture" in addition to "the taste you crave," whereas the single-sense ad promised "the rich barbecue flavor" and "the delicious salty taste." The results revealed that those persons who processed the multiple-sense ad had more positive sensory thoughts, which led to higher taste ratings than the single-sense ad after they were given an opportunity to eat the potato chips. Similar results were obtained when the experiment was repeated using chewing gum and popcorn.

On the basis of these studies, Elder and Krishna concluded that advertisers are missing out if they only mention taste in their advertisements and fail to mention other senses. A simple rewording of ad copy to emphasize more than a promise of good taste can enhance a product's appeal and potentially lead to higher levels of buyer satisfaction. The research results also have value for restaurants, where the descriptions of items on menus can be expected to alter the taste experience, as well as for product manufacturers, whose food descriptions on product packaging can influence the perceived taste quality of foods consumed in the home.

The taste research described here represents only one example of what investigators are learning about potential avenues for influencing consumers' product experiences which, to date, have largely been ignored by marketing practitioners. For example, although advertisements rarely, if ever, ask consumers to imagine the smell of a product (so-called "smellizing"), recent research reveals that imagining a smell can indeed increase consumers' desire to consume and purchase food products. Krishna, Morrin, and Sayin found that when they asked their research participants to imagine what a tasty food smells like, smellizing had an effect on salivation, desire, and actual food consumption—but only when the consumer also sees a picture of the advertised product.[100] The need for a pictorial identification of the product apparently has something to do with the fact that humans are quite poor at identifying the odors they smell, despite their facility to discriminate among thousands of different odors and to recognize odors they have smelled before. The visual element provides the necessary identification for associating the imagined smell to the advertised food product—another example of how consumers' experiences are shaped by polysensuality.

Engagement

There is a sea change in contemporary marketing that can best be summed up in one word: engagement. Much has been written about the ongoing paradigm shift in regards to the ways consumers interact with each other and with marketers. In my book *Connecting With Consumers: Marketing for New Marketplace Realities*, I described how consumers are increasingly taking control of the marketplace and are no longer merely passive participants in the wide array of activities that comprise the marketing enterprise.[101] To a great extent, these changes have to do with the evolution of new technologies that are serving to connect consumers with a facility few could have imagined as recently as a couple decades ago. Marketers are quickly learning that consumers have become averse to traditional communication campaigns and other unidirectional targeting efforts. As Idris Mootee, CEO of the digital innovation company Idea Couture Inc., explained in his blog:

> the first generation of marketing took a pure functional view and was entirely tactical in nature, dominated by the 4P's . . . focusing on pushing mass market product messages and driving store promotions. The next generation of marketing takes a "customer" view: uncovering unmet needs, facilitating conversations, realizing, and delivering real customer value through "customer engagement."[102]

Indeed, a growing number of firms are turning to *engagement* (or *participation*) *marketing* approaches in order to enter into the consumer conversation and establish a dialogue with their customers. To a great extent, this requires that firms engage in true, ongoing conversations with consumers, typically by generating online dialogues through the sharing of relevant knowledge.

As the chief marketing officer at KidZania observed: "Content is no longer something you push out. Content is an invitation to engage with your brand."[103] This is something Dell Computers pursued following a wave of online criticism in 2005 from disgruntled consumers about the company's customer service. In an effort to join the conversation that Dell's customers were having without the participation of the firm, Dell established a corporate blog, Direct2Dell. Characterized under the blog's logo as a conduit for "one-2-one conversations with Dell," the blog provided the company with a means to transmit timely information to customers (e.g., an initial topic pertained to a burning battery problem) by incorporating moderated postings and reader comments. Accompanied by a useful search engine for Dell-related issues, the blog also operates as a forum that engages consumers with Dell and with each other. In 2007, Dell launched IdeaStorm.com, a website that serves as a collaborative environment by inviting consumers to suggest ideas for Dell products and services, which are then voted on by the community, the most popular ideas ultimately being implemented by Dell (see Chapter 5). More recently, in partnership with Intel, Dell turned to Twitter as a new channel for engaging potential customers throughout the buying process, launching a marketing program called "Dell Swarm." The program invites people to join a "swarm" through invitations sent out over social networks, and the more people who join, the lower the price for every participant in the swarm.[104] Such Internet-based programs that encourage open dialogue and exchange between consumers and companies are likely to become the norm in the not-too-distant future.[105]

Although much attention has been focused on the increasing engagement between consumers and firms, far less has been devoted to consumers' engagement with products, yet the opportunity for engagement can be considered as another important contributor to product desirability, along with pleasure and sensory gratification. Not unlike the trend that finds consumers demanding more of a two-directional interaction with companies, the consumer relationship to products is moving from one in which an individual acts upon the product, exploiting its functions to accomplish a task or to satisfy a need, to one involving an interaction with the product that is more symbiotic in nature. The interactive nature of products is perhaps best exemplified by the emerging concept known as the "Internet of Things," which involves equipping everyday objects with sensors and then connecting them to the Internet. These objects then can be controlled by smartphones or other devices to provide various monitoring and security functions for the consumer (e.g., detecting drastic changes in moisture levels, air quality, and temperature in the home), to enable the consumer to manipulate objects from a distance (e.g., programming a television, turning on lights in the home when one is away), and a wide range of other possible uses.[106] Wearables represent another example of interactive products that are likely to diffuse rather rapidly across the consuming public, such as smart watches and fitness bands that can track activity levels and monitor the user's health status (see Chapter 6).

A variety of products answer the consumer's call for greater engagement, interactivity, monitoring, and feedback: touch-screens, the computer mouse, interactive software, software updates, video games (see Box 3.9), DVRs, the Internet and social media (e.g., Facebook fan pages), smart clothes, apps that connect portable devices to televisions, Google Glass, smart forks that inform their users that they are eating too quickly,[107] and so on. Such products are forging a new kind of relationship between people and objects, one not unlike that described by Baudrillard, in his description of recent trends in interior furniture design:

> Human beings and objects are indeed bound together in a collusion in which the objects take on a certain density, an emotional value—what might be called a "presence." There is progress . . . : between the individual and these objects, which are now more supple in their uses and have ceased to exercise or symbolize moral constraint, there is much more liberal relationship, and in particular the individual is no longer strictly defined through them relative to his family [but relative to society at large].[108]

BOX 3.9 CONSUMERS AND VIDEO GAMES

The interactive nature of video games accounts for much of that category's attraction for consumers worldwide. As a result of aggressive marketing tactics, video games are no longer the sole province of young males; indeed, although the most prevalent demographic of online gamers consists of males aged 15–24 years, female gamers over the age of 55 spend by far the most amount of time online gaming.[109] Many gamers are high-income, educated, and professional persons who utilize the Internet for social networking, information searches, and e-commerce. In recent years, seniors residing in nursing homes have taken to multiple-player games, such as Nintendo's Wii bowling game, as a much appreciated form of recreation and social interaction.[110]

According to the president of Pod Digital, Steve Curran, the new generations of video games have certain distinctive characteristics that set them apart from other media: (1) they are interactive in nature, and thus provide an engaging and involving means of getting messages across to consumers; (2) they provide an ideal opportunity for social networking, in that players recommend games to friends and compete with their peers and with strangers; (3) they represent a compelling medium to inform, educate, and entertain, because they are capable of capturing the focused attention of players; (4) they can be used on every major digital platform, including televisions, mobile phones, personal computers, tablet PCs, game consoles, handheld devices, and PDAs; and (5) their appeal for consumers crosses demographic and gender boundaries.[111]

New technology is creating even greater opportunities for game designers to connect with consumers, through the maximization of visual and motion possibilities that enhance realism and augment reality. In describing the great potential of reality augmentation in 2007, game designer Will Wright foretold the creation of Google Glass, as well as the computer plaything envisioned by filmmaker Spike Jonze in *Her* (2013), a futuristic film about a man who falls in love with his computer's operating system:

> This [reality augmentation] is the idea that there are computer overlaps on top of the real world. For example, I might be wearing a set of glasses that can project computer images, and mix them with the real world. I can imagine something . . . where you have two kids wearing these things . . . and all of a sudden, little army men appear in dirt running around having battles. The kids are playing in the real world, but with this computer partner helping their imagination. . . . It's a shared point of imagination for the two kids, so that their two imaginations run in sync. The computer in that sense is a third playmate.[112]

Engagement with products is also reflected in the strong attachments that consumers form with some products and brands (see Chapter 1). An examination of the ways in which people become emotionally attached to products has led designers to identify the power of product stories or "narratives" as a main tool for engagement and the development of such attachments. As described in the published proceedings for a 1997 conference on product design convened in the Netherlands by the designer group The Eternally Yours Foundation, "products need to express through design a story that one can identify with and explain to others. That is what makes them personal."[113] One simple, yet potentially effective, narrative that manufacturers often neglect in favor of a fictional advertising scenario is to inform consumers about how the product was originally created. Telling a story about the company's heritage and founder, ideology or values, the people who work behind the scenes for the company, and the firm's special or unique skills or services also can result in consumers becoming attached to the firm's products. Nike, for example, effectively communicated the footwear and apparel company's ideology through its "individual achievement through perseverance" narrative, as succinctly summarized by the slogan "Just do it." Apple capitalized on the "inspired inventor" brand story archetype, particularly in the case of the iPhone, by carefully constructing a narrative about the company's founder Steve Jobs and his vision for products that people need, but are not necessarily aware that they do. Southwest Airlines effectively utilized its corporate blog to engage consumers with stories about travel and the lives of the company's employees, with an emphasis on service and family.

The Eternally Yours group described three ways that narratives can become attached to products: (1) through traditional advertisements and endorsements; (2) through users' collective appreciation of products that culminates in "cult" status, as exemplified by product and brand discussions and sharing online (e.g., social networks, official and unofficial owners' clubs and fan sites, customer forums, blogs); and (3) through specific events that turn products into mementos or souvenirs (e.g., creation of personal associations, having the product thought of as not unlike a family heirloom). Combining the first two means, the Swiss luxury watch manufacturer Patek Philippe launched a print ad campaign depicting various scenes emphasizing how a father treats his Philippe Patek watch with great care so that it can eventually be passed down to his child; the tagline, translated from the French, was "one wears it, preciously maintaining it for future generations."

Saatchi and Saatchi CEO Kevin Roberts coined the term "lovemarks" to describe a brand with loyal followers that invokes stronger emotions than "I want it," but rather feelings of love, warmth, affection, and undying devotion.[114] In short, a lovemark is a respected product, service, or entity that inspires loyalty beyond reason. Some examples of lovemarks that have created well-developed, concise narratives over the years are Coca-Cola, Harley-Davidson, Apple, and Whole Foods Market. According to Roberts, lovemarks are not only known for things that are different, but are known for things that people care about, thereby increasing the likelihood that consumers will be moved to advocate the brand to others through word of mouth—in short, the product becomes "talkable."

Conclusion

By elucidating what contemporary consumers expect from marketplace offerings, the challenge for product designers and innovators becomes clearer: while there certainly are exceptions, such as when the consumption choice is impulsive or urgent, or when choice is lacking, consumers are moved to acquire things that go beyond the capacity to perform promised functions effectively and efficiently. Call it what you will—greed, hedonism, or a logical effort to maximize the price/quality relationship in a difficult economic climate—consumers want more. Consistent with their predilection to multitask in an effort to save or recuperate precious lost time, their efforts to arrive at the best purchase decisions in the context of a marketplace that is glutted with efficient and increasingly similar offers, and their desire to derive some degree of comfort and pleasure from the things they possess in a world filled with unpleasant pressures and frustrations, consumers also demand products that are useful, desirable, and engaging. This is not to denigrate the importance and value of product usability, in the sense of product efficiency, which remains of primary importance to consumers.

If we return to the question posed earlier in this chapter—"What do consumers want?"—the answer may now be clearer, but no less daunting. Products must fulfill some requisite usage situation in an engaging and personally satisfying way, without compromising functionality, practicality and convenience, or comfort. Human motivation and desire are complex determinants of consumer behaviors that are shaped in myriad ways by a multitude of factors, including past experiences, culture, lifestyle, demographic characteristics, and situational context. This does not make the job of developing and designing products any easier, but it does provide extensive opportunities for the creative application of talents and skills to create products that are capable of satisfying needs and shaping consumer preferences and loyalties.

Further reading

My 2012 book *Psychological Foundations of Marketing* (Routledge) provides in-depth coverage of the concepts, processes, and principles that determine consumer behavior, with extensive focus on the consumer decision-making process. The book also examines the impact of psychology on marketing practice, and highlights the applied aspects of psychological research in the marketplace.

Originally published in 1968, Jean Baudrillard's *The System of Objects* (Verso) still holds sway as a fascinating and original attempt to deconstruct the meaning and classifications of everyday objects. Proceeding from more of a philosophical approach couched in semiological analysis, Baudrillard provides numerous practical examples that help us better understand the nature of human relationships with objects.

French sociologist Gérard Mermet is the author of the annually published book *Francoscopie* (Larousse), which extensively tracks the changes and trends in everyday life of the French, with a focus on their consuming habits. Although written in French and focused on the French populace, the book is replete with useful summary charts and figures about consumers and products that resonate far beyond France's borders.

A recommended starting point for comprehensive coverage of usability issues is the 2002 volume edited by Judy Hammond, Tom Gross, and Janet Wesson, *Usability: Gaining a Competitive Edge* (Springer Science+Business Media), which includes expanded versions of the papers presented at the IFIP 17th World Computer Conference held in Montreal, Canada.

Notes

1 Baumgartner, H. & Pieters, R. (2008). Goal-directed consumer behavior: Motivation, volition, and affect. In C. P. Haugtvedt, P. M. Herr, & F. R. Kardes (Eds.), *Handbook of consumer psychology* (pp. 367–392). New York: Psychology Press, p. 367.
2 Lewin, K. (1997). *Resolving social conflicts and field theory in social science.* Washington, DC: American Psychological Association.
3 Solomon, M. R., Bamossy, G., Askegaard, S., & Hogg, M. K. (2010). *Consumer behavior: A European perspective*, 4th ed. Upper Saddle River, NJ: Prentice Hall.
4 Choudhury, U. (2004, September 23). India's rich buy into "lifestyle." *International Herald Tribune*, p. 22.
5 Reynolds, S. (2011). *Retromania: Pop culture's addiction to its past.* London: Faber and Faber, p. 96.
6 Reynolds, S. (2011), p. 111.
7 Kessler, S. (2012, December 11). How Google's designers are quietly overhauling search. *Fast Company*. Available: http://www.fastcodesign.com/1671425/how-googles-designers-are-quietly-overhauling-search.
8 Bevan, N., Kirakowski, J., & Maissel, J. (1991). What is usability? In H. J. Bullinger (Ed.), *Proceedings of the 4th international conference on human–computer interaction*, Stuttgart, Germany. London: Elsevier.
9 Bevan, N. (1995, July). Usability is quality of use. In Y. Anzai & K. Ogawa (Eds.), *Proceedings of the 6th international conference on human–computer interaction*, Yokohama, Japan. London: Elsevier.
10 Krajicek, D. (2014, January 1). Perfecting the no-hassle brand experience. *American Marketing Association*. Available: https://www.ama.org/publications/MarketingInsights/Pages/brand-experiences-loyalty-crm-customer-satisfaction.aspx.
11 Bevan, N. (1995, July).
12 Goffin, K., Lemke, F., & Koners, U. (2010). *Identifying hidden needs: Creating breakthrough products.* Basingstoke, UK: Palgrave Macmillan.
13 Von Hippel, E. (1986). Lead users: A source of novel product concepts. *Management Science, 32*, 791–805.
14 Pew Research Center. (2010, February). *Millennials: A portrait of generation next.* Available: http://pewsocialtrends.org/files/2010/10/millennials-confident-connected-open-to-change.pdf.
15 Read, M. (2010, August 6). Market research: Young people neither "hate" anything, nor "love" anything. *Gawker*. Available: http://gawker.com/5606055/market-research-young-people-neither-hate-anything-nor-love-anything.
16 Twenge, J. M., Campbell, W. K., & Freeman, E. C. (2012). Generational differences in young adults' life goals, concern for others, and civic orientation, 1966–2009. *Journal of Personality and Social Psychology, 102*, 1,045–1,062.

17 Levere, J. L. (2013, June 16). A campaign from Marriott aims younger. *The New York Times*. Available: http://www.nytimes.com/2013/06/17/business/media/a-campaign-from-marriott-aims-younger.html.

18 Mermet, G. & Hasterok, R. (2009). *Francoscopie 2010*. Paris: Larousse.

19 Bracetti, A. (2013, June 30). The most useless gadgets ever. *The Complex Newsletter*. Available: http://www.complex.com/tech/2013/06/most-useless-gadgets-ever/.

20 Adams, D. (2002). *The salmon of doubt: Hitchhiking the galaxy one last time*. New York: Ballantine, p. 115.

21 Papanek, V. (1984). *Design for the real world: Human ecology and social change*. Chicago: Academy Chicago Publishers, p. ix.

22 Rawsthorn, A. (2012, March 5). Farewell, pocket calculator? *International Herald Tribune*, p. 8.

23 Kimmel, A. J. & Tissier-Desbordes, E. (1999). Males, masculinity and consumption: An exploratory investigation. In B. Dubois, T. M. Lowrey, L. J. Shrum, & M. Vanhuele (Eds.), *European advances in consumer research*, Vol. 4 (pp. 243–252). Provo, UT: Association for Consumer Research.

24 Solomon , M. R., Bamossy, G., Askegaard, S., & Hogg, M. K. (2010).

25 Quenqua, T. (2011, December 20). Men change. (Products do, too). *The New York Times*. Available: http://www.nytimes.com/2011/12/22/fashion/men-once-again-invest-in-skin-care-skin-deep.html.

26 United Nations Population Division. (2010). *World population prospects: The 2010 revision*. New York: United Nations.

27 Senior Care Products. (2014). Top 10 technology devices for seniors. *HomeCare*. Available: http://homecaremag.com/top-10-technology-devices-seniors.

28 Floor, K. (2006). Branding a store: How to build successful retail brands in a changing marketplace. Amsterdam: Ko Floor and BIS Publishers.

29 Onishi, N. (2006, September 4). In a graying Japan, lower shelves and wider aisles. *The New York Times*. Available: http://www.nytimes.com/2006/09/04/world/asia/04japan.html.

30 "My goal is to simplify complexity."—Jack Dorsey on The Charlie Rose Show—Watch it ASAP! *JASONPOLLOCK.TV*. Available: http://jasonpollock.tv/2011/01/my-goal-is-to-simplify-complexity-jack-dorsey-on-the-charlie-rose-show-watch-it-asap/.

31 Mermet, G. & Hasterok, R. (2009).

32 Trop, J. (2014, January 26). Makers pack new cars with technology, but younger buyers shrug. *The New York Times*. Available: http://www.nytimes.com/2014/01/27/automobiles/makers-pack-new-cars-with-technology-but-younger-buyers-shrug.html.

33 Rawsthorn, A. (2010, January 25). When more is decidedly less. *International Herald Tribune*, p. 9.

34 Maeda, J. (2006). *The laws of simplicity*. Cambridge, MA: MIT Press.

35 Rawsthorn, A. (2010).

36 Rawsthorn, A. (2012, March 25). Genius and tragedy at dawn of computer age. *The New York Times*. Available: http://www.nytimes.com/2012/03/26/arts/design/genius-and-tragedy-at-dawn-of-computer-age.html.

37 Reynolds, S. (2011), p. 70.

38 Desta, Y. (2014, March 24). 9 super simple apps that will make your life easier. *Mashable*. Available: http://mashable.com/2014/03/24/super-simple-apps.

39 Stout, H. (2013, October 9). For American consumers, next level of instant gratification is on its way. *The New York Times*. Available: http://www.nytimes.com/2013/10/08/technology/for-shoppers-next-level-of-instant-gratification.html.

40 Rawsthorn, A. (2011, November 28). Innovations that make everyday life a little easier. *International Herald Tribune*, p. 11.

41 Conlin, J. (2012, September 14). Maps go in new directions, and don't require folding. *The New York Times*. Available: http://www.nytimes.com/2012/09/15/travel/15iht-gear15.html.

42 Meece, M. (2010, April 28). Bringing an innovative razor to the masses. *The New York Times*. Available: http://www.nytimes.com/2010/04/29/business/smallbusiness/29sbiz.html.

43 Kim, S. (2011, September 20). Heinz redesigns the ketchup packet. *SmartPlanet*. Available: http://www.smartplanet.com/blog/decoding-design/heinz-redesigns-the-ketchup-packet/.

44 Curtin, M. (2013, January 16). EU car sales slump. *The Wall Street Journal*. Available: http://online.wsj.com/news/articles/SB10001424127887323468604578244981638540410.

45 Ford, D. (2012, March 16). As cars are kept longer 200,000 is new 100,000. *The New York Times*. Available: http://www.nytimes.com/2012/03/18/automobiles/as-cars-are-kept-longer-200000-is-new-100000.html.

46 Packard, V. (1960). *The waste makers*. New York: Ig Publishing.

47 Cooper, T. (2012). The value of longevity: Product quality and sustainable consumption. Paper presented at the Global Research Forum on Sustainable Consumption, Rio de Janeiro.

48 Cooper, T. (Ed.). (2012). *Longer lasting products: Alternatives to the throwaway society*. Farnham, UK: Gower, p. xv.

49 Boorstin, D. (1961). *The image: A guide to pseudo-events in America*. New York: Vintage, p. 232.

50 Leeflang, P. S. H. & van Raaij, W. F. (1995). The changing consumer in the European Union: A "meta-analysis." *International Journal of Research in Marketing*, *12*, 373–387.

51 Le Nagard, E., Monkel, I., & Kimmel, A. J. (2005). *Actimel case study*. Paris: ESCP Europe.

52 The Danone Actimel Success Story. (2000). *The Irish Times Business 2000*, 7th ed. Available: http://business2000.ie/pdf/pdf_7/danone_7th_ed.pdf.

53 World Health Organization. (2009, September). Europe puts health claims to the test. *Bulletin of the World Health Organization*. Available: http://www.who.int/bulletin/volumes/87/9/09-020909/en/.

54 Milutinovic, R., Gibault, A., & Kimmel, A. J. (2011). *Tropicana ESCP Europe case*. Paris: ESCP Europe.

55 Report shows fitness industry back in growth. (2012, June 6). *SPORTS think tank*. Available: http://www.sportsthinktank.com/news/2012/06/report-shows-fitness-industry-back-in-growth.

56 IHRSA. (2013, October 16). IHRSA releases new European health club report. *IHRSA Media Center*. Available: http://www.ihrsa.org/media-center/2013/10/16/ihrsa-releases-new-european-health-club-report.html.

57 Fitness Industry Analysis 2014—Cost & Trends. (2014). *Franchise Help*. Available: https://www.franchisehelp.com/industry-reports/fitness-industry-report/.

58 Gym, Health & Fitness Clubs in the US: Market Research Report. (2014, February). *IBISWorld*. Available: http://www.ibisworld.com/industry/default.aspx?indid=1655.

59 Scelfo, J. (2009, January 14). The stuffing dreams are made of? *The New York Times*. Available: http://www.nytimes.com/2009/01/15/garden/15mattress.html.

60 Vora, S. (2012, March 28). Starting early, and young. *The New York Times*. Available: http://www.nytimes.com/2012/03/29/fashion/beauty-products-for-babies.html.

61 Hennen, L. (2005, September 8). Rocking the baby products cradle. *The New York Times*. Available: http://www.nytimes.com/2005/09/08/fashion/thursdaystyles/08skin.html.

62 *MarketingCharts* staff. (2010, January 21). Nine in 10 consumers put "green" in daily routine. *Marketing Charts*. Available: http://www.marketingcharts.com/wp/television/nine-in-10-consumers-put-green-in-daily-routine-11698/.

63 Gleick, J. (1999). *Faster: The acceleration of just about everything*. New York: Pantheon.

64 Gleick, J. (1999).

65 *MarketingCharts* staff. (2010, August 10). Latin America, Asia Pacific watch most TV. *Marketing Charts.* Available: http://www.marketingcharts.com/wp/television/latin-america-asia-pacific-watch-most-tv-13826/.

66 Bureau of Labor Statistics. *American time use survey—2011 results.* US Department of Labor. Available: http://www.bls.gov/news.release/archives/atus_06222012.pdf.

67 Gleick, J. (1999), pp. 230–231.

68 Gleick, J. (1999), pp. 231–232.

69 Soojung-Kim Pang, A. (2013). *The distraction addiction.* New York: Little, Brown.

70 Baudrillard, J. (1994). The system of collecting. In J. Elsner & R. Cardinal (Eds.), *The cultures of collecting (critical views)* (pp. 7–24). London: Reaktion Books.

71 Dua, A., Hersch, L., & Sivanandam, M. (2009, October). Consumer electronics gets back to basics. Available: http://www.mckinsey.com/insights/consumer_and_retail/consumer_electronics_gets_back_to_basics.

72 Tian, K. & Belk, R. W. (2005). Extended self and possessions in the workplace. *Journal of Consumer Research, 32,* 297–310.

73 Hardy, Q. (2013, July 30). New habits transform software. *The New York Times.* Available: http://www.nytimes.com/2013/08/01/technology/as-work-habits-change-software-makers-rush-to-innovate.html.

74 Sennett, R. (1996). *Flesh and stone: The body and the city in Western civilization.* New York: Norton.

75 Lévy, M. & O'Donoghue, D. (2005). New trends in the promotion of companies and brands to stakeholders: A holistic approach. In A. J. Kimmel (Ed.), *Marketing communication: New approaches, technologies, and styles* (pp. 11–22). Oxford, UK: Oxford University Press.

76 Clifford, S. (2011, August 1). The airport experience now includes shopping for the family. *The New York Times.* Available: http://www.nytimes.com/2011/08/02/business/the-airport-experience-now-includes-shopping-for-the-whole-family.html.

77 "Transumers." (2006, November). *trend watching.com.* Available: http://www.trendwatching.com/trends/TRANSUMERS.htm.

78 Gardiner, B. (2013). Big European players embrace the car-sharing trend. *The New York Times.* Available: http://www.nytimes.com/2013/11/20/business/international/big-european-players-embrace-the-car-sharing-trend.html.

79 Gardiner, B. (2013).

80 Weber, L. (2007). *Marketing to the social web.* Hoboken, NJ: John Wiley, p. 4.

81 Wong, D. (2013, October 16). Shareaholic report: Facebook, Pinterest and Twitter traffic referrals up 54%. *Social Media Today.* Available: http://socialmediatoday.com/dannywong1190/1830681/report-facebook-pinterest-and-twitter-traffic-referrals-54-past-year.

82 Now called The Free Music Archive: http://freemusicarchive.org.

83 Reynolds, S. (2011), pp. 106, 107.

84 Macht, M. & Simons, G. (2000). Emotions and eating in everyday life. *Appetite, 35,* pp. 65–71. Mattila, A. S. & Enz, C.A. (2002). The role of emotions in service encounters. *Journal of Service Research, 4,* 268–277.

85 Kimmel, A. J. (2013). *Psychological foundations of marketing.* Hove, East Sussex, UK: Routledge. Norman, D. A. (2005). *Emotional design: Why we love (or hate) everyday things.* New York: Basic Books.

86 Patrick, V. M. & Hagtvedt, H. (2011). Aesthetic incongruity resolution. *Journal of Marketing Research, 48,* 393–402.

87 Postrel, V. (2003). *The substance of style: How the rise of aesthetic value is remaking culture, commerce, and consciousness.* New York: HarperCollins.

88 Meyer, C. & Schwager, A. (2007). Understanding customer experience. *Harvard Business Review, 85,* 117–127. Jaakkola, E., Aarikka-Stenroos, L., & Kimmel, A. J. (2014). Leveraging customer experience communication. In J. Kandampully (Ed.), *Customer experience management: Enhancing experience and value through service management* (pp. 45–72). Dubuque, IA: Kendall Hunt.

89 Reynolds, S. (2011), p. 126.
90 Tournier, P. (1966). *The meaning of gifts*. (trans. J. S. Gilmour). Richmond, VA: John Knox, p. 5.
91 Milutinovic, R., Gibault, A., & Kimmel, A. J. (2011).
92 Gopnik, A. (2010, April 5). No rules! *The New Yorker*. Available: http://www.newyorker.com/magazine/2010/04/05/no-rules-2.
93 Wansink, B. (2006). Mindless eating: Why we eat more than we think. New York: Bantam.
94 Baudrillard, D. (1996). *The system of objects*. London: Verso.
95 Batey, M. (2008). *Brand meaning*. New York: Routledge.
96 Titterton, G. & Fioroni, M. (2009). *Brand storming: Managing brands in the era of complexity*. Basingstoke, UK: Palgrave Macmillan, p. 83.
97 Hultén, B., Broweus, N., & Van Dijk, M. (2009). *Sensory marketing*. Basingstoke, UK: Palgrave Macmillan.
98 Elder, R. S. & Krishna, A. (2010). The effect of advertising copy on sensory thoughts and perceived taste. *Journal of Consumer Research, 36*, 748–756.
99 Elder, R. S. & Krishna, A. (2010).
100 Krishna, A., Morrin, M, & Sayin, E. (2014). Smellizing cookies and salivating: A focus on olfactory imagery. *Journal of Consumer Research, 41*, 18–34.
101 Kimmel, A. J. (2010). *Connecting with consumers: Marketing for new marketplace realities*. Oxford, UK: Oxford University Press.
102 Mootee, Idris. (2007, July 11). Open source advanced branding masterclass—program framework. *Innovation Playground*. Available: http://mootee.typepad.com/innovation_playground/2007/07/page/2/.
103 Elliott, S. (2006, October 9). Letting consumers control marketing: Priceless. *The New York Times*. Available: http://www.nytimes.com/2006/10/09/business/media/09adcol.html.
104 Acker, O., Gröne, F., Yazbek, R., & Akkad, F. (2010). *Social CRM: How companies can link into the social web of consumers*. Booz and Company. Available: http://www.strategyand.pwc.com/media/ uploads/Strategyand-Social-CRM.pdf.
105 Kimmel, A. J. (2010).
106 Wortham, J. (2014, January 20). Computerized homes finding a mainstream market. *The International New York Times*, p. 15.
107 Saint Louis, C. (2014, March 10). Better eating with smart scales and forks. *The New York Times*. Available: http://well.blogs.nytimes.com/2014/03/10/better-eating-with-smart-scales-and-forks/.
108 Baudrillard, D. (1996), pp. 15–16.
109 Wayne, T. (2010, August). Women set the pace as online gamers. *The International New York Times*. Available: http://www.nytimes.com/2010/08/09/technology/09drill.html.
110 Baig, E. C. (2009, January 8). Older folks like Wii, PCs and cellphones, too. *USA Today*. Available: http://usatoday30.usatoday.com/tech/columnist/edwardbaig/2009-01-07-seniors-tech-products_N.htm.
111 Curran, S. (2007). Changing the game. In J. Kirby & P. Marsden (Eds.), *Connected marketing: The viral, buzz and word of mouth revolution* (pp. 129–47). Oxford, UK: Butterworth-Heinemann.
112 Moggridge, B. (2006). *Designing interactions*. Cambridge, MA: MIT Press.
113 Parsons, T. (2009). *Thinking: Objects—contemporary approaches to product design*. Worthing, West Sussex, UK: AVA, p. 28.
114 Roberts, K. (2004). *Lovemarks: The future beyond brands*. New York: powerHouse Books.

4

PRODUCT DESIGN AND AESTHETICS

By the end of this chapter, you will:

- understand what is meant by the term "design" from the point of view of designers and consumers;
- gain insight into the relationship between form and function in product design within the context of modernism and post-modernist approaches;
- learn about the influence of product form and aesthetics on consumer behavior;
- recognize the role of ergonomics and natural mapping in product design;
- be aware of the relationships between product design, consumer perception, and brand meaning;
- appreciate the evolving role of touch in the consumer/product dynamic;
- discern the functions of product packaging and the influence of package design and redesign on consumer behavior.

Discussing the intricate relationship between story and cinematography in film, renowned filmmaker Jean-Luc Godard once opined that "to me, style is just the outside of content, and content the inside of style, like the outside and inside of the human body—both go together, they can't be separated."[1] Godard's famous quote has resonance not only for the art of film-making, but also for the development of consumer products, whose internal functional components and exterior aesthetical design must blend effectively and coherently before products can become, in the words of architectural historian Adrian Forty, "objects of desire."[2]

Product design is an essential element for business success and a central consideration for meeting the needs and expectations of the buying public. Prior to the modern era, the acquisition of goods and services was based almost entirely on their functional, need-satisfying qualities, with little consideration of the design and style of the offerings. As the number of products and services began to proliferate, branding emerged as an essential means of differentiating one's goods from those of competitors. By the late 1950s, consumers had begun to base their purchase and product usage decisions not only on what products and brands could do for them, but also on the basis of subjective dimensions, including the psychological, sociological, and symbolic—each dimension in part determined by product form, design, and aesthetical considerations.[3]

The importance of the design or form of a product as a key to marketplace success was emphasized in marketing professor Peter Bloch's influential 1995 article "Seeking the Ideal Form: Product Design and Consumer Response." Bloch questioned the lack of attention given to the topic of product design in the marketing literature, despite the fact that "a good design attracts consumers to a product, communicates to them, and adds value to the product by increasing the quality of the usage experiences associated with it."[4] Two decades after Bloch's paper appeared in the influential *Journal of Marketing*, product design continues to be a neglected topic in the marketing literature, despite the significant attention given to it by marketing managers. With technological innovations continuing to evolve at an exponential rate, the objective characteristics and design qualities of products, packaging, and services can increasingly be seen as enhancing the overall desirability of marketplace offerings, the combination of which can better satisfy the evolving demands of consumers.

In this chapter, our attention turns to a number of design considerations that are essential to understanding the dynamic interplay between people and products. A primary focus of the discussion is the importance of style, aesthetics, and design from both the consumer and designer's perspective in terms of usability and marketing considerations. Along the way, I will tackle what some design and marketing experts consider to be the fundamental ingredients for successful product design. First, however, it is important to consider how the term "design" can best be understood in light of its changing meaning in the world of objects.

Capturing the illusory meaning of "design"

One reason why "design" can be considered an illusory term is that, like much technical terminology that has entered everyday parlance, it can mean various things to different people in different circumstances: it could refer to an intention, as when a person has designs on someone who takes on the aura of an object of intrigue; it might be understood as a blueprint, sketch, or graphic drawing; it could refer to an object's aesthetics or style; or the term could be used to describe an individual's proposal (as in "designing a plan for a new hospital or an annex to one's house), aim ("to design a corporate strategy"), fabrication ("to design a dress or menu"), or invention ("to design a voice-activated computer program or gene-splicing technique"). Originating from the Latin verb *designare*, meaning to trace, describe, and plan, design is perhaps best understood as referring to means by which people seek to improve their surroundings.[5] In this light, design refers to anything from the prehistoric development of making clay bowls for drinking, as opposed to cupping one's hands, to the modification of household cleaning products so that they have a bend in the container's neck, making it easier to clean hard-to-reach areas in kitchens and bathrooms and offering consumers greater convenience and practicality of use.

Unlike the term *invention*, which has retained a more or less consistent meaning over time since it was first defined in 1509 as "the action of coming upon or finding; discovery," design has acquired new meanings over the centuries, some of which diverge from earlier ones. Originally used as a verb ("to designate or indicate"), it was not long before people began using "design" as a noun to refer to finely calibrated technical specifications or to a specific profession.[6] According to Alice Rawsthorn, one consistency in its various guises is that design is typically viewed as an agent of change in the sense of helping us translate developments in different domains—such as the scientific, technological, political, and cultural—into something that might be useful or emotionally satisfying. This also is true of inventions, with the caveat that the outcome is something new: the end result of the design process may be new or a modification and improvement of something that already exists. These distinctions are evident in the case of the first computers, developed in the late 1940s by a team of scientists at the University of Manchester in the UK:

> They [the British scientists] can be described as having invented the computer, but it required the work of the designers at IBM in the United States to transform an inscrutable labyrinth of wires and dials into a marketable machine that fulfilled a useful function. The result, the IBM 701, went on sale in 1952. Even so, the 701 and other early computers were enormous, prone to overheating and could only be operated by trained technicians. To this day, Apple, Samsung and other computer makers are still wrestling with the design challenge of making them ever smaller, safer and easier to operate, often deploying scientific inventions to do so.[7]

A further difficulty in pinning down exactly what we mean by the term "design" is the fact that few professional designers agree on a definition. As product designer Tim Parsons explained in his book *Thinking: Objects—Contemporary Approaches to Product Design*,[8] in the past, answers to questions about what product design connoted were a simple matter of aligning oneself with one of the major design movements, which definitively spelled out what design is, what its purpose should be, and what should be considered "good" design. Over time, however, these views have been subject to numerous critiques, leading to a fragmentation of opinion among designers as to how design should be viewed, as the following definitions illustrate:

- "'Design' means how something works, not how it looks—the design should evolve from the function" (James Dyson).[9]

- "The act of imposing one's will on materials to perform a function" (Ron Arad);[10]
- "Design is about creatively exploiting constraint" (Nick Crosbie);[11]
- "an iterative decision-making process that produces plans by which resources are converted into products or systems that meet human needs and wants or solve problems" (America's International Technology Education Association);[12]
- "the creative invention of objects destined for serial reproduction" (Guy Julier);[13]
- "a plan for arranging elements in such a way as best to accomplish a particular purpose" (Charles Eames).[14]

These views are typical in conceiving of design as (a) something that follows, and is secondary to, a manufacturing innovation; (b) the innovative manipulation of materials to serve some utilitarian function; or (c) a creative process that attempts to answer the challenge of limited resources. Product design within the marketing discipline is arguably more closely aligned with the second of these conceptualizations (b) in considering design as the process of creating an innovative product that can be offered to consumers by a business.[15] However, as Parsons concludes, each of these perspectives has merit; accordingly, design in the contemporary era must be considered within a context of pluralism, in which the individual designer, client, or collaborators must decide their own set of rules as to what good design represents:

> The search for "good design" therefore becomes the search for definitive results identified according to the designer's own intentions and the specific conditions of each project. If we are to judge products holistically, we therefore need access to this information, along with some insight into the social fabric into which they are introduced.[16]

What is evident from this discussion is that for professionals involved in the business of design, design is a process that stops once the product is manufactured. As design journalist Marcus Fairs observed, with the rise of sophisticated consumers, design has taken on a meaning that pertains more to the end result of the manufacturing process and qualities related to the objects themselves, as evidenced by the expressions, "good design," "contemporary design," "Dutch design," or "design hotels":

> When most people talk about design these days they are referring to "stuff," not method. Sentences such as "I'm interested in design," and "that's a beautiful piece of design" are now widely understood to be referring to the outcome of the process rather than the process itself. To consumers, design is something they experience in the finished object.[17]

Whether this consumer-oriented perspective on design pertains to an object's stylistic or aesthetical characteristics (i.e., qualities the object possesses; its style or fashion) or to its functional or process-related aspects (i.e., characteristics of the plan or arrangement scheme related to product usage, as suggested by "the design of the keyboard is rather awkward for typing") depends on the specific context in which the term is employed and the intentions and tastes of the user. Perhaps the clearest description of design was offered by Fairs, following his comprehensive survey of the term's various meanings:

> [Design is] the outcome of the creative process called designing . . . a status conferred upon selected examples of this output by a discerning (but increasingly diverse) elite, according to their taste. . . . [I]t is a term used by consumers to denote objects that have emotional or sensual appeal beyond their usefulness.[18]

A more original way of putting it, according to design historian John Heskett, is to say that "design is to design a design to produce a design" (see Figure 4.1).[19]

Form and function: From modernism to post-modernism

A comprehensive survey of design trends during the past century is beyond the scope of this book, but one long-standing theme that merits our attention in terms of the consumer-related implications of product form and design is the well-known dictum that "form follows function." Dating back to architect Louis Sullivan's 1896 assertion that "form ever follows function," the essence of this idea is that an object's physical appearance is dictated by how the object works and what it does.[20] Sullivan, whose steel-framed buildings represent examples of the earliest skyscrapers, strongly believed that a building's design should logically

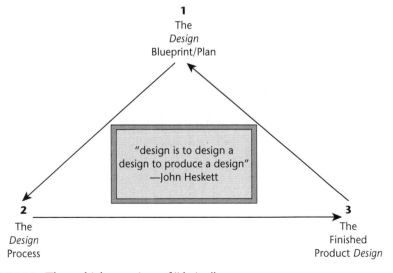

FIGURE 4.1 The multiple meanings of "design"

follow not from historical precedence or traditional aesthetics, but from the building's purpose, in the sense of signaling a "correct" form. This view was adopted as a standard by other architects and used as a guide by industrial and product designers for much of the twentieth century (see Box 4.1).

BOX 4.1 THE GUGGENHEIM MUSEUM: FORM FOLLOWS FUNCTION

American architect Frank Lloyd Wright (1867–1959) worked during the early part of his much-heralded career as an assistant to Louis Sullivan, who became his mentor and to whom he later referred to as his *lieber Meister* ("dear master"). Wright adhered to Sullivan's "form follows function" philosophy, to the point of modifying the phrase to "form and function are one." During his illustrious career, Wright designed numerous buildings of renown, including his home in Oak Park, Illinois and the Fallingwater residence in Mill Run, Pennsylvania. Arguably his most famous creation is the Solomon R. Guggenheim Museum in New York City, which opened in October 1959 and whose design thoroughly reflects the merging of form and function. The museum's spiral shape functions as a kind of user's guide for visitors, who enter the building, take an elevator to the top floor, and descend along a spiral ramp to the bottom while enjoying an unimpeded and uninterrupted art-viewing experience.

Like many great original designs, the Guggenheim polarized critics and received its share of scorn, with some arguing that the building's design would overshadow the artwork, and others criticizing the shallow, windowless concave spaces in which paintings were displayed. Wright's response to such criticisms reflected his strong belief in the unity of form and function. Shortly before his death, he penned a letter that emphasized the connection between the Guggenheim's design and the artwork it exhibited, stating:

> Yes, it is hard . . . to understand a struggle for harmony and unity between the painting and the building. No, it is not to subjugate the paintings to the building that I conceived this plan. On the contrary, it was to make the building and the painting a beautiful symphony such as never existed in the World of Art before.[21]

The originality of the Guggenheim design is reflected in one of the museum shop's best-selling items, its coffee mugs. As a souvenir of one's visit to the museum, instead of the expected name and picture of the museum, each plain white ceramic mug bears a smooth groove that winds along the surface from the bottom to the top, subtly referencing the shape of the museum's famous rotunda. According to Tim Parsons, this approach breaks the mold of the design of typical souvenirs:

Sadly, the design approach taken to most souvenirs is immature and the results are kitsch. Form is transposed but often in crass and obvious ways—onto dolls or soft toys, into snow domes, vials of sand and other charity-shop fillers. These archetypal blank canvasses of the souvenir merchant, once emblazoned with place names, shout for attention and once bought, continue shouting "look where we've been" with the subtlety of a megaphone. [The Guggenheim mug] subverts the "souvenir as show-off accessory" and directs its power to evoke memories towards their source.[22]

The "form follows function" axiom was adopted as a touchstone of *modernism*, a theoretical framework that emerged in Europe around the turn of the twentieth century, and which served as a kind of universal ideology for design, the arts, and architecture. The basic tenets of modernism, which still have relevance today, include (1) the pursuit of human progress through the applications of technological and social innovations; (2) harnessing machines and manufacturing to achieve democratic ends; and (3) the idea that superior aesthetic and moral values result from pure geometric forms and undecorated materials. Following from these ideas—considered as absolutes, rather than tied to a particular designer, group, or culture—modernists believed that the successful design of an object would render it timeless and continuously desirable.

For modernists, design is a noble undertaking whose goal is to harness mass production so as to provide people with affordable and functional products that will improve their lives. Products are designed to reflect a so-called "machine aesthetic," meaning that their form is consistent with machine-made objects: pared down, devoid of decorative embellishments, and characterized by a geometric purity.[23] Some adherents of this view, such as the Austrian architect Adolf Loos, went so far as to proclaim in 1908 that architectural "ornament was a crime."[24] An example of a product that typified the modernist perspective is the Bauhaus lamp, an unadorned desk lamp designed by Wilhelm Wagenfeld and K. J. Jucker in the Bauhaus Metal Workshop (1923–24), which consists of simple and parsimonious geometric shapes—a circular base, cylindrical shaft, and spherical opaque glass that helps diffuse the light. Consistent with the "form follows function" axiom, the Bauhaus lamp, whose working parts are all visible, is described in the Museum of Modern Art's collection catalog as having achieved both maximum simplicity and economy in terms of time and materials.[25] Another household product whose design is consistent with modernist tenets is the upright Dyson DC01 cyclonic vacuum cleaner, whose visible, industrial-like components convey the impression that engineering is tantamount to any secondary concerns regarding the product's basic form (see Figure 4.2). The DC01 became the best-selling vacuum cleaner in the UK in 1995.[26]

FIGURE 4.2 The Dyson DC01 cyclonic vacuum cleaner

Source: Dyson.

The values and aesthetics of modernism may have been espoused as reflections of technological progress, but by the mid-1960s its notions were undermined by arguments that pointed to its various failures and contradictions, the foremost being the inadequacies of the "form follows function" axiom. In his book *The Nature of Design* (reprinted as *The Nature and Aesthetics of Design*), professor of furniture design David Pye struck at the heart of the "form follows function" axiom with two sharp blows by contending that: (1) although the form of an object might affect that object's ability to function, there is far greater latitude in what the shape of the object can be than modernist proponents are willing to admit; and (2) the purpose assigned to an object is highly personal and variable, and thus what is understood as "function" is not necessarily straightforward or predetermined.[27] Products, for example, may be used by consumers in creative ways that were not intended by the product designer or manufacturer, as illustrated by the IKEA hackers discussed in Chapter 5. Pye argued that the fact that objects can serve multifunctional uses counters the modernist notion that a product's function implies a singular or "correct" form.

Some postmodernists specialize in "reinventing functionality" by designing products in surprising ways and, in so doing, end up enhancing the product's functionality when compared with more traditional designs. A well-known example of this approach is designer Joris Laarman's Heat Wave radiator, whose baroque wall design across a relatively large surface area functions not only as an effective heating device, but also as a work of art. Made from fiber-reinforced concrete and sized to buyer specifications, the radiator is more aesthetically pleasing than the typical room radiator and more efficient, given that its greater surface dimensions result in better heat distribution.[28] Laarman hoped to demonstrate with his innovative radiator design that a decorative form could function as well, if not better, than a conventional geometric form.

According to some, the true death knell for the freeing of form from function coincided with developments in digital technology, specifically the microchip, which ensured that the relationship between an object's power and size no longer held sway. This became evident in the design of early mobile devices like the iPod and BlackBerry, whose exterior ("that tiny slither of metal, glass, [and] plastic"[29] in the case of the BlackBerry and the "clean lines, uniform radii and undecorated surfaces"[30] in the case of the iPod) belied any evidence of the ability of those devices to harness new technology—storing huge amounts of data; providing access to the Internet and electronic communication with others; and carrying out the functions of traditional products like the camera, watch, diary, and sound system in the process. Imagine showing a tablet PC or a smartphone to someone from an earlier era—it is improbable to imagine that they could guess what the device does. According to Alice Rawsthorn: "By liberating design from functionalism, the microchip has, in theory, given the designers the chance to radically re-define the type of objects they produce, and to make them more humane."[31] The humanizing aspect that Rawsthorn alludes to is evidenced in Apple designer Jonathan Ive's reflections:

> An object exists at the meeting of technology and people. As designers we not only influence the nature of that meeting but by creating something physical we have a potent and immediate means of communicating the identity and very meaning of an object. Far from designing enclosures around anonymous, albeit powerful logic boards, our real challenge is to make relevant and extend technological capability.

> Searching for wholly new approaches to product configuration and manufacturing requires the development of fundamentally new materials and processes. Significant solutions tend to emerge when new production technologies are exploited as a means to a greater end; the crafting of objects that stand testament to people rather than manufacturing or functional imperatives.[32]

Ive's comments have obvious relevance for consumers because they suggest the importance of designers considering the needs and desires of the end users during the design process. From an end user perspective, the freeing of form from function, ushered in as it were by the postmodern movement, represented a significant development that, in part, bestowed greater power on consumers to actively participate in the design of products (see Chapter 5). In the past, modernist designers tended to serve as arbiters of taste, operating under the belief that they knew best what was correct and appropriate, and unwilling to concern themselves with what the end user thought or desired. The recognition that a product's features, form, design, and aesthetical value might have different degrees of appeal across varying consumer subgroups, contexts, and circumstances has led product developers and manufacturers to attend more closely to what consumers want and desire. The emergence of new technologies has facilitated the means by which consumers can take advantage of their growing power in the marketplace to provide input into the design, innovation, and marketing of new products and the modification of existing ones (see Chapter 5).

Product form and consumer response

In this section, our consideration of product design turns to focus on form, arguably a primary means by which designers can engage in a dialogue with the consuming public (see Box 4.2). As defined by Peter Bloch in his influential paper on the topic: "a *product's form* represents a number of elements chosen and blended into a whole by the design team to achieve a particular sensory effect."[33] A product whose form has been carefully and strategically designed can affect multiple senses, arouse emotions, serve as an integral element of daily life, reflect the user's identity and aspirations, and can convey meanings that lead to differentiation and a distinct image in the consumer's mind. Product form is determined by a variety of design choices, involving such characteristics as shape, proportion, scale, color, materials, ornamentations, and texture. The choices and combinations of these elements can have profound effects on potential customers and current product users.

BOX 4.2 THREE DESIGNERS ON DESIGN AND PRODUCT FORM

To say that product form represents a primary means by which an object can engage in a dialogue with consumers suggests a function that goes beyond a product's ability to provide an aesthetic appeal. When Charlotte and Peter Fiell interviewed 100 contemporary designers for their book *Designing the 21st Century*, the communicative aspect of product form was mentioned again and again, as evidenced by the views of the three designers who are quoted below.

Reiko Sudo, head designer and one of the founders of the Nuno Corporation, a company that creates and sells innovative and functional fabrics, believes that her company's products not only bring "pleasure and lustre to everyday life," but communicate a message about a creative blending of the new and the old:

> As a textile designer my aim is to create textiles that our times (the present moment) will regard as beautiful. At Nuno, we believe that

"fabric"—one of the oldest materials known to humankind—can still speak to people in this day and age, and so we set our sights on "contemporary fabric-making." While deriving inspiration from the age-old history of fabrics and weaving culture, we give free rein to new ideas and employ the latest technologies in the quest for the most up-to-date creative expressions.[34]

One example of Sudo's reinterpreting of textile traditions is evidenced by a scarf that she created based on the traditional Japanese method of dying known as *shibori*. By placing dye-coated paper on top of silk, the fabric is pinched through holes in the paper and flattened before the dye is heat-transferred to the fabric. The resulting crushed and twisted fabric provides a contemporary, edgy look to the traditional *shibori* scarf.[35]

Award-winning form-finder and designer Arnout Visser understands the importance of having everyday products forge emotional attachments with their users:

A beautiful product alone is not enough, we like to hear the story and see the marks of craftsmanship and not the influence of a "styling" designer. The ideal situation would be the designer looking over the shoulder of the consumer at the product and sharing his or her enthusiastic wonder about how it works. The product should be a life-long friend.[36]

Applying this philosophy to the creation of everyday products, such as tableware, Visser's objective is to captivate the product's end user in elegantly simple ways. For example, his Salad Sunrise oil and vinegar bottle is designed so that the oil floats on top of the vinegar, creating a container with two distinct levels, either of which can be dispensed by using one of two glass tubes attached to the side of the bottle at different heights. Visser's microwavable plates skirt the problem of putting metal in a microwave oven through their unique design. The plates are composed of a special glass with metal ingredients and a printed pattern on the bottom. When placed in the microwave, the pattern heats the inner area of the plate while the edges stay cool.[37]

Dutch industrial designer Hella Jongerius, whose specialty is fusing opposites—industry and handmade crafts, the traditional and the contemporary, high and low technology—has been described as "bringing sensuality and sophistication to the sanitary industrial design." Jongerius has professed a greater interest in the social and human implications of designs rather than in the form of the objects themselves:

From my point of view, a product communicates with its environment and imbues its owner with an identity. Because of this, I search for the

(Continued)

(Continued)

character that lurks within so that my designs are first and foremost a means of creating a dialogue with the future user. Just as material research is crucial to final creations in avant-garde fashion, so the materials used in my designs often determine the final product's form and function at an early stage. As hyper-modern alchemists, today's designers should use and abuse traditional techniques so as to create new and better solutions.[38]

Jongerius' 2014 East River Chair, which was developed in 2014 for the United Nations delegates' lounge, is a solidly constructed, lightweight, and mobile armchair composed of textile, leather, and wood.[39] According to Jongerius, heavy furnishings are counterproductive in a neutral space like a lounge, which is used for spontaneous meetings and interactions. Thus, her chair was intended as a means for facilitating conversations in a casual atmosphere. The look of the chair is rather unique, each sporting one of several combinations of colors ranging from muted and calm to cheerful and bright. Leather covers serve the practical function of protecting the armrests from dirt and wear, and two front wheel rollers and a strap handle attached to the backrest provide for easy mobility.

Functions of product form

Product developers and marketers are well aware of the importance of form (or external design) for a product's success, with several studies demonstrating the link between a new product's performance in the marketplace and its physical form or design.[40] One of the basic ways that product form can contribute to success is by serving as an important means by which a product can get noticed in a cluttered, competitive marketplace. For example, in recent years, US brewers of domestic beers have attempted to fight the competition coming from the growing wine and liquor categories by experimenting with new and unusual looks to the traditional beer bottle. Anheuser-Busch has done this by adding chic and colorful aluminum packaging for some of its benchmark beers, including Budweiser and Michelob, that proffer those beers with a funky, postmodern aesthetic. The company also resurrected some of its early packaging from the 1920s through the 1950s to add a retro-chic look to some of its standard bottles. These alterations in bottle design convey a hipper, more sophisticated image to beer drinkers, and also help the brands stand out among the array of more traditional bottles on the store shelf to capture the attention of shoppers.

Another way form is linked to a product's success is evident in the way that it communicates information to consumers regarding corporate and brand identities and other product attributes. For example, the unadorned exterior appearance of the aforementioned Dyson cyclonic vacuum cleaner is such that all of the product's key functional components are apparent due to its see-through design, thereby conveying industrial strength and efficiency (see Figure 4.2). By contrast, the simple compact appearance of many smartphones and other portable devices transmits the message of user-friendliness and ease of use. Some firms take great care in adhering to consistency in external design to reinforce their corporate character, an approach that is readily evident in the form of Bose speakers and home sound systems, with their unmistakably sleek designs enhancing the upscale, high-quality image of the Bose corporate brand.

For consumers, product form can affect quality of life, both in terms of the sensory pleasures and stimulation that elegantly designed products can provide as well by facilitating product usage by offering greater efficiency, multifunctionality, and time savings. For example, the Royal VKB Boomerang wok has a unique patented curved end that is aesthetically pleasing, but also more functional than the conventional cooking wok. When the stir-fried food is pushed toward the cupped edge with a spatula, the food is easily turned, avoiding the need to lift the pan and overcoming the likelihood that some of what is being cooked will end up outside of the wok (see Figure 4.3).

The Dyson vacuum cleaner was designed to improve life via its innovative cyclonic suction system, which eliminates the need for the user to replace bags or filters, thereby offering the consumer greater convenience and functionality. In recent years, makers of external computer peripherals have begun to replace traditional connection cables with flat ribbon cables that eliminate the frequent problem of tangling that computer users are all too familiar with.

A unique or aesthetically designed product form can extend the life of a product long after its functional utility has passed. Consumers are wont to hold on to such products rather than discarding them, choosing to incorporate them as part of their sensory environment. A good example of this was provided by one of my students, who described her disappointment with the taste of the coffee brewed by her new Senseo pod coffee maker. Although she decided to replace it with a drip coffee maker, she kept the Senseo on her kitchen counter because she was impressed by its uniquely designed cylindrical shape and bright color, and believed that it helped smarten the look of her kitchen. Twinings of London promoted its teas by highlighting the stylish design of its reusable tea container cans, boasting in ad campaigns that "people have been storing things for 150 years, yet we only make tea."

FIGURE 4.3   Product form and life quality

Despite the various ways a product's form adds value from the point of view of both the marketer and consumer, design experts remind us that external design is not always critical to success, particularly in industries where the virtues of the tools of the trade are based primarily on the results they achieve rather than on the impressions they make on their end users. For many consumer products, however, external design is a fundamental determinant of consumer choice and satisfaction. This point was evoked by visual arts critic Peter Dormer in his book *Meanings of Modern Design*, in which he claims that "the closer one gets to the public or home, the greater the need for the stylist to intercede with a repertoire of visual good manners."[41] As Tim Parsons points out, Dormer's use of the term "manners" to describe a product's external design is significant:

> Manners are culture-specific and constantly evolving. What is considered polite in one situation may be embarrassingly out of place in another. As with manners, so with objects. We may choose to surround ourselves with objects of pedigree, displaying the latest style, prefer an eclectic mix or find matters of style pedantic in relation to function.[42]

The stylistic aspects of a product, such as a dinner plate or fruit bowl, are more likely to take precedence because the object's functionality is reduced, compared to a more complex product like a camera, where functional qualities (ease of focusing, comfort to carry and hold, and the like) must be considered in tandem with stylistic considerations. According to Parsons: "By concentrating upon the aspect of the object that is first seen, and not those that are discovered through use, the designer attracts accusations of putting style before substance."[43]

Relating product form to consumer response

Bloch's conceptual model of consumer responses to product form provides a good starting point for a more in-depth examination of the relationship between external design and consumers' psychological and behavioral reactions toward a product (see Figure 4.4).[44] A consideration of the model begins with the product form itself, whose stylistic and functional external characteristics are based on the designer's goals and management approval. A product's design must be consistent with its ultimate purpose, the target market, and desired performance specifications, which in turn are determined within the context of performance, ergonomic, production and cost, regulatory and legal, and designer constraints. Performance goals, for example, which often represent the primary constraint for a design project, pertain to the target consumers' desired level of a product's functional (e.g., power, shelf life, maintainability), aesthetic (e.g., sensory, experiential), and environmental (e.g., recyclable, energy savings) performance. Product design is pragmatically determined in part by the tools required for production, as when the choice between, say, a baroque or more geometric style is resolved by taking into consideration the relative costs and ease of production involved. With materials like glass and ceramics, an organic or baroque style

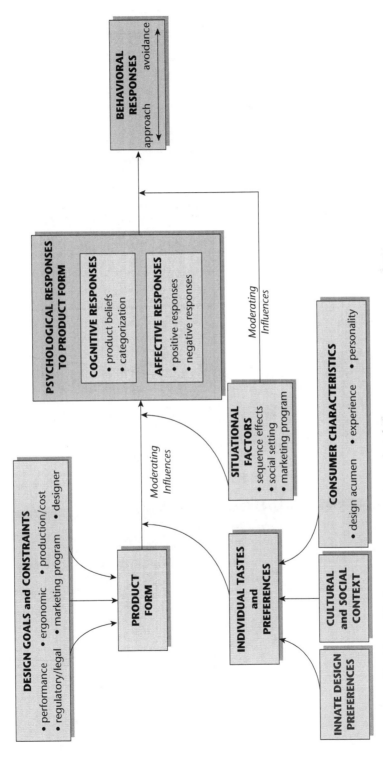

FIGURE 4.4 Bloch's model of consumer response to product form

is likely to be easier and cheaper to produce, but in most other cases, machinery and tools favor the manufacturing of geometric, straight-lined objects.[45]

Another important area that poses constraints for product design is *ergonomics*, which pertains to the match between product form and human capabilities. Ergonomics takes into account the physical measures and cognitive processes of potential users to enable the creation of objects that are more comfortable and more intuitive to use. Decisions about weight, texture, size, and shape must be considered in terms of ease of use, efficiency, comfort, and safety for target users. In light of the consumer demands discussed in Chapter 3, the aesthetical appeal of a product may not be enough to attract consumers if it becomes apparent that the product is difficult and overly complex to use, inconvenient, or impractical.

Certain aspects of product design can overcome usage constraints through the intelligent and creative application of ergonomic principles. In his 1988 book *The Psychology of Everyday Things*, Donald Norman argued for product forms that incorporate visible cues as to how they should be operated and that limit behaviors to correct usage (e.g., tools with finger grooves that make it obvious where one's fingers should be placed to grip the object for maximum efficiency).[46] Such signals represent a fundamental element of *natural mapping*, an approach to design that makes evident the relationship between a product's controls and their resulting functions, so that the product is easy and intuitive to use, without need for labels or an instruction manual (see Figure 4.5). In the traditional arrangement of stove top burners (top), it is not entirely clear which dial operates which burner, without a more significant learning effort or the reading of labels. A more innovative design (bottom) in which the dials are arranged in rows

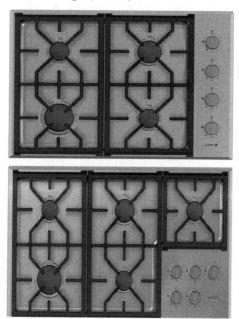

FIGURE 4.5 Natural mapping and stove-top design

Source: http://www.subzero-wolf.co.uk +44 845 250 0010.

provides a natural map for usage that eliminates the need for labels and facilitates learning. Natural mapping typically takes advantage of physical analogies (as evidenced by the "good" stove-top design depicted in Figure 4.5) and cultural standards (e.g., a rotating volume control is understood in many cultures as requiring a clockwise rotation to increase volume). Inattention to ergonomic factors in the development of a product's external design is likely to result in high levels of consumer dissatisfaction (see Box 4.3).

BOX 4.3 ERGONOMICS AND THE DESIGN OF DOORS

If there is one unarguable assertion regarding our relationship to products, it is that poorly designed objects often result in frustration and dissatisfaction. Something as apparently trivial as a microwave oven's door requiring excessive force to close can be particularly irritating, especially if the user is elderly and has frail hands, or if the noise that results prevents someone from preparing a midnight snack due to fear of waking up everyone in the apartment. Speaking of microwaves, I was struck by the inexplicable number of ovens at the stores where I recently shopped that had dark, opaque glass fronts, making it impossible to see what one is heating, even with an interior illuminated light. For someone who is concerned about spoiling a cup of coffee should it be heated to boiling, a non-transparent glass could be a deal killer. Small details in external design matter, as the following review comments from a recent purchaser of a microwave oven at Amazon.co.uk attest:

> It has a stunning look and a very sleek design. My only slight gripe with it so far is that the + button to alter the cooking time is quite annoying as you have to press it hard and at the right position (to the left), as if you miss the exact spot, it doesn't press. So, it can take a few attempts before finding the right spot. Our last one was press button, but also dial, so to alter the timing it was done by the dial.

Such comments reflect the importance of ergonomic design from the consumer's perspective, and also highlight how "the ideal product is not necessarily that which is most beautiful."[47]

In *The Psychology of Everyday Things*, Donald Norman describes how he is often perplexed by doors—an observation that most of us surely can identify with: "I push doors that are meant to be pulled, pull doors that should be pushed, and walk into doors that should be slid." As Norman goes on to explain, a door design requires the solution to two basic questions from the user's perspective: (1) In which direction does the door move? (2) On which side should the door be operated? In France (as in other countries), one rarely has to contemplate such questions, because most public doors bear the words *pousser* (push) and *tirer* (pull), yet Norman correctly avers that the design of a door—or any other everyday object, for that matter—should

(Continued)

(Continued)

make evident its correct usage "without any need for words or symbols, certainly without any need for trial and error."[48]

The French solution to the door problem demonstrates the essential nature of visual cues in external design. The correct parts for product use and manipulation should be apparent, while at the same time conveying a clear and correct message—for example, doors that require pushing should provide clear signals that the door should be pushed, and not pulled, and on which side the pushing should occur—signals that Norman refers to as "natural signals," in that they are naturally interpreted, without any conscious need for contemplation. A good illustration of what Norman had in mind is apparent in the two door photos below that were posted at the Ergonomic Design blog.[49]

For these examples of push-handled doors, the better-designed door handle is clearly the one on the left (sometimes referred to as a "crash bar" or "panic bar" because of its ease of opening during an emergency), where it is intuitively apparent how the door opens and on which side it should be pushed. Although it is rather evident that the door on the right must be pushed, it is unclear on which side it opens without trial and error on the part of the user.

For the pull-handled doors above, the handles invite users to wrap their hands around them to pull. Both sides of the doors have visible pull handles, yet the doors cannot be pulled from both sides to open, requiring the user to guess the correct solution.

The two door designs below eliminate any confusion on the part of the user through the elegantly simple application of visible natural signals.

Returning to Figure 4.4, Bloch maintains that consumer reactions to a product's form, once it is determined, do not occur in isolation, but rather are moderated by a variety of individual (e.g., design acumen, experience, personality characteristics) and situational (e.g., cultural values and social norms) variables. At the outset, it is important not to lose sight of the fact that response to a product's form is dependent upon one's personal taste, which, according to design critic Peter Jones, reflects "the discrimination of beauty from deformity and is shown in the preference for one object over another."[50] Although it may be stating the obvious to say that consumers are more likely to respond positively toward a product whose external design is consistent with their taste preferences, and vice versa, taste was not always considered a relevant consideration in product design. Recall the modernist design philosophy that viewed the aesthetic preferences of users as a primary obstacle to "true" objective forms, so much so that the modernist approach can be described as one oriented to the creation of design beyond taste. As Jones explains, in the context of the more affluent economy that began to manifest around the end of the 1980s, consumer culture shifted away from the modernistic focus on the satisfaction of purely functional needs toward being characterized by an indulgence in taste and appreciation.

There is evidence that some consumer taste preferences are innate or acquired early in life, such as a predilection for organized and unified designs.[51] "Organized" in this context means that there is a logical arrangement of design elements such that together they provide symmetry, unity, and harmony. Consistent with established principles of perceptual organization, in addition to leading to greater preference among consumers, organized elements are easier to recognize, perceive, and remember. An overriding Gestalt idea, first developed by a group of German psychologists around the turn of the twentieth century, is that in its entirety, perception—a term that technically refers to how individuals experience and make sense of their surrounding environment—is fundamentally different from the sum of individual sensations (such as those emanating from colors, texture, and shapes). A preference for organized designs apparently has its limits, however, thus posing a serious challenge for designers: to create an object's external design so that there is harmony among elements, while providing at least some degree of variety, novelty, and complexity so that an object is noticeable and engaging. Satisfaction with objects appears to fall somewhere between boredom and confusion, in the sense that overly conventional designs will not provide enough stimulation or arousal, whereas extremely novel and disorganized designs may evoke too much.[52]

Cultural and social forces are among the various situational factors that significantly influence consumer preferences for product form. Appreciation for a product's design is likely to be associated with various extrinsic factors, with differences emerging between cultures in terms of colors, materials, and shapes, or the result of general philosophies of aestheticism linked to a region's heritage or tradition (see Box 4.4). Colors, a critical element in international marketing, have varying symbolic meanings for people as a result of religious, political, cultural, and aesthetical factors, and such meanings impart a significant influence on why certain product styles are preferred over others. In Western cultures, white is a color that typically connotes goodness, purity, cleanliness, and refinement, whereas in Asian cultures it is the color for mourning. These associations are strong determinants of the preferred color of a wedding dress, with Chinese and Indian brides preferring a red gown, which for them conveys happiness, joy, and good fortune. Some online suppliers of Asian bridal wear reaffirm these associations with descriptive names for their companies, such as Redd Bridal Couture for a London-based specialist in Indian bridal wear and Red Hot Brides for a Chinese online bridal wear firm.

BOX 4.4 JAPANESE AESTHETICS AND *MONO NO AWARE*

The Japanese aesthetic concept *mono no aware*, literally translated as the pathos of things or a bittersweet awareness of the transience of things, signifies "a sad, fleeting beauty that is conspicuous in traditional Japanese cultural expressions."[53] *Mono no aware* is reflected in the passion the Japanese have for cherry blossoms (*Sakura*), one of the national flowers of Japan. Cherry blossoms appeal to the aesthetic sensibility of the Japanese, who often find beauty in transient things. Beautiful in full bloom and gracious when scattered, cherry blossoms are short-lived, and thus symbolize both new beginnings and the transience of life. According to one Japanese blogger: "I always feel happy when I see them, but at the same time its short life makes me sad."[54]

The implications of this greater sensitivity to ephemeral things for preferences in product design is aptly suggested in the following passage from designer Jaitra:

> *Mono no aware* states that beauty is a subjective rather than objective experience, a state of being ultimately internal rather than external. Based largely upon classical Greek ideals, beauty in the West is sought in the ultimate perfection of an external object: a sublime painting, perfect sculpture or intricate musical composition; a beauty that could be said to be only skin deep. The Japanese ideal sees beauty instead as an experience of the heart and soul, a feeling for and appreciation of objects or artwork—most commonly nature or the depiction of—in a pristine, untouched state.[55]

The attraction to ephemeral things may also be assumed to manifest itself in Japanese consumer behavior in terms of an appreciation for the temporal pleasures that can be derived from product offerings, rather than from their long-term permanence. Consistent with this presumption is the popularity of sampling salons (e.g., Sample Lab) and temporary ownership among the Japanese discussed in Chapter 2. Yet it must also be remembered that cultural traditions often fall victim to mobility and globalization. As Japanese culture has become more Westernized in recent decades, and as the world's economic climate has changed, consumer preferences in turn have undergone significant shifts. The appeal of luxury products has diminished as Japanese consumers strive to cut costs and economize, as seen in the booming sales of private-label products, casual clothing, and low-cost skin care products. In stark contrast to their long-standing inclination to pay for convenience, a recent survey found that a majority of Japanese respondents (53%) agreed that they were more likely to "spend time to save money" rather than "spend money to save time."[56]

The Japanese have long held the reputation of being quintessential imitators and borrowers, preferring to master established artistic traditions until confidence is reached and original touches and creative variations can be added.[57] In the recent past, the adoption of Western products, such as food items that are not indigenous to the country, would likely be customized and made more exotic so as to conform to the high value placed on high-quality luxury goods.[58] In the contemporary context, this predilection has begun to wane as growing materialism and more pragmatic concerns about value have begun to take precedence.

In addition to these broad cultural differences, it is also the case that design preferences vary according to basic individual differences, such as age, gender, social class, and ethnic subcultures. According to some American product designers, lower-income consumers prefer simpler colors (i.e., those that can be easily described, like "grass green" or "sky blue"), whereas higher-income consumers show a greater preference for more complex colors (such as "gray-green with a hint of blue"). Lower-income consumers tend to view complex colors as "dirty" or "dull."[59] The popularity of colors waxes and wanes over the years, a considerably important point for automobile makers, given that about 34% of car buyers will opt for another model if their first choice of color is unavailable. During the first decade of the current century, silver mixed with tints of cool blue, and green and grays infused with more hues in red, blue, and purple were among the emerging color trends in the car industry. White, black, and silver reigned as the world's most popular automobile colors in 2012.[60]

Another way that culture influences design preferences is in terms of the prevailing trends in style and fashion of the era. As suggested by Tim Parsons' notion of the "aesthetics of progress," in which a design language is constructed from visual cues derived from contemporary symbols of progress, it is possible to discern how a consensus among product designers and, in turn, consumers, forms around a particular style during a particular period. For example, the skyscraper was viewed as the symbol of progress during the 1930s, giving rise to an emphasis on vertical lines in the design of products. A subsequent wave of influence took hold as long-distance train travel and intercontinental flight became fashionable, leading to the popularity of a design movement known as "Stream-form." Corresponding with this design trend, products took on more of a streamlined aesthetic than was previously the case. The influence of developments in nuclear energy and space travel is apparent in the styling and enhanced efficiency of household appliances and furniture (e.g., lunar landing pad feet on furniture) and, more recently, advances in biological science (e.g., gene mapping) have resulted in designers moving toward working with more natural and embellished organic forms in product design (e.g., Senseo's highly stylized pod coffee maker).

Situational factors represent another category of moderating influences on consumer response to product form. This is evidenced when a product is encountered in a social setting, as when a person's preferences are shaped by the behaviors and reactions of others present in the situation. As discussed in Chapter 2, the growing popularity of Apple's iPod portable music player was publicly evidenced by the appearance of the product's white earbud headset (see Box 4.5). The prevalence of the white headset, denoting iPod ownership, was taken as a sign of the product's popularity, thereby conveying an implicit message about its quality. Moreover, researchers have found that people tend to like objects— be it an advertisement, product, salesperson, song, or work of art—that they have been exposed to repeatedly.[61] The *mere exposure effect*, which describes the positive effects of repeated exposures on the shaping of attitudes, has been demonstrated across a wide range of stimuli, including music, photographs, paintings, and faces. One explanation as to why repeated exposure results in the acquisition of positive attitudes maintains that recognition plays a mediating role in linking exposure to liking.[62] In other words, the more we are exposed to some stimulus—say, Apple's iconic headset—the more recognizable it becomes to us, and people prefer things that they recognize to things that are unfamiliar to them. In short, familiarity reduces uncertainty—a point we will return to in the discussion of changes in product packaging.

BOX 4.5 APPLE'S SUCCESS FROM A DESIGN STANDPOINT

Among the keys to Apple's enormous marketplace success are product design elements that go far beyond adding a white color to the iPod's iconic earbud headset. Apple's Jonathan Ive was influenced by the product design movement sparked by the work of Dieter Rams, a prominent German designer for Braun products and whose modernistic philosophy focused on creating product forms that offered a clarity of function devoid of superfluous details. By the 1980s, this approach had taken hold among manufacturers of electronic products, which attempted to adhere to a rigorous design aesthetic without sacrificing usability, with few controls, dials, and buttons visible to the naked eye. Ive successfully achieved a purity of form of this nature with the design of the original Apple iMac, a style that continued with designs for the Apple Powerbook laptop, iPod, iPhone, and iPad. Consider this description of the iPod's success from Bill Moggridge, designer of the original laptop computer (the GRiD Compass, 1981):

> When the first iPod was launched, the beautiful design was captivating, but the integration with iTunes really made the interactivity irresistible. It was so convenient to be able to use your personal computer to download music from the Internet, or copy it from your CD collection, and then sort your play list before you copied it onto the iPod. The first version had separate switches as controls, with wonderful tactile feedback, so the feel of using the product was delightful.[63]

According to Paul Mercer, a member of Ive's design team, the success of the iPod can be attributed to a great extent to its simplicity:

> The iPod is very simple-minded, at least in terms of what the device does. It's very smooth in what it does, but the screen is low-resolution, and it really doesn't do much other than let you navigate your music. That tells you two things. It tells you first that the simplification that went into the design was very well thought through, and second that the capability to build it is not commoditized.[64]

(Continued)

(Continued)

It is interesting to note that the exterior design of the iPod—thin block of metal, rounded corners, unembellished face consisting of a small screen and simple, intuitive touch controls—exemplifies the separation of form from function, meaning that the appearance of the product belies its actual purpose. This point is apparent in Alice Rawsthorn's description of the iPod Shuffle:

> How could you be expected to guess what that tiny metal box does by looking at it?
>
> There are no clues to suggest that it might play music. Like most other digital devices, the Shuffle is (literally) an inscrutable box of tricks. Apple's designers conceived the latest model as a subtle joke on the demise of "form follows ...". [The Shuffle] gives no hint as to its . . . important role of storing and playing hundreds of songs.[65]

Consistent with social psychological research on the structure of *attitudes*—the evaluative reactions people have toward the things they encounter in their social world—it is understood that consumer responses to product form can fall within one of three categories:

1. cognitive, which refers to beliefs about the product;
2. affective, which consists of feelings toward the product;
3. conative, which refers to intentions toward behaving in a certain way toward the object (see Figure 4.4).[66]

The concept of hierarchy of effects has been proposed to describe the various relationships between attitudinal components, and is based on the idea that the components are organized in a sequential and consistent fashion. For example, it is reasonable to assume that if a consumer holds several positive beliefs about a product, those beliefs give rise to positive feelings (i.e., strong liking) toward the product, thereby moving the consumer to purchase or use it should the opportunity arise. Product form can exert a clear influence on each of the three attitudinal components, which, in turn, can affect each other.[67] Beliefs about a product's durability, price/quality ratio, ease of use, prestige, and technical sophistication are likely to be shaped at least in part by external design. The streamlined features of an automobile's exterior convey the belief that the car is fast; handsome design features such as a glossy or sleek casing suggest to shoppers that a laptop is expensive and has high prestige value; and a microwave oven with several dials and buttons on its front face communicates the idea that the product requires a high level of technical sophistication.

In Figure 4.4, categorization is included as another potential cognitive response to product form. In an effort to understand a product, a typical initial consumer reaction is to attempt to classify the product into an appropriate product category. To do so requires that one compare the perceived characteristics of the focal product with those possessed by representative examples of products within various product classes and sub-classes. As an example, a recent addition to the plethora of mobile devices on the market is the large-screen smartphone, which has led to the coining of the term "phablet," a portmanteau of the words phone and tablet PC. The phablet's design characteristics, as well as the product's functions, straddle both the mobile phone and tablet PC categories. Assessing such a product from the consumer point of view poses a problem in terms of categorization given that the phablet possesses characteristics that would readily suggest a fit into either product category. If the consumer has owned a small-sized Kindle e-book reader, the phablet's external design could suggest a better fit in the tablet category. Understanding the product in that way would ultimately have an effect on the consumer's subsequent response to it, including a purchase decision. As Bloch cautions, it is in the best interest of marketers to take proactive steps to assist consumers so that consumers will be more likely to classify a product in the most strategic category (e.g., by emphasizing the phone features of the phablet).

As indicated in Figure 4.4, the psychological reactions to a product's form are likely to give rise to a subsequent behavioral response, the nature of which falls somewhere on an approach/avoidance continuum. Approach responses would result from a favorable evaluation and initial liking of the design, moving the consumer to further explore the product (e.g., by touching it, visually examining it, and probing its features more carefully), seek additional information about it, and perhaps purchase it. Once purchased, the product's desirable aesthetics could motivate the owner to prominently display the product, as a way of enhancing one's self-image or to improve the décor in one's office or home, the latter being the case with my student and her Senseo coffeemaker.

Product design and consumer perception

In a psychological sense, the fundamental processes that lie at the heart of our reactions to product design are perceptual in nature. People depend on the information they acquire from their surrounding environment to interpret and assign meaning to what is going on around them. This is how we react to many marketing stimuli as well, in the sense that meanings are primarily influenced by the stimuli we encounter from our interaction with products and brands (see Box 4.6). Perception encompasses active cognitive processes that are typically referred to as "higher-order," in the sense that they go beyond the merely physiological processes (collectively referred to as "sensation") that make it possible for us to receive information about the world around us. Unprocessed information (e.g., light, sound, texture) received via the sensory systems provides the basic raw material for vision, hearing, taste, and touch. For example, our eyes contain specialized receptor cells (rods and cones) that are responsive to a small range of electromagnetic energy, enabling us to recognize something visual in the environment through electrical impulses transmitted to the brain. The raw information is perceived—that is, rendered meaningful—on the basis of innate human abilities, prior learning, and past experiences. A bulbous, orange–shaped object resting on a table might be perceived at a quick glance as an Orangina fruit drink, without any apparent indication of the brand name.

BOX 4.6 PRODUCT DESIGN AND CONSUMER RECYCLING BEHAVIOR

A product's design changes over time with usage: features wear away, smudges appear, materials develop various imperfections. At some point, consumers are compelled to make choices about whether to replace a product, recycle it, or throw it into the garbage, among other possible disposal options (see Chapter 6). An interesting question that served as the focus of recent research asks how product design can influence consumer recycling behavior. The answer apparently can be found in design cues indicating whether or not the product is trash, and less so in whether the product itself is recyclable. Marketing researchers Remi Trudel and Jennifer Argo conducted a series of studies to determine the link between a product's form and size and the consumer's decision to recycle a product.[68] The most compelling finding that emerged from their research was that the extent to which a product has been distorted during the consumption process is a key determinant as to whether a consumer decides to recycle a product or throw it away. When usage distorts a product's size or appearance sufficiently from its original form, consumers are likely to perceive the product as less usable, and thus as something to be disposed of as garbage.

In one of Trudel and Argo's studies, participants were asked to test a pair of scissors provided to them by the researchers. Half of the participants were told to use the scissors by cutting paper, whereas the others were left to evaluate the scissors without testing them in practice. When they exited the laboratory, participants saw two bins, one of which was labeled for recyclables and the other for trash. Those persons who had cut up sheets of paper were much less likely to recycle the fragments (44%) compared with those who carried whole sheets of undamaged paper (86%), despite the fact that both groups had the same amount of paper at the outset and had been pre-screened as being aware of the importance of recycling. In a post-experiment follow-up, the researchers determined that the participants with cut-up paper perceived it as less useful than the whole sheets, and that this no doubt influenced their ultimate decision about whether or not to recycle it. In another study, participants were given one of two different-sized aluminum soft drink cans (12 or 7.5 fluid ounces). In this case, the smaller can was less likely to be recycled than the regular-sized larger can. Recycling likelihood decreased for either can if it was slightly crumpled, although there was still a bias toward recycling the regular-size, but dented, can.

Together, these studies reveal that both size and appearance can influence consumer choices regarding product disposal and recycling. Trudel and Argo concluded that changes in a product's size and original form have a significant impact on the product's perceived usefulness, with usefulness then serving as a category-defining attribute for recyclables and trash. In this light, product designers can enhance the environmental impact of products by creating forms that are capable of maintaining their original shape and appearance through continued use and aging, or that can readily be reshaped after they have been distorted.

The perceptual process is stimulated when raw data are received by one of the basic human senses (sight, smell, taste, touch, or sound). This, of course, requires that a person is first exposed to a stimulus to which one of the senses can respond. For consumers, exposure requires proximity to something in the marketing landscape that is capable of capturing attention, which is one reason why in-store displays that allow the consumer to interact with a product are an important aspect to the shopping experience (see "Designing packages to capture attention" below).

The perceptual process can be understood as comprised of a chain of events that begins with sensorial input (i.e., the immediate response of our sensory receptors to basic stimuli like light, sound, and texture) and ends with the conscious recognition (i.e., a meaningful perception) of an external event (e.g., "Aha, there's an Orangina on the table"). This sequence may or may not stimulate a specific response (e.g., tasting the Orangina). In other words, perception is not a single, discrete experience, but rather the conscious determination of a sequence of non-conscious processes. This point helps us understand why certain stimuli may not be noticed by individuals even after exposure to the stimulus has occurred (e.g., "I didn't even see the bottle on the table because I was concentrating on the song that was playing in the background").

From a design perspective, the appearance attributes of objects are capable of accomplishing various functions for the marketer, from gaining exposure and maintaining the consumer's attention to overall product appraisal and the construction of brand meaning. At the outset, how these functions are accomplished requires a better understanding of how consumers perceive a product's exterior design. According to one simplistic view,[69] product appearance perception involves two steps: (1) Upon exposure to a product, consumers first perceive the physical properties that comprise the product's design, such as its color (including hue, saturation, and combinations), texture, shape, surface, size, symmetry, and weight; for example, a clothes dryer is rectangular and has a smooth white surface.

(2) The combination of the physical attributes then conveys a look that suggests a more abstract appearance attribute for the consumer, such as modernity, simplicity, fashion, high-tech, old-fashioned, unity, and the like. An external speaker for portable devices that is sharp-edged and has a metallic and smooth-looking black exterior might create an overall impression that the product is modern. Based on consumer descriptions of the appearance of various durable products, researchers Blijlevens, Creusen, and Schoormans found that consumers in general typically use three appearance attributes to distinguish between different product appearances: modernity (oldish, modern, and futuristic), simplicity (simple, plain, and minimalistic), and playfulness (funny and playful).[70]

Designers hope to objectify a certain meaning in the appearance of the products they develop, but must be attentive to the risk that consumers may not derive the same product attributes and meaning from a product's appearance as was intended. This possibility typically compels marketers to convey the desired product meaning through high-cost promotional campaigns, which might not have been necessary had proper product testing been carried out prior to launch. According to some studies, ordinary consumers distinguish fewer product attributes and possess a more shallow understanding of similarities and differences between objects than design experts.[71] Such differences point out the subjectivity in the perception of product appearance and design, as reflected in the following informal comments from British industrial designer Sam Hecht about reactions he encountered to design simplicity:

> We've just done a project for LaCie and when it came out there was an enormous amount of criticism because "it was just a box" and "it wasn't design," that "you could have designed that in five minutes. Why did it take two years?" . . . It was a real shocker for me because it means that a designer can't make the simplest of solutions because "that's not design." . . . Whereas if something looks styled, has got fancy materials or interesting sprays and all these sorts of things, then that's seen as something that is more worthy—"that's design."[72]

According to Hecht, the moral of this anecdote is that clients must be capable and willing to consider the life of the product after it is purchased and to evaluate its design from the consumer's perspective beyond the short-term "wow" factor—that is, in terms of whether it will satisfy needs in the long term through everyday use. As it turns out, in the example above, the firm LaCie was not among those who criticized Hecht's product, the sales of which turned out to be robust. Apparently, from the consumer perspective, the simplicity of design and LaCie's strong reputation trumped the lack of a fancy design for a product designed to be used for utilitarian purposes.

Product design perception is in part determined by prior experience with objects. In this regard, designers sometimes utilize familiar size and shape dimensions (so-called "proportional analogies") that connect with consumers by evoking physical and visual memories of other objects. The smallest versions of pocket hard drives, for example, are reminiscent of Zippo lighters, with larger models roughly the size of a package of cigarettes. A desk lamp developed by designer Naoto Fukasawa copied the shape and size dimensions of a ream of A4 photocopier paper. Such proportional analogies are not intended as literal translations of dimensions, but rather are designed to evoke a familiarity based on experience and product use context. Like cigarettes and lighters, pocket hard drives and other USB devices are carried in the pocket, whereas both the desk lamp and photocopier paper are used in the office. Sam Hecht reflected on the underlying logic of designing products on the basis of a proportional analogies approach:

> [The LaCie hard disk] was originally provided to us more the size of a MiniDisc cassette (long, wide and thin). After much experiment with re-orienting the components we came up with something similar in size to a packet of cigarettes. People are already familiar with this proportion inside their top pockets—much more than an MD [MiniDisc]—as something compact. However, the dimensions are not governed by the cigarette packet. It's more a feeling.[73]

Another approach to product design perception is suggested by a framework developed by researchers Robert Kreuzbauer and Alan Malter, which focuses on the various stages that occur during the perceptual process of design information processing and that ultimately influence consumers' knowledge about brands. In developing their theoretical framework of product perception, the researchers started with the assumption that perceptual processes are critical to understanding how product design becomes embedded within one's knowledge and memory about a brand.[74] Their model suggests that product design information is initially "picked up" by consumers' sensory systems and then integrated into their cognitive understanding as a mental concept of the focal brand via a sequence of information processing stages. The mental concept then guides the consumer in determining the appropriate category in which the product or brand belongs.

To be more specific, the framework proposes that consumers process product design elements when they are exposed to relevant product form stimuli. In an initial step, sensory information results in a two-dimensional retinal image that provides a first impression of the visually observed product's design elements. The retinal image is further processed so that its basic elements like lines, curves, and edges are detected and sharpened (image-based processing). In the next stage, a consideration of surface and spatial information occurs (surface-based processing), which is next related to general stored knowledge about the nature of the three-dimensional object (object-based processing). Returning to the example of a person catching a glimpse of an Orangina bottle on a table, let's assume that the bottle is partially hidden by a vase holding a bouquet of flowers so that only a portion of the bottom half of the bottle is within the individual's line of vision. By simply perceiving a portion of the curved surface of the bottle, the observer could logically predict the probable appearance and properties of the object in its entirety, which would then enable classification of the object into its appropriate category and perhaps even correct identification of the brand. Parallel to this "bottom-up" sequence is a "top-down" process in which an existing concept influences the focused attention to and perception of product design stimuli, suggesting that product design perception is in part controlled by previously stored knowledge about products and brands.

Product design and brand meaning

Kreuzbauer and Malter's product design information processing framework further explains how one's perception of product design influences brand knowledge. According to the framework, the processes by which this occurs require a consideration of two concepts—(1) product affordances, and (2) categorization of the product and brand—both of which are described below.

Affordances of objects

The term "affordance" was introduced by psychologist James Gibson in his 1977 chapter "The Theory of Affordances" to refer to the unaided clues and signals by which a product reveals its use, as when one considers "affords" in the sense of "is for."[75] In his book *The Design of Everyday Things*, Donald Norman elaborated on the concept, defining affordance as:

> the perceived and actual properties of the thing, primarily those fundamental properties that determine just how the thing could possibly be used. . . . Affordances provide strong clues to the operation of things. Plates are for pushing. Knobs are for turning. Slots are for inserting things into. Balls are for throwing or bouncing. When affordances are taken advantage of, the user knows what to do just by looking: no picture or instruction is required. . . . When simple things need pictures, labels, or instructions, the design has failed.[76]

From the consumer's perspective, product affordance is perceptual in nature because it concerns how one perceives what one is able to do with an object—how one can go about using and operating it (pull? twist? turn? press?). Returning to the discussion of doors in Box 4.3, I pointed out how poor design often results in misuse—a door meant to be pushed is pulled, a door that opens from the left is pushed on the right. In such cases, the design failed in terms of signaling proper use, and to overcome the problem would require descriptive labels "Push" and "Pull" affixed to the doors as aids. In what is arguably the best design from among the illustrated examples in Box 4.3, the next to last in the series, we see that the handles on either side of the doors are different, with a pull handle on one side and a push bar on the other. In this case, the affordances are clear: a handle is meant to be grabbed and pulled, whereas a metal bar can only be pushed. Any confusion about how to use the door is avoided as a result of perceived affordances that focus on the intended action. When designed with affordances in mind, an object can instinctively suggest how it should be used, or else it can bring to the user's mind previous experiences involving interactions with other similar things.

Kreuzbauer and Malter argue that product affordances can be ascertained during the visual perception of design elements at both the surface-based and object-based stages. As an example, a rough texture on an otherwise smooth surface, as in the case of notches or ribs on one side of a felt-tip pen, would serve as a subtle cue as to how the object should be grasped, and that affordance would then be incorporated as part of the product/brand concept. However, Kreuzbauer and Malter caution that for more complex products, affordances will not be enough to convey the essential functional properties without additional information provided from another source, such as an instruction manual, advertising, online frequently asked questions (FAQs), and direct experience with the product: "a consumer can directly perceive that a mobile phone handset affords grasping and carrying but would need additional input to understand its function as a communication tool, portable music player or camera."[77]

Feedback represents another important component of proper product usage, and one that should go hand in hand with product affordances. People typically need to be aware of the consequences of the actions they exert in using a particular object. In the case of simple mechanical objects like doors, the feedback is obvious—the door either opens or it does not. Electronic devices are often more perplexing when feedback is lacking. When we plug a device into an electrical outlet and nothing happens, we may first wonder if the device is receiving power and charging. An LED power indicator light that varies in color according to the power status of the device would provide the necessary feedback to rule out one possible problem, as would an identifiable sound that suggests that a device has begun to be charged. Similarly, a noticeable clicking sound informs the user that a cap or lid on a product container has been firmly affixed; a dark bar that grows longer from left to right indicates the progress of a download; and a small, spinning animation is a sign that a browser window is in the process of opening.

Brand categorization and meaning

In addition to making product affordances salient to consumers, product design perception influences brand knowledge in terms of the ways consumers ultimately categorize a certain product and brand. To better understand this process, it is helpful to have some insight into the psychological concept of *schemas*. As a consumer encounters various sensations within the context of a specific marketing environment, the information those sensations provide is considered relative to recalled knowledge acquired from prior experiences. It is in this sense that schemas—mental templates or organized structures of beliefs and feelings—play a pivotal role in determining the interpretations or assumptions arrived at by the perceiver. A schema reflects one's expectations and knowledge about some particular aspect of the world that has previously been experienced by the individual.[78] Once encountered, objects and events are assigned to schemas comprised of elements with similar characteristics; thus, the schema to which a perceived element is assigned will play a crucial role in terms of how that element is later evaluated. This process is akin to what Kreuzbauer and Malter refer to as "brand-product categorization." Visual input relating to design elements, say, of a Mercedes, is matched against a *structural* representation of the generic object in the brain—in this case, the general concept of car. Thus, both design knowledge about, for example, Mercedes car models as well as generic knowledge about the concept of car will determine how the consumer mentally categorizes the Mercedes brand.

Consider for a moment what a schema for the brand Mercedes might encompass—that is, the elements or characteristics that are integrated as a cognitive representation of Mercedes in the consumer's mind: automobile, transportation, sedan, coupe, luxurious, expensive, silver, big, well-engineered, and so on. Now compare this with the elements associated with a schema for snack foods: small, savory, sweet, crackers, chips, cheap, plastic wrapper, and the like. Whenever a consumer encounters an object that could be a Mercedes, a snack, or something else, it is mentally compared with the associations within one's various schemas to determine which meaning is most appropriate.[79]

In his 2008 book *Brand Meaning*, brand consultant Mark Batey suggests that some brand meanings are archetypal in nature, establishing an emotional affinity and strong connections with consumers as a result of tapping into "deep, primordial experiences and motivations."[80] Saying that a brand's symbolic meaning is archetypal is to suggest that its meaning is universal and iconic. Considering the long-term associations linked to the Harley-Davidson brand, we recognize that the archetypal meaning of the outlaw/outsider/rebel consists of attributes such as rebellious, revolutionary, disruptive, and iconoclastic. The outlaw is a person who exists on the fringes of society, is an outsider to the community, and is characterized as possessing an undercurrent of brooding tension and rejection of prevailing societal conventions and mores. Such archetypal meanings no doubt underlie the way consumers perceive some brands, but for the majority of brands, image and meaning are based on individualistic, subjective processes. According to Batey, brand meanings are perceptual in nature and resonate at both the conscious and subconscious levels:

> [Brand meaning] refers to the semantic and symbolic features of a brand, the sum of the fundamental conscious and unconscious elements that compose the consumer's mental representation of the brand. Brand meaning both defines and is defined by the territory where the meaning derived from brand associations corresponds with consumer needs and aspirations. It is where the concrete qualities of the product meet the abstract qualities of the brand.[81]

The subjective nature of brands and brand meaning was initially elucidated in the marketing literature in a seminal *Harvard Business Review* paper authored by Burleigh Gardner and Sidney Levy in which they argued that brand image is based on much more than a product's objective qualities or characteristics, but also on the brand's psychological, social, and symbolic dimensions of meaning.[82] Recently, branding expert Marty Neumeier echoed this point in his attempt to answer the question "So what exactly is a brand?":

> A brand is a person's gut feeling about a product, service, or company. It's a gut feeling because we're all emotional, intuitive beings, despite our best efforts to be rational. It's a person's gut feeling, because in the end the brand is defined by individuals, not by companies, markets, or the so-called general public. Each person creates his or her own version of it. While companies can't control this process, they can influence it by communicating the qualities that make this product different than that product. When enough individuals arrive at the same gut feeling, a company can be said to have a brand. In other words, a brand is not what you say it is. It's what they say it is.[83]

Of course, what consumers say a brand is, or the meanings they associate with it, is strongly influenced by the sensory stimuli they encounter as they interact with the brand.

Neumeier acknowledges this when he points out that companies can communicate qualities in an effort to shape consumer perceptions, and the more brands can leverage multiple sensory touch points (smell, touch, sight, etc.), the stronger and more vivid a brand meaning becomes for the consumer. Dove soap's pure whiteness conveys purity, and its oval shape triggers positive associations regarding touch (such as creamy and soft), and these associations in no small way reinforce Dove's positioning as a moisturizing beauty bar.

Product design and the touch factor

It is becoming a rare sight indeed to come upon a fellow commuter who does not have some sort of mobile device literally in hand—be it a smartphone, mp3 player, tablet PC, or e-book reader. Devices are held expectantly, as their owners eagerly await a message from a friend; they are grasped defensively, for fear of dropping them or having them snatched away by a thief; they are repeatedly tapped and swiped by fingers as one composes a text, surfs the Internet, or searches for a song; they are rubbed and caressed as if one is magically trying to conjure up a text, tweet, or Facebook update; they are brought to the lips, as one discretely completes a phone conversation. Our borderline erotic relationship with portable devices—estimates are that more than 65% of young Americans aged 18–29 sleep with a cell phone, smartphone or tablet in their bed—is a reflection of a relatively recent development in which people have become more tactile-oriented with regard to the ways they interact with technology.

Consumers have made a swift and smooth transition from the traditional keyboard to touch-screen devices like ATM machines, mobile phones, mp3 players, tablets, and e-book readers. Compare the more natural, intimate, and intuitive shift to touching screens with the more difficult assimilation in the late nineteenth century from pen and pencil to the typewriter. The typewriter proved to be difficult for people to master at first because of the odd arrangement of the letter keys and the fact that people had no familiarity with putting words on paper in such a different way.[84] The transition from typewriter to computer was easier than that from pen or pencil to the typewriter in part because of the similarities of the computer and typewriter keyboards. The transition to touch-screens from keyboards has proven even easier, not only because our behavior has been gradually shaped over time through our use of automated teller machines (ATMs), the computer mouse, and the like, but also because touch is the human sense that most directly facilitates our interaction with material objects. Some trend watchers are predicting that the next generation of portable device screens will signal a move beyond touch to devices that can respond to users' gestures, eye movements, and spoken commands, but for the present, people are spending an increasing amount of their everyday lives touching, tapping, swiping, and texting on electronic screens. Marketers are well aware of the importance of tactile stimulation for consumers, given the compelling need for shoppers to be able to feel the texture of a product prior to purchase and the importance of touch in sales interactions (see Box 4.7).[85]

BOX 4.7 TOUCH AND THE WILLINGNESS TO PAY MORE

Researchers have determined that touch is sometimes implicated in consumer behaviors in less than obvious ways. Imagine the following scenario: You are at a fine restaurant. It's getting late, and after a terrific appetizer and main dish, you're feeling kind of sated. So now you must decide whether or not to order a tasty dessert. Which do you think would be most likely to influence your decision: reading a listing of available desserts on the menu, perhaps with a brief description included for each; seeing colorful, glossy pictures of the desserts; or having the dessert cart brought to your table with the choices available in plain view?

A growing body of research suggests that the form in which products are presented matters a lot, especially in monetary terms, so the chances are that your decision about whether to spend the additional money for a dessert that you could live without may well be influenced by the way the dessert options are presented to you. This is precisely what was learned in a series of studies conducted by a team of researchers at the California Institute of Technology, whose experiments demonstrated that the form in which objects are presented has a significant impact in monetary terms. Research participants placed on average a 50% higher value on the food presented on a tray in front of them, whereas there was no difference in bids placed on the food presented either in a text-only format or as a high-resolution photo. To rule out the possibility that the appealing smell of the food explained the differences, the researchers conducted the same experiment using trinkets from the university store in place of food and obtained identical results.

A critical determining factor in these studies was the influence of touch, given that subjects were willing to pay more for items they could reach out and touch than for those presented in text or picture form. The role of touch was confirmed by a third experiment, which was conducted exactly like the others, but with one exception—a Plexiglass barrier was placed between the research participant and the products on display, thereby eliminating the possibility of touch. This time, the average monetary amount bid on the items decreased to the level of the text- and picture-based conditions. According to researcher Antonio Rangel: "behavioral neuroscience suggests that when I put something appetizing in front of you, your brain activates motor programs that lead to your making contact with that item and consuming it. Even if you don't touch the item, the fact that it is physically present seems to be enough."[86] Eliminate the possibility of touch, however, and all bets are off, a point worthy of consideration for the growing number of bricks and mortar retailers who are shifting their strategies and resources to the digital marketplace.

Haptics and consumer behavior

The sense of touch (also referred to as *haptics*) plays an important role in capturing consumers' attention as well as in helping to shape reactions to product offerings. An advertisement printed on a heavier or coarser paper will stand out against the promotional clutter in a magazine and have a better chance at capturing the attention of the reader. Frizz Salon & Spa exploited this strategy by issuing a poster ad for which the top half of the page was heavily wrinkled and the bottom half nice and smooth. The ad copy running vertically down the page read, "skin that feels like this to skin that feels like this," effectively causing the poster to stand out while emphasizing how the spa could assist in the transformation of unhealthy to healthy skin. Beyond their effects on selective attention, tactile cues also convey symbolic meanings for consumers, leading people to link underlying product qualities to varying textures.[87] Fabrics that are smooth to the touch, such as silk, are typically equated with luxury and thus are perceived as classy and expensive, whereas denim is perceived as lower-class, practical, and durable. Marketers often frame their promotional messages to suggest implicit haptic connotations, as evidenced by expressive slogans and taglines like "smooth as silk" (Thai Airways, Kessler Whiskey), "reach out and touch someone" (AT&T), "let your fingers do the walking" (Yellow Pages), "the Midas touch" (Midas Auto Service), "touching is believing" (iPhone), and "a touch more" (Acer). The long-term slogan for Allstate Insurance, "you're in good hands with Allstate," along with the corresponding symbol depicting two open hands, successfully conveys the promise that personal care and competent service will be offered by the company.

Despite the fact that researchers to date have devoted relatively less attention to the sense of touch and its implications for marketing than other sensory modalities, interest in haptics appears to be on the rise as marketers investigate the impact of virtual and catalog shopping, and other situations in which the physical examination of products is not possible. Research has focused on differences in product attributes that encourage touch and individual motivations to touch.[88] As for product attributes, when products vary in a diagnostic way on a property such as texture, softness, weight, and temperature, they are more likely to be touched by shoppers prior to purchase.[89] Thus, clothing, which varies on texture and weight, will encourage more touch than DVDs, which vary little on material attributes that would provide useful diagnostic or comparison information. Researchers have found that consumers show a greater preference for products varying in diagnostic properties (e.g., bath towels, carpeting) when they are presented in an environment that allows for physical inspection than a non-touch environment (e.g., the products are verbally described).[90] No such difference was apparent for products lacking in variation on material properties (e.g., videotape, rolls of film), suggesting that written or verbal descriptions can compensate for the lack of touch.

People differ in the need to extract and use information obtained through touch, and it appears that this individual difference—the so-called "need for touch" (NFT)—serves to moderate the relationship between direct experience with a product and confidence in judgments about the product, as well as the amount of time people spend touching a product to extract information about it. High-NFT consumers report less confidence than low-NFT consumers in their judgments about products they are unable to touch;[91] however, for all material properties other than texture, high-NFT persons spend less time than those with low NFT exploring a product with their hands, perhaps because of the former's greater efficiency in extracting the information.[92]

Natural user interface

At the core of consumers' touch interactions with technological devices is *natural user interface* (NUI), which pertains to the design of product interfaces based on ingrained, intuitive human movements and gestures that do not have to be learned, as opposed to interfaces centered on the keyboard, mouse, and cursor. The intuitive tendency to touch is evidenced even in the youngest of children, who will instinctively interact with the screen of a portable device through touch. The makers of computers and other technological devices are now operating under the assumption that people increasingly expect to be able to interact with digital content as they have interacted with physical objects, and natural interfaces essentially emulate everyday human gestures. This is perhaps most evident in the design of e-book readers, which include a page flip feature that enables readers to swipe from page to page as if they were actually skimming the pages of a physical book. This more natural way of interacting with an e-reader was apparent in focus groups organized by Sony to assess consumer reaction to its early non-touch reading devices.[93] Participants automatically tried swiping the screen before they realized that pages had to be turned by pressing buttons on the side of the device—a gesture that is completely foreign to reading physical versions of books and magazines.

Amazon, the company that launched the original e-reader, the Kindle, boasted that the device offers pages that "are virtually indistinguishable from a physical book."[94] Indeed, certain other features of physical books that serve little if any utilitarian functions are being retained so that the digital version mimics the physical version to the greatest extent possible. E-book copies can be downloaded to a virtual bookshelf; author autographs can be embedded in electronic titles; readers can highlight key passages and add comments in the margins; and illustrative covers continue to be provided, despite no longer being needed to entice shoppers in a crowded bookstore. E-books offer a number of other advantages over the traditional book form beyond the touch factor: (1) they are immediate (e.g., after reading an intriguing review of a book that may not yet be available in local stores, the e-book version can be ordered and delivered with the click of a button); (2) they are incorporeal (e.g., several volumes in the digital format can be carried weightlessly as one travels; they do not take up space on bookshelves); (3) e-books can be read in the dark, and font sizes and type can be varied to accommodate older readers or those with visual impairments; (4) there are frequent indicators of reading progress; and (5) factual information and the meaning of obscure words can be instantly obtained on an interactive device.

Despite conforming to consumer demands for efficacity, convenience, practicality, and time saving, e-readers, like other NUI touch devices, are not without their detractors. One criticism concerns the intrusive nature of such devices, particularly the ease of access they provide to a wide range of content at the touch of a finger, which distracts from a focused reading experience. This is a concern that was voiced by Pakistani writer Mohsin Hamid when he was asked how e-books have changed the reading experience:

> E-reading opens the door to distraction. It invites connectivity and clicking and purchasing. The closed network of a printed book, on the other hand, seems to offer greater serenity. It harks back to a pre-jacked-in age. Cloth, paper, ink. They afford a degree of protection and make possible a less intermediated, less fractured experience. They guard our aloneness.[95]

Other critics of e-books have bemoaned the loss of the emotional relationships and nostalgic intimacies we form with physical books as we carry and handle them, pull them off a bookshelf to revisit a favorite passage, pass our favorites along to friends and lovers, or covet the ones given to us and inscribed by loved ones. Vinyl record aficionados express similar points about how digitized music fails to elicit the enjoyments that come from handling physical records, reading record covers, flipping through the albums in record shop bins, and the like. It is rather ironic that a great appeal of the digital book version may be the touch element, yet we never actually touch the book at all, and for traditional readers, the ephemeral nature of e-books diminishes the reading experience. *The New York Times* editor Verlyn Klinkenborg poignantly summarized this argument:

> When I read a physical book, I remember the text and the book—its shape, jacket, heft and typography. When I read an e-book, I remember the text alone. The bookness of the book simply disappears, or rather it never really existed. . . . All of this makes me think differently about the books in my physical library.
>
> They used to be simply there, arranged on the shelves, a gathering of books I'd already read. But now, when I look up from my e-reading, I realize that the physical books are serving a new purpose—as constant reminders of what I've read.
>
> They say, "We're still here," or "Remember us?" These are the very things that e-books cannot say, hidden under layers of software, tucked away in the cloud, utterly absent when the iPad goes dark.[96]

With developments in natural user interface, including voice recognition, gestural interactions, and body movement detection, the upsides of digital readers and other mobile devices eventually may very well overcome the concerns of all but hard-core traditionalists. Yet, this is not meant to imply that physical objects like books are doomed to extinction. A decisive factor in determining whether endangered objects will be deemed necessary or desirable and continue to survive is design. According to some design experts, where e-books fall short compared to physical books is in terms of their aesthetics. Even with a likely improvement in the visual standards of digital books over time, a well-designed and printed book holds the advantage of being more aesthetically pleasing, with, in the words of Alice Rawsthorn, "the sensual charm of the scent and feel of wonderful paper."[97] According to American philosopher David Rothenberg, objects like physical books conform to the principles of "aesthetic selection" or "survival of the beautiful." In other words, if an important feature of an analogue object is its aesthetic value, it may endure even if its digital counterpart is more efficient. As discussed in Chapter 3, the superior quality of music played over a traditional music system at home is a basic reason why some music enthusiasts have rejected the idea of listening to music on digital devices and continue to purchase vinyl records or CDs. Vulnerable objects are those that have nothing to offer that could offset their comparative inconvenience, which is another reason why the days of typewriters, pocket calculators, and telephone kiosks are surely numbered.

To be sure, the e-reader does not represent the only noteworthy example of NUI; another can be found in the domain of gaming, as exemplified by Microsoft's foray into full-body gaming known as Kinect. Originally launched in 2009 as Project Natal, Kinect controls the Xbox 360 and Xbox One video game systems. The natural user interface senses the player's body movements and voice commands rather than requiring input devices such as a keyboard or touch-screen. Motion control gaming systems have since been launched for other home consoles, including Nintendo's Wii and PlayStation's Move/PlayStation Eye and PlayStation Camera. Among other emerging computer/human interface developments is voice recognition technology, by which computers type as the user speaks or launch software applications in response to voice commands; head movement tracking technology, which enables computers to respond with computer mouse movements and is being tested for future television remote control functions; and eye tracking, which some foresee as an eventual preferred method for computer cursor control.[98]

Although promising, these NUI developments are not likely to transform the world of consumer/technology interactions quite yet. Interface technologies that rely on gestures, for example, suffer from their lack of feedback and knowledge of results, which are essential to learning and mastering a skill. That is, gestures are ephemeral, leaving little record of their precise path, so if the desired response fails to emerge, there is little information available to serve as feedback for the user to understand what went wrong. A conventional graphic user interface, by contrast, facilitates one's ability to remember actions and to grasp what actions are possible and how to invoke them through the use of visible icons and visible menus. According to Don Norman, the feedback limitation of purely gestural systems can be overcome by "adding conventional interface elements, such as menus, help systems, traces, tutorials, undo operations, and other forms of feedback and guides."[99]

Returning full circle to our discussion of touch, a more intuitive emerging NUI technology is tactile feedback, which overcomes the knowledge of results deficiency of other approaches. This is accomplished through the use of tactile feedback hardware that provides users with the ability to "feel" their computer interfaces. An example of the tactile feedback approach that is currently available is Immersion's CyberGlove, a wired glove that prompts the user's computer to track and translate detailed hand and finger movements. Tiny force feedback generators that are mounted on the glove deliver the sensation of touch or vibration to one's fingers. SensAble Technologies is another company involved in the development of tactile feedback technologies, including its Phantom devices that facilitate users' ability to construct and "feel" three-dimensional objects in virtual space. With proper software translation, these innovative technologies provide users with the ability to manipulate virtual objects using their hands. As described by technology writer Mike Adams: "It's an intuitive way to manipulate objects in virtual space, since nearly all humans have the natural ability to perform complex hand movements with practically no training whatsoever."[100]

Design and product packaging

Considerations relating to design extend beyond the product itself. Product packaging and in-store display are likely to have a greater impact on many shoppers at the point of sale than the product itself, especially for unplanned purchases. From a marketing standpoint, product packaging fulfills a variety of important functions. In a utilitarian sense, efficient packaging protects and preserves products during transit, while they remain in the store prior to purchase, and in the home prior to consumption. In pharmaceutical, food and beverage, and other product categories, concerns about product tampering and contamination have led to the introduction of multiple safety and security features in packaging. Johnson & Johnson, for example, was plagued by a tampering crisis involving its benchmark Extra-Strength Tylenol pain relief capsules (see Box 4.8). In another case, Colgate-Palmolive added a safety cap to the bottle of the firm's multi-use cleaner Fabuloso after learning that numerous consumers had inadvertently drunk it after confusing the color and packaging with a sports drink. The company also changed the label to more clearly indicate the product's intended use.

BOX 4.8 PACKAGING AND THE TYLENOL CRISIS

Over the course of a dramatic few days beginning on September 29, 1982, seven people in the Chicago area died from cyanide poisoning after using Johnson & Johnson's (J&J's) painkiller product Extra-Strength Tylenol capsules. To this day, the crime remains unsolved, but it appears that someone had removed some of the Tylenol bottles from supermarket shelves, laced their capsules with cyanide, resealed the packages, and then replaced them on store shelves. Using an astute public relations strategy, the company nonetheless managed to avert disaster through a combination of quickly implemented marketing measures.

From the very first day, the poisoning scare was the leading story reported in print and broadcast news reports, and marketing experts were predicting that the Tylenol brand, which represented 17% of the company's net income in 1981, would never recover.[101] However, this time the experts got it wrong. Within two months of the onset of the crisis, a modified Tylenol was back on the store shelves in a new tamper-proof packaging, and within one year its market share of the US$1.2 billion analgesic market was nearly back to its pre-crisis level. With the stakes so high, and facing an unprecedented crisis in the history of consumer goods marketing, it is informative to consider how Johnson & Johnson managed to rebound so quickly.

According to company officials, at the heart of their handling of the crisis was a firm commitment to placing consumers before profits at any cost, consistent with J&J's long-standing commitment to a decentralized management approach, ethical principles, and an emphasis on managing the business for the long term.[102] This set the tone for the immediate key business decisions that were made both during the Tylenol crisis and in its aftermath. Although J&J took a number of steps to deal with the crisis, the actions most closely related to the Tylenol package and packaging design are summarized below:[103]

- More than 31 million bottles of Tylenol capsules were recalled from shelves in all of the U.S. states in which the product was distributed. The media were informed so that they could warn consumers and all Tylenol advertising was suspended. (Prior to 1982, product recalls were virtually never carried out by consumer goods firms.)
- Warnings about the tainted capsules were sent out to the medical community through more than 450,000 Mailgrams, and special telephone hotlines were set up to respond to anxious consumers and the medical profession.
- Production of Tylenol capsules was halted on October 1.
- Tylenol capsules were reintroduced in November in a triple-seal tamper-resistant package, which began to appear on retail shelves the following month. As a result, Johnson & Johnson represented the first company to respond to new US Food and Drug Administration (FDA) regulations requiring tamper-resistant packaging.
- On October 24, the company ran a television announcement featuring one of their medical directors who talked about Tylenol's twenty-year history, offered to replace capsules with tablets, and asked the public to maintain their trust in Johnson & Johnson.
- Following another Tylenol poisoning episode in February 1986 and a much smaller recall of the product than during the original tampering crisis, J & J discontinued the manufacture and sale of all its over-the-counter medicines in capsule form. At the same time, the company offered at its expense to replace nearly 15 million packages of its capsule products in homes and retail stores with an easier-to-swallow tamper-resistant caplet. A free-trial coupon for a package of the new Tylenol caplet was distributed. Together, these later efforts resulted in an estimated cost of US$150 million for the company.[104]

The quick decision to pull Tylenol off the market, the company's straightforward approach in dealing with the media and the public, and the redesign of the product and its packaging are widely considered to be the most instrumental components of the successful outcome to the Tylenol story. According to one recounting of the crisis: "Tylenol made a hero of Johnson & Johnson."[105]

Related to the safety and security function in packaging decisions is environmental protection. Companies that once used several layers of packaging have moved to simpler designs to avoid charges of "over-packaging," without neglecting the security aspects. Environmentally friendly packaging lessens ethical criticisms regarding a firm's apparent desire for profits at the neglect of the health of the planet, adds value to the brand, and is a practice that is preferred by consumers. An example is shrink-wrapping, which involves the redesign of packages so that they use less or different material, while maintaining the original volume of the product. One company that has successfully utilized this approach is McDonald's, which in the 1990s replaced its plastic foam clamshell sandwich holders with recyclable, biodegradable cardboard. Coca-Cola redesigned its iconic soda bottle to make it smaller and lighter without altering its familiar shape, resulting in reduced environmental costs, and materials and transportation savings.

From a marketing communication perspective, packaging can be seen as a means of building brand image and the last chance to persuade consumers before they make a brand choice. In fact, the package may well be the only source of information available to the consumer while evaluating the product at the point of sale. Although we are not yet at the stage where shoppers pass down an aisle at their local grocery and have packages call out to them, as was depicted in the futuristic film *Minority Report*, some products at least figuratively beg to be selected. One brand of barbeque sauce bore the words "Try Me! Try Me!" along the plastic covering on the bottle's neck. A container of cough syrup included a sticker asking the cold sufferer not to forget corresponding products ("Need facial tissue?").

Certain packages and products often become inseparable in consumers' minds, providing instant recognition and differentiation. The aforementioned Coca-Cola bottle, perhaps the most recognizable product package in the world, is unlikely to be confused as any brand other than Coca-Cola—a point that also applies to our example above involving Orangina's unique orange bottle. A few years ago, Nestlé changed the packaging of one of its lines of instant coffee so that the product was sold in an elegant black tin container. Although the intent was to enhance the overall image of the brand, the strategy backfired when consumers perceived the brand as too expensive.

It is not surprising to find a proliferation of brand lookalikes on the market that mimic the packaging of brand leaders in the hopes that consumers will respond more favorably—a practice referred to by marketers as "passing off." In fact, researchers have demonstrated that imitative brands often result in "brand confusion," in the sense that consumers misperceive lookalikes and mistakenly select them rather than the intended original brands. For example, 42% of consumers confused the aperitif Fortini with the original and better-known brand Martini. Passing off, whereby a business implies or claims its product is another better-known one, is a common practice in the packaging of private label brands, which are typically offered at a lower price than leading brands.

Designing packages to capture attention

One of the most difficult challenges for contemporary marketers is to simply get their offerings noticed. Thus, it may not be much of an exaggeration to suggest that package design and store placement are everything in the retail setting—a point aptly underscored by Paco Underhill's insight into shopping:

> Where people go, what they see and how they respond determine the very nature of their experience. They will either see merchandise and signs clearly or they won't. They will reach objects easily or with difficulty. They will move through areas at a leisurely pace or swiftly—or not at all. And all of these . . . factors come into play simultaneously, forming a complex matrix of behaviors that must be understood if any environment is to adapt itself successfully to our animal selves.[106]

Consider the many multi-faceted stimuli to which one is exposed upon entering a typical supermarket. This includes the visual stimulation associated with window displays, the layout of merchandise on sales racks, end-of-aisle displays ("end-caps"), product packaging, and point-of-purchase (POP) communications (store flyers, posters, signs, and mobiles); the aromas emanating from fresh produce and the in-store bakery; the texture of products that are squeezed, poked, and stroked; the tastes derived from any food or drink sampled from in-store displays; the auditory stimulation coming from such sources as the in-store radio or promotional announcements, a customer loudly complaining to the store manager, and the screams of a tearful young child who is trying to convince her mother to purchase a particular brand of breakfast cereal. As described by consumer researchers Peck and Childers, all of this stimulation provides a "window to the world" that, when integrated, comprises the overall experience (in this case, of the supermarket) for the shopper:

> Our judgments about a store, its products, and even its personnel, are driven in part by the smells we encounter (our olfactory system), the things we hear (our auditory system), the objects we come into physical contact with (our tactile system), our taste experiences (the gustatory system), and what we see (the visual system).[107]

Thus, exposure to a diverse range of stimuli provides an opportunity for consumers to notice and pay attention to products and promotional messages, although there is no guarantee that will actually happen. In retail settings, where the number of stock-keeping units (SKUs) continues to rise—the average number of products carried by a typical supermarket has quadrupled since 1980, from 15,000 to 60,000—effective product packaging and display are required so as to be noticed and selected by shoppers.[108] Given all the competitive stimuli in a typical supermarket, the average package has about one tenth of a second to make an impression on the shopper. As a result, many consumer goods companies now view product packages not only as containers for shipping and storing products, but as three-dimensional ads for grabbing shopper attention.[109] This is seen in Pepsi's striking bottle designs for its Mountain Dew soft drink, Evian's luxurious glass container for a line of bottled water, rounded Kleenex packages bearing artistic imagery, the growing line of high-concept design vodka bottles, and NXT's men's body care products bearing LEDs that light up the product every 15 seconds to illuminate air bubbles suspended in the clear gel.

Given that the visual properties of stimuli influence visual attention, and attention is known to influence choices, package design attributes and aesthetics can prove to be determining factors in the retail context for capturing the attention of shoppers and influencing the choice of a product that must compete with multiple similar brands. In a recent series of experiments, researchers tracked the eye movements of participants as they navigated a simulated shopping environment.[110] Operating under the assumption that "perceptual processes happen in the brain in parallel with economic value computations and thus influence how economic decisions are made," the studies showed that the aesthetics of a package can predetermine how long consumers spend looking at certain items and ultimately influence which product is chosen for purchase. In one experiment, participants were instructed to scan and choose a snack food item from among four alternatives as eye tracking equipment recorded in real time which items were viewed and for how long. The options were varied in terms of overall salience and attractiveness, based on color, brightness, and other visual packaging features. The results revealed that visual fixations are driven by a combination of the product's visual attractiveness and consumer preference information. Although the visual attractiveness of product packaging was found to have a comparatively smaller influence than food preferences, it nonetheless had a significant impact on consumer choice preferences. Marketers have long operated under the assumption that people's choices are driven by past experience and personal preferences when it comes to deciding what food to eat, yet, according to these research results, they would be wise to also recognize the important role of the general appearance of the package for capturing attention and influencing the buying decisions of consumers.

Package design and behavior

A number of packaging design decisions are based on practical considerations related to consumer shopping and usage behavior, as well as basic in-store concerns. Package shape can provide useful information about how to open, use, and reseal the product. Moreover, the shape of a product container may reflect a physical attribute of the product itself. This is evident in certain packages that are designed with a primary emphasis on facilitating usage, as is the case with squeezable containers for condiments like ketchup and mustard. When Lever Brothers conducted focus group interviews with homemakers to identify ideas for improving the firm's household cleaners, participants revealed their difficulties attempting to clean hard-to-reach areas of sinks and toilets. As a result, Lever Brothers designed its range of Domestos cleaning bottles with a slight bend in the containers' neck to facilitate ease of application—now a common feature of a range of household cleaning products. Other product packaging includes nozzles or applicators to facilitate use, such as thin plastic straws for aerosol bug sprays and multi-purpose oils.

Packaging design decisions regarding volume and size dimensions are often based on the shopping and consumption habits of target consumer markets, who may vary in terms of the desired amounts of product to purchase and frequency of use. For example, low-income households tend to have lower usage rates for many everyday consumables and thus favor small package sizes or, conversely, prefer to economize by purchasing inexpensive bulk, generic goods.[111] Households with several children are likely to consume large amounts of certain products like toothpaste, soap, milk, and laundry detergent, resulting in a desire to "stock up" by purchasing multi-packs or large-sized packages. For many years in Guatemala, the majority of laundry care was done by hand and, as a result, through the early 1990s, the most popular detergent package type was a single-usage pouch. In the US, by contrast, the most popular size of detergents was likely to be one of 500 grams or more.[112] In recent years, however, Guatemalan washing habits have changed and laundry care has registered significant steady growth in the retail sector, now representing the largest category in home care. This shift in part has been attributed to the ethnic diversity of the Guatemalan population, with different consumer groups having different needs related to home care, and an increased awareness of the importance of cleaning and disinfecting the home from a health perspective.[113] To take another example, in Brazil, there has been a migration from powdered detergents, until recently the only type of laundry detergent available, to liquid detergents, a result of rising income levels and multinational manufacturers' investments in product and packaging innovations.[114]

The consumer demand for convenience is another consideration to take into account for packaging design, with a number of relevant dimensions affected: ease of package opening, closing, and resealing; screw-top or flip-top containers; metal cans with a self-opening device; gripping contours on large glass containers; squeeze bottle or pump devices; and large-sized containers with built-in handles for portability (see Box 4.9). Certain conveniences will add value to many products and serve to distinguish brands from competitors, albeit while adding to the price of the product.

BOX 4.9 FLIP-TOP OR SCREW-TOP?

Although the number of toothpaste brands appears to be declining, with 352 distinct types or sizes of toothpaste sold in US retail shops in 2011, down from 412 in 2008, the category offers something for everyone, with

(Continued)

(Continued)

specialized pastes and gels promising various benefits to the user (teeth whitening, reduction of plaque, reduced sensitivity, etc.), flavors, and packaging variations (sizes, tube or pump, etc.).[115] The numerous offerings pose a bewildering array of choices for the shopper, recalling the ongoing "more is less" paradox of choice issue in the consumer behavior literature, which holds that consumer decision making would be easier and more satisfying if there were fewer alternatives to choose from.[116]

Concerning toothpaste choice, a colleague recently informed me that he had switched his brand fidelity after hearing that his former brand purportedly contained an ingredient that had been linked to cancer. Satisfied with what he perceives as a safer choice, my colleague nonetheless laments the loss of a flip-top cap, which was a feature of his previous brand's squeeze tube which he had become accustomed to using for several years. The flip-top cap—a relatively recent packaging development—serves as an interesting case example of how seemingly minor changes in design can have a significant impact on product desirability and consumer preferences. Unlike the traditional screw-top toothpaste container, the flip-top offers practicality and convenience, and can save time. Based on the author's own rudimentary tests, it takes approximately two-and-a-half seconds (a conservative estimate) to open and close a screw-top tube of toothpaste, a full two seconds longer than a flip-top toothpaste container. Assuming my 42-year-old colleague lives another 36 years—a figure representing his projected life expectancy—and brushes his teeth twice a day, he stands to lose more than a day or two of his life if he continues to use the screw-top brand, factoring in the additional lost seconds for those times he misplaces or drops the screw-top, and an occasional leap year. With these data in hand, will the promises of an additional couple of days of life and greater convenience convince my colleague to go back to his original brand (which he still perceives as bearing a safety risk) or try another brand with a flip-top cap, or will he remain faithful to his new brand, with its more time-consuming screw-top? Such considerations, while apparently mundane, are reflected in the following posts that appeared in an online forum discussion on the relative merits of the flip-top versus screw-off toothpaste caps:[117]

> I like flip tops because it saves me time in opening and closing the tube. I'm usually in a hurry so I have to do things fast. As for the mess created with flip tops, I have to keep reminding people to use it neatly so it can be closed well. It's sort of annoying to keep reminding them but I just have to. This is the only cap that works for me. In fact I want flip tops with almost everything I use: shampoos, lotion and all other bottled and tubed things I use daily.

> I like the screw tops better. Right now we are using a tube with a flip top and it's been driving me crazy. If it's not perfectly clean it won't

close all the way and will leak all over the place. I love the toothpaste but hate the cap.

An additional one or two days of life may seem like a trivial consideration in the grand scheme of things, especially when compared to the far greater risks associated with the use of potentially harmful products, such as tobacco and alcohol. Nonetheless, the seconds add up when one considers the amount of time people spend engaged in other everyday product-related activities, such as opening shrink-wrapped packages, carrying leftover food to the microwave and warming it, recycling newspapers, text-messaging, booting up and shutting down computers and mobile devices, surfing the Internet, locking and unlocking doors, shaving, choosing and tying a necktie, and so on.

From the retailer's point of view, packaging design can prove to be a hindrance to stocking and shelving in the store. If, for example, brands in a particular category, such as breakfast cereals, are packaged in similarly sized rectangular boxes, a uniquely dimensioned package for a brand alternative will pose a problem in terms of fit on the supermarket shelf. Such boxes may end up on the top of the shelving unit, or the retailer may not bother displaying the item at all—in either case, the shopper is likely to select another brand, no matter how much care and imagination went into the novel design. It is possible to circumvent this problem, as the clothing firm Hanes demonstrated when it introduced its L'eggs line of pantyhose, an innovative brand that was packaged in a plastic container shaped like an egg. The product's name, packaging, and logo were created by designer Roger Ferriter, with each element serving to reinforce brand meaning and differentiation. Recognizing that the odd shape of the package would pose a significant problem for in-store shelving, Hanes offered retailers a special end-of-aisle display comprised of several tiers designed like egg cartons, with oval slots into which each package could be neatly placed. The display added extra value to the retail setting, captured the attention of shoppers, and in no small part contributed to the rapid success of the brand. L'eggs essentially revolutionized the pantyhose and nylons category, which previously consisted of mainly generic no-name brands.

Much of the research into the relationship between packaging and consumer behavior has focused on food products, particularly in terms of issues related to obesity. Consumer researchers have investigated such design elements as food package size and the nature of packaging labels in efforts to ascertain the extent to which these and other product factors prompt overindulgence. For example, it is widely believed that people consume more junk food when they eat from large packages as opposed to small ones; in response, food companies have taken to decreasing portion sizes and offering single-serving packages, such as multi-pack snacks, cereals, and ice cream. However, studies have shown that this strategy may have the opposite effect on consumers, leading them to consume more from small packages as a result of blunted wariness about how much they have consumed.[118] That is, because small or single-serving packages are typically consumed in full, self-regulatory behaviors may not be activated as they would be when eating from larger, bulk containers that enable consumers to more effectively monitor their total consumption.

In one series of controlled studies, Coelho do Vale, Pieters, and Zeelenberg activated participants' thoughts about their body shape and dietary concerns, and then provided participants with potato chips to consume while watching a television program. Nearly twice as many chips were eaten by persons who were given nine small bags of chips (an average of 46.1 grams) as opposed to those given two large bags (an average of 23.5 grams), and the smaller bags were opened with far less hesitancy. Based on these findings, the authors argue that multi-packs of single-serving portions, like Haagen-Dazs's "Little Pleasures" mini-ice cream cups, may appear to consumers as innocent little treats that will help them keep their shape, when the chances are that the product will be consumed at an even higher rate, leading to over-consumption.

The tendency to finish an entire package of chips or cookies in a single sitting may also have something to do with the external cues people attend to while they are eating (see Box 6.5, p. 277). For example, Brian Wansink, director of the Food and Brand Lab at Cornell University, and his colleague Pierre Chandon found that low-fat nutrition labels have an influence on consumers not unlike food size labels: they increase perceptions of the appropriate serving size of a food product, while at the same time decreasing consumption guilt, leading consumers—especially those who are overweight—to overeat snack foods.[119] The researchers also found that providing salient, objective serving-size information (e.g., "Contains 2 Servings") can reduce over-eating among guilt-prone, normal-weight eaters, but not for those who are overweight.

Changing packaging and logo design

Within the marketing context, a common strategy in efforts to maintain a brand's reputation or market value is to institute some sort of modification of external brand identifiers, such as the brand logo or packaging (see Box 4.10). In many cases, this practice is carried out by companies behind long-term, successful brands in order to keep the product looking contemporary and fresh, perhaps at the same time conveying the impression that the product's quality has been improved. Such changes are often implemented in minimal increments over time rather than in dramatic makeovers, so that the original brand continues to be recognizable and loyal buyers are not misled into thinking that their beloved brand has been significantly altered. The contour shape of the Coca-Cola bottle, introduced in 1916, has undergone many subtle changes over the years, including changes in the bottle's size and in the elaborate Spencerian script that comprises the "Coca-Cola" logo on the bottle's face.[120] Comparing an early 1900s Coke bottle with its counterpart in the early 2000s, it is obvious that the original bottle has changed, yet modifications were made gradually over time without alerting consumers or posing any threats to the brand's reputation. Similarly, both General Mills' Betty Crocker logo and Quaker Oat's Aunt Jemima have been subtly updated over the years to overcome the stereotypical images that both logos conveyed in the contemporary era.

BOX 4.10 TYPOGRAPHY MATTERS

The importance of typography and graphic design for products and product packaging cannot be underestimated. *Typography* refers to the selection and arrangement of the type that appears on products, product packaging, and in various advertising formats. Well-designed and carefully thought out typography facilitates consumer perception of brands, can add equity to a brand name, can capture consumer attention, and makes it easier for consumers to read and process textual marketing content. Without doubt, the most ubiquitous typeface in the contemporary era is Helvetica, a sans-serif typeface (i.e., one whose letters bear no projecting features) first developed in 1957 by typeface designer Max Miedinger and Haas Typefoundry head Eduard Hoffmann in Switzerland. The simplicity of Helvetica underlies its versatility, as evidenced by its ever-present appearance in a variety of contexts: storefronts, product packaging, advertising, street signs, public transportation systems, government forms, and newspaper vending boxes. The great appeal of Helvetica stems from its apparent neutrality, such that meaning emerges from the content of the text rather than in the typeface itself. According to filmmaker Gary Hustwit, Helvetica is "an emblem of the machine age, a harbinger of globalization, and an ally of modern art's impulse toward innovation, simplicity and abstraction."[121]

Perhaps the best way to emphasize why typography matters is to hear what graphic designers have to say about the significance and meaning of their craft. To do so, one need search no further than Gary Hustwit's fascinating feature-length film about typography, graphic design, and global visual culture, *Helvetica—A Documentary Film* (2007). Some of the most noteworthy interview comments from the film concerning typography and its significance in the marketing context appear below:

> The way something is presented will define the way you react to it. So you can take the same message and present it in three different typefaces. The response to that, the immediate emotional response will be different, and the choice of typeface is the prime weapon in that communication. I say "weapon" largely because these days with commercial marketing and advertising, the way the message is dressed is

(Continued)

going to define our reaction to that message in the advertising. So if it says "buy these jeans," and it is a grunge font, you would expect it to be some kind of ripped jeans or to be sold in some kind of underground clothing store. If you see that same message in Helvetica it's probably on The Gap—it's going to be clean, you're going to fit in, you're not going to stand out.

(Graphic designer Neville Brody)

I'm very much a word person, so that's why typography for me is the obvious extension. It just makes my words visible.

(Typographer and designer Erik Spiekermann)

Type is saying things to us all the time. Typefaces express a mood, an atmosphere. They give words a certain coloring. Graphic design is the communication framework about what the world is now and what we should aspire to. It's the way they reach us. The designer has an enormous responsibility. Those are the people, you know, putting their wires into our heads. . . . All of us, I would suggest, are prompted in subliminal ways. Maybe the feeling you have when you see particular typographic choices used on a piece of packaging is just "I like the look of that, that feels good, that's my kind of product." But that's the type casting its secret spell.

(Design writer Rick Poyner)

Another situation that can spark a need for product packaging changes arises when the current packaging results in consumer misperceptions or product misuse. The previously mentioned example of Colgate-Palmolive's cleaning product Fabuloso, which was mistakenly drunk by consumers who misperceived the product as a sports drink, is a case in point. In a similar example dating back to 1982, Lever Brothers distributed free samples of its new Sunlight dishwashing liquid to households in several US Mid-Atlantic States.[122] However, nearly a hundred consumers were misled by the product's name, the yellow container with its images of lemons, and information on the label reading "with lemons," and ended up drinking what they believed to be a lemon juice substitute. Apparently, those perceptual cues were more salient to consumers than labeling information, which stated in two places that the contents contained detergent not intended for consumption. In most cases, such unfortunate outcomes can be prevented if firms test consumer reaction to product and packaging prototypes prior to launch. In the Sunlight case, appropriate changes were made only after the onset of negative publicity, with product warnings emboldened and an image of a sparkling drinking glass replacing those of lemons on the label.

A common marketing mistake is to institute design changes without any carefully considered purpose. In early 2009, Pepsico's Tropicana orange juice brand announced that it was changing its long-standing carton design, replacing its familiar orange and straw logo with an image of an orange juice-filled glass and adding a squeeze cap shaped like an orange.[123] As explained by Omnicon's Arnell Group CEO Peter Arnell at a press conference announcing the Tropicana repackaging, the logic behind the new design was "to give a new, refreshed energy to Tropicana, to evolve it to a more current or modern state."[124] However, consumer response to the design was swift and overwhelmingly negative, with many loyal Tropicana orange juice buyers chastising the change throughout the blogosphere and demanding that the company return to the original design. Consumers described the new, rather generic-looking packaging as "ugly," "stupid," and resembling a "store brand." Given the intense consumer backlash, which was beginning to represent a public relations fiasco for Tropicana, the brand announced only a few weeks later that it was dropping the new packaging and switching back to the original design, while retaining the new orange squeeze cap.

Other successful brands have encountered similar consumer resistance in the face of a logo change (e.g., Starbucks, Gap, the University of California) or alteration in packaging (e.g., Pepsi's Sierra Mist)—signifying how tinkering with a long-standing, familiar brand element is a risky proposition, particularly among loyal customers who perceive such changes as a threat to what the brand represents for them. In a psychological sense, consumers often respond negatively to change because, in their minds, change alters what a brand subjectively represents to them. Although innovation is the lifeblood of the consumer marketplace, it also is true that consumers generally are more comfortable with the familiar than they are with surprises. Evaluating Tropicana's short-lived packaging modifications, Interbrand's North American executive creative director Fred Richards explained that:

> design companies should be asking far smarter questions at the outset of the changes to really understand the reasons for the change. Sadly, many [of these] companies enjoy the design process so much that design for design's sake takes over, and all reason jumps out of the window for the benefit of a trend or effect they've wanted to try.[125]

These points recall the comments made by Paul Capelli, McCann-Erickson senior vice president and group creative director for Coca-Cola Classic, in describing his approach to advertising for the well-known brand:

> I certainly have to look at things through the eyes of Coca-Cola—that is ultimately my responsibility, to make sure that they're getting what I sold them as the idea and concept of the commercial. I have to make sure that we don't become sometimes too artsy, and make sure that we're selling. We're selling here, I mean, this is a business proposition more than it is an artistic proposition. So I have to make sure that there's

plenty of their product in the commercial because, after all, it is *their* commercial, not mine.[126]

Conclusion

At the outset of this chapter, I emphasized how product design and aesthetics are critical to business success and central to understanding the consumer/product dynamic—a message that bears repeating here. Our relationships with objects are complex and multi-faceted, and to be fully understood, require a close examination of the objectives and insights of designers, their clients, and the consumers who serve as end users. As product design expert Tim Parsons implied in his discussion of product aesthetics, this is no small task because attempts to fathom the nature of the finer points of product design are like dancing about architecture: "there are things we can only experience through sight and touch and that cannot be adequately expressed in words."[127] Indeed, it is only through actual direct interaction with products that our needs and desires can be fulfilled and the relationship between product form, function, and aesthetics fully discerned. For marketers, this poses a particular challenge in terms of their need to gain insight into product design from the consumer point of view—a topic I address more fully in Chapter 5.

It is interesting that Parsons references architecture in his discussion of the intuitive decision-making approach used by many product designers. The famous design dictum that "form follows function" originated in the context of architecture, and its application quickly migrated from buildings to objects. In the remarkable book *Avian Architecture: How Birds Design, Engineer and Build*, author Peter Goodfellow elucidates the behavior and design acumen of 600 species of birds through a discussion of the how and why of nest construction.[128] Suggestive of the proliferation of products and brands in the consumer marketplace, the vast diversity of nest types, evident even among related species, reflects the engineering skills of "birds as builders," where form and function are inseparably linked. For example, male bowerbirds build nests out of grass or sticks on the ground, and then decorate them with leaves, stones, or other objects. There is evidence that over time, the birds improve on the quality of their structures, which primarily serve as courtship displays intended to signal their mating potential to their female counterparts. The female song thrush uses intricate engineering skills in the construction of a cup-shaped nest built on a foundation of sturdy twigs and dried grass, which is lined with wood pulp and mud. The structure then is camouflaged against predators with an outside decoration composed of moss and leaves—a perfect blending of behavior, function, and design.

It is easy to extrapolate from the nest-building skills of bird species to the design of homes in the human species, yet the dynamic interplay between product usage, function, and design is equally evident in even the most mundane, everyday consumer objects, such as toothpaste tubes, woks, desk lamps, external hard drives, microwave ovens, and doors. Product form, function, and aesthetics engage consumers in a fluid drama that defines how people relate to objects in the material world, and at certain levels compares with the relationships people have with each other. It no longer makes sense, if it ever did, to consider the role of products in consumer behavior purely in terms of their functional, need-satisfying properties. As Alice Rawsthorn observed, this is especially true in the contemporary digital era, which sees "the dislocation of form and function" that poses "a new challenge for designers: how to help us operate ever more complex digital products."[129] As designers are now able to incorporate multiple functions into the tiny containers that operate as computers, smartphones, mp3 players, and tablets, the appearance of such products no longer bears any relevance to their purpose or what they do for us. In this light, it is clear that the relationship between product design and consumer response will continue along an evolutionary path that will prove to be an increasing focus for designers and marketers for years to come.

Further reading

There are a number of excellent books on design that could be recommended here, but the one that proved especially useful for the completion of this chapter is Tim Parsons' *Thinking: Objects—Contemporary Approaches to Product Design* (AVA Publishing, 2009). Parsons' book is a comprehensive guide to understanding objects from the designer's perspective, providing deep insight into the nature of the design process and an appreciation of the multi-disciplinary nature of product design.

Another book that is particularly useful for understanding contemporary approaches to product design is Charlotte and Peter Fiell's *Designing the 21st Century* (Taschen, 2001), which surveys the thinking and creations of a cross-section of the world's most influential designers.

Award-winning designer Bill Moggridge's book *Designing Interactions* (Massachusetts Institute of Technology, 2007) is a compendium of interviews with 40 influential designers who have shaped our interaction with technology, including the creators of the computer mouse, the Palm organizer, The Sims, and Google. Moggridge, the designer of the original laptop computer (the GRiD Compass, 1981), keeps his interviews focused on the interactions between users and objects and the integration of ergonomics into design practice.

The Design of Everyday Things (Basic Books, rev. ed., 2013), by Donald A. Norman, is an enlightening overview of the design of products from the end user's perspective. The book provides numerous examples of flawed designs and offers guidelines for enhancing the usable design of everyday objects.

Also highly recommended are design critic Alice Rawsthorn's informative essays on how design affects our lives, which are occasionally published in the international edition of *The New York Times*, as well as her more comprehensive coverage of the topic in the book *Hello World: Where Design Meets Life* (Pearson, 2013). Finally, no matter what the reader's level of interest in product design may be, the trilogy of documentary films on design by Gary Hustwit should not be missed: *Helvetia* (2007) focuses on graphic design and typography; *Objectified* (2009) emphasizes industrial design; and *Urbanized* (2011) covers architecture and urban planning. *Objectified* was projected on a wall in a continuous loop as part of an installation at the Dansk Design Center in Copenhagen during my visit there in 2010, and planted the seed of inspiration for the writing of this book.

Notes

1 Roud, R. (1967). *Godard*. London: Martin Secker & Warburg.
2 Forty, A. (1986). *Objects and desire: Design and society since 1750*. London: Thames and Hudson.
3 Gardner, B. B. & Levy, S. (1955). The product and the brand. *Harvard Business Review*, *33*, 33–39.
4 Bloch, P. H. (1995). Seeking the ideal form: Product design and consumer response. *Journal of Marketing*, *59*, 16–29.
5 Rawsthorn, A. (2011, October 2). Can anybody be a designer? *The New York Times*. Available: http://www.nytimes.com/2011/10/03/arts/design/can-anybody-be-a-designer.html.
6 Rawsthorn, A. (2013, April 22). Designers versus inventors. *International Herald Tribune*, p. 10.
7 Rawsthorn, A. (2013, April 22).
8 Parsons, T. (2009). *Thinking: Objects—contemporary approaches to product design*. Worthing, West Sussex, UK: AVA Publishing.
9 James Dyson—Dyson—how I got started in business. (2012, July 20). *Wildfire Hub*. Available: http://www.wildfirehub.com/blog/james-dyson-dyson-how-i-got-started-in-business.
10 Fairs, M. (2004, December). What is design? *Icon*, *18*. Available: http://www.iconeye.com/component/k2/item/2674-what-is-design?-|-icon-018-|-december-2004.
11 Fiell, C. & Fiell, P. (2001). *Designing the 21st century*. Cologne, Germany: Taschen.
12 Fairs, M. (2004, December).
13 Fairs, M. (2004, December).
14 Gillin, J. (2011, June 21). Unseen Eames: Films from the vault. *Dwell*. Available: http://www.dwell.com/dwell-design/article/unseen-eames-films-vault.
15 Ryan, V. (2007). What is product design? *A Design and Technology Site*. Available: http://www.technologystudent.com/prddes1/prody1.html.
16 Parsons, T. (2009).
17 Fairs, M. (2004, December).
18 Fairs, M. (2004, December).
19 Heskett, J. (2002). *Design: A very short introduction*. Oxford, UK: Oxford University Press, p. 3.
20 Sullivan, L. H. (1896, March). The tall office building artistically considered. *Lippincott's Magazine*, *57*, 403–409.
21 Frank Lloyd Wright to Harry Guggenheim. (1958, July 15). *Frank Lloyd Wright: From within outward*. Exhibition catalog. New York: Solomon R. Guggenheim Foundation, p. 268.
22 Parsons, T. (2009), p. 69.
23 Parsons, T. (2009).
24 Loos, A. (1998). *Ornament and crime: Selected essays*. Riverside, CA: Ariadne Press, p. 20.
25 Wilhelm Wagenfeld, Carl Jakob Jucker. Table lamp. 1923–24. (2014). *MoMA. The Collection*. Available: http://www.moma.org/collection/object.php?object_id=4056.
26 Dyson vacuum cleaner. (2005, April). *The Great Idea Finder*. Available: http://www.ideafinder.com/history/inventions/dysonvac.htm.

27 Pye, D. (1964). *The nature of design*. London: Barrie and Jenkins.
28 Fehrenbacher, J. (2006, February 13). Joris Laarman's Heat Wave radiator. *Inhabitat*. Available: http://inhabitat.com/heat-wave-radiator/.
29 Rawsthorn, A. (2010, November 22). Freeing form from function. *International Herald Tribune*, p. 14.
30 Parsons, T. (2009), p. 18.
31 Rawsthorn, A. (2010, November 22).
32 Fiell, C. & Fiell, P. (2001), p. 132.
33 Bloch, P. H. (1995), p. 17.
34 Fiell, C. & Fiell, P. (2001), p. 290.
35 Warner, J. (2013, July 9). Reiko Sudo—Nuno Corporation. *twofold Contemporary Textiles*. Available http://www.twofoldstyle.com/blogs/blog/8295865-reiko-sudo-nuno-corporation.
36 Fiell, C. & Fiell, P. (2001), p. 313.
37 Salad Sunrise. *Arnout Visser*. Available: http://www.arnoutvisser.com/saladsunrise.html. Microwave plates. *Arnout Visser*. Available: http://www.arnoutvisser.com/microwaveplates.html.
38 Fiell, C. & Fiell, P. (2001), p. 144.
39 East River Chair. *Jongeriuslab*. Available: http://www.jongeriuslab.com/work/east-river-chair.
40 Bruce, M. & Whitehead, M. (1988). Putting design into the picture: The role of product design in consumer purchase behavior. *Journal of the Market Research Society*, *30*, 147–162. Cooper, R. G. & Kleinschmidt, E. (1987). New products: What separates winners from losers? *Journal of Product Innovation Management*, *4*, 169–184.
41 Dormer, P. (1990). *Meanings of modern design*. London: Thames & Hudson.
42 Parsons, T. (2009), p. 53.
43 Parsons, T. (2009), p. 52.
44 Bloch, P. (1995).
45 Parsons, T. (2009).
46 Norman, D. A. (1988). *The psychology of everyday things*. New York: Basic Books.
47 Bloch, P. (1995), p. 18.
48 Norman, D. A. (1988), p. 3.
49 Push sign on a pull door. *Ergonomic Design*. Available: http://blogs.evergreen.edu/brookewalsh/push-sign-on-a-pull-door.
50 Jones, P. L. (1991). Taste today: The role of appreciation in consumerism and design. New York: Pergamon, p. ix.
51 Simonson, I. & Sela, A. (2011). On the heritability of consumer decision making: An exploratory approach for studying genetic effects on judgment and choice. *Journal of Consumer Research*, *37* (6), 951–966.
52 Gombrich, E. H. (1979). *The sense of order*. Ithaca, NY: Cornell University Press. Holbrook, M. B. & Zirlin, R. B. (1985). Artistic creation, artworks, and aesthetic appreciation. *Advances in Non-profit Marketing*, *1*, 1–54.
53 Meli, M. (2002). Motoori Norinaga's hermaneutic of mono no aware: The link between ideal and tradition. In M. F. Marra (Ed.), *Japanese hermeneutics: Current debates on aesthetics and interpretations* (pp. 60–75). Honolulu, HI: University of Hawai'i Press, p. 60.
54 Abe, N. (2014). The Japanese and cherry blossoms—from Nihonjin to Sakura. *About.com*. Available: http://japanese.about.com/od/namikosbloglessons/a/lesson14.htm.
55 Jaitra. (2008, July 25). Mono no aware: Beauty in Japan. *Sensitivity to Things*. Available: http://sensitivitytothings.com/2008/07/25/mono-no-aware-beauty-in-japan/.
56 Salsberg, B. (2010, March). The new Japanese consumer. *McKinsey Quarterly*. Available: http://www.mckinsey.com/insights/consumer_and_retail/the_new_japanese_consumer.
57 Reynolds, S. (2011). *Retromania: Pop culture's addiction to its own past*. London: Faber and Faber.

58 Brannen, M. Y. (1992). Cross-cultural materialism: Commodifying culture in Japan. In F. W. Rudmin & M. Richins (Eds.), *Meaning, measure, and morality of materialism* (pp. 167–180). Provo, UT: Association for Consumer Research.

59 Kanner, B. (1989, April 3). Color schemes. *New York Magazine*, pp. 22–23.

60 DuPont. (2012). 2012 automotive color popularity report showcases global preferences. *DuPont News*. Available: http://www2.dupont.com/media/en-us/news-events/december/2012-automotive-color.html.

61 Zajonc, R. B. (1968). Attitudinal effects of mere exposure. *Journal of Personality and Social Psychology Monographs, 9* (2, Pt. 2), 1–27.

62 Birnbaum, M. H., & Mellers, B. A. (1979). Stimulus recognition may mediate exposure effects. *Journal of Personality and Social Psychology, 37*, 391–394.

63 Moggridge, B. (2007). *Designing interactions.* Cambridge, MA: MIT Press, p. 305.

64 Moggridge, B. (2007), p. 315.

65 Rawsthorn, A. (2009, May 30).

66 Eagley, A. H. & Chaiken, S. (1998). Attitude structure and function. In D. T. Gilbert & S. T. Fiske (Eds.), *The handbook of social psychology* (pp. 269–322). Boston: McGraw-Hill.

67 Kimmel, A. J. (2013). *Psychological foundations of marketing.* Hove, East Sussex, UK: Routledge.

68 Trudel, R. & Argo, J. (2013). The effect of product size and form distortion on consumer recycling behavior. *Journal of Consumer Research, 40*, 632–643.

69 Blijlevens, J., Creusen, M. E. H., & Schoormans, J. P. L. (2009). How consumers perceive product appearance: The identification of three product appearance attributes. *International Journal of Design, 3*, 27–35.

70 Blijlevens, J., Creusen, M. E. H., & Schoormans, J. P. L. (2009).

71 Hsu, S. H., Chuang, M. C., & Chang, C. C. (2000). A semantic differential study of designers' and users' product form perception. *International Journal of Industrial Ergonomics, 25*, 375–381. Tanaka, J. W. & Taylor, M. (1991). Object categories and expertise: Is the basic level in the eye of the beholder? *Cognitive Psychology, 23*, 457–482.

72 Parsons, T. (2009), p. 63.

73 Parsons, T. (2009), p. 63.

74 Kreuzbauer, R. & Malter, A. J. (2007). Product design perception and brand categorization. *Advances in Consumer Research, 34*, 240–246.

75 Gibson, J. (1977). The theory of affordances. In R. Shaw & J. Bransford (Eds.), *Toward an ecological psychology* (pp. 67–82). Hillsdale, NJ: Erlbaum.

76 Norman, D. A. (2013). The design of everyday things: Revised and expanded edition. New York: Basic Books, p. 9.

77 Kreuzbauer, R. & Malter, A. J. (2007), p. 243.

78 Batey, M. (2008). *Brand meaning.* New York: Routledge.

79 Babin, B. J. & Harris, E. (2011). *CB3.* Mason, OH: South-Western.

80 Batey, M. (2008), p. 36.

81 Batey, M. (2008), p. 111.

82 Gardner, B. B. & Levy, S. (1955). The product and the brand. *Harvard Business Review, 33*, 33–39.

83 Neumeier, M. (2006). *The brand gap.* Berkeley, CA: New Riders, pp. 2–3.

84 Ierley, M. (2002). *Wondrous contrivances: Technology at the threshold.* New York: Clarkson Potter.

85 Kimmel, A. J. (2013).

86 California Institute of Technology. (2010, September 9). Consumers will pay more for goods they can touch. *ScienceDaily*. Available: http://www.sciencedaily.com/releases/2010/09/100908160358.htm.

87 Solomon, M. R., Bamossy, G., & Askegaard, S. (1999). *Consumer behavior: A European perspective.* Upper Saddle River, NJ: Prentice Hall.

88 Peck, J. & Childers, T. L. (2008). Effects of sensory factors on consumer behavior: If it tastes, smells, sounds, and feels like a duck, then it must be a . . . . In C. P. Haugtvedt, P. M. Herr, & F. R. Kardes (Eds.), *Handbook of consumer psychology* (pp. 193–219). New York: Psychology Press.

89 Klatzy, R. L. & Lederman, S. J. (1992). Stages of manual exploration in haptic object identification. *Perception & Psychophysics*, *52*, 661–670. Klatzy, R. L. & Lederman, S. J. (1993). Toward a computational model of constraint-driven exploration and haptic object identification. *Perception*, *22*, 597–621.

90 McCabe, D. B. & Nowlis, S. M. (2003). The effect of examining actual products or product descriptions on consumer preference. *Journal of Consumer Psychology*, *13*, 431–439. Peck, J. & Childers, T. L. (2003). To have and to hold: The influence of haptic information on product judgments. *Journal of Marketing*, *67*, 35–48.

91 Peck, J., & Childers, T. L. (2003).

92 Peck, J., & Childers, T. L. (2005). Self-report and behavioral measures in product evaluation and haptic information: Is what I say how I feel? *Advances in Consumer Research*, *32*, 247.

93 Cain Miller, C. (2010, September 1). To win over users, gadgets have to be touchable. *The New York Times*. Available: http://www.nytimes.com/2010/09/01/technology/01touch.html.

94 Streitfeld, D. (2013, December 13). Digitally, books remain strangely familiar. *The International New York Times*, pp. 1, 16.

95 Hamid, M. (2013, December 31). How do e-books change the reading experience. *The International New York Times*. Available: http://www.nytimes.com/2014/01/05/books/review/how-do-e-books-change-the-reading-experience.html.

96 Klinkenborg, V. (2013, August 10). Books to have and to hold. *The New York Times*. Available: http://www.nytimes.com/2013/08/11/opinion/sunday/books-to-have-and-to-hold.html.

97 Rawsthorn, A. (2012, June 18). When form trumps function. *The International New York Times*, p. 13.

98 Adams, M. (2004, July 14). The top ten technologies: #8 computer/human interface systems. *Natural News*. Available: http://www.naturalnews.com/000304_technology_movement_eye.html.

99 Norman, D. A. (2010, May–June). Natural user interfaces not natural. *Interactions*, *17*, 6–10.

100 Adams, M. (2004, July 14).

101 Rehak, J. (2002, March 23). The recall that started them all. *International Herald Tribune*, p. 15.

102 Johnson & Johnson. (1982). *The Tylenol comeback*. New Brunswick, NJ: Johnson & Johnson Corporate Public Relations.

103 A more complete discussion of Johnson & Johnson's approach can be found in Kimmel, A. J. (2004). *Rumors and rumor control: A manager's guide to understanding and combatting rumors*. Mahwah, NJ: Lawrence Erlbaum Associates.

104 McFadden, R. D. (1986, February 18). Johnson is ending all capsules sold over the counter. *The New York Times*, pp. A1, B4.

105 Rehak, J. (2002, March 23).

106 Underhill, P. (2009). *Why we buy: The science of shopping*. New York: Simon & Schuster, p. 40.

107 Peck, J. & Childers, T. L. (2008), p. 193.

108 Food Marketing Institute. (2014). Supermarket facts: Industry overview 2013. Available: http://www.fmi.org/research-resources/supermarket-facts.

109 Story, L. (2007, July 3). Engaging at any speed? Commercials put to test. *The New York Times*. Available: http://www.nytimes.com/2007/07/03/business/media/03adco.html.

110 Towal, R. B., Mormann, M., & Koch, C. (2013). Simultaneous modeling of visual saliency and value computation improves prediction of economic choice. *Proceedings of the National Academy of Sciences*, *110*, E3858–E3867.

111 Sarathy, R., Terpstra, V., & Russow, L. C. (1999). *International marketing*, 9th ed. Hinsdale, IL: The Dryden Press.

112 Griffin, T. (1993). *International marketing communications*. Oxford, UK: Butterworth-Heinemann.

113 Euromonitor International. (2014, April). *Home care in Guatemala*. Available: http://www.euromonitor.com/home-care-in-guatemala/report.

114 Euromonitor International. (2014, April). *Laundry care in Brazil*. Available: http://www.euromonitor.com/laundry-care-in-brazil/report.

115 Byron, E. (2011, February 23). Whitens, brightens and confuses. *The Wall Street Journal*. Available: http://online.wsj.com/news/articles/SB10001424052748703373404576148363319407354.

116 Schwartz, B. (2004). *The paradox of choice: Why more is less*. New York: HarperCollins.

117 Stealthy. (2007, August 6). Toothpaste caps. *myLot*. www.mylot.com/post/1233140/toothpaste-caps.

118 Coelho do Vale, R., Pieters, R., & Zeelenberg, M. (2008). Flying under the radar: Perverse package size effects on consumption self-regulation. *Journal of Consumer Research, 35*, 380–390.

119 Wansink, B. & Chandon, P. (2006). Can "low-fat" nutrition labels lead to obesity? *Journal of Marketing Research, 43*, 605–617.

120 Coca-Cola Great Britain. (2010). History of the Coca-Cola logo. Available: http://www.coca-cola.co.uk/125/history-of-coca-cola-logo.html.

121 Seitz, M. Z. (2007, September 12). Helvetica (2007): The life and times of a typeface. *The New York Times*. Available: http://www.nytimes.com/2007/09/12/movies/12helv.html

122 Dunn, M. (1982, July 23). Dish detergent mistaken for lemon juice. *Kentucky News Era*, p. 5.

123 Elliott, S. (2009, February 22). Tropicana discovers some buyers are passionate about packaging. *The New York Times*. Available: http://www.nytimes.com/2009/02/23/business/media/23adcol.html.

124 Levins, H. (2009, February 26). Peter Arnell explains failed Tropicana package design. *AdAge*. Available: http://adage.com/article/video/peter-arnell-explains-failed-tropicana-package-design/134889/.

125 Gidman, J. (2009, March 16). Packaging: Lessons from Tropicana's fruitless design. *Interbrand Brandchannel*. Available: http://www.brandchannel.com/features_effect.asp?pf_id=469.

126 Advertising Educational Foundation. (1990). *Behind the scenes: The advertising process at work*. Available: http://www.aef.com/on_campus/classroom/educational_materials/1755.

127 Parsons, T. (2009), p. 53.

128 Goodfellow, P. (2013). *Avian architecture: How birds design, engineer and build*. Lewes, East Sussex, UK: Ivy Press.

129 Rawsthorn, A. (2009, May 30). The demise of "form follows function." *The New York Times*. Available: http://www.nytimes.com/2009/06/01/arts/01iht-DESIGN1.html.

5

CONSUMERS AS ACTIVE PARTICIPANTS IN THE PRODUCT DESIGN PROCESS

By the end of this chapter, you will:

- become aware of the multi-faceted nature of the prosuming consumer as consultant, co-creator, and creator;
- recognize the importance of listening to and engaging consumers in the processes of product conception, design, and marketing;
- gain insight into methods for advancing inclusive product design;
- appreciate the emerging role of crowdsourcing and open innovation in the product co-creation process;
- understand the nature of product customization and consumer personalization and their impact on product design.

> We see a progressive blurring of the line that separates producer from consumer. We see the rising significance of the prosumer. And beyond that we see an awesome change looming that will transform even the role of the market itself in our lives and in the world system.
>
> *(Alvin Toffler, futurist, 1980)*[1]

> The power is with the consumer. Marketers and retailers are scrambling to keep up with her. . . . Consumers are beginning in a very real sense to own our brands and participate in their creation.
>
> *(A. G. Lafley, chief executive at Procter & Gamble, 2006)*[2]

Alvin Toffler introduced the term *prosumer* in 1980, yet it took a couple of decades before the concept began to resonate within the consumer marketplace. During the ensuing years following publication of his book *The Third Wave*, Toffler's has become a prophesy foretold as we have seen a dramatic rise in technological advances that have facilitated the means by which people connect with businesses and with one another, providing consumers with new, efficient channels for engaging in conversations with product designers, manufacturers, and product and brand managers. By the early 2000s, some pundits were arguing that the term *consumer* had become archaic in the new millennium, suggestive of a passive participant in the marketing process who merely buys and consumes what is offered, "a gullet whose only purpose in life is to gulp products and crap cash."[3] Although it would be an exaggeration to say that consumers are in control— think about all those recent frustrating experiences you have had with products, salespersons, service representatives, and the like, and how helpless you may have felt at those times—it is now clear that consumers have more power than ever before and have become more active participants in the marketing process, no longer merely engaging in the consumption of products and services. Is it time to retire the word "consumer" in deference to "prosumer," as some have suggested? Probably not, yet it is an unarguable fact that prosumption—in the sense of "proactivity"—has become a well-integrated element within the profile of a growing number of consumers.

The collaborative interaction between marketers and consumers is especially evident with regard to one fundamental element of the marketing function— product. For many years, new product managers preferred to work in rather closed and secretive ways, fiercely protective of their intellectual property, insulated from external input, and content to rely on the findings of their own new concept research. Many companies still operate in this way when it comes to new product development although, sooner or later, they are likely to be left in the dust by more forward-thinking competitors. The new business environment is one in which companies have become more openly collaborative, not only with consumers, but with other companies. Don Tapscott and Anthony D. Williams famously coined the term *wikinomics* to describe how an increasing number of twenty-first-century companies are relying on a combination of mass collaboration and open-source technologies to fundamentally alter the face of marketing innovation.[4] At the heart of wikinomics (and business success) are four principles—openness, peering, sharing, and acting globally— which, according to Tapscott and Williams, effectively serve to "tap the torrent of human knowledge and translate it into new and useful applications."[5] The authors explain:

> People, knowledge, objects, devices, and intelligent agents are converging in many-to-many networks where new innovations and social trends spread with viral intensity. Organizations that have scrambled to come up with responses to new phenomena like Napster or the blogosphere should expect much more of the same—at an increasing rate—in the future.[6]

Another term that increasingly comes up in discussions of consumer/firm collaboration in the new-product development process is *customer-made*, which describes:

the phenomenon of corporations creating goods, services and experiences in close cooperation with experienced and creative consumers, tapping into their intellectual capital, and in exchange giving them a direct say in (and rewarding them for) what actually gets produced, manufactured, developed, designed, serviced, or processed.[7]

The customer-made trend is given impetus thanks to some of the benefits consumers can accrue from their participation in the collaborative process, including the status that is derived from showing off their creative skills; the guarantee that goods, services, and experiences will be tailored to their needs; monetary rewards and possible job employment for assisting companies in the development of successful innovations; and the pleasure and satisfaction that come from co-creating with preferred brands.

A growing number of businesses have gotten the message that a deeper and more sympathetic engagement with customers can result in the development of ground-breaking, inspirational products that satisfy real consumer needs, while generating brand loyalty in the process.[8] Unfortunately, a sizable number of players in the consumer products industry are still operating as if times have never changed, disinterested in or ignorant about how to engage with consumers. According to French entrepreneur Carlos Diaz's social media maturity model, businesses that engage in one-way communication with customers are operating at a "pre-social" stage, believing that by establishing a website and sending out emails without the possibility of a reply, they are sufficiently relating with consumers.[9] Needless to say, with such a strategy, customer engagement is virtually non-existent. Pre-social firms are those tenaciously clinging to the traditional "top-down" marketing philosophy described in Chapter 1, deciding what is best for consumers and what kinds of products people need and desire. A truer form of social media involvement occurs at the "engagement" or "functional" stage, which typically involves participating in two-way communication with consumers (e.g., responding to comments posted on a firm's blog or Facebook page, or participating in consumer-to-consumer conversations), with social media utilized for well-defined purposes and integrated within marketing campaigns. At this functional level of social media maturity, borders between corporate divisions fade because of the use of social media throughout a firm, the development of a social media policy, and the establishment of a structure for responding to consumers and entering into consumer conversations. At the other end of the engagement spectrum is "social advantage," a term descriptive of firms that not only actively encourage two-way communication with customers, but take advantage of opportunities to make the conversation actionable. Truly social businesses are those that engage deeply with consumers through multiple social media channels, inviting input about how products can be modified and improved, and soliciting ideas for new product innovations. For such firms, the implicit message is: "Okay, you don't like my product, let's go online to a community, understand why, and figure out a solution together."

Within the field of industrial design, the prevailing approach to product development has long adhered to the pre-social modus operandi, with designers following a primarily client-centered approach in efforts to generate desirable products, while largely neglecting the end user. By the 1960s, this short-sighted approach began to change, in no small part due to the publication of designer Henry Dreyfuss' *The Measure of Man: Human Factors in Design*.[10] Dreyfuss argued for the use of design methods based on *anthropometrics*, the study of the measurements of the human body, and his book featured numerous body measurements and drawings relating the human body to the designed environment. As a user-centric approach, this work represented an important development in facilitating the design of objects that were attuned to the requirements of users. Nonetheless, such an approach has been characterized as failing in terms of social inclusiveness, in part because designers excluded a wide range of body types and ability levels from consideration, but more so because the input of end users during the creative process was largely neglected.[11] In other words, designers continued to proceed with little attention to how and why products are actually used, whether they are meeting the needs of users, and whether they are effective. In recent years, there has been a change in the way design is perceived by businesses, as suggested by Rama Gheerawo, deputy director of the Helen Hamlyn Centre for Design:

> If a design is described as a purely aesthetic process, it makes for a one-dimensional relationship with business and society that weakens its effectiveness in both arenas. But if design is described as a way of thinking about and visualizing people's real needs and aspirations, it becomes a powerful tool for change.[12]

On the heels of this philosophical shift among industrial designers, and with evolving technologies that provide a more fully developed engagement with consumers, we have begun to enter into an era in which consumers themselves are increasingly taking on the roles of co-creators and designers. That they have come to occupy a more central place in the design process in recent decades as prosumers underlines how consumer "do-it-yourself" (DIY) creation, co-creation, and crowdsourcing have moved front and center into the strategic thinking and planning of designers and marketers. These and other developments, which envision consumers as taking on an active role in the product design process, serve as the focus for the remainder of this chapter. The discussion proceeds through a consideration of three evolving prosuming roles assumed by the product end user: consultant, co-creator, and creator.

Consumers as product consultants

As one of the new "faces" of the proactive consumer, the term "consultant" is used here to refer to the functions consumers can fulfill as product experts, advisers, counselors, and guides. For consumers to serve as effective product consultants, it is essential for designers, product manufacturers, and marketers to first recognize the utility of considering the product end user's perspective, and then to provide channels for engagement and active listening in order to have access to customer advice, recommendations, and feedback. In the context of the growing influence of social media and word-of-mouth conversations, listening to consumers has begun to occupy a central position within the strategic thinking of astute marketing professionals.[13] When asked about the secret of marketing success at the 2010 Marketing 2.0 conference in Paris, the reply of president and CEO of Procter & Gamble's Tremor brand advocacy program Steve Knox was short and simple: "Listen, listen, listen to your consumer"—a refrain that is frequently echoed by other social media experts.[14] With the rise of social networks, consumer forums, and blogging, the consumer conversation is in full swing, providing product designers, manufacturers, and marketers with numerous opportunities to follow and respond to what people are saying about products and brands (see Box 5.1).

BOX 5.1 LISTENING TO CONSUMERS

Listening to consumers is a task that is foremost on the radar of firms that recognize the potential merits of *inclusive design*, defined by The British Standards Institute as "the design of *mainstream* products and/or services that are accessible to, and *usable* by, *as many people* as reasonably possible . . . without the need for special adaptation or specialised design."[15] Inclusive design is an orientation that is followed during the product design and development process to better satisfy needs and improve the product experience across a broad range of users. As a starting point, many organizations involved in the development and marketing of products either conduct or commission market and user research to gain *consumer insight*, a term used to refer to the in-depth understanding of customers to better fulfill their needs. Although a discussion of the traditional research methodologies typically used in such efforts is beyond the scope of this book, it suffices to say that the more widely used approaches are self-report methods (such as in-depth interviews, focus group discussions, and standardized surveys) and behavioral observations in product use and shopping situations, each of which are described at length in my book *Ethical Issues in Behavioral Research* and various marketing research texts.[16]

Another approach to listening to consumers is oriented toward tapping into the ongoing consumer conversation as it naturally occurs online in the context of social networks, user forums, newsgroups, blogs, and company websites. One advantage of using these channels to listen to what consumers are saying about products and brands is that they allow one to capture consumers' opinions and

(Continued)

(Continued)

insights in a setting conducive to natural conversation. By contrast, contrived research surveys are more likely to pose questions about products and brands in terminology that is first and foremost on the mind of the researcher, not the consumer. Among the millions of Internet user forums, chat groups, and blogs that have proliferated in recent decades are a growing number specifically dedicated to brands. For the most part, such websites operate completely independently from the companies that own the brands; however, companies are increasingly recognizing the impact of these customer-created forums for discussion and have begun to use them as an informal channel for gauging consumer opinion. For example, according to executive Ken Ross of the movie rental company Netflix: "In addition to viewing blogs as another media channel, it allows us to keep our pulse on the marketplace."[17] One blog, Hacking Netflix,[18] created by a consumer in 2003, tallies more than 100,000 readers per month, with representative postings about scratched disks or torn return envelopes generating numerous comments from readers. Such online commentary provides consumers with a sense of ownership and a stake in defining the brand's image, while at the same time serving as a potentially fruitful source of feedback for the company.

Companies that fail to attend to the online commentary are missing an important opportunity to learn how consumers really feel and what they think about brands, and stand to lose valuable insight into how products and services can be improved. Experts who follow the impact of consumer websites tend to agree that the in-depth customer feedback should be embraced by firms. As professional blogger Steve Rubel suggested, a consumer forum, newsgroup, website, or blog can be viewed as a kind of "24/7 focus group that's transparent and out in the open," and it provides companies with the opportunity to find their product consultants and brand ambassadors.[19]

If those on the business and production sides of product design are to become truly serious about listening to and engaging current and potential customers, it is important to be clear about just what those terms entail. In a marketing sense, the terms are not really new, as marketers have long recognized the importance of gaining the attention of consumers (from the original hierarchy of effects models of the early 1900s) and generating consumer interest, involvement, and commitment (in the sense of marketing offers that have personal relevance and importance for targets). Once we put consumers first, the essence of marketing relationships changes. This point was emphasized by marketing consultant Joseph Jaffe, author of the 2007 book *Join the Conversation*. In his book, Jaffe argues that in contrast to traditional marketing communication, which involves a one–way, unidirectional, and carefully controlled process of marketer-initiated messaging, marketing conversation is:

a two-way dialogue or a stream of messaging between two or more parties with likeminded or shared beliefs, wants, needs, passions, or interests. Conversation is not initiated by any one person, side, or organization. It is organic, nonlinear, unpredictable, and natural.[20]

Good conversation is productive because it can result in tangible or concrete assets for a firm (see Box 5.2). According to James J. Schiro, past CEO of Zurich Financial Services, approaches for opening up the conversation with consumers can bring success because they are based on two fundamental ingredients: inclusion and listening. When asked to describe the most important leadership lesson he had learned at the helm of his financial institution, Schiro responded:

> It's the ability to listen, and to make people understand that you are listening to them. Make them feel that they are making a contribution, and then you make a decision. I don't think any one individual is so brilliant that they know all of the answers. So you've got to have a sense of inclusiveness. The other most important thing is making people understand the strategy and the message, and be out front of the people so that they actually understand the mission.[21]

BOX 5.2 BREWTOPIA'S PRODUCTIVE ENGAGEMENT

To say that listening to and engaging with consumers is productive is more than saying that it is valuable, because the inclusion of consumers in the product design process can lead to tangible, profitable results. As an example, consider the 13-week open-source marketing campaign that was launched in 2002 by the Australian start-up beer company Brewtopia.[22] The objective of the campaign was to generate demand for a custom-built boutique beer among consumers who were given the opportunity to vote on each aspect of the beer's development and marketing. The firm's founder, Liam Mulhall, and his staff distributed an email to 140 of their close friends and family, inviting them to register as members of a new beer website in exchange for the opportunity to vote on a variety of choices related to Brewtopia's as-yet non-existent benchmark beer—the name, style and taste of the beer, logo, type of bottle and packaging, pricing, where it would be sold, and so on. If the company succeeded with the launch, participants would receive a single share of stock for each vote they cast, carton of beer they purchased, and registered friend they referred.

Decisions regarding the product and its marketing were enacted immediately after votes were cast, and the details, along with a picture of the product, were immediately made known to participants. Although the campaign was

(Continued)

(Continued)

limited in scope, the email medium enabled the Brewtopia team to imbue the project with a high degree of timeliness. For example, on two occasions when the voters' decisions could not be honored due to unforeseen expenses, the company quickly emailed a personal apology and honest explanation. All registered members were then invited to a launch party in Sydney, where they could purchase the beer via mail order directly from Brewtopia.

It should be noted that Brewtopia's pre-launch campaign was followed up by post-launch actions in the form of a variety of sales growth campaigns, which included a focus on feedback from influentials, the employment of third-party press coverage to accelerate the buzz, and continued incentives to encourage the spread of word of mouth. Participants in such open collaborations typically have an intrinsic motivation to spread the word on their own as a result of their involvement in the product's design and, in Brewtopia's case, part-ownership. However, these marketing activities were essential to maintain and exploit the initial consumer excitement for the product, Blowfly Beer. Overall, Brewtopia's reliance on the principle of getting potential users involved in developing the product effectively put the successful customized brewing company on the beverage industry map. Explaining the brand's success, Liam Mulhall, a co-founder of Blowfly Beer, summed it up this way:

> You've got to keep moving [a reference to the pop star Madonna and continuous reinvention] and really listening to customers. We've gone away from selling a proprietary product to custom-made and customer-made product. People can create their own brand of beer using Blowfly as the source. A kind of mass customisation.[23]

Although Schiro's comments were specifically intended as recommendations for proper employee management, they also have resonance within the context of product development, where inclusive design now plays an increasingly vital role for firms, not only in terms of targeting a wider range of potential end user groups, but also in terms of soliciting active participation from those groups.

From a product design standpoint, the extent to which consumers are welcomed as consultants can be viewed as falling along a continuum of user involvement in the design process, which ranges from designers not considering end users at all to situations in which designers seek to collaborate with users as co-creators, with consumer participants becoming directly engaged in configuring and ultimately designing products themselves. Falling between these extremes of the continuum are opportunities in which the user is invited to consult with designers, by providing feedback and advice about existing products as well as those that are in the development process.[24] According to Keith Goffin and Fred

Lemke, authors of the book *Identifying Hidden Needs: Creating Breakthrough Products*, from the perspective of involving users in product development and design, customers vary in terms of their level of expertise and interest in products:

> it is difficult for customers to articulate the type of features they would like, particularly if they are unaware of the technological possibilities. However, some customers do have the expertise to know what is technologically possible, and others may have already modified their existing equipment to cope with its limitations. Some consumers are interested to have their views heard by their favorite companies, and yet others are even willing to assist with product development.[25]

Overall, there are a variety of ways to garner ideas from consumers and to exploit their expertise to fulfill product-related objectives and better satisfy consumer needs. These approaches are discussed below.

Reaching out to those who care

A company's coterie of loyal customers represents a ready and willing source for potential product consultants, and social networking has facilitated the means by which such individuals can be identified and engaged. Unlike more traditional marketing approaches, which are designed to bring attention to one's products and brands, social media marketing efforts tend to succeed when they spotlight loyal customers. The cosmetics firm Bare Escentuals[26] does this in part by highlighting a "Fan of the Week" post on its Facebook page to recognize top contributors to its online community, which consists of more than a half million people. Although the company's policy is not to ask directly for customer testimonials, its Facebook fans leave hundreds of them, which in turn drives traffic to the firm's resellers and shops. Bare Escentuals' fan conversations on Facebook have also resulted in numerous recommendations for improving the company's offerings.

Some firms make concerted efforts to support communities of loyal consumers of the firm's products and brands. For example, Saab maintains a close relationship with brand admirers, providing direct access to the company president for comments, supporting Saab owner clubs, sponsoring annual events at which owners are invited to display their cars and attend seminars, and soliciting feedback from dedicated owners prior to car design changes. In this way, the company gains access to community information sources and thus is in a better position to identify, and perhaps affect, the information that is being relayed to and by the community.[27]

Increasingly, potential consultants are solicited from among product and brand bloggers. Analyses of several hundred French and American bloggers have revealed that bloggers appreciate learning that a company is reading something they have written and are willing to be contacted by marketing professionals, for instance by personalized email.[28] As Sernovitz points out: "many bloggers are (pleasantly) shocked when they find out that a company is actually reading what they write. Post a note when you read something you like. Post replies and comments when you see unfair criticism."[29] A 2005 online survey of 821 bloggers conducted by Edelman and Technorati found that although a majority of respondents said they were open to receiving contacts from companies, only 16% reported that companies attempted to interact with them in a personalized way.[30] The poll also revealed that more than half of the bloggers surveyed wrote about a company or product at least once per week. In recent years, there have been more concerted efforts to connect bloggers with firms, as evidenced by the Bloggers Required website,[31] which assists companies with blogger outreach by assigning specialized blog owners to specific brands that have registered at the website. Corporate participation in the blogosphere provides an effective channel for establishing an open, ongoing dialogue with consumers.

Inclusive design toolboxes

Within the design industry in recent years, there have been efforts to advance more specific techniques and tools for involving consumers in the design process, including the British Standards online Inclusive Design Toolkit, Bill & Melinda Gates Foundation's HCD Connect, Designing With People, the Include Toolbox, the UCD Toolbox, the UX Toolbox, and the 55plus Toolbox.[32] These toolkits lay out the stages for a design process that is oriented toward developing products that match the skills and values of diverse user groups, and propose various methods for each stage. For example, the Designing With People online resource,[33] created by the Helen Hamlyn Centre for Design at the Royal College of Art, includes such user involvement methods as the user forum, which is an interactive session involving designers and users where attendees express their opinions about a variety of design issues, and the participatory design game, a prototyping kit in which participants express their needs and preferences through the actions of a board game. The participatory design game incorporates architectural models or abstract parts derived from prior research that are placed on the game board, with individual participants or small groups assigned the task of constructing different scenarios and design outcomes in a workshop setting.

The lead user approach

Like avid brand loyals and bloggers, the underlying assumption regarding lead users (a concept briefly introduced in Chapter 3) suggests that certain categories of consumers may be in a better position to serve as product consultants than others. The lead user technique, first introduced by management professor Eric von Hippel, is based on the understanding that the product insights generated by typical users tend to be limited by those users' own real-world experience.[34] For example, research on problem-solving has shown that familiarity with an object interferes with one's ability to imagine novel attributes and uses for that object; that the more recently persons have used an object in a familiar way, the more difficult it is for them to employ it in a novel way; and that typical users of existing products perform poorly on problem-solving tasks requiring them to assess unfamiliar products and their potential uses.[35] By contrast, lead users have a high level of expertise with a particular product, currently possess strong needs that are likely to become prevalent in the marketplace at some time in the future, and are already experienced at contemplating how those needs might best be satisfied. As a result, lead users can serve as need forecasters for marketers and as useful resources for providing new product concepts and design ideas. In terms of new product adoption, lead users are *innovators*—consumers who are open and willing to try new products and services as soon as they become available (see Chapter 2).

A number of leading companies around the world have pursued the lead user approach for solving ongoing product-related problems and for discovering new avenues for product design and improvement (see Box 5.3). Some firms, such as Hilti, a global building construction and maintenance products company, recruit lead users from technical institutes to consult with in-house experts, while others utilize customer surveys to identify customers who have an interest in contributing to product development.[36] Once recruited, workshops are typically held to develop product concepts, and product prototypes derived from the workshop collaborations are then tested with selected consumers.

BOX 5.3 THE LEAD USER TECHNIQUE IN ACTION

The lead user technique has been successfully utilized by firms in a variety of industries. In their book *Identifying Hidden Needs: Creating Breakthrough Products*, authors Goffin and Lemke describe the 1998 case in which LEGO engaged the services of lead users in an effort to improve the firm's successful LEGO Mindstorms robot kit. Initially, LEGO connected with four teenage users who were enthusiastic about engineering and invited them to meet with the director of Mindstorms to exchange ideas about the existing product. Subsequently, the teens were encouraged to stay in close contact with the company and asked to share their recommendations for how the product could be improved. This approach led to the launch in 2006 of a significantly different Mindstorms product that utilized an improved programming language and an advanced array of components. Despite the fact that LEGO did not offer payment to its lead users, the participants were allowed to keep the prototype product kits and were sufficiently motivated by the opportunity to have a say in the firm's decisions about product development and to influence the design of the new product.

More recently, the lead user approach was employed in the medical products industry by 3M in an attempt to address recent increased demands for

(Continued)

(Continued)

hygiene, resistance against antibiotics, and cost pressures.[37] The company used a networking approach to identify doctors working under extreme conditions, such as in developing countries, as well as users from the analogous fields of microbiology and cosmetics who assisted in the development of materials that adhere comfortably and reliably to human skin. The involvement of these lead users resulted in the development of improved protective coverings, a microbiotic-treated incisions foil, and a radical new approach for controlling individual infection that allows hygienic measures to be tailored to specific patient needs.

Within the IT industry, the lead user technique was used by Nortel Networks in developing a global system for mobile communications (GSM) tracking for use in different applications.[38] Nortel went about seeking lead users for whom the positioning of objects and the transfer of data played significant roles in their work, including so-called "storm-chasers," who locate and track tornados, and "animal trackers," who often must determine the position of wild animals from a moving vehicle. The company's collaboration with these lead users resulted in the creation of applications for mobile tracking systems that permit the transfer of multiple types of data. This included the evolution of a mobile smart system that can control various home appliances from a distance, including switching on a heater or pre-heating the oven as one leaves work at the end of the day. (In 2009, Nortel sold its GSM business to Ericsson and Kapsch for US$103 million.)

More specifically, there are four distinct stages involved in the lead user technique: (1) conducting a trend analysis (to identify relevant trends in customer and user requirements, industry, technology, etc.); (2) recruiting lead users (i.e., identifying customers who have extreme needs for particular product categories through the use of surveys, telephone interviews, and recommendations); (3) holding workshops with lead users at a company's site (i.e., subgroups are assigned to consider possible solutions relative to the trends identified by the company, with the entire group taking those solutions judged as most original and feasible and merging them into one or more concepts); and (4) developing product concepts (i.e., the most promising concepts that emerge from the workshops are tested with a wider selection of consumers to determine the relevance of the idea to mainstream users). The identification of lead users to participate in such a program is not always straightforward and can pose a significant challenge for firms attempting to use this approach. Attentiveness to customer service records and conferring with service technicians can be useful in pointing to extreme users of goods that happen to fail or break down on numerous occasions. In this sense, extreme users are those who place heavy demands on products and have significant in-depth knowledge about how to adapt products to suit a variety of needs. Lead users can also be identified through an investigation of analogous markets, social networks, and customer online forums.

In-house customer interaction centers

As a variation of sampling salons and the tryvertising approach described in Chapter 2, a number of firms have begun to establish customer interaction centers on company premises in efforts to involve consumers early in the product creation process in a close-up and personal fashion. Typically, customers are invited to a center to test products prior to their launch in the marketplace. For example, the French cosmetics company L'Oréal operates several test labs around the world to observe how consumers apply beauty products. Using this process, the company learned that many Chinese consumers have adopted the habit of washing themselves and shampooing their hair over a bowl to conserve water in cities and towns with frequent water supply interruptions. This led L'Oréal to develop an easy-to-rinse shampoo that would appeal to those consumers by satisfying an ongoing need. In 2013 L'Oréal created a research and innovation center in Mumbai that serves as a hub for developing products locally. Using "model bathrooms" in which customers are invited to test out products in the presence of observers who note their usage habits and obtain product-related feedback, this approach is oriented toward obtaining a deeper understanding of Indian consumers' beauty expectations and needs that can translate into innovative cosmetic and personal hygiene products.[39]

Other test centers similarly strive to gain consumer insight into the product design process. The Indian multi-business conglomerate ITC Ltd. set up a 3,050 square meter customer interaction center in Bangalore for its personal care division in 2011. The center includes specialized rooms for consumers to test out various elements for skin and hair products that are in development, the results of which are used to determine how the products are ultimately designed. As Godrej Industry's chief strategy officer Vivek Gambhir revealed in discussing his company's Hair Care Institute in Mumbai, "the recent rebranding of hair color brand Godrej Expert with additional benefits was a direct outcome of the research we collected at the institute."[40] As part of its product testing lab institute, Godrej also operates a Design Lab in which designers work closely with consumers in efforts to innovate new product and packaging designs.

There are some concerns that inviting consumers inside a company's premises could lead to more biased results in the testing process when compared with engaging with consumers in their homes or a neutral setting. However, such concerns are probably unwarranted in cases in which consumers are assured that their honest feedback will be given serious consideration in the design of products they evaluate and that they have a vested interest in the products' ultimate success—a point that also applies to the other consumer consulting approaches discussed in this section.

Consumers as co-creators

Another approach to engaging consumers in the product development and design process is to cede power to the consumer collective for specific decision-making tasks. This process of co-creation is commonly referred to as *crowdsourcing*, whereby tasks typically performed by employees are outsourced to consumers via an open call or challenge, and whose responses are then voted on by other consumers online (the so-called "crowd"). Returning to the different stages of social media maturity described above, such efforts reflect the most advanced maturity level, the "social advantage" or "transformation" stage, where organizations take steps to make conversations actionable through co-creation and collaborative problem-solving.[41] This approach to product design via social media channels, exemplified by well-known crowdsourcing projects such as Dell's IdeaStorm, BMW's Virtual Innovation Agency, LEGO's Mindstorms, and Starbucks' My Starbucks Idea, involves the formulation and employment of a social media strategy that eliminates divisions between internal and external stakeholders, enabling the firm to establish a truly cooperative network.[42]

One company that can be identified as a pioneer in the consumer as co-creator movement is Dell Computers, which, during the first decade of the new millennium, took steps to address some customer service issues and growing levels of consumer dissatisfaction with some of the computer maker's products by directly engaging with customers. In an initial phase, Dell attempted to resolve dissatisfaction, contain negative customer feedback, and communicate the Dell story.[43] A second phase involved an appeal for a more constructive form of consumer participation, beginning in 2007 with company founder Michael Dell's introduction of IdeaStorm.com, a website that serves as a collaborative environment by inviting consumers to tell Dell what to do. IdeaStorm provides an opportunity for people to suggest ideas for Dell products and services ("Post"), asking the general community to comment on and rate the ideas ("Vote"), and invites site visitors to find out how Dell has put consumer ideas into practice ("See"). IdeaStorm has operated as an effective tool for Dell in terms of product development (in this case, the product begins from the consumer side of the marketing equation) and customer relationship management. The success of IdeaStorm is evidenced by the numbers: to date, it has resulted in more than 21,000 ideas generated by the community, 744,500 promotions of ideas (i.e., favorable votes), 100,500 comments, and 550 ideas implemented by Dell (e.g., backlit keyboards, rubberized netbook cases, the decisions to sell Linux computers and reduce the promotional "bloatware" that clogs machines).[44] A rough breakdown of consumer-generated ideas reveals that approximately 12% received are classified as unusable (i.e., no action needed), 4% as innovative (i.e., possible game-changing ideas), and 80% as improvements (i.e., including incremental ideas for next-generation products as well as improvements for existing products and services).[45]

An analysis of the progress of IdeaStorm over time revealed two outcomes that companies must prepare for if they choose to follow in Dell's footsteps by initiating a similar participatory mechanism: (1) an initially dramatic spike of ideas (e.g., Dell received about 2,000 ideas within IdeaStorm's first two weeks), and (2) the community's expectations for an immediate response to, or engagement with, their ideas.[46] Timely feedback, clear status updates, and "thank you" mechanisms are thus essential, as well as providing a link to the company's blog. Dell now provides a means for customers to rate its products on the IdeaStorm site, and has begun to integrate IdeaStorm with social networks so as to extend the reach of the community (e.g., by encouraging friends to participate on ideas) and use the technology to address specific business needs and interest groups (e.g., soliciting ideas for the health care industry; partnering with the University of Texas for a competition to solicit innovative ideas that can change the world).

Dell's IdeaStorm has spawned a variety of similar programs on the heels of its success in generating participation from the online community. A nearly identical program, My Starbucks Idea, was initiated by Starbucks soon after IdeaStorm began to reap benefits for Dell. Like IdeaStorm, My Starbucks Idea solicits customer ideas, shares them with visitors to the website, invites discussion, and implements the ideas that receive a sufficient number of favorable votes from the community (e.g., a spicier chai offering, more Verismo pods per pack, and new sliced loaf cake recipes). Another co-creator program is PlayStation.Blog Share,[47] which invites PlayStation gamers to submit their ideas for improving PlayStation products. Launched in 2010 as an integral element of PlayStation's enormously successful blog, the sharing program allows visitors to the blog to submit ideas to the PlayStation.Blog team about anything related to the brand. The "submit your idea" program is described on the blog's website as follows:

> Do you have an idea for how to improve the PlayStation experience? If so, Share it! PlayStation.Blog Share is a place to formally submit your best ideas on how we can improve all PlayStation products. It's also a place where you can discover and vote on other people's ideas, as well as communicate with us and other PlayStation fans about how to bring great ideas to life. You can only submit one idea per week. Make it count![48]

Submitted ideas are posted so that other users can vote, enabling the PlayStation. Blog team to track their popularity as well as the volume of interest they generate within the PlayStation community. The users who submit the most popular ideas are acknowledged by PlayStation at the top of a leader board that appears on the website.

A number of companies have jumped on the crowdsourcing bandwagon during the past decade, going beyond merely soliciting and capturing consumer input to inform product and packaging designs, service experiences, and advertising promotions, by offering consumers a more active role in their co-creation (see Box 5.4). There are no hard-and-fast guidelines for a crowdsourcing campaign, meaning that the process provides great leeway in terms of the scope and the specific nature of its operation. For example, in 2014 the snack foods company Frito-Lay, which regularly solicits consumer input on flavor extensions, launched its "Do Us A Favor" campaign, inviting its Facebook fans to devise an original potato chip flavor, with the winner standing to earn US$1 million or 1% of the chip's yearly net sales, whichever is higher. The initial attempts at this promotion globally inspired more than 12 million flavor idea submissions.[49] The campaign, which incorporates an easy-to-use, engaging app for portable devices, cedes nearly complete control to the "crowd," with participants invited to name their flavor, choose its ingredients, promote it, and help devise other marketing elements for the new Frito-Lay addition.

BOX 5.4 MOUNTAIN DEW'S "DEWMOCRACY" CROWDSOURCING CAMPAIGN

In what has proven to be one of the more unique and successful online crowdsourcing efforts, PepsiCo launched its "DEWmocracy" campaign in 2007, empowering consumers to choose among ideas for new beverage flavors for its Mountain Dew soda brand. The execution of the campaign involved much more than simply having fans of the brand cast their votes in a poll for their preferred new flavor, instead taking advantage of the collective intelligence of consumer communities in several phases and on various levels. Described in a PepsiCo press release as "the first-ever interactive, story-based online game that will result in a consumer-generated beverage innovation," it was clear from the start that the firm intended to make heavy use of social media channels and active consumer participation.[50] This was accomplished with the creation of a three-minute film involving the collaboration of actor/director Forest Whitaker, an online role-playing game, and social networking devices that engaged the online crowd.

In the campaign's first phase, the short film appeared online, presenting a scenario in which a savior arises to rebel against a fictitious oppressive governmental regime, promising an elixir to reintroduce creativity and "restore the soul of mankind." At the same time, a massive multi-player game was launched on the "DEWmocracy" website, which involved having participants navigate through various online "worlds," selecting the attributes they desired for an ideal Mountain Dew beverage, including flavor, ingredients, color, name, and logo design. According to PepsiCo, the "DEWmocracy" website received more than 700,000 unique visitors, with 200,000 registered users participating in the first phase of the game.[51] The second phase consisted of narrowing down the submitted choices to three flavor finalists, which were given fan-chosen names, colors, and overall designs: Voltage, Supernova, and Revolution. The three flavors were released in small batches and sampled by the public throughout North America on a short-term basis during the summer of 2008. Those who had tasted the samples were invited to visit the campaign's official website to vote for their favorite, with Voltage ultimately emerging as the winner, which PepsiCo subsequently added to its Mountain Dew offerings.

As a follow-up to the successful campaign, PepsiCo soon after launched "DEWmocracy II" in 2009, which was similarly oriented to having Mountain Dew fans design and select the next new flavor to be added to the brand's line. In this case, Mountain Dew started out with seven experimental new flavors and distributed applications in 17 US cities from which "super fan" Web influencers were selected to test out the new flavors.[52] The 50 selected applicants were mailed test kits consisting of the seven flavors, along with video cameras with which they were to record their reactions to each flavor and upload the resulting video commentaries on the Internet. The 50 testers then were assigned to one of three "Flavor Nations," each representing one of the three most favored flavors (Typhoon, Distortion, and White Out) from among the original seven, and were asked to promote their flavor throughout their social networks and online communities. At the same time, samples of the three finalists were distributed to the public. White Out emerged as the flavor that received the most votes by the public on such online channels as Twitter, Facebook, and DEW Lab's YouTube channel, and was subsequently made a permanent addition to the Mountain Dew product line. The "super fans" were responsible for decisions that were made about the flavors at every step of the campaign: they named and designed the three finalist flavors and were responsible for all aspects of marketing and branding of the new White Out flavor.

PepsiCo's "DEWmocracy" program turned out to be a social media hit, resulting in an increase in Mountain Dew's social networking presence in a competitive product category. As described by the brand's marketing director, Brett O'Brien, in a 2010 interview:

> With "DEWmocracy II," you started to see a great deal of people feel like they could have a say in the direction of the brand, now that their voices meant something. You saw a great increase in traction on Facebook and we had an almost 800,000 fans increase from the time we started the program in June 2009 until today, where we are at 920,000 Facebook fans. And honestly, what I think has driven that has been word of mouth and enthusiasm for the brand.[53]

Crowdsourcing approaches like "DEWmocracy" communicate the message to consumers that participating firms are willing to give them the power not only to choose what they want, but to play a significant part in creating it themselves. As one observer adroitly noted regarding "DEWmocracy II," White Out "was chosen for the people, by the people."[54]

Some companies cede control to consumers not for the creation of specific products, but to satisfy other objectives, such as management of a corporate online social network presence, which can provide openings for further customer engagement. The confectionery firm Skittles tapped the consumer collective by designating the redesign of its corporate website as entirely open source, incorporating widgets for capturing unmoderated consumer-generated content feeds from Twitter, Facebook, and YouTube. The website connects visitors to Skittles-related digital content on several other social media websites created and managed by consumers, including a Facebook fan page that serves as Skittles' website homepage, a news update from Twitter, and a product information tab that is fed from Wikipedia. By leaving its website content completely in the hands of consumers, Skittles' online presence reflects the consumer conversation about the brand in real time, with corporate messaging noticeably absent in the image of the firm that is presented to the public.[55]

Some companies, such as Coca-Cola and Ferrero's Nutella, have relinquished control over the creation and management of their social media sites to brand devotees, offering assistance and input only when requested. When Coca-Cola decided to launch its Facebook fan page, it was learned that such a page already existed, having previously been created by two young Coke enthusiasts. Rather than demanding that the duo shut their page down or attempting to take control over it, Coca-Cola gave them its blessing and empowered them to keep running the Facebook fan page. The company also rewarded the fan page creators by flying them to corporate headquarters in Atlanta, giving them a tour of the facilities, and inviting them to make a video about the history of the fan page, all of which conveyed the message to future brand enthusiasts that cooperative engagement with Coca-Cola can result in rewards and recognition.

Crowdsourcing has to date become a common aspect of the connected marketing toolbox for several of the world's top global brands, as evidenced by the following sampling of campaigns:

- Nescafé's "Reinvent Instant Coffee" campaign—Nescafé challenged the eYeka online global community (consumer members who offer their creative skills to solve brand-related problems) to propose ideas on how to reinvent instant coffee for in-home use.
- Nespresso's design competitions—Nespresso launched its first design competition in 2005, aimed at imagining the future of coffee rituals. Some of the novel submissions included the Nespresso InCar coffee machine and the Nespresso Chipcard, a device to store coffee preferences for registered consumers and communicate with a central database to produce a personalized cup of coffee for them. For its second competition in 2008, first prize was awarded to two French students from the Université Toulouse Le Mirail for their creative design of a coffee maker resembling a thermo-sensitive work of art that gradually changes appearance according to the heat of the water.

- General Electric's "Healthymagination" program—GE's six-year, US$6 billion program focused on collaborating with consumers and professionals to find new ideas in health diagnosis, patient stratification, and cancer treatment ("Committed to creating better health for more people. Together"). For example, as part of the program's US$1 billion Cancer Commitment, five seed winners were awarded US$100,000 each for their breakthrough work in emerging breast cancer research innovation.
- Nokia's "Calling All Innovators" contest—Nokia regularly launches competitions inviting innovative consumers (students, entrepreneurs, Facebook fans, etc.) to devise new phones and applications for mobile devices, with winners offered large cash payments, devices, and other prizes. During the summer of 2005, the firm created the Nokia Concept Lounge,[56] inviting designers from the Benelux countries to share ideas and design the next new cool phone. The winning concept, chosen from among entries submitted around the world, was a flexible wristband-style phone, the Nokia 888, created by a Turkish designer, Tamer Nakisci.
- Google's "Doodle 4 Google" competition—Google's program annually challenges schoolchildren to create a doodle in response to a particular theme. For example, the 2014 challenge was "If I Could Invent One Thing to Make the World a Better Place …." The 11-year-old winner received a US$30,000 college scholarship and a US$50,000 Google for Education technology grant for her school for an animated doodle showing her vision of a machine to help clean polluted water. Google also donated US$40,000 in her name for a project intended to provide clean water to schools in Bangladesh.
- LEGO's "LEGO Factory"—The toy manufacturer offers this create-and-sell service, which invites children and other building enthusiasts to design their own virtual LEGO models, using free downloadable software. Pending approval from LEGO, the models then can be ordered from the company and shipped in custom packaging. Creators can upload their models online to share with the community of LEGO users, who can purchase each others' creations as an actual set or download models to view or modify.

Types of crowdsourcing

The examples above reflect the breadth of possibilities for corporate approaches to crowdsourcing. Despite the numerous forms that crowdsourcing might take, it is possible to distinguish between four broad types of crowdsourcing campaigns: (1) crowdsource design, (2) crowdfunding, (3) microtasking, and (4) open innovation.

Crowdsource design

Nearly anything—a company logo, products, product packaging, in-store displays, websites, corporate facilities, advertisements, fashion, and so on—can be designed. Crowdsource design involves sending out an open call to professionals, or non-professional consumers who assume the role of designers, to submit a design for something the company is developing or intends to change. This approach is typically more cost-efficient than engaging a design firm or an online freelancer and is likely to result in a wider selection of creative, high-quality ideas and concepts. Nokia's "Calling All Innovators" campaign represents an example of this approach, whereby Nokia obtains original design concepts for new mobile phones and applications from the very people who will be using them.

Western companies may have turned their focus overseas during recent decades, seeking out cheap labor in India, China, and southeast Asia, but today, as *Wired* magazine contributor Jeff Howe points out, it really does not matter where the laborers are located, be it down the street or in Indonesia, so long as they are connected to an online network.[57] Some people have dubbed the emerging consumer generation as "Generation-C," referencing the rise of the consumer as creator (see Box 5.7). According to Howe, this new consumer face owes its arrival to technological advances in product design software, digital cameras, online publishing tools, and the like which, in effect, are serving to destroy the monopoly of professional designers and breaking down the cost barriers that once separated professionals and amateur creators:

> Hobbyists, part-timers, and dabblers suddenly have a market for their efforts, as smart companies in industries as disparate as pharmaceuticals and television discover ways to tap the latent talent of the crowd. The labor isn't always free, but it costs a lot less than paying traditional employees. It's not outsourcing; it's crowdsourcing.[58]

A recent example of a crowdsource design campaign was initiated by the German automaker BMW in 2012, with a pair of contests seeking ideas for cars specifically designed for the megacities of the future. Dubbed the "BMW Urban Driving Experience Challenge," the company offered a US$7500 top prize and a trip to Munich, along with runner-up prizes, for a future car design sketch, perhaps embellished with a video or animated GIF, consisting of features that would be functional on a premium car consistent with impending lifestyle shifts in future urban environments. The megacity concept is based on trends reflecting lifestyle changes in young adult millennials, an increasing number of whom are gravitating to larger urban areas where there are better economic opportunities for employment and more desirable settings for raising a family. By attracting young, talented urban dwellers, it is expected that such megacities will spawn an improved economy and higher standard of living. Among the concerns a futuristic car designer would have to accommodate are those related to problems of pollution and parking—cars of the future will need to be energy-efficient, non-pollutant, small, and smart (e.g., capable of knowing where available parking spaces are located). BMW specified that for a design to be seriously considered, "feature or form must be realistic; i.e., must be grounded in some science. Vehicles that are driven telepathically from a distance, for example, are not realistic."[59]

For its campaign, BMW partnered with Local Motors of Phoenix, an auto-maker that sells the crowdsourced Rally Fighter, a US$75,000 vehicle that can be built by two people in one week in a microfactory, with the assistance of an expert. Companies like BMW have relied heavily on more traditional research approaches, such as focus groups, for obtaining ideas and insight from consumers; however, such approaches are typically constrained by having a small number of participants who are asked to respond to ideas that are already under consideration by the automaker. This limits the degree of change that could be effected by creative individuals responding to an open challenge.

The potential utility of crowdsource design for business and socially oriented problem-solving was evidenced by a campaign launched in 2013 by the Bill & Melinda Gates Foundation, which involved a challenge to the online crowd to create a condom that men would actually use. According to the foundation, the crowdsourcing contest was aimed at decreasing sexually transmitted diseases and unintended pregnancies through the creation of "a next-generation condom that significantly preserves or enhances pleasure."[60] In response to the challenge, the foundation received 812 condom design recommendations, with 11 winning applicants, including an Indian condom manufacturer, American chemical engineers, and British design consultants, each receiving a US$10,000 award and the possibility of up to US$1 million if their product ideas are ultimately developed. Many of the ideas recommended alternative materials to latex, with one winning proposal consisting of an "ultrasensitive reconstituted collagen condom" that would be made from collagen fibers that would feel like skin and a "wrapping condom" made of polyethylene plastic that clings like Saran Wrap rather than squeezes. For the most part, the submitted proposals tackled ongoing product-related problems, such as the need to improve lubrication, provide internal and external friction, and enhance heat transfer.

Some makers of beloved brands have bypassed the opportunity to engage with consumers prior to making significant alterations in familiar products or brand signifiers, such as logos, brand names, packaging, ingredients, or components, and have learned the hard way that customers usually know better what they want or need than the companies that serve them. In Chapter 4, I mentioned how some firms have encountered resistance from loyal customers after altering long-standing brand logos. Such was the case in October 2010, when Gap, the well-known American clothier, made a business move it would immediately regret: it unveiled a new company logo that was intended to convey a "more contemporary, modern expression." This consisted of replacing the iconic logo in white capitalized serif type on a navy blue background with one featuring black Helvetica lettering partially superimposed on a small blue square at the right-hand corner. According to company spokesperson Louise Callagy, it was believed that the logo change would signify Gap's transition from "classic, American design to modern, sexy, cool."[61] However, as soon as the announcement was made, negative reactions spread like wildfire on the Internet, with critics posting numerous comments that derided the new logo design and mocked Gap's decision-making approach through thousands of tweets appearing on Twitter and Facebook status updates. A marketing move that Gap had hoped would generate praise and positive feedback from the consuming public had instead brought an embarrassing degree of negative publicity. According to Sandra Fathi, president of the social media firm Affect Strategies: "It shows you the power of social media. What people might have privately said walking into a store—now they can actually share their view with others and rally around a cause to change back the logo."[62] To its credit, Gap had listened to the consumer conversation and quickly reacted. Within days, the company announced that it would be returning to its twenty-year-old original logo design, stating on its Facebook page: "Ok. We've heard loud and clear that you don't like the new logo. We've learned a lot from the feedback. We only want what's best for the brand and our customers . . . we're bringing back the Blue Box tonight."[63]

Gap, like other companies that have run into similar problems after deciding to take a significant marketing action without first consulting with customers, could have circumvented a public relations disaster by outsourcing the task to consumers through some sort of engaging crowdsource design effort. As it turns out, this is exactly what Gap decided to do, but only after the initial wave of customer backlash. Within days after negative comments began appearing online, Gap announced that it would welcome design suggestions from its brand followers, announcing on its Facebook page:

> We know this logo created a lot of buzz and we're thrilled to see passionate debates unfolding! So much so we're asking you to share your designs. We love our version, but we'd like to see other ideas. Stay tuned for details in the next few days . . . .[64]

Instead of following through with this effort, however, Gap announced less than a week later that it had decided to revert back to the old logo—a move that further alienated consumers. By reneging on the offer to let customers decide what the logo should look like, Gap further undermined those customers' sense of ownership and pride in the brand. In light of the formidable power of social media, a better tactic for Gap would have been to solicit feedback about a logo change through such channels as Facebook and Twitter before taking the one-sided step of unveiling the new design. Given that the company went back to the original logo anyway, such a strategy might have saved Gap millions of dollars and untold embarrassment throughout the online social media community.

Crowdfunding

A form of peer-to-peer collaborative investment, crowdfunding involves inviting people, typically through an online channel, to donate a small amount of money to help fund an inventor's project. Using a particular crowdfunding platform, a monetary amount is set as a goal along with any reward that is offered to donors. Unless the project attracts 100% of the goal by a designated deadline (typically less than 60 days), all of the donations are returned and the creator walks away with nothing. As an example, if a musician wants to raise US$20,000 within one-and-a-half months to record a new CD or to create a short documentary film, crowdfunding represents a way that goal could be achieved. There are various types of crowdfunding approaches, including those that are reward-based (i.e., entrepreneurs pre-sell a product or service to launch a business concept without having to forgo equity or shares), equity-based (i.e., donors receive finance in the form of equity in exchange for contributing money to a project or company), donation-based (i.e., people raise money for personal or social causes, such as covering health care costs), and credit-based (i.e., raising credit for loans by non-bank entities, with lenders matched with a pool of investors who are willing to accept credit terms).

Crowdfunding has been given impetus in recent years in large part as a result of certain economic realities, including widespread job cuts and stricter banking terms, which have driven innovators to seek funding from online investment communities. Although there are no guarantees that well-known crowdfunding platforms such as Kickstarter and Angel's Den will generate sufficient funding, they have proven to be viable options even for more radical, creative ventures and can provide a means for testing ideas that otherwise would not draw much attention through more conventional channels. Kickstarter, for example, which is limited to fundraising for creative projects, has brokered nearly US$1.2 billion in investment pledges since its launch in 2009 (see Box 5.5).[65] Angel's Den, established in 2007, initially began as a funding model that matched business owners and investors online, but ultimately introduced the concept of SpeedFunding, whereby innovators and entrepreneurs present their ideas to Angel investors on a one-to-one basis. At the time of this writing, the platform provides a pool of 6,000 business "angels" with investment funds. Scottish entrepreneur Ryan O'Rorke obtained £150,000 in funding through the Angel's Den platform, enabling him to launch Flavorly, a successful gourmet food and niche beer business. O'Rorke's project was the quickest to be equity crowdfunded in the UK, having reached its funding target after only one day of appealing to investors. According to O'Rorke, who was initially able to raise only £500 from private investors and his own savings, crowdfunding has several advantages:

> By going down the crowd route we've gained access to a pool of 12 investors who together bring financial, marketing and customer acquisition skills to the table. For a young company like ours, that's invaluable. We wanted the added value, the connections, the help with marketing. The risk of seeking investment is that the due-diligence process can take months and investors could still say no at the end of it. And if you go down the crowdsourcing route you need to be ready to act once you've raised the funds. But this is a channel that's worked well for us.[66]

BOX 5.5 OCULUS RIFT: A KICKSTARTER SUCCESS STORY

According to data provided by Kickstarter, one of the original and better-known crowdfunding platforms, less than 40% of the more than 187,000 project applications posted on the Kickstarter website are successfully funded, with a majority of those that are funded raising less than US$10,000.[67] At the time of this writing, 1,452 projects had successfully raised funding exceeding US$100,000. A majority of Kickstarter-funded projects fall within the categories of the arts (music, film, theater), publishing, design, and technology. A range of other project types have received Kickstarter support, in categories such as food, fashion, crafts, and restaurants. Although about 10% of project applications never receive a funding pledge, about 80% of those that raise at least one-fifth of their funding objective tend to go on to be successfully funded. Unlike some other crowdfunding platforms, investors receive no monetary return for supporting a project, although incentives may take more psychologically gratifying forms. For example, an investor who supports the making of a documentary film may receive a copy of the film or the inclusion of his or her name in the film credits, whereas a speaking role or appearance as an extra may be available for a fictional film. One lauded Kickstarter story is the Oscar-nominated documentary film about the 2011 revolution in Egypt, *The Square*, which raised over US$100,000 through Kickstarter.[68]

On the technology front, one of the more successful Kickstarter-funded projects is Oculus VR's Rift, an immersive reality headset for video games, funded in September 2012 after meeting a US$250,000 goal with pledges donated by 9,522 backers.[69] Based on a technology that provides immersive stereoscopic 3-D rendering in a head-mounted device, the Rift offers a high-end virtual reality experience for the average video game player, at a price that is more affordable than other existing virtual reality devices. According to Oculus VR founder Palmer Luckey, who designed the Rift in collaboration with developer John Carmack, one of the main appeals of using Kickstarter, in addition to the obvious financial one, was to get development kits for his new product into the hands of developers as quickly as possible so that they could try out the device for themselves and begin to integrate support into their games. Oculus also hoped to receive feedback from the developers that could be incorporated into the design of the final consumer version of the product. In exchange for their US$275 or higher financial pledge, developers received the Rift development kit, a copy of the first Oculus-ready game, Doom 3, and other perks depending on the size of the donation. Pledges of lesser amounts received minor tokens of appreciation, such as Oculus T-shirts and posters, or a promise to be kept informed about the company's developments.

Although its pioneering Rift device was still only limited to release as a development prototype, Oculus VR was acquired by Facebook in March

2014 for US$2 billion—a deal that included US$400 million in cash, 23.1 million common shares of Facebook (valued at US$1.6 billion), and additional possible monetary incentives. According to some, the Oculus deal represents an important milestone for crowdfunding because it proves the model's viability and is likely to attract more entrepreneurs to Kickstarter and other platforms. However, not everyone was happy about this deal at the time, and the criticisms point to some of the imperfections in the crowdfunding model that will have to be addressed in order for this promising form of crowdsourcing to continue to evolve. For example, some Oculus Rift backers were critical of the sale of what was originally perceived as a creative start-up to a corporate tech giant, viewing the move as a kind of sell-out, whereas others criticized the fact that they had no say in Oculus' financial decisions. According to one frequent Kickstarter backer:

> I felt a little used, I guess. Maybe I was naive. I thought it was more just like someone doing it for a hobby and just wanted to do something fun for the community. I didn't know it was going to turn into a $2 billion deal.[70]

Such comments could portend a growing skepticism among potential backers that certain projects are more commercially oriented, whereas their motivations as donors are more altruistic in nature or focused on a social cause that they wish to support. Adding insult to injury, whereas the venture capital firms Spark Capital and Matrix Partners stood to make a 2,000% return on their early investments in Oculus VR, the 9,522 Kickstarter donors received nothing from the Facebook deal, with a majority left with nothing more than a T-shirt or poster. As one disgruntled user on Kickstarter's comments page noted: "I think I would have rather bought a few shares of Oculus than my now worthless $300 obsolete VR headset."

Despite these criticisms, defenders of the crowdfunding model point out that backers need to have clearer expectations and a better understanding of their role in the process from the outset, as one Kickstarter adroitly observed:

> Kickstarter is for doing exactly what it's called. It's for kick starting projects and the companies that create them. We "donated" (really we just preordered a product) and they used the money to create the product and deliver it to us. Now that the product we paid for is finished and in our hands we are no longer entitled to any say about what the company does. We are not investors in the company. . . . You have no extra entitlements or rights because you were a backer. You should not feel personally insulted by this deal.[71]

Another crowdfunding success story is a new product project initiated by Bike Systems, a small UK company that offers innovative technology for motorbike enthusiasts. As an initial venture, owner Dave Vout developed the idea for Bike-HUD, a "head-up" display for motorcyclists that projects information in a display within the rider's helmet, including speed, revolutions per minute, and speed camera alerts. Vout initially built a prototype using a 3-D printer and conducted feasibility studies and research into the legalities of the product. With an initial goal of £90,000, he eventually obtained financial backing through Seedrs,[72] a European equity crowdfunding platform through which early-stage start-ups are funded. To date, over a hundred start-ups have met their investment targets on Seedrs. Following two rounds of funding, Vout ended up raising a total of £120,000 from 180 small investors. Summing up his experience, Vout stated: "If I was raising more funds, I'd definitely go the crowd route first. Otherwise, it's a case of who you know rather than the strength of your idea, and that's very frustrating."[73]

There are other variations on the crowdfunding horizon that suggest the range of possibilities for this type of consumer involvement in the product development process. One approach is exemplified by Crowdemand, a consumer-powered fashion website that provides a low-risk venue for fashion designer experimentation, using a method akin to Kickstarter to connect designers directly with consumers. Unlike the typical crowdfunding platforms, Crowdemand does not involve consumer donations to determine whether a product venture gets off the ground, but rather calls for votes and pre-orders. Designers are invited to post their work on the website, where consumers can pre-order items during a two-week campaign period. If the number of orders reaches a specified number, the designs go into production and are shipped to customers. Crowdemand suggests an interesting concept, as observed by co-founder Yaniv Reeis: "sharing for the purpose of getting something made," with customers deciding what they want for themselves. As Reeis further explains: "It's all about consumers and their own self expression. What we're trying to do here is let the market dictate what consumers really want."[74]

Microtasking

This form of crowdsourcing involves breaking up a project into many clearly defined, small tasks that are then delegated to the wider consumer community, with participants receiving a small payment for each completed task (usually no more than a few cents). The tasks might include scanning images, proofreading, transcribing audio files, and so on. A website owner who has thousands of photos on his or her site that need captions can ask thousands of people each to add a caption to an individual photo.

Microtasking is an approach that is relatively inexpensive and has proven to be quite efficient in terms of speed and accuracy. An important component of microtasking as a form of crowdsourcing is that the tasks that are involved cannot be completed by a computer software program, but require human participation and intelligence, as is the case for the creation of textual content that describes a photo or the determination of whether two images correspond to the same place or setting. It is for this reason that one of the more popular microtasking platforms, Amazon Mechanical Turk (AMT), refers to the tasks that it delegates out as "Human Intelligence Tasks" (HIT).

According to AMT's vice president Sharon Chiarella, Amazon's platform divides its microtasks into four types: (1) translation tasks (smaller fragments of a text, such as sentences or paragraphs, are translated, rather than the text as a whole); (2) transcription tasks (the content of an audio, video, or image file is transcribed into writing); (3) research tasks (volunteers are solicited to respond to standardized questionnaires, such as those that are a component of a behavioral or social science study); and (4) classification tasks (a variety of categorization undertakings, such as adding tags to describe images or the aforementioned captioning of photographs). A number of microtasking websites have emerged on the Internet in recent years, providing opportunities for a widely diverse and flexible crowd consisting of the unemployed, retirees, and individuals in developed and developing nations who are seeking to supplement their income. Microtasking websites typically earn money by charging a fee to the task creator.

Open innovation

As the name suggests, open innovation is a type of crowdsourcing in which the creative process does not originate with a specific product concept or goal in mind, but is an open-ended effort oriented toward discovering new ideas for business opportunities. The open innovation process encourages collaborations between individuals from different fields and levels of expertise, including designers, investors, inventors, marketers, and consumers.

An increasing number of firms are beginning to recognize the merits of establishing open collaborations with external innovators. One example is the consumer goods company Procter & Gamble, which launched an open innovation program, "Connect+Develop," in 2001.[75] As defined by P&G, open innovation is "the practice of tapping externally developed intellectual property to accelerate internal innovation and sharing our internally developed assets and know-how to help others outside the Company."[76] In addition to soliciting ideas from innovators about the company's needs posted on the Connect+Develop website, P&G employs a global team assigned with the task of searching for innovations from a variety of prospective partners. According to a P&G press release, since the creation of its open innovation program, the firm "has developed more than 2,000 global partnerships, delivered dozens of global game-changer products to consumers, accelerated innovation development and increased productivity, both for P&G and its partners."[77] P&G receives about 20 innovation idea submissions daily, or about 4,000 each year, from around the world (the website includes translations in Chinese, Japanese, Spanish, and Portuguese).

Another example of an open innovation program, and a reflection of the recent trend toward humanitarian and sustainable design, is the biannual €500,000 Danish project known as the INDEX: Design to Improve Life Award, which since 2005 has sought out design ideas oriented toward enhancing quality of life. Among numerous other design competitions, INDEX: is distinguished by its mission to promote "the humanist qualities of Danish modernism by celebrating exemplars of the emerging disciplines of environmentally and ethically responsible design."[78] Indeed, the competition's winning concepts tend to make useful contributions to human well-being and the environment, while also raising awareness of issues related to good practice both within and outside the design community. For example, in 2005, the five winners, each of whom received a €100,000 award, conceived of projects consisting of a social housing program in Chile, an urban development initiative in South Korea, a free eyeglasses project in Mexico, and an Indian program to empower children worldwide. A 2011 winner, Hövding's "invisible" bike helmet, was developed by two design graduates from the University of Lund, Anna Haupt and Terese Alstin. The unique design aspect of the helmet is its invisibility; essentially, the product is worn not on the head, but around the neck as a collar. Sensors included within the collar detect unusual movements on the part of the bicyclist, and an airbag begins to inflate within one-tenth of a second, quickly covering a much larger proportion of the head, neck, and face than a traditional cycle helmet. Hövding's helmet recently underwent rigorous testing by three major European agencies for road safety and scored significantly higher on all safety parameters than conventional bike helmets.[79]

The establishment of relationships with third parties in an open development environment offers several potential benefits, including reduced research and development costs, improved product development productivity, attraction of customers early in the product development process, extending the capabilities of the existing workforce by tapping knowledge skills that fall within other domains of expertise, and the building of profitable customer and business networks. Survey research by the management consulting and technology firm Accenture revealed that companies that are more effective at open innovation are more likely to meet or exceed their new-product launch plans.[80] The French and German companies included in Accenture's survey that involved third parties and customers in their new product development process tended to have an average launch time for new products of less than three months, whereas the average new product launch time across a global sample was six months. European companies were found to be significantly more willing to use an open innovation model than their American counterparts. The merits of open innovation are evident when one considers some of the hurdles to innovation that were identified by 270 communications executives across Europe, Asia, and North America who responded to Accenture's survey. According to the results, projects running over budget and slow development time (i.e., the time lag in moving from concept to prototype) represented the primary constraints to new product development. Among other problems cited were lack of new ideas for innovative services, lack of incentives for innovation, and inability to attract the right level of in-house talent. A well-managed open innovation program has the potential to overcome each of these potential barriers to new product innovation and development.

By its very nature, open innovation does pose certain risks and challenges, foremost of which is the possibility of revealing proprietary information to competitors and other parties outside the firm, perhaps resulting in a loss of competitive advantage. Implementing an open innovation model increases the complexity of managing and controlling innovation, regulating the input of external contributors to projects, realigning innovation strategies to extend beyond the firm, and engaging the cooperation of more conventionally inclined employees who occupy product development positions within the firm. These issues notwithstanding, when a company adopts the open collaboration model as a long-term commitment, there is a good chance that it will lead to the creation of a more extensive pool of new ideas and an increase in the potential customer base.[81]

Consumers as creators

Though a common complaint may be that technology is turning consumers into increasingly passive individuals, ceding their intellectual skills and abilities, as well as emotional and physical functioning, to an array of gadgets and devices, for many people, nothing could be further from the truth. An increasing number of consumer end users are approaching technology as an open-ended set of tools that enable them to become the creators of the things they consume. Prosuming is no longer a vision of the future or an emerging trend, it is a basic reality of the contemporary consumer marketplace. Consumers are designing their own music, films, clothing, and other products; sharing with their peers through the development of social software; and distributing and paying for products and services with no need for marketing intermediaries (see Box 5.6).

BOX 5.6 CAN'T FIND IT AT THE MALL? THEN MAKE IT YOURSELF

There's no better inventor than a frustrated consumer. You can be a frustrated consumer at any age and see an opportunity to make something better and fill a void.[82]

These comments by Sara Blakely, founder of the female undergarment company Spanx, could be understood as a clarion call to contemporary

(Continued)

(Continued)

entrepreneurs, both young and old. A case in point is the story of American teenager Megan Grassell, who, at the age of 17, in an effort to fundamentally change the bra industry, founded her own company, Yellowberry. Ms. Grassell had been frustrated when shopping for a bra for her 13-year-old sister by her inability to find choices that were appropriate for young girls. Most of what she came across in shops were push-up styles with padding and underwiring that were appropriate for more mature consumers, with the only exceptions being a limited range of training bras offered by companies like Maidenform and Hanes. Recognizing that the 11–15-year-old female demographic had largely been ignored by the bra industry, Grassell first set out to familiarize herself with fabrics and sketch designs. Using her own savings, she hired a local seamstress to assist her in creating bra prototypes and sought mentors from among local businesses for advice on product development, marketing approaches, and basic financial considerations, such as cash-flow management and profit margins.

One of the persons whose assistance proved invaluable in helping Grassell get her fledgling company off the ground was Stephen Sullivan, founder of the outdoor apparel companies Cloudveil and Stio, who recognized that the young entrepreneur had a well-executed idea that could provide a solution to a real marketplace need. He informed Grassell how the garment industry is volume-driven, which poses a difficult challenge in finding a manufacturer willing to produce small batches of product. This underlined the need for the development of a finely tuned prototype in the form of a polished and production-ready sample. Although she encountered some expected resistance based on her age and inexperience—one reaction was, "Oh, honey, why don't you finish high school first and then think about it?"—Grassell eventually partnered with a Los Angeles manufacturer and began selling Yellowberry bras online from her home. With funding raised on Kickstarter's crowdfunding website, Grassell has been able to expand her Yellowberry business.

Yellowberry's success illustrates the growing involvement of consumers in the product conception and design process, and is not as rare as one might imagine. As another example, 12-year-old California student Shubham Banerjee, relying on nothing more than a LEGO toy kit and family support, invented a low-cost Braille printer to help the visually impaired. Shubham's invention, the Braigo, was created through the use of a LEGO Mindstorms EV3 set and a modified "Robot" model. It functions through the use of push-up pins that act as the print head, impressing Braille characters onto the paper. At the time of this writing, the Braigo was not yet a profit-making venture, but rather a conception that Banerjee desired to maintain as open source so that others could learn to make similar devices at a low cost. As he explained on his Facebook page:

> My dad mentioned to me yesterday night, not to jump off the gun if I
> have to execute my vision of a sub $150 Braille printer. I need to make
> the prototype first and show everyone that it is possible. If I go to the
> crowd for funding, then it is a big responsibility because people will
> entrust me with their own hard earned money to support me. I agreed
> that over summer I will work on making the prototype ready and show
> it to all of you. I don't know if it will be feasible but I will try.[83]
>
> From an entrepreneurial perspective, consumer creation does not always equate
> with business success. Perhaps even more essential than the financial resources
> and business acumen required to launch a business is a clear vision and sincere
> belief in the legitimacy of the product venture—in short, a good idea.

In the Marketing 2.0 era, we have seen the proliferation of consumer-generated content (CGC), with text, images, video, and audio content having rapidly accumulated on the Internet. This content can be attributed on the one hand to the creative talents of consumers and, on the other, to the manufacturing of content-creating and publishing tools that facilitate the production and sharing of consumers' creations. Moreover, where once consumer inspiration for product creation typically remained as mere unfulfilled dreams, crowdfunding is now providing the financial means, credibility, and confidence for dreams to manifest as reality: "Mike Whitehead's big idea was to design a better cast-iron skillet. Stephanie Turenko's big idea was to make an animated short film about her Ukrainian grandmother. Colin Owen's big idea was to manufacture a hard-to-steal bike light."[84] Each of these visions, as described in a *New York Times* article, came to fruition as a result of the good faith of other consumers who recognized good ideas when they saw them and were willing to support product development, market research, and the raising of much-needed capital to get the projects off the ground.

Content-creation: From blogs to body parts

The content-creating consumer crowd (the so-called *Generation-C*) is actively creating content in both the online and offline contexts (see Box 5.7). A good example of an online CGC tool is blogging, which I discussed briefly in my consideration of sharability in Chapter 3. Blogging emerged during the late 1990s along with the creation of Web publishing tools that facilitated the posting of content by individuals with little technical expertise. Whereas at one time publishing content on the Internet required proficiency in Internet file transfer protocols such as HTML and FTP, today even the novice Internet user is likely to find the website and blog creation process to be relatively painless and easy, with a variety of services and online tutorials providing useful insights into the process. Although I would hardly consider myself a high-tech whiz, I was able to set up and publish my restaurant review blog[85] in less than 30 minutes.

BOX 5.7 WELCOME TO GENERATION-C

According to management professors Jan Kietzmann and Ian Angell, who coined the term, *Generation-C* refers to a generational movement of consumers who are "constantly connected citizens—creative, capable, content-centric, and community-oriented—who collectively communicate, collaborate, copy, co-develop, combine, contribute and consume common content."[86] Although that is a lot of "Cs" to process, Kietzmann and Angell more simply suggest that the contemporary youth generation is actively involved in marketplace activities that go beyond the traditional buying and selling structure of marketing. Increasingly, young people—although these activities are by no means restricted to youthful consumers—are exchanging ideas online for improving products and modifying proprietary offerings, with the resulting creative content then utilized by other members of society. These developments in part are attributed to the high degree of *malleability*, or range of possible uses for a product, that characterizes many new marketplace offerings, particularly those that are technological in nature.

Even as companies make strides to protect their products from all but intended modifications or extensions, such as by integrating built-in limitations for operating systems or write-protected software, creative consumers are finding ways to change products to increase their functionality and uses. Some more familiar examples of these modifications are "jailbreaks" for game consoles, unlocked mobile phones, video and audio mashups, adding storage to TiVo personal video recorders, controlling vacuum cleaners via mobile phone applications, and tuning cars so that they can exceed top speed limiters. The Generation-C movement reflects the rising power of consumers in terms of their efforts to alter the marketplace of products so that offerings are more attuned to their own needs and desires, as opposed to those that are oriented more toward increasing profits for manufacturers and retailers. However, Kietzmann and Angell stress that consumer alterations of proprietary offerings are resulting in a number of moral and legal controversies associated with existing intellectual property rights (IPRs). In their view, by taking legal steps to protect against the infringement of IPRs, companies that hold IPRs are actually doing more harm than good because such a strategy ultimately blocks innovation, particularly in cases where firms do little to develop their own inventions. (This point is very similar to the ongoing issues regarding patent rights discussed in Box 2.3.) In France, as in some other countries, governmental regulations require that an invention be exploited, and regulatory bodies will award a license to others who desire to take advantage of a protected invention. Kietzmann and Angell argue that firms, IPR lawyers, governments, and politicians need to reconsider the impact that restrictions on proprietary product modifications have, not only on the members of Generation-C who engage in hacking activities, but on consumers in general.

Underlying the current proliferation of blogs are a variety of characteristics that make them so appealing to Internet users.[87] For example, blogs are quickly indexed by search engines; easy to update and add instantly viewable new content to; easy to attract Web traffic to; rise up search engines quickly; and are relatively simple to develop and design. As a reflection of the sharing aspect of CGC, blogs use tags that allow them to be tracked through specialized blog search engines, such as Technorati. A *tag*, which is a relevant keyword, phrase, or label assigned to a blog entry, tends to increase the visibility of the blog and its capacity for drawing Internet traffic, and provides ready accessibility to sharable content.[88] For example, I regularly post photographs of the dishes I order in the restaurants I review for my blog. Because I added tags to many of the photographs, the images often appear elsewhere on the Internet, such as among the results of a Google image search. This is just one small way that CGC enters the online public domain; another is by retweeting on Twitter, where reposting or forwarding a message posted by another user is as easy as the click of an appropriate icon.

Offline, consumer creation of products promises to thrive with the evolution of 3-D printing, which enables people to "print out" objects like tools, toys, clothing, food, furniture, product parts and components, and even human tissue and body parts. The technology of 3-D printing, invented in the 1980s by American technologist Charles Hull, is part of a process known as "additive manufacturing," which involves the production of three-dimensional solid objects from digital files. This is accomplished with the aid of additive processes, which lay down successive layers of material until the desired object is created, with each layer serving as a thinly sliced cross-section of the eventual object. The process is initiated through the creation of a blueprint or virtual design of the object one intends to print. This design can be developed through the creation of an original design using modeling software like Blender, an open-source platform suite of tools for 3-D creation, or from visiting websites like Shapewaves, iMaterialise, or Cubify to find objects other users have 3-D-modeled. Based on the design data, renewable bioplastic spools on the back of home 3-D printing devices pull the material through a tube, melt it, and then deposit it to the plate, where it cools instantly. A completed 3-D structure is eventually formed through the addition of material, one layer at a time. Although plastic is the most common material used in 3-D printing, other materials allow for the creation of a wide range of intriguing product possibilities, including food and bio-materials for regenerative medical uses. Currently under testing in the medical domain, doctors are finding it possible to use a patient's cells as the basis for 3-D printing small body parts (such as ears and noses), tissue, bones, and organs for transplant.

At present, 3-D printing is more at the stage of ruminations about its potential as opposed to actual practical applications, but as the technology is becoming more efficient, inexpensive, and versatile, it is beginning to change the nature of product design and the way people produce and use objects. Small, consumer-friendly 3-D printers have begun to bring additive manufacturing to homes and businesses, leading to the customization of everyday items (personalized coffee mugs, wedding cake toppers, clothing accessories), the completion of inexpensive and time-efficient repairs (the replacement of small plastic or rubberized parts for kitchen accessories or automobiles), and the creation of customized adaptors and connectors that merge products that were never meant to be used together (brackets, mounts, gimbals, and housings). Perhaps more important than these applications are the ways in which 3-D printing technology is likely to encourage and facilitate learning, invention, and the building of new product prototypes. According to technology consultant Justin Levinson: "It's not about printing. It's about how you start to look at the world. You start to think, 'I can solve my own problems.'"[89]

In terms of the farther-reaching design implications of 3-D printing, advances in digital production promise to provide designers with opportunities to realize previously inconceivable shapes in complex geometries. An example that foretells this possibility is suggested by the Collagene project, a series of 3-D printed masks developed at MHOX, a generative design studio that creates objects that serve as body extensions intended to "integrate the human body to mutate its aesthetic, sport and medical potential."[90] The polyamide-based masks were fashioned by Italian designers Filippo Nassetti and Alessandro Zomparelli, who developed a software and digital fabrication technique to create customized masks based on scans of human faces and game console sensors. The intricately designed masks take the shape of a tangle of twigs which, as design critic Alice Rawsthorn describes, have "the futuristic air of things that could only have been made by advanced technology, and look significantly different to the products of traditional mass-manufacturing" (see Figure 5.1 and this book's cover illustration).[91] The intent, according to MHOX's DOTHEMUTATION blog, is to imagine "the mask as the product of the growth of a virtual organism on the human face. The object keeps its traditional functions of body prosthesis, providing identity alteration and concealment, stimulating viewers' imagination and visual association."[92]

In addition to stimulating a rethinking of the nature of product structures and shapes that cannot be produced through the use of traditional technologies, 3-D printing poses other new challenges for designers. Because the technology will empower consumers to produce accurate replicas of lost or damaged parts and components of the products they own, designers will need to develop original objects that allow for those possibilities. Moreover, as Rawsthorn predicts, digital production will also force designers to forge new relationships with manufacturers, in addition to the consumers who use their work. In the near future, every town is likely to establish a sophisticated 3-D printing facility, where local residents can

FIGURE 5.1   Collegene mask by MHOX

Source: Collagene masks. Design and photography by MHOX; production by CRP Group/Windform

order customized products or repair existing ones. One result of these develop-ments is that designers would be less beholden to manufacturers who are willing to realize their ideas, preferring instead to become more entrepreneurial by creating prototypes and selling their original concepts directly to consumers.[93]

Designers and design-related organizations are increasingly open to the cre-ative potential of consumers, establishing relationships with educational institu-tions, engaging students in competitions, and sponsoring graduate design research projects with live clients. For example, the non-profit technical organization ASME sponsors a Student Design Competition that provides a platform for the more than 30,000 student members to present their solutions in the form of an operable prototype responding to a range of design problems, from everyday household tasks to more complex science and technology issues, such as space exploration. Student teams of four compete annually for a variety of awards and cash prizes, with award-winning teams invited to present their work at the ASME International Mechanical Engineering Congress and Exposition (IMECE). The Design Academy Eindhoven in the Netherlands provides an online showcase of the design projects of its graduating class of students, highlighting the range of creative possibilities for new product ideas.[94] Volvo recently sponsored a research project in collaboration with Harvard University's Graduate School of Design, entitled "Transforming Urban Transport—The Role of Political Leadership," engaging students in an effort to advance understanding about the role of political leadership in the adoption of innovative and transformative transportation policies. Such projects underscore the increasing range of opportunities for young creators to play a significant part in the dynamic field of design.

Customization and consumer personalization

Although marketers typically approach customer targeting by attempting to segment the consumer marketplace into groups according to similarities in demographics, geographic demarcations, and personality and lifestyle characteristics, the typical consumer tends to perceive himself or herself as a unique individual, with personal needs and tastes, and strives to project that uniqueness by personalizing the products he or she possesses. If everyone in one's clique owns an iPhone, one's own can be distinguished by a uniquely colored or textured protective skin. All one's friends may have a discreet tattoo, but the specific nature of the tattoo's design no doubt reflects how each friend sees himself or herself or desires to be perceived by others. Personalization is reflected in a variety of marketplace preferences, including food products in individual portions or mini-sizes, clothing accessories (body piercing jewelry, pins, scarves), options and accessories for cars, on-demand television, specialized salons, special interest magazines, regional newspapers, and the like.

In light of the consumer desire for personalization, designers and marketers are increasingly recognizing the value associated with providing customers with opportunities to create their own unique products or to personalize their buying experiences. Dell Computers is an example of a growing number of companies that have successfully demonstrated how complex manufactured products can be customized to satisfy diverse needs and provide unique value for customers. As mentioned in Chapter 1, companies like Converse and Nike enable their customers to customize their online athletic apparel purchases by providing a variety of possible stylistic choices. Amazon personalizes its webpage displays on the basis of customer purchasing and browsing behavior, offering customized recommendations and links suggesting prospective future purchases. Presenting personalized product choices to their customers has proven to be a key driving force underlying Amazon's phenomenal success and dominance of the market.

Capabilities for providing consumers with product customization options have advanced in recent years, resulting in more flexible, digitally controlled manufacturing processes and the integration of online design with distribution supply chains. Online companies like Fluid now offer e-commerce retailers specialized software and services that make it relatively easy to satisfy the customer demand for customized products. From the consumer perspective, the customization process has become a relatively painless experience as a result of superior computing power, speedier Internet connections, and the greater convenience proffered by mobile devices and applications.

Insights into product customization were derived from a 2013 survey of more than a thousand online shoppers conducted by the global management consulting firm Bain & Company.[95] Although less than 10% of the respondents claimed to have already tried customization options, nearly 30% indicated a desire to do so, more so in terms of design, aesthetics, and user-generated content than basic specification options like fit and size. Younger shoppers were more likely than their older counterparts to demand more individualized products. The survey also pointed to the importance of offering consumers the opportunity to return goods within a reasonable period. In fact, the tendency to customize appears to decline considerably if online shoppers fear that they will be stuck with a customized product they are dissatisfied with.

As a growing number of consumers take advantage of customization opportunities, companies will be in a better position to glean insight from the sorts of customized designs and personalized products that appeal to consumers. What companies learn as they follow real-time customer shopping preferences can be systematically used to enhance online customization offers. In addition to providing an impetus for sales, firms stand to gain much from providing their customers with the possibility of personalizing the products they buy from them. The Bain survey revealed higher levels of customer engagement for consumers who had customized a product online: they visited the website more often and lingered there longer, and were more loyal to the brand, as measured by the Net Promoter Score (NPS), which reflects the extent to which people say they would recommend the brand to others.

Among Bain's conclusions that are relevant to companies contemplating the addition of product customization as an element of their business plan, two recommendations stand out. The first is the need to modulate the degree of customization on offer. Whereas some firms provide consumers with the possibility to design a unique product that can be built to order with a range of features that can be added, others allow for only minor customization options, such as the addition of monograms for clothing or luggage, or personalized designs for product packaging. Some retailers simplify the customization process by offering "consumer-choice bundling," whereby customers are able to choose purchase combinations (such as the addition of pillow cases to an order for sheets). This is the simplest personalization approach for a firm because it merely requires the provision of goods from a standard line of merchandise. Although it only provides the perception of customization without actually offering it, evidence suggests that the average order value for bundled purchases tends to exceed those of customers whose purchases are item-by-item.[96]

The second recommendation from Bain acknowledges the social aspect of consumer behavior. Consumers who take advantage of customization offers typically want to share their creations with persons in their social networks, which provides a means for companies to engage with their current customers while attracting new ones. For example, Levi's links its online apparel catalog to a Facebook application that encourages consumers to share the outfits they "like" among their Facebook friends. Urban Outfitters set up a Flickr pool, inviting its customers and fans to post photographs of themselves wearing the brand's clothing and accessories ("Show us how *you* wore it"), effectively creating a virtual catalog of their creative fashion statements. Urban Outfitters has included some of the customer photos on a rotating basis on its various websites, thereby inspiring consumers to purchase and wear the company's offerings. In short, given the range of possible online resources and portable device applications, it is relatively easy for firms to expand the customization offer by collaborating with customers in the sharing of those customers' creations with others.

Do-it-yourself and product hacking trends

Another manifestation of consumer creation is apparent in the growing trend for customers to modify or maintain manufactured goods beyond their intended nature, use, or lifespan. A term that is increasingly used to refer to this tendency is "hacking," a word that more commonly connotes subversive online activity involving the breaching of computer security weaknesses for illicit purposes (and which in itself reflects another form of consumer creativity). Consumers may view a new possession as a sort of work in progress, recognizing uniquely different possibilities for usage, beyond what the manufacturer had in mind when the product was conceived of and produced. For example, "IKEA Hackers" represent a loosely connected community of consumers who regard the well-known Swedish furniture company IKEA's final products merely as starting points for creations that can be put to alternative uses.[97] Some actual examples of consumer-generated IKEA product reinventions include music speakers made from IKEA salad bowls, children's clothes produced from IKEA quilt covers and pillow cases, a blond electric guitar body created from an IKEA pine tabletop, a cat litter box simultaneously used as a living room end table, and a waterproof dress produced by a consumer who altered an inexpensive IKEA shower curtain. In 2006, the IKEA Hackers website[98] was created by IKEA fan Jules Yap to provide a forum for the sharing of modifications on and repurposing of IKEA products ("If you hack IKEA, we want to see it"). To date, IKEA's reaction to the IKEA Hackers community has been somewhat contentious, suggesting that it is missing an opportunity to further promote its goods by engaging some of the company's more resourceful fans.[99]

A different variation of product hacking pertains to the Newton, Apple's early line of personal digital assistants (PDAs). Much to the chagrin of loyal Newton owners, the company decided to take the product off the market in 1998. However, long after it was abandoned by Apple, thousands of Newton enthusiasts essentially took over the product and continue to use it. Consumers have upgraded the device over the years through the development of new software, giving it functions it was never meant to perform. It can now connect to Macs, PCs, and Unix machines, as well as a variety of networks (from wi-fi networks to the always-on GPS mobile phone networks); it streams mp3 files off the Internet; and it can audibly read headlines that have been retrieved automatically from online news sites. According to brand community experts

Albert Muñiz and Thomas O'Guinn: "Newton users fulfill the role advertising and branding would normally play. They've taken possession of the product and the brand away from Apple, and when you talk to them you get the sense that it's *their* brand."[100]

Product hacking represents one of several options available to consumers who are ready to dispose of an acquisition that has run its course or no longer functions as intended. Disposal options basically boil down to three possible courses of action: keep an item (e.g., storing it in the hopes it will become useful again in the future), get rid of it permanently (e.g., throw it away, give it away, trade or sell it), or get rid of it temporarily (e.g., loan it or rent it). One recourse when the decision is made to keep an item that is no longer serving its original purpose is for its owner to convert, modify, or transform the product so that it can serve a new purpose. This could range from having the product fulfill a decorative function (e.g., an elegant empty vodka bottle used to adorn a living room shelf) to serving an unintended utilitarian function (e.g., adapting outdated floppy disks to function as an office organizer; using a malfunctioning Macbook charger as a bottle opener; constructing a workbench by supporting a cracked surfboard with broken IKEA chairs).[101]

As an increasing number of consumers are beginning to engage in more creative activities in terms of the ways they interact with products, it is interesting to consider what some of the broader consequences are from a consumer psychology standpoint. Researchers have only recently begun to consider the impact of DIY and hacking activities on the psyche and self-concept of consumers. We might imagine that wielding creative control over products via tangible improvements or modifications would enhance a consumer's sense of self-worth and could provide a means for satisfying various altruistic motivations. Moreover, joining an online DIY network is likely to broaden one's social network and boost one's image in the eyes of others. In one recent investigation of American men, consumer researchers Risto Moisio, Eric J. Arnould, and James Gentry postulated that DIY home improvement could serve as a means by which men develop or enhance their masculine identities.[102] Their interviews revealed that financial pressures and workplace stress were central factors compelling American men to engage in home improvement projects. An interesting finding was that social class determined whether the respondents envisioned themselves as either suburban craftsmen or family handymen. DIY home improvement provided upper-class male consumers with a means to unleash their inner suburban craftsman persona as one who takes pleasure from engaging in physical labor. Being able to toil away on various projects provided a respite from their stressful full-time jobs and provided feelings of self-fulfilment. By contrast, work around the house for lower-class male consumers served as a means to assert their identities and construct an identity of the family handyman. DIY home improvement projects enabled lower-class men to project a masculine form of caring for their families and improving their homes—more so than was possible due to their economic and social standing. The researchers concluded:

For upper class men, DIY home improvement is a therapeutic escape from the burdens of knowledge work, allowing them to experience a blue-collar fantasy by working with their hands. In contrast, lower class men treat DIY home improvement as a chore rather than a therapeutic outlet. Projects around the house represent an essential part of their male territory and housework repertoire.[103]

Conclusion

Tapscott and Williams were not exaggerating when they proclaimed in 2006: "Millions of people already join forces in self-organized collaborations that produce dynamic new goods and services that rival those of the world's largest and best-financed enterprises."[104] In a nutshell, that statement summarizes how the status of consumers has evolved in recent years to one of greater self-sufficiency and control, less beholden to the whims of corporate entities within the consumer goods industry. Perhaps a function of necessity as much as opportunity, businesses are finding that their survival depends on the establishment of a more symbiotic relationship with their consumer targets than has ever previously been the case. The relationship between designers, marketers, and consumers is being transformed as consumers are increasingly invited into the product development and marketing processes as advisors and co-creators. As some have predicted, the boundaries between these various participants in the marketplace of things will become even more blurred as technologies like 3-D printing and digital production techniques allow consumers to participate more fully in the design process so as to personalize the end result.[105]

The customer-made trend in part offsets the ethical concern that many products in the consumer marketplace have been developed primarily to provide value to the manufacturer and retailer, without regard to the satisfaction of essential customer needs. In fact, in most industrialized nations, one can observe a proliferation of products that offer little real value to consumers, such as mascara for babies, salted bandages, silicon thigh implants, and a growing range of pet products and services, the latter ranging from Halloween costumes and limousine services for cats and dogs to pet spas, fitness centers, vacation resorts, and retirement homes.[106] Although such ostensibly useless products may provide a certain degree of novelty to the purchaser, one may argue that they merely serve to encourage consumers to "buy and have" regardless of the need-satisfying properties of the acquisitions. In addition, it is argued that many products merely add to the creation of false wants and the encouragement of materialistic values and aspirations discussed in Chapter 1, thereby influencing consumers to value material objects more than personal development and socially oriented causes. As more businesses mark a shift in the ways they communicate with consumers, from a monologue to a dialogue, there should be a sea change in terms of the kinds of products that appear in the marketplace. Thus, the more active involvement of consumers in the product development and design processes has ethical and social implications in addition to marketing-oriented ones.

As a prelude to Chapter 6, director of MIT Media Lab Joichi Ito's musings on the impact of an open-source society perhaps represent the most appropriate way of bringing the current chapter to a close:

> Today we are seeing the emergence of a community of hardware hackers and designers very reminiscent of the developers who wrote the original open standards of the Internet. An explosion of grass-roots innovation in hardware is coming—freely designed and freely shared—as it did in software. . . . Neoteny . . . means the retention of childlike attributes in adulthood: idealism, experimentation and wonder.

> In this new world, not only must we behave more like children, we also must teach the next generation to retain those attributes that will allow them to be world-changing, innovative adults who will help us reinvent the future.[107]

Further reading

My 2010 book *Connecting With Consumers: Marketing for New Marketplace Realities* (Oxford University Press) goes into much greater detail about the evolving collaborative relationship between marketers and consumers than I was able to cover in this chapter. In the book, I provide a comprehensive description of the emerging set of tools that can empower marketers to more fully engage with consumers so as to encourage their active participation in the marketing process.

Don Tapscott and Anthony D. Williams' best-seller *Wikonomics: How Mass Collaboration Changes Everything* (Portfolio, 2006) is a pioneering reference for insight into how companies are embracing new technologies and incorporating collaboration into their business models. The authors provide numerous examples of how consumers, as individual creators and as members of online communities, are exploiting new platforms to become active participants in the content-creation process.

Although I have already included Tim Parsons' *Thinking: Objects—Contemporary Approaches to Product Design* (AVA Publishing, 2009) as further reading for Chapter 4, I feel compelled to recommend it again here, particularly in terms of Parsons' detailed discussion of social inclusion and user-centered thinking within the design industry. Parsons describes the ways that designers are increasingly moving toward models of inclusivity, prioritizing needs from the consumer's perspective, and recognizing the value of establishing a deeper, more empathetic relationship with their customers.

A useful reference resource for research on customization and personalization trends in the contemporary marketplace is the two-volume *Handbook of Research on Mass Customization and Personalization* (World Scientific, 2010), edited by Frank T. Piller and Mitchell M. Tseng. Inspired by the 4th World Conference on Mass

Customization and Personalization, the book compiles recent research advances from an international lineup of leading practitioners and scholars in the areas of mass customization and open innovation in a wide variety of business domains.

Notes

1 Toffler, A. (1980). *The third wave.* New York: Bantam Books, p. 267.
2 Elliott, S. (2006, October 9). Letting consumers control marketing: Priceless. *The New York Times.* Available: http://www.nytimes.com/2006/10/09/business/media/ 09adcol.html.
3 Michalski, J., as quoted in Locke, C., Levine, R., Searls, D., & Weinberger, D. (2000). *The cluetrain manifesto: The end of business as usual.* New York: Perseus Book Group, p. 78.
4 Tapscott, D. & Williams, A. D. (2006). *Wikinomics: How mass collaboration changes everything.* New York: Portfolio.
5 Tapscott, D. & Williams, A. D. (2006), p. 30.
6 Tapscott, D. & Williams, A. D. (2006), p. 31.
7 Customer-made. (2006). *trendwatching.com.* Available: http://trendwatching.com/ trends/CUSTOMER-MADE.htm.
8 Parsons, T. (2009). *Thinking: Objects—contemporary approaches to product design.* Worthing, West Sussex, UK: AVA.
9 Diaz, C. (2010, March). *Successfully tie in traditional social media techniques within your existing multi-channel marketing strategies.* Paper presented at the Marketing 2.0 Conference, Paris, France.
10 Dreyfuss, H. (1960). *The measure of man: Human factors in design.* New York: Whitney Library of Design.
11 Parsons, T. (2009).
12 Gheerawo, R. (2007). Vital signs. *Helen Hamlyn Research Associates Catalogue.* London: Royal College of Art, p. 3.
13 Kimmel, A. J. (2010). *Connecting with consumers: Marketing for new marketplace realities.* Oxford, UK: Oxford University Press.
14 Knox, S. (2010, March). *Perspectives on innovative word-of-mouth advertising—P&G learnings and future outlook for brand markers.* Paper presented at the Marketing 2.0 Conference, Paris, France.
15 What is inclusive design? (2013). *Inclusive Design Toolkit.* Available: http://www. inclusivedesigntoolkit.com/betterdesign2/whatis/whatis.html.
16 Kimmel, A. J. (2007). *Ethical issues in behavioral research: Basic and applied perspectives.* Oxford, UK: Wiley-Blackwell. Iacobucci, D. & Churchill, G. A. (2010). *Marketing research: Methodological foundations* (international ed.), 10th ed. Mason, OH: South-Western.
17 Ralli, T. (2005, October 24). Brand blogs capture the attention of some companies. *The New York Times*, p. C6.
18 http://www.hackingnetflix.com/.
19 Ralli, T. (2005, October 24).
20 Jaffe, J. (2007). *Join the conversation.* Hoboken, NJ: John Wiley, p. 3.
21 Bryant, A. (2009, May 11). Inclusion and listening are key to success. *International Herald Tribune*, p.17.
22 Mulhall, L. (2006). Brewing buzz. In J. Kirby & P. Marsden (eds.), *Connected marketing: The viral, buzz and word of mouth revolution* (pp. 59–70). Oxford, UK: Butterworth-Heinemann.
23 Moore, J. (2005). Blowfly podcast. *Johnnie Moore.* Available: http://johnniemoore. com/blowfly-podcast/.
24 Parsons, T. (2009).
25 Goffin, K. & Lemke, F. (2010). *Identifying hidden needs: Creating breakthrough products.* New York: Palgrave Macmillan, p. 153.

26 www.bareescentuals.com.

27 Muñiz, A. M., Jr., & O'Guinn, T. C. (2005). Marketing communications in a world of consumption and brand communities. In A. J. Kimmel (Ed.), *Marketing communication: New approaches, technologies, and styles* (pp. 63–85). Oxford, UK: Oxford University Press.

28 abourdaa. (2008, January 14). BuzzParadise publishes the results of its survey about French bloggers. *vanksen*. Available: http://www.vanksen.com/blog/buzzparadise-publishes-the-results-of-its-survey-about-french-bloggers/. Lenhart, A. & Fox, S. (2006). *Bloggers: A portrait of the Internet's new storytellers*. Washington, DC: Pew Internet & American Life Project. Available: http://www.pewinternet.org/files/old-media/Files/Reports/2006/PIP%20Bloggers%20Report%20July%2019%202006.pdf.pdf.

29 Sernovitz, A. (2007, July 25). Dealing with negative word of mouth. *Andy Sernovitz's Damn, I Wish I'd Thought of That!* Available: http://www.damniwish.com/dealing-with-ne/.

30 French, R. (2005, October). Edelman/Technorati blogger study update. *Auburn Media Infopinions*. Available: http://www.auburnmedia.com/wordpress/2005/10/12/edelmantechnorati-blogger-study-update/.

31 http://bloggersrequired.com.

32 Zoon, H., Cremers, A., & Eggen, B. (2014). "Include," a toolbox of user research for inclusive design. In J. P. van Leeuwen, P. J. Stappers, M. H. Lamers, & M. R. Thissen (Eds.), *Creating the difference: Proceedings of the Chi Sparks 2014 Conference*, The Hague, The Netherlands: The Hague University of Applied Sciences & Chi Nederland.

33 http://designingwithpeople.rca.ac.uk.

34 Von Hippel, E. (1986). Lead users: A source of novel product concepts. *Management Science, 32*, 791–805.

35 MacLeod, C. M. (2007). The concept of inhibition in cognition. In D. S. Gorfein & C. M. MacLeod (Eds.), *Inhibition in cognition* (pp. 3–23). Washington, DC: American Psychological Association. Von Hippel, E. (1982). Appropriability of innovation benefit as a predictor of the source of innovation. *Research Policy, 11*, 95–115. Birch, H. G. & Rabinowitz, H. J. (1951). The negative effect of previous experience on productive thinking. *Journal of Experimental Psychology, 41*, 121–125.

36 Goffin, K. & Lemke, F. (2010).

37 Kulkarni, R. (2008, February 6). Lead users. *SlideShare*. Available: http://www.slideshare.net/idrushi/lead-user.

38 Kulkarni, R. (2008, February 6).

39 Penning, A. (2013, January 13). L'Oréal unveils new Indian research and innovation center. Available: http://www.cosmeticsandtoiletries.com/networking/news/company/LrsquoOreacuteal-Unveils-new-Indian-Research-and-Innovation-Center-186324642.html.

40 Khicha, P. (2011, September 21). Consumers lead the way: FMCG companies are involving customers early in the product co-creation cycle. *Business Standard*. Available: http://www.business-standard.com/article /management/consumers-lead-the-way-111092100046_1.html.

41 Van Luxemburg, A. (2011, March 17). Social media maturity model. *M&I/Partners*. Available: http://www.mxi.nl/publicaties/904/www.socialmediamodellen.nl.

42 Kimmel, A. J. (2010).

43 Kimmel, A. J. (2010).

44 http://www.ideastorm.com.

45 Killian, V. (2009, April). IdeaStorm overview. *SlideShare*. Available: http://www.slideshare.net/Dell/ideastorm-overview.

46 Killian, V. (2009, April).

47 http://share.blog.us.playstation.com.

48 http://share.blog.us.playstation.com.

49 PR Newswire. (2014, January 14). Lay's "Do Us a Favor" contest is back. *MarketWatch*. Available: http://www.marketwatch.com/story/lays-do-us-a-flavor-contest-is-back-fans-invited-to-submit-next-great-potato-chip-flavor-idea-for-the-chance-to-win-1-million-2014-01-14.

50 Tanner, S. (2008, February 27). Commentary: DEWmocracy and Mountain Dew's online marketing. *BevReview*. Available: http://www.bevreview.com/2008/02/27/commentary-dewmocracy-and-mountain-dews-online-marketing/.

51 Tanner, S. (2008, February 27).

52 DEWmocracy II. *Mtn Dew wiki*. Available: http://mountaindew.wikia.com/wiki/DEWmocracy_II.

53 Wong, E. (2010, June 16). What Mountain Dew learned from "DEWmocracy." *Adweek*. Available: http://www.adweek.com/news/advertising-branding/what-mountain-dew-learned-dewmocracy-107534.

54 Mountain Dew's innovative campaign quickly goes viral. (2011, September 15). *Grand Social Central*. Available: http://www.grandsocialcentral.com/hustler-marketers/brand-managers/mountain-dew/mountain-dews-innovative-campaign.

55 Fournier, S. & Avery, J. (2011, May–June). The uninvited brand. *Business Horizons*, *54*, 193–207.

56 http://conceptlounge.nokia.be.

57 Howe, J. (2006, June 14). The rise of crowdsourcing. *Wired*. Available: http://archive.wired.com/wired/archive/14.06/crowds.html.

58 Howe, J. (2006, June 14).

59 Howard, B. (2012, October 5). BMW to crowdsource the design of its megacity-centric future car. *ExtremeTech*. Available: http://www.extremetech.com/extreme/137343-bmw-crowdsource-megacity-future-car.

60 Belluck, P. (2013, November 20). Condom contest produces 812 ideas for improvement. *The New York Times*. Available: http://www.nytimes.com/2013/11/21/health/condom-contest-produces-812-ideas-for-improvement.html.

61 Flinn, R. & Townsend, M. (2010, October 8). Gap's new "modern, sexy, cool" logo irks shoppers, designers. *Bloomberg*. Available: http://www.bloomberg.com/news/2010-10-08/gap-s-new-modern-sexy-cool-logo-irks-shoppers-designers.html.

62 Flinn, R. & Townsend, M. (2010, October 8).

63 Torossian, R. (2011). *For immediate release*. Dallas, TX: BenBella, p.63.

64 Ogg, J. C. (2010, October 8). Gap's logo change adding brand damage. *24/7 WALLSt*. Available: http://247wallst.com/retail/2010/10/08/gaps-logo-change-adding-brand-damage-gps/.

65 Tabbitt, S. (2014, June 4). Crowdsourcing for startup success. *The Guardian*. Available: http://www.theguardian.com/small-business-network/2014/jun/04/crowdsourcing-banks-startup-investment.

66 Tabbitt, S. (2014, June 4).

67 https://www.kickstarter.com/help/stats.

68 Rose, C. (2014, March 20). Charlie Rose talks to Kickstarter's Yancey Strickler. *Bloomberg Businessweek*. Available: http://www.businessweek.com/articles/2014-03-20/kickstarters-yancey-strickler-on-1-billion-pledge-mark-no-ipo.

69 Oculus. (2012). Oculus Rift: Step into the game. *Kickstarter*. https://www.kickstarter.com/projects/1523379957/oculus-rift-step-into-the-game#.

70 Luckerson, V. (2014, March 26). When crowdfunding goes corporate: Kickstarter backers vent over Facebook's Oculus buy. *Time*. Available: http://time.com/39271/oculus-facebook-kickstarter-backlash/.

71 Summers, N. (2014, March 26). Enjoy your $500 t-shirt: Kickstarter backers get nada in Oculus sale. *Bloomberg Businessweek*. Available: http://www.businessweek.com/articles/2014-03-26/enjoy-your-500-t-shirt-kickstarter-backers-get-nada-in-oculus-sale.

72 https://www.seedrs.com.

73 Tabbitt, S. (2014, June 4).

74 Goldin, M. (2014, April 14). Crowdemand is like Kickstarter for fashion designers. *Mashable*. Available: http://mashable.com/2014/04/13/crowdemand-fashion/.

75 http://www.pgconnectdevelop.com.

76 What is Connect+Develop? *P&G connect+develop*. Available: http://www.pgconnectdevelop.com/home/pg_open_innovation.html.

77 P&G Connect+Develop launches new open innovation website. *P&G Corporate Newsroom.* Available: http://news.pg.com/press-release/pg-corporate-announcements/pg-connectdevelop-launches-new-open-innovation-website.
78 Rawsthorn, A. (2011, September 5). In this contest, we're all winners. *The International New York Times*, p. 9.
79 Airbag for cyclists tests almost 100% in preventing fatal head injuries. (2014, April 7). *INDEX: Design to Improve Life.* Available: https://designtoimprovelife.dk/invisible-bike-helmet-tests-almost-100-ability-prevent-severe-head-trauma/.
80 Reznik, G. & Morelli, A. (2009, October). Open innovation: How to create the right new products, the right way. *Outlook.* Available: http://www.accenture.com/SiteCollectionDocuments/PDF/OutlookPDF_Innovation_02.pdf.
81 Reznik, G. & Morelli, A. (2009, October).
82 Martin, C. (2014, May 10). Can't find it at the mall? Make it yourself. *The New York Times.* Available: http://www.nytimes.com/2014/05/11/business/cant-find-it-at-the-mall-make-it-yourself.html.
83 https://www.facebook.com/BraigoPrinter.
84 Murphy, K. (2014, January 22). Crowdfunding tips for turning inspiration into reality. *The International New York Times.* Available: http://www.nytimes.com/2014/01/23/technology/personaltech/crowdfunding-tips-for-turning-inspiration-into-reality.html.
85 http://parisrestaurantreviewsandbeyond.blogspot.com.
86 Kietzmann, J. H. & Angell, I. (2013). Generation-C: Creative consumers in a world of intellectual property rights. *International Journal of Technology in Marketing*, 9, 86–98.
87 One new blog created every second means yours is irrelevant unless. (2011, August 22). *Blog Blog Baby.* Available: http://www.blogblogbaby.com/one-new-blog-created-every-second-means-yours-is-irrelevant-unless/.
88 Rainie, L. (2007, January 31). *28% of online Americans have used the Internet to tag content.* Available: http://www.pewinternet.org/files/old-media/Files/Reports/2007/PIP_Tagging.pdf.pdf.
89 O'Leary, A. (2013, June 19). 3-D printers to make things you need or like. *The New York Times.* Available: http://www.nytimes.com/2013/06/20/technology/personaltech/home-3-d-printers-to-make-things-you-need-or-just-like.html.
90 About. *DOTHEMUTATION.* http://dothemutation.wordpress.com/about/.
91 Rawsthorn, A. (2013, July 21). Catching up to 3D printing. *The New York Times.* Available: http://www.nytimes.com/2013/07/22/arts/design/Catching-Up-to-3D-Printing.html.
92 Collagene. *DOTHEMUTATION.* Available: http://dothemutation.wordpress.com/collagene.
93 Rawsthorn, A. (2013, July 21).
94 See, for example, DAE Graduation Show 2012. *Design Academy Eindhoven DESIGNDAELY.* Available: http://www.designacademy.nl/portals/0/www/events/daegs12/#.
95 Spaulding, E. & Perry, C. (2013, September 16). Making it personal: Rules for success in product customization. *Bain & Company.* Available: http://www.bain.com/publications/articles/making-it-personal-rules-for-success-in-product-customization.aspx.
96 Spaulding, E. & Perry, C. (2013, September 16).
97 Green, P. (2007, September 6). Romancing the flat pack: IKEA, repurposed. *The New York Times.* Available: http://www.nytimes.com/2007/09/06/garden/06hackers.html.
98 http://www.ikeahackers.net/.
99 Alexander, H. (2014, June 25). IKEA backs off from legal action against IKEA hackers site. *SFGate.* Available: http://www.sfgate.com/homeandgarden/article/Site-that-brought-us-Texas-Ikea-cat-playground-5576633.php.

100 Muñiz, A. M., Jr., & O'Guinn, T. C. (2001). Brand community. *Journal of Consumer Research, 27*, 412–431.

101 Koerber, B. (2014, May 12). 17 DIY office hacks to make work more tolerable. *Mashable.* Available: http://mashable.com/2014/05/12/diy-office-hacks-tips-tricks/.

102 Moisio, R., Arnould, E. J., & Gentry, J. (2013). Productive consumption in the class-mediated construction of domestic masculinity: Do-it-yourself (DIY) home improvement in men's identity work. *Journal of Consumer Research, 40* (2), 298–316.

103 Moisio, R., Arnould, E. J., & Gentry, J. (2013).

104 Tapscott, D. & Williams, A. D. (2006), p. 11.

105 Rawsthorn, A. (2013, April 22). Designers versus inventors. *International Herald Tribune*, p. 10.

106 Tanikawa, M. (2004, January 24). Addiction on a "cellular" level. *The New York Times.* Available: http://www.nytimes.com/2004/01/24/business/worldbusiness/24iht-itaddict_ed3_.html.

107 Ito, J. (2011, December 5). In an open-source society, innovating by the seat of our pants. *The New York Times.* Available: http://www.nytimes.com/2011/12/06/science/joichi-ito-innovating-by-the-seat-of-our-pants.html.

6

THE FUTURE OF THINGS

By the end of this chapter, you will:

- gain insight into how the modern era was envisioned in the past;
- become familiar with some future trends and directions for products and product design;
- recognize some of the emerging product-related issues in ethics and environmentally friendly consumption;
- understand the concept of sustainability and its relevance to consumer products;
- appreciate the emerging role of services and the service experience for consumers.

Predicting the future is no small task. Few could have foreseen the dramatic changes that have taken place in the consumer marketplace within such a relatively short period: the central role of the Internet and the evolution of portable computing, mobile devices, social networking, virtual reality, e-commerce, 3-D printing, wearable smart devices, wi-fi, on-demand television, radio streams and podcasts, crowdsourcing, and so on. Fifty years ago, all of these developments were largely unimaginable to most people, perhaps with the exception of a small number of forward-looking scientists, engineers, and science fiction writers.

It is exceedingly difficult to forecast the future even in the short term with any degree of accuracy because those attempts are invariably restricted by the blinders of the present. For example, the invention of the automobile around the end of the nineteenth century may have logically led dreamers to envision flying cars as a common feature of the early twenty-first century, but unforeseen environmental developments and social trends have instead brought us energy-efficient cars, electric car sharing programs, driverless cars, and more efficient mass transportation systems. These current realities were in no small part shaped by the environmental impact of the automobile, traffic congestion, the rising population of urban areas, the evolution of commuter lifestyles, and the like. Nobody talks about flying cars anymore, which does not necessarily mean they will not become a common fixture of the twenty-second-century transportation landscape. As marketing professor James Fitchett astutely observed, a credible imagining of the marketplace of the future can only emerge when we approach the future "as a continuation of prior social trends and cultural dynamics."[1] In the chapter "The Twenty-First-Century Consumer Society," Fitchett explained:

> One of the recurrent problems with many futuristic accounts of consumer society is that beneath the creativity of potentials we often find deeply engrained tropes of the present. Thus, for example, imagining a future of high-speed data transfer is probably best understood as a manifestation of present-day frustrations with slow download times and poor interconnectivity rather than a rational analysis of possible technological developments.[2]

In short, however tempting it may be, technology does not by itself represent a coherent vision of the future, only the means of shaping possible futures. Thus, it is not enough to focus solely on potential technological advances and their likely impact on consumers, especially without considering the broader cultural, social, and physical developments that are likely to shape the needs and behaviors of future consumer markets. In this chapter, we will look for lessons from past attempts to imagine the present and, however tenuous the effort may be, contemplate what can be expected from products and our relationships with them in years to come in an effort to identify what future consumer societies might look like. The discussion will include a specific focus on some areas that have begun to capture the attention of contemporary designers, product manufacturers, and marketers, including environmental sustainability and the growing role of experiential marketing and service-dominant logic.

Imagining the present

There is perhaps no better place to turn for insight into what imaginings of the current era looked like in the past than science fiction, in both its literary and cinematic versions. Although an admirer and consumer of both artistic forms, I hardly profess to possess sufficient breadth of knowledge to provide a complete survey of future visions here, but I hope a few noteworthy examples will suffice. It should come as no surprise that visions of the future that have captured the imagination of children, filmmakers, science fiction writers, and ordinary consumers range from the misguided to the prescient, the ridiculous to the profound. One early classic of the science fiction film genre, *Things to Come* (1936), dubbed "a landmark of cinematic design" by cultural historian Christopher Fraying, charts a future history that unfolds from 1940 to 2036, as originally conceived in literature by H. G. Wells' "great dream of the future," *The Shape of Things to Come* (1933). Wells disparaged the future as portrayed in Fritz Lang's 1927 classic class warfare-themed *Metropolis*, with "all that balderdash . . . about 'robot workers' and ultra-skyscrapers."[3] Wells' vision of a future city ("Everytown") was largely couched within a grander political treatise on how we would arrive there, following a course of war, anarchy, reconstruction, and a new society. As a result, the film itself, like many other early science fiction films depicting a near or distant future, had very little to suggest about products and technology within the context of an evolved consumer landscape. A noteworthy exception is seen in the production design of *Things to Come*'s furniture of the distant future, which director Vincent Korda based on a 1933 exposition of the designs of architect Oliver Hill at the Exhibition of British Industrial Art in London.

Things to Come does stand out as an exception among the fantasy films of the Depression era in its depiction of the promises and threats of technology. At that time, for the general public, science essentially connoted more and bigger machines and engineering, as opposed to great breakthrough discoveries. When spectacular technology did appear in films—a mid-ocean airport in *F.P.1 Does Not Answer* (1932), a tunnel constructed under the ocean linking England to America in *Transatlantic Tunnel* (1933)—its effects were far more limited in scope than, for example, the underground cities and moon flights of *Things to Come*. For the most part, however, the emphasis in cinema focused more on an individual's personal plight, as opposed to what invention could mean for humankind as a whole.[4] This changed with the onset of World War II and the development of the atom bomb, which quickly led to the realization among the general public that science could drastically affect them en masse, not simply in isolated groups. Post-World War II realistic fantasies were apt to feature technology as more pervasive than it had previously been portrayed, not something constricted to a single invention or a private laboratory.

More recent musings on the present era are evident in a variety of disparate sources, ranging from classic French cinema to American television pop culture—yet they provide an uncanny similarity in terms of their depiction of the influence of technology on modern consumer lifestyles. Jacques Tati's acclaimed 1958 film *Mon Oncle* is a pointedly observed comedy that sheds light on the clash between tradition and modernity. Its early scenes depict the quiet and charming community in a quaint French village, with scenes of vegetable stands and horse-drawn carriages, a street sweeper, and impudent children playing harmless practical jokes on unsuspecting adults. The leading character, Monsieur Hulot (played by filmmaker Tati himself), is unquestionably low-tech: in one scene, we watch as he manipulates his apartment's window so that it reflects the sun onto birds perched on a neighbor's window sill, causing them to sing. In another scene, Monsieur Hulot uncovers the solution to why customers are being overcharged by a produce seller working out of a delivery truck. The seller's scale needle exaggerates to the right, not because of some sly, high-tech maneuver, but because of a flat tire that is causing the truck to tilt.

This mirror of decidedly old-fashioned small-town life is quickly contrasted by scenes set at the ultra-modern house in the suburbs where the family of Monsieur Hulot's sister resides. Madame takes obvious pride in her fully automated abode, replete with a variety of futuristic elements, including the push-button delivery of meals, self-functioning vacuum cleaner, electric eyes, and the like. No convenience is spared: the cabinets, doors, and gate are fully automatic; the house is centrally air conditioned; the kitchen is equipped with sterilization and ventilation systems, and a steak in a frying pan is flipped with the push of a button. We hear Madame repeatedly assure her guests how the house is coming along: "it's so practical, everything is connected," with "connected" in this sense falling well short of how we apply that term today. Undeniably fallible in terms of reliability, the futuristic gadgets and trimmings in Tati's imagined futuristic home leave much to be desired (see Box 6.1). The atmosphere is cold and clinical, gadgets repeatedly malfunction and break, and overall, the modern trappings come off as overly pretentious and ridiculously superfluous. Despite the added conveniences, modernity brings more work, not less, as Madame admits—"oh, you know with these modern homes . . . a house like this is such a job"—the complaint repeatedly affirmed as she frantically runs around the house pushing buttons to turn things on or off. In one scene, we watch as Monsieur Hulot's young nephew takes greater pleasure in the simple toy offered by his uncle than in the higher-tech offering of his father; in another, the noise from modern appliances prevents Madame and her husband from communicating effectively with each other. When asked to rescue her employers after their accidental entrapment in the garage due to their walking past the electronic garage door sensor, the maid recoils in fear: "Oh no, I'll be electrocuted. I'm so afraid of electricity!" Reflecting on the film, design expert Tim Parsons suggests that Tati's comedy represents "a heartfelt polemic against what he saw as the inhumanity of contemporary 'progress'":

> A naïve but likeable everyman, Hulot is unacquainted with, and therefore bemused by, anything remotely modern. Even the simplest of mechanisms can confound him. Hence, as he appears on screen with objects, we predict their behaviour long before he does. . . . Tati produced the perfect weapon for satirising "progressive" design and, by implication, its designers. The joy he uncovered by showing objects out of place, being misread or misused, has been emulated by Castiglioni and others in the world of design. Like Tati's films, these designs become an effective foil to po-faced, dogmatic modernism.[5]

BOX 6.1 MEET THE JETSONS

Recalling some of the same themes as those conveyed in one of the last great films of the silent era, *Modern Times* (1936), in which Charlie Chaplin's factory worker character struggles with the frustrating and overwhelming demands imposed by the machine age, the implicit message taken from Jacques Tati's *Mon Oncle* (1958), and others that followed in its wake—such as Tati's own *Playtime* (1967), Jean-Luc Godard's *Alphaville* (1965), and George Lucas' *THX-1138* (1971)—is that technological progress does not always turn out to be as ideal as one might hope. This idea was popularly echoed during the early 1960s in an unlikely American source—a Hanna-Barbera cartoon series, *The Jetsons* (1962–83). As the Space Age counterpart to the already successful Stone Age cartoon *The Flintstones* (1960–81), from the first episode of this long-standing television success story we are presented with a glimpse into the ultramodern world of the twenty-first century, as seen through mid-twentieth-century eyes, and the results are not entirely hopeful. Although ostensibly set in the year 2062, several of the high-tech developments are familiar to us today, including 3-D flat-screen TVs, videophones, and moving walkways; some, such as push-button appliances and paper money, are oddly archaic; and others, such as flying saucer cars and spaceboots for walking on the ceiling, are rather far-fetched.

Throughout the series' episodes, characters repeatedly marvel at the convenience and practicality of their high-tech age while bemoaning its various downsides. Homemaker Jane Jetson is reduced to morning "push-button finger exercises" to overcome the finger cramps caused by repeatedly operating automatic push-button appliances (reminiscent of the hazards of contemporary texting on mobile devices), while her husband George—a "digital index operator" who spends "a hard day at the button" at the Spaceley's Sprockets Company—complains of persistent back pain ("compact saucer cramp") induced by his constrictive flying saucer transport. As with *Mon Oncle*'s Madame, Jane complains about the hard work involved in managing her completely programmable kitchen, with the push-button preparation of meals from a selection panel ("Thank goodness that's over with!"), and having to deal with the persistent malfunctions of the "antique monster" (instead of scrambled eggs, Jane's son is presented with a "hot fudge pizza"). Fortunately, all is not lost, as lazy George has his job saved in the series' initial episode by an outmoded rent-a-maid robot whose pineapple upside-down cake seduces George's cantankerous boss.

Perhaps it is not surprising to find that many of the past contemplations of what early twenty-first-century living would have in store for consumers centered on the kitchen—a focal point for musings on what technology offered for facilitating ease of living, convenience, practicality, time savings, and pleasure. This is evidenced in a variety of short industrial films produced during the 1950s and 1960s, each of which provides a vision of what we could anticipate as the approaching millennium began to take shape. Some of the more noteworthy films were General Motors' *Design for Dreaming* (1956), which envisioned a "Frigidaire Kitchen"[6]; the "Kitchen of Tomorrow" (source unknown), with video screens exhibiting recipes at one's fingertips[7]; and the 1967 Philco-Ford Corporation short film *1999 A.D.*, with its "Kitchen of Future" segment. As in the others, the latter showcases familiar themes of the future household as being characterized by automation, health concerns, and push-button technology. The three-and-a-half-minute segment portrays a housewife at the dawn of the next millennium preparing lunch for her family in a mere two minutes, selecting dishes from her computer screen based on their calorie content (a cold roast beef and beans lunch is selected as a healthier alternative to her husband's requested cheeseburger and fries), turning on her microwave oven, and retrieving the fully cooked meal in a matter of seconds from a tray that automatically slides out from the side of the oven. As a narrator explains:

> Split-second lunches, color keyed disposable dishes, all part of the instant society of tomorrow. A society rich in leisure and taken-for-granted comforts. At the turn of the next century, most food will be stored frozen in individual portions. The computer will keep a running inventory on all foodstuffs and suggest daily menus based on the nutritional needs of the family. When the meal has been selected, the various portions are fed automatically into the microwave oven for a few seconds of deep thawing or warming.[8]

Some of the technological, social, and lifestyle changes such prescient depictions of modern living failed to anticipate, however, are noteworthy, and serve to further illustrate my point at the outset of this chapter about how predictions of the future are typically framed within the mindset of the present. For example, the kitchen remained the sole province of women adorned in aprons, as eventual shifts in gender roles remained largely unforeseen. Similarly, whereas convenience and time saving were recognized as essential requirements of the ideal kitchen for the consumer of the future, the rise of fooding and comfort dining (see Chapter 3), gourmet cooking, and DIY meal preparation (including the 3-D printing of food) were also unanticipated. On the technological front, push-buttons connoted ease of use and modernity (as they did in popular feature-length films about the future), whereas present-day consumers are more apt to touch and swipe—bearing in mind that gestural and retinal communication with devices are developments on the horizon. Although the rudimentary idea was evident in the industrial videos of the ideal kitchen, a fully functioning Internet of Things was off the radar of prognosticators.

Imagining the future

If our ability to predict the future was hit or miss in the past, what about our contemporary efforts to preordain the future consumer landscape? An argument can be made that given dramatic technological developments during the past half-century, we are in a better position to anticipate what is to come than ever before. Advances in technology in the contemporary era, as Ray Kurzweil pointed out in *The Singularity is Near*,[9] tend to build on those that precede them, and computer modeling and simulation techniques have progressed significantly in recent decades, with the speed of computing continuing to increase exponentially. In fact, more recent attempts to forecast the future have been undeniably perceptive. As I have mentioned in previous chapters, futurist Alvin Toffler discussed the growing power of the prosumer in his 1970 book *Future Shock*. In that book and his 1980 sequel *The Third Wave*, Toffler covered other concepts and ideas that are common fixtures of our present-day lexicon, including the promise of renewable energy, embedded sensors in household appliances, corporate social responsibility, information overload, and the DIY revolution. Toffler, along with his wife, Heidi Toffler, recognized the potentially far-reaching effects of advanced communication technology while others did not. They foresaw the impact that communication devices and virtual worlds would have on people, and warned of threats to privacy and problems of overstimulation decades before these became mainstream issues. The Tofflers conducted no scientific research themselves, but instead implicated themselves among those individuals who were at the cutting edge of scientific and industrial developments, conducting on-site visits and extensive interviews with the people who had special insight into where technology and science were heading. In a sense, we might say that the Tofflers were early pioneers in crowdsourcing, taking what they could from the crowd to methodically piece together an elusive future.

Another literary source of prescient forecasting is the science fiction subgenre known as *cyberpunk*, which is typified by fictional accounts of the near future, with an emphasis on the central role of high-tech in the lives of the authors' protagonists. As described by science fiction writer Lawrence Person:

> classic cyberpunk characters were marginalized, alienated loners who lived on the edge of society in generally dystopic futures where daily life was impacted by rapid technological change, an ubiquitous datasphere of computerized information, and invasive modification of the human body.[10]

Among the standout authors in this subgenre are William Gibson (*Neuromancer*, 1984; *Idoru*, 1997) and Neal Stephenson (*Snow Crash*, 1992; *The Diamond Age*, 1995), whose books provide a number of guideposts as to where emerging technologies were heading. For example, in his 1992 classic *Snow Crash*, Stephenson imagines an information age in which virtual reality, avatars, computer viruses, microcoding, hacking, GPS, digital smartwear, and, it might be added, high-speed pizza delivery are common fixtures.[11] The brilliance of Stephenson's prophetic imagination is apparent in his description of the aforementioned high-tech pizza delivery:

> they went with a quick cheap technical fix: smart boxes. The pizza box is a plastic carapace now, corrugated for stiffness, a little LED readout glowing

on the side, telling the Deliverator how many trade imbalance-producing minutes have ticked away since the fateful phone call. There are chips and stuff in there. The pizzas rest, a short stack of them, in slots behind the Deliverator's head. Each pizza glides into a slot like a circuit board into a computer, clicks into place as the smart box interfaces with the onboard system of the Deliverator's car. The address of the caller has already been inferred from his phone number and poured into the smart box's built-in RAM. From there it is communicated to the car, which computes and projects the optimal route on a heads-up display, a glowing colored map traced out against the windshield so that the Deliverator does not even have to glance down.[12]

Despite various spot-on projections into the not-too-distant future, as suggested at the outset of this chapter, predicting what lies ahead is precarious business. To elucidate the complexity of future forecasting, *The New York Times* science writer Gina Kolata described how her prediction twenty-five years earlier that within one year the effectiveness of gene therapy would be demonstrated and begin to rapidly transform medicine has yet to come to pass. In defense of her failed prognostication, Kolata deferred to two Nobel laureates: Joseph L. Goldstein, who revealed that "I've learned over the years that the best predictor for what will be new and exciting is, 'Expect the unexpected,'" and David Baltimore, who observed: "If you could predict it, it wouldn't be breakthrough."[13] These observations notwithstanding, others suggest that once it appears that a particular area of science, medicine, or engineering is beginning to undergo certain advances, it is possible to project how subsequent events will likely unfold, even if predicting a particular major discovery remains unlikely. In essence, there is a tipping point at which an important advance is recognized for what it is once its generality becomes apparent. This is what some claim is occurring in stem cell research or is just around the corner for researchers seeking a cure for Alzheimer's disease.[14] Given that these observations pertain to the scientific and medical domains, it is logical to ask whether they also apply to developments in new product design and the impact of objects on consumer cultures.

New product development and design had for years proceeded in an incremental fashion, with gradual improvements made in products like telephones (from rotary dials to touch tones) and televisions (from black and white to color). Today, changes appear to be more revolutionary, with the emergence of previously unimaginable innovations like the Internet, personal digital assistants, satellite navigation, and 3-D printers. As advances in technology continue to accelerate and as demands for more environmentally responsible alternatives to existing products increase, predicting the future is perhaps more challenging than ever. In the following sections, I will describe some of the possible developments in a sampling of representative product domains according to experts from a variety of fields.

The future of computing

The personal computer as we know it is already undergoing significant changes, with desktops and laptops rapidly being supplemented or replaced by tablets, phablets, and smartphones. In the near future, keyboards and mice are likely to become irrelevant as touch-screen, voice-operated, and motion-sensitive systems gradually take hold, promising to reinvent computer design. A 2011 exercise conducted by *The New York Times* challenged readers and technology experts to imagine the future of computing over the next couple of centuries. Predictions included the following:

- By 2020, Google real-time language translation will permit people to communicate with each other via their smart phones, regardless of the specific language they speak.
- By 2022, a "halo of data" will constantly accompany people, keeping them informed on their portable devices of what and who is around them.
- By 2031, most people will engage in full-life recording, storing full video and audio of their daily lives in searchable archives, dramatically augmenting their effective memory.
- By 2078, it will be possible for people to connect their brains to the Internet via wi-fi, providing unlimited memory and communication ability.
- By 2114, humans will be able to sync, restore, and back up their entire memory to a computing cloud.
- By 2170, as people become more integrated with electronics, more people will die from computer viruses than biological ones.
- By 2025, "we'll be laughing at these predictions."[15]

In the same *The New York Times* project, bioengineer Drew Endy advised that the future value of computers should be considered in terms of the type of information being computed, and of when and where these computations occur, as opposed to the speed, scale, and efficiency with which computations are performed. For example, a smartphone that computes a person's route home when lost has more personal value than a powerful, but inaccessible, home computer—at least, that is, until the connectivity between our various devices, wherever they are located, becomes more ubiquitous. In Endy's vision, the future of computing is likely to be one in which people and things literally merge, a development he envisions in one variant as silicon computers in the form of miniature implants that could be installed within a person's body's cells. Such implants, individually consisting of only a modicum of data storage (about 8 bits), could have significant value, with the potential to assess how many times each cell divides in order to control aging, development, and the emergence of cancers, the latter of which could be offset through the programmed destruction of cells before a tumor has the chance to form. The prospects for such computers, which could have great promise for basic research and medical biotechnology, would be unimaginable without the proper tipping point—in this case, as Endy suggests, from research conducted by biologists:

Fortunately, sustained basic research since the early 1980s has taught us how natural biological systems might be adapted to store information and compute upon it. Now, researchers are starting to systematically apply this knowledge to develop scalable living data storage systems and simple computational interfaces. For example, digital information can be stored inside cells by flipping DNA sequences back and forth or by controlling protein levels and locations. Other research is exploring how RNA, for example, can be engineered to control the reading and writing of information to synthetic biological bits.[16]

Whereas Endy focuses on the potential power of small data, others see future developments as evolving from large data stores and greater computing power, such as computer scientist David Patterson, who envisions Big Data, sophisticated statistical algorithms, and crowdsourcing as keys in the fight to cure cancer.[17] Physicist and scientific computing expert Larry Smarr also sees power in greater computing speed, storage, and data ubiquity. With billions of processors and sensors embedded in a growing range of products (including smartphones, cars, appliances, and buildings) and capable of sending out a steady stream of data about their surroundings, Smarr envisions the evolution of vast clouds of "spatially aware" data, centralized among large corporations like Google, Amazon, Microsoft, Yahoo!, and Apple:

> Smart electric grids are measuring our homes' use of power; active people are tracking their heart rates; and hundreds of millions of us are uploading geo-tagged data to Flickr, Yelp, Facebook and Google Plus. As we look 10 years ahead, the fastest supercomputer (the "exascale" machine) will be composed of one billion processors, and the clouds will most likely grow to this scale as well, creating a distributed planetary computer of enormous power. . . . With the continuing exponential increase in the power of the planetary computer, one has to wonder whether we stand at the beginning of what Isaac Asimov's "Foundation" series, more than 60 years ago, called "psychohistory." His visionary forecasting of human society's actions would be possible with data from enough people throughout the galaxy.[18]

Although we are only at the outset of realizing such a global vision, Starr points to the example already set by Google Maps, which utilizes data in the cloud to sample the locations and movement of drivers' mobile phones in order to develop real-time pictures of traffic congestion.

The future of cars

If it is now becoming relatively easy to track traffic congestion, more efficient routes for reaching one's destination, and the location of available parking spaces[19] based on available technologies, it is reasonable to question how the nature of our relationship with cars is likely to change in the future. One development is rendering drivers superfluous, as the analysis of traffic data, in-car radar, and autopilot electronics have begun to provide the software control of robot-driven electric cars. At the time of this writing, Google had taken the lead with the creation of driverless cars and several countries had begun testing robotic cars in traffic.

As cars are becoming less dependent on people, the means and circumstances in which the product is used by consumers are also likely to undergo significant changes, with higher rates of participation in car sharing and short-term leasing programs. In the not-too-distant future, a driverless car could come to you when you need it, and when you are done with it, it could then drive away without any need for a parking space.[20] Increases in car sharing and short-term leasing are also likely to be associated with a corresponding decrease in the importance of exterior car design. Rather than serving as a medium for personalization and self-identity (see Chapter 1), car exteriors might increasingly come to represent a channel for advertising and other promotional activities, including brand ambassador programs, such as those offered by Free Car Media (FCM).[21] As a result, the symbolic meanings derived from cars and their relationship to consumer self-identity and status are likely to change in turn.

With electric cars and other energy-efficient alternatives to gas-powered vehicles likely to become the norms, it is interesting to conjecture about the potential effects of this development on the urban landscape. Telephone booths and parking meters—both presently heading toward obsolescence as a result of mobile phones and the possibility of paying for parking with one's portable devices—could provide ready-made sources of electricity for recharging electric cars and other consumer devices, as well as wi-fi stations for car sharing, traffic, weather, and parking information. Such changes are well underway, with the Spanish government having taken steps in a pioneering effort to convert underused phone booths into electric vehicle charging stations.[22]

A focus on car design changes reveals a number of trends over the years, corresponding to societal patterns, technological advances, and consumer preferences. Major changes in car design seem to occur about every ten to twelve years.[23] For example, during the 1950s, as a reflection of the American public's growing fascination with modernity and the emerging so-called "jet age," car designers began to add stylistic flourishes, such as rear fins, wraparound windshields, and turbines in the front grill, to the mundane designs of mainstream family cars of the era. Meanwhile, European vehicles showed less radical changes, although the stylishly rounded, clean lines of vehicles popular at the time, including sports cars designed by Ferrari, Porsche, and BMW, influenced the design of cars during the following decades.[24] Car designs require a careful balance between aesthetics and ergonomics because, however appealing a stylistic attribute may be, it cannot undermine the driver's ability to control and manage the vehicle, block sightlines, or add discomfort to the driving experience.

Contemporary car designers have borrowed ideas from consumer product design in their attempts to integrate new communication technologies and respond to environmental demands. For example, it has been observed that the look of the ultra-compact Smart car connotes more of the idea of a gadget than a motor vehicle.[25] The growing symbiosis between the design of cars and other consumer product categories is evident in emerging developments in computer software (such as Solidworks and Rhinoceros) and ongoing technological advances (see Box 6.2). One new development consists of producing products with the use of "bulkypapers"—ultra-tough, extremely lightweight sheets of matter developed through the use of nanotechnology. Although only as wide as a sheet of paper, bulkypaper material is many times stronger than steel.[26] Weight continues to be a concern in the production of electric cars and batteries; however, responding to such problems, automotive designer Jeff Teague reflected the optimism among designers in his field when he observed: "it's just a matter of time. Green vehicles will be 100% green and will run on plastic. But when continues to be the question."[27]

BOX 6.2 THE CHANGING CAR LIGHT: A GLIMPSE INTO THE FUTURE OF DESIGN?

An element of automotive design that has gone largely unheralded in recent years has to do with the transformation of the car light. New vehicle lines offered by Audi, Ford, Mercedes, Opel, and Range Rover, in addition to London buses, have made use of new technologies in the design of front and rear lights, altering their aesthetic appeal ("dazzling assortments of tiny light sources, filters and reflectors cast in alluringly futuristic shapes") and functionality ("adjusting their beams in response to obstructions on the road, approaching vehicles or changes in the weather").[28]

What is particularly interesting about this apparently minor development in product design is that the technological innovations that have led to the transformation of automotive lighting, including sophisticated light sources and sensor control systems, are beginning to have an impact on the design of other consumer products. This is particularly evident in the recent proliferation of the more energy-efficient, miniature light-emitting diode (LED), which consumes less power and has greater flexibility than other light sources. Because of their small size, they can be arranged in novel configurations and, when combined with reflectors and filters, can have a significant aesthetic impact, as described by design expert Alice Rawsthorn:

> The results have the improbably complex air of objects that could only have been created by advanced technology, and share the surreally intricate forms of the abstract digital images we see in data visualizations and the experimental objects produced by advanced manufacturing technologies, like three-dimensional printing, which will be increasingly common in future. The dominant shapes of the immediate future

will look not unlike the strange, rippling structures you can now see inside headlights and brake lights.[29]

As for functionality, advances in the performance of car lights, with their ability to detect and respond to changes in their surroundings through the use of adaptive light sensors, are also likely to become evident in future applications, in home and office lighting, as well as in the development of driverless vehicles. LED bulbs, for example, generate less heat and can be utilized in more imaginative ways than traditional light bulbs, such as by placing them underneath cabinets or inside closets. Some new lighting systems come equipped with dedicated apps so that they can be controlled by mobile devices, allowing the consumer to change colors manually or according to predetermined settings. A consumer who has difficulties falling asleep or waking up could program ambient lighting colors as necessary.

New trends in smart devices

It is likely that some of the elements of the kitchens of the future imagined in the past (see above) will soon be among several new innovative fixtures in households, especially as greater connectivity between devices, now commonly referred to as the "Internet of Things," becomes more pervasive (see Box 6.3). Computer scientists and technology experts are working toward putting the digital "smarts" into a vast array of products, with smart products invariably able to interact intelligently with people and the physical world. One representative example introduced in 2011 is Nest Labs' digital thermostat, which combines sensors, machine learning, and Internet technology to sense changes in air temperature along with the movements of people in a house, adjusting room temperatures accordingly as people enter or leave rooms, saving energy in the process. It is noteworthy that Google acquired Nest Labs, a maker of Internet-connected home products, for US$3 billion in early 2014, further legitimizing the nascent Internet of Things industry.[30] Products are well on the way to being transformed by sensors and computing intelligence and, in the process, the ways in which consumers interact with products and the contexts in which they use them also are undergoing significant changes. According to research conducted by the management consulting firm McKinsey & Company, there are three key technological trends at the root of these changes, which are briefly described below.[31]

BOX 6.3 THE DOWNSIDE OF THE INTERNET OF THINGS

Despite the apparent attractiveness of having an Internet-connected home, there are certain hurdles that need to be overcome before the Internet of Things diffuses across consumer populations and becomes a reality. As with

(Continued)

(Continued)

most new innovations, expense is an issue. At present, it is expensive to set up a connected home, given that smart products cost much more than their traditional counterparts. Three other challenges that must be overcome before we see the widespread diffusion of smart, connected products are summarized below:

1. Many of the new smart products already available on the market do not function together seamlessly because the companies that produce them are competing to become dominant in the market. As a result, consumers are faced with having to acquire more and more apps and digital services, which many are reluctant to do. This drawback was concisely described by tech columnist Dan Tynan, who wrote: "Unfortunately, it turns out that the future is kind of a mess. The stuff that was supposed to make our lives easier has created a fresh new hell of apps and gadgets all clamoring for our attention. Efforts to stitch them together into one seamless interface range from hopelessly complex and costly home automation systems to promising-yet-still-buggy upstarts. Frankly, it's still easier to just walk over and flip the switch yourself."

2. A corresponding concern is that the many devices that comprise a household's Internet of Things all generate a flood of data, information, and alerts which is likely to be perceived as overwhelming by the typical consumer, until the companies that provide the products are able to convince customers that all this information will contribute more to their safety, comfort, and well-being. However, according to the Cédric Hutchings, CEO of the Internet-connected health care products firm Withings, his company has seen rapid growth in recent years because an increasing number of people "are keen to put metrics on everything and analyze any aspect of their lives and improve it."[32] Whether Hutchings is characterizing a relatively small segment of the population engaged in monitoring their lives remains to be seen.

3. Privacy and security concerns collectively represent another significant hurdle to overcome before companies can hope to entice consumers to adopt more smart-connected devices. Access to the steady flow of information about one's personal life and possessions represents a source of further concern among people who are growing increasingly unsettled by the thought that companies and governments are infringing on the privacy rights of ordinary citizens. The possibility that a smart lock, home security system, or other household objects could be hacked is another issue that raises a red flag for consumers.[33] Companies that manufacture smart products typically scan for weaknesses in the software of their devices but, as has been the case with the Internet, experienced hackers seem to have an uncanny ability to stay one or more steps ahead of the safeguards.

At present, it is uncertain whether these concerns will prove to be obstacles that are perceived by consumers as not worth the potential advantages that can be derived from opting into the Internet of Things. Many within the technology industries, however, believe that the widespread adoption of connected smart devices is inevitable within the next ten years, and unlikely to be limited to a niche market.[34] Such predictions are buttressed by Acquity Group's 2014 Internet of Things research revealing that two-thirds of consumers surveyed plan to purchase connected technology for their homes and nearly half expect to adopt wearable technology by 2019.[35]

Seamless low-power connectivity

One significant trend driving smart device innovations is the widespread availability of low-power connectivity, which is contributing to the increasing flexibility of mobile intelligence. Central to this development is Bluetooth low energy (LE), a low-power interface that uses wireless sensors to provide consumers with the ability to interact with household appliances. For example, if a consumer wanted to control a room lamp with his or her smartphone, such an action would not necessitate the constant passing of high volumes of data back and forth between the devices. Only a handful of data bytes would be required to tell the lamp to turn on or off, or to report its current status, and the sending of low volumes of data would only have to occur at infrequent intervals. Because the duration of a connection need only be long enough for the user to send a command, the reduction of data transfer would reduce energy usage, and this process is enabled via the new low-power Bluetooth LE connectivity. With such developments, consumers will be able to interact with their homes and offices even from a distance, securing locks, controlling the lighting, programming appliances, and so on.

Sensor innovations

A second important trend in smart devices identified by McKinsey pertains to the emergence of a variety of types of miniature sensors, which are extending the capabilities of smartphones and other mobile devices through a range of innovative applications. Based on the microelectromechanical systems (MEMS) technology of small devices, it is now relatively easy and inexpensive to embed sensors into nearly every physical product. For example, wearable sensors can be integrated into clothing in order to convey physiological data about the wearer. The French smart textile firm Cityzen Sciences has led the way with this technology, specializing in the creation of smart textiles that are embedded with micro-sensors that monitor temperature, heart rate, speed and acceleration, as well as the energy output of users' muscles and the severity of physical impact. The Kolibree toothbrush is a sensor-embedded toothbrush that collects data on the user's brushing habits, including duration and frequency of brushing and the zones that were missed, and then sends that data to one's smartphone via Bluetooth technology.

Wearables, or the so-called "Internet of You," represent a burgeoning area in which sensor technology is playing a key role. In recent years, a range of innovative products similar to the Cityzen Sciences smart textiles have appeared that use embedded sensors to collect information about the user and his or her body, promising a variety of applications for the health care sector, especially for the senior consumer segment. Wearable devices such as the wristbands, bracelets, and other products offered by Fitbit[36] and Jawbone[37] collect and report data on physical activity (steps taken, distance, stairs climbed, calories burned), eating (intake and healthfulness), weight, and sleep (duration and quality), and allow the user to sync the measurements to multiple devices. Unobtrusive technology is now progressing for sensors in shoes that are capable of measuring and providing active feedback about how well the user is walking. It is hoped that such a development could be used to help amputees adapt to their prosthetic limbs, assist patients in their recovery from joint replacements or stroke, or alert seniors when they may be in imminent danger of falling. Other sensor-based wearable products are now available for monitoring pulse rate, blood pressure, glucose levels for diabetics, and exposure to sunlight, with the latter providing alerts about the need to apply sunscreen or wear sunglasses.[38] Such devices are particularly compelling for consumers who, as discussed in Chapter 3, are increasingly concerned about health and fitness.

An extension of the sensor technology is evident in mainstream wearable computers: a range of products consisting of a screen that augments vision with information and media, typically with data communicated back to a smartphone. Led by Google, which introduced its connected eyewear, Glass, in 2012, and Samsung Electronics, which released a smartwatch in 2013, wearable computing represents a trend in technology that further blurs the real and virtual worlds. Recently, Google partnered with Novartis' eye care division Alcon to develop smart contact lenses which, it is hoped, will serve a variety of ocular medical uses. Ophthalmic electrochemical sensors are embedded in the contact lenses to measure glucose levels and offer real-time updates on a connected mobile device for diabetics, and the lenses also may ultimately provide vision correction for elderly consumers.[39]

Materials innovation

Several years ago, marketers marveled over a new innovation on the horizon: the flexCD—a thin, ultra-flexible, high-storage data disc which was lauded as the next "hard-to-miss" trend.[40] Pioneered by the German media giant Bertelsmann, the flexible CD was made of polyester foil rather than the conventional polycarbonates, resulting in such a high degree of flexibility that it could be wrapped around innumerable products, from soda cans to detergent bottles, placed in magazines, and so on. Flexible CDs were compatible with mainstream CD players and computer CD-ROM drives, and were produced at half the cost of traditional hard CDs. At the time, however, research consultant David Miller, in response to the new developments in compact discs, opined that "the technology is ahead of the application." Before applications were pursued with the flexible CDs, digital content and online streaming became pervasive and, perhaps as a result, the innovation never got off the ground. Now, more than a decade later, new materials are emerging that promise to make flexible and bendable devices a reality, which is the third significant new trend identified by McKinsey's researchers. An example is the South Korean electronics firm LG's transparent, big-screen TV, which is so flexible that it can be rolled up like a poster. Using a polymer as the backplane of the panel instead of conventional plastic, it was possible for LG to increase the flexibility of the display panel and reduce its thickness. Provisioned for 2017, the product's flexibility is likely to have a huge impact on the shipping, storage, and portability of televisions.[41]

Although the career advice given to Dustin Hoffman's young leading character in the 1967 film *The Graduate* was summarized in one word, "plastics," a remake would likely change that counsel to "graphene." Graphene, which is a transparent form of carbon, is considered to be both the hardest and the thinnest material in the world, and one of the most pliable. It can conduct electricity and heat more efficiently than any other material, and the results of scientific experiments with graphene suggest that it has great commercial potential for the creation of flexible devices, electronic clothing, supercharged quantum computers, and computers that can interface with human body cells.[42] In one example of how graphene can be commercially produced, Chinese scientists used a gel to create a graphene aerogel which is one-seventh the weight of air. As for the potential applications of this innovative material, it is believed that it will provide greater freedom to design thinner and faster electronic devices that are clear and flexible; long-lasting batteries that can be submerged in water; touch-screen electronics in the form of paper-thin portable phones and tablets; flexible wearables and displays; and electronic gadgets that can be implanted in the human body to interact with biological systems. Perhaps the best news for consumers is that graphene is inexpensive, meaning that most products in the contemporary electronics industry can be made cheaper, smaller, and more flexible.

The design implications for new materials like graphene in terms of the appearance, feel, and utilization of products are likely to be formidable. As discussed in previous chapters, the contemporary smartphone bears little resemblance to the rotary-dial telephones of the past, as technologies enhanced the conventional product not only with new functions, but also with unique forms, varying sizes, and greater interactivity. With new materials, it seems logical to surmise that the primarily rectangular objects we utilize as smart devices today could be replaced by something unrecognizable in the near future. Graphene and other emerging materials are similarly likely to have a significant impact on the design of innumerable other products, including household appliances, computers, children's toys, weapons, money, cars, houses, food, and clothing.

Products, ethics, and sustainability

Marketers have long been the targets of a number of social criticisms regarding the potential negative impact of their practices on consumers (e.g., deception in practices and promotion; the setting of high prices), society (e.g., promotion of materialism; cultural pollution), and other businesses (e.g., unfair competitive practices). These criticisms bring us within the realm of *marketing ethics*, which pertains to considerations of right and wrong (or appropriate and inappropriate) in the context of marketing practices, policies, and systems.[43] Previously, I have briefly discussed some of the ethical issues perhaps most closely linked to new product development and design, including the planned obsolescence of products (Chapter 3) and concerns about whether marketers are developing and marketing products that consumers could live without, creating false wants and a rise in materialism within societies in the process (Chapter 1). In recent years, the impact of product manufacturing, production, distribution, and disposal on the environment has moved front and center among the critical issues facing designers and marketers of consumer products, bringing into the debate a rapidly evolving emphasis on sustainable development. In the remainder of this section, we will turn our attention to some ethical issues pertaining to product design and marketing not yet addressed that are likely to be especially salient as we move deeper into the twenty-first century.

Product pricing and ethics

One of the long-standing social criticisms of marketers is that their practices serve to raise the cost of products beyond what is justified by their utility and economic value. In part, excessive prices are attributed to the high costs of advertising, promotion, and packaging, which may add to the psychological value of a product, but are unlikely to provide additional functional value. The cost of distribution is believed to be another source of price increases, as multiple intermediaries mark up prices beyond the value of their services, with some intermediaries merely unnecessarily duplicating the services of others. Although space does not permit a comprehensive discussion of the ways in which prices are set, it is important to note that a product's price is determined differently according to the type of product and the nature of the selling situation.[44] Wholesale prices are determined by what it costs the manufacturer to produce an item, plus a mark-up that is added so that the manufacturer can derive a profit. The retail price, which is what the product is sold for in real or virtual stores, reflects the wholesale price that the retailer paid for the product, plus the retailer's mark-up. Additional mark-ups are added at each stage of the distribution process and, combined with national and local taxes, the paying of staff and other business operating expenses, designer's royalties, and the like, the actual retail price of a product in shops will far surpass the actual cost price of manufacturing a product. Overall, mark-ups will vary according to what each participant in the supply chain—the manufacturer, the wholesaler, and the retailer—believes it can charge, based on economic equations, to ensure that it will not incur a loss on a sale.

Although from the consumer perspective certain objects have subjective, intrinsic value, the financial value of a product or good is ultimately determined by what customers are willing to pay for it—that is, by whether it sells at its retail price (see Box 6.4). In this sense, a number of sales at a similar price can act as a gauge to provide a collective idea of what a product is worth.[45] This is where the notion of supply and demand comes into play, with the supply of a good reflected by how much producers are willing to make at a given price and the demand determined by how much consumers are willing to buy at a given price. It is important to add that an object generally loses value, or depreciates, as soon as it is purchased, except where it is a limited edition or collector's item, in which case the item is likely to gain in value over time.

BOX 6.4 PRICE AND PERCEPTION

Although it may not be an inherent attribute of a product, price is nonetheless capable of capturing attention and influencing consumer reaction to a marketplace offering. This is especially true for price-conscious shoppers or in situations where price exceeds one's limits of acceptability. Studies have demonstrated that consumers often rely on price as an indicator of quality and, in so doing, may attribute different qualities to identical products that bear different price labels. The perception of price as an indicator of quality is more likely to influence a shopper when other cues are lacking, such as when one has limited experience with brands in the category under consideration and is unfamiliar with a store's image. For example, if you know little about wine and have been asked by your host to "bring a good Bordeaux" to her party, you might choose the most expensive bottle (albeit within your budget) from the choices before you in the wine shop, assuming that the quality of the selected bottle will be satisfactory.

Marketers often resort to various pricing strategies to lead consumers to perceive a price as less expensive than it actually is. For example, *odd pricing* consists of establishing a price for a product or service at an amount ending in an odd number like 9 or 5. Because people are more likely to remember the larger (leftward) digit positions in a series of numbers, a price of US$29.99 may be recalled as closer to US$20 than US$30, and to assume that greater precision was used in establishing the odd price. Perceptually, odd pricing tends to connote savings, and is frequently employed by discount stores, whereas even pricing (such as US$50) tends to connote status, and is often evident in prestige or fashion retail settings. It also has been found that partitioning the base price and the surcharge (e.g., the cost of shipping and

(Continued)

(Continued)

handling) typically results in consumers perceiving the total price as cheaper than had the all-inclusive price been given.

Another price-related tendency is for people to perceive lower numbers (such as 2 and 3) as further apart than higher digits (such as 8 and 9). As a result, when retailers establish a price reduction for an offering using lower digits, consumers are likely to believe that the savings will be greater than if the same reduction had employed higher digits. In one test of this effect, researchers presented consumers with print ads announcing that a US$233 pair of skates had been marked down to US$222.[46] When compared with another group of consumers presented with a markdown of US$199 to US$188 for the same skates, those given the lower-digit figures believed they would receive a larger discount (5.53%) than those shown the higher-digit figures (4.18%). Although the absolute markdown (US$11) was the same for both groups, price perceptions based on digit size made a big difference. This effect suggests that comparative price advertising can distort consumers' perceptions in ways that may not have been intended by the seller.

Method of payment has also been found to have an influence on the nature of the items that are purchased. An analysis of 1,000 consumer households revealed that when shoppers used credit or debit cards to pay for their purchases, their shopping baskets contained a larger proportion of impulsive and unhealthy food items than those of shoppers who paid in cash. According to the study's researchers, paying by credit card is a relatively less painful activity than cash payment, resulting in a weakening of consumers' impulse control.[47]

The ethical responsibility of the marketer is to be sensitive to these tendencies and to recognize that consumers may unintentionally be influenced by perceptual forces that lead them to make choices that are not entirely rational. To offset perceptual influences, marketers could attempt to better inform consumers about product details that are likely to be useful for decision making. Point-of-purchase displays that provide clear price comparisons can also assist the consumer in selecting those items that are likely to maximize value. As an example, the French hypermarket chain Carrefour periodically sets up a prominent display in its stores consisting of two shopping carts, each filled with the same items, the only difference being that one cart is loaded up with national brands and the other with the private label Carrefour brand. A poster mounted above each cart lists all the individual items contained in the cart, with their corresponding prices, and in front of each cart is a sign exhibiting the total price of the cart's contents and an indication of whether the items are national brands or Carrefour brands. Needless to say, the private label brands' total is significantly lower than the national brands'—a difference that is unlikely to be influenced by any particular perceptual bias.

In response to the social criticisms pertaining to high prices, some marketers point out that perceptions of unfairness are at least in part a function of consumers' lack of understanding about the complexities of price setting and the reasons why some products appear to be disproportionately marked up in relation to others.[48] For example, mark-ups for pharmaceutical and perfume products cover many costs, including research and development in efforts to discover and test new medicines and fragrances. Rising retailer mark-ups also are a function of improved services that consumers themselves increasingly demand, including greater convenience, larger stores and a greater assortment of goods, longer store opening hours, and return privileges. The intensity of competition among retailers is high in most sectors, with customers shopping around for the best price for an item, which they often now find online. Moreover, the costs of operating brick-and-mortar stores continues to rise, with many retailers going out of business as a result of exorbitant rents alone. In New York City's Manhattan borough, for example, rising rents have forced out numerous booksellers, restaurateurs, florists, and other shop owners in recent years.[49] As a result of these trends, retailer profit margins actually tend to be quite low.

In recent years, consumer-to-consumer selling has proliferated with auction sites like eBay and a multitude of classified advertising services, and this trend has added a degree of fluidity to product pricing and perceptions of worth. This process provides a means for consumers to circumvent some of the ethical concerns they have about how prices are set in conventional marketplace selling contexts. As with more traditional auction sales of high-priced art objects and antiques, prices are set for online auctions for inexpensive items by those taking part in the transaction, without the intervention of any marketing agents. Sellers may or may not set a reserve price, which denotes the minimum payment they will accept for the item, and then it is up to the bidders to determine the maximum value they are willing to pay according to their perceptions of the item's worth. Because this process, including the winning bid, is typically publicly open to the wider online community, the number of bidders and the final selling price serve as mechanisms for affecting the collective's notion of the value of the object and others like it.[50] In essence, consumer perceptions of the value of an object can be significantly influenced by the nature of the buying and selling activity they follow online. It is likely that other emerging developments, such as the greater acceptability of virtual money and the possibility for consumers to use their portable devices to buy from each other with credit cards, will also influence perceptions of product value in the future.

In the context of the product design process, another relatively recent trend with ethical implications is a phenomenon that has been labeled "design art," which refers to the tendency for a growing number of designers to produce one-off or limited batch-produced items that are sold at auction for significantly higher prices than would be the case had they been mass-produced and sold by retailers. Design art to date has largely been confined to such product categories as furniture and lighting fixtures, and the significant mark-up of price, which has an open-ended ceiling depending on what bidders are willing to pay, is attributed to the perceived status of the designer. For example, designer Zaha Hadid's uniquely shaped Aqua table, whose organic form was created using a translucent silicon gel to emulate the "dynamic gestures of liquid," was manufactured by Established & Sons in limited editions.[51] One version of the table in red was produced for an AIDS awareness campaign sponsored by Bono, thereby providing the added cachet of associating the table with the successful pop star. The table sold at auction for US$300,000, well above its functional value for ordinary consumers. According to designer Tim Parsons, this tendency among collectors to own an object that has literally been touched by its prestigious creator—which is akin in intensity to the desire among some extreme fans to possess something that has been owned or worn by idolized celebrities—is a last vestige of design's arts and crafts heritage.[52] One ethical consideration related to this tendency to possess a designer item at any price that is presumed to have received the "personal touch" of the designer, whose name appears on the product and its packaging, is apparent in Parsons' observation that the "hand of the creator" is more often than not a myth in the contemporary marketing landscape:

> With computers and rapid prototyping interjecting in the once very physical sculpting of product form, nowadays, the "hand of the creator" may touch little more than a computer mouse, yet this seems to have done nothing to diminish the perceived value of their output. The new breed of design-artists have fully embraced this new technology rather than shying away from it, using it to manufacture spectacular one-offs—a state of affairs that could hardly be further from the social project of harnessing production methods to provide quality goods for all.[53]

In certain respects, the "design art" phenomenon can be seen as a subtle form of deception in packaging—a social concern that will be addressed in more depth in the next section.

Ethical issues involving product packaging

Of the various ethical issues concerning product packaging, those pertaining to deception stand out as the most noteworthy. A substantial body of evidence points to declining levels of trust among consumers toward marketers and their practices, thus accounting for the dramatic rise in recent decades in consumers' reliance on word-of-mouth recommendations and advice about products and brands.[54] Marketers are frequently accused of engaging in a wide range of practices that mislead consumers to their detriment. "Deceit" and "deception" are elusive terms, and there is no consensus as to their meaning. According to consumer researchers Joëlle Vanhamme and Adam Lindgreen, deception occurs when people hold false beliefs or a distorted perception of something they encounter in the (marketing) environment.[55] One example involves the design of product packaging intended to imitate more popular brands or brands of higher quality, leading consumers to unintentionally select the wrong brand (see Chapter 4).

Although Vanhamme and Lindgreen's definition would likely be considered adequate from the consumer's perspective, it is important to note that people may hold false beliefs for reasons that may not be a function of intentionally misleading practices on the part of the marketer. These could include inattentiveness on the part of message recipients, a lack of shared knowledge or the experience required to correctly interpret the message, or distortions caused by the content of the marketing message itself (such as ambiguous or vague words). Regulatory bodies typically assert that deception exists if there is a misrepresentation, omission, or practice that is likely to mislead the consumer acting reasonably in the circumstances, to the consumer's detriment.[56] This definition recognizes that deceit may be actively or passively conveyed, and thus should be anticipated by ethical marketers even when there is no intent to deceive.

As a form of point-of-purchase promotional material, product packaging serves as a last means of communicating with and persuading shoppers before they make a product or brand choice. Marketers can engage in a variety of ethically questionable packaging practices so as to induce consumers to select or misuse products that will ultimately prove disappointing, unsatisfactory, or harmful (see Box 6.5). For example, package contents may be exaggerated through subtle design or misleading artwork; product size may be described in misleading terms; an oversized package may not be completely filled; and misleading labeling (e.g., "new and improved") may be used. Some products that are specifically intended for adults, such as alcoholic goods, may be packaged in such as way as to appeal to children. This was the case for the product known as Zippers, a 24-proof, fruit-flavored, gelatin product containing 12% alcoholic content. Zippers' packaging consisted of bright-colored plastic containers that closely resembled those of popular gelatin snacks for children that are often packed in their school lunches. The makers of the product became the target of concerned parents and school administrators, who complained that Zippers made it too easy for children to sneak alcohol into school. Various drug prevention coalitions have underscored these complaints by charging that Zippers was being marketed in ways that appealed to under age consumers.[57]

BOX 6.5 PACKAGING: A KEY TO OVEREATING?

As obesity rates soar worldwide and other health considerations are increasingly being taken into account by food and beverage manufacturers, marketing researchers have turned their attention to the psychology of eating behavior

(Continued)

(Continued)

and, more specifically, the packaging cues that stimulate overeating. One source of those cues is food labels, in that people will often eat more of something if the label suggests that the portion is "small." This tendency was observed in a series of studies conducted by researchers Nilufer Ayinoglu and Aradhna Krishna, in which they manipulated the size labels on food products.[58] In one of their experiments, participants were given two packages of nuts, one clearly containing more nuts than the other. For some participants, the packages bore the labels "small" and "medium" in accordance with their actual contents, whereas for others, the labels were reversed. As predicted, the mislabeling resulted in people underestimating both the content weight of the medium-sized package bearing the "small" label and the amount they consumed from the package. When people consume a large item that is labeled "small," they tend to feel less guilty about how much they have eaten—a tendency the researchers term "guiltless gluttony." Participants were not found to overestimate the actual package size or consumption when the small packages were labeled "medium."

The researchers explained that the pattern of results points to two conflicting motivational goals that are salient for consumers when making food consumption decisions: the hedonic goal of taste enjoyment (along with the urge to eat more) versus the utilitarian goal of maintaining good health (and corresponding concerns about body image and self-presentation). Consumers can reconcile these conflicting goals by responding selectively to the product information at hand in a way that minimizes their guilt while satisfying their hedonic urges. Thus, people may be automatically more willing to believe a product label that claims that a large-sized item is "small" or "medium" than a small-sized item that is mislabeled as "large" or "medium." The relevance of these tendencies should be apparent in light of the increasing portion sizes of many products now commonly available in supermarkets, cafés, snack counters, and restaurants.

Something as apparently innocuous as the choice of package colors can be seen to have ethical implications. In the case of the marketing of "light" or "low-tar" cigarettes, the tobacco companies have been criticized for their use of subtle and light colors, along with other packaging cues, which consumers tend to perceive as implying that the cigarettes inside are less harmful than conventional cigarettes (i.e., "the whiter the pack, the healthier they are"). The notion that such cigarettes are less dangerous comes from a combination of the brand names used (Misty, Kiss, etc.), the lower tar and nicotine content labels on the packs, and the light package coloring. In fact, it has been documented that the use of "low-tar," "mild," or "light" cigarettes is not any healthier than conventional cigarettes and does not reduce the risk of disease.[59] Similar issues have begun to emerge regarding alternatives to traditional tobacco products, such as electronic cigarettes (e-cigarettes). For example, stimulants known as "e-liquids," which are the key ingredients in e-cigarettes, can be toxic when ingested or absorbed through the skin. Public health officials have voiced concerns that such products pose a significant health risk to children, who are attracted by the products' bright colors and fragrant flavorings.[60]

In his creative rendering of the coming decades, James Fitchett foresees a consumer society not unlike the one depicted in the futuristic film *Minority Report* (2002), with marketers able to collect personal identity information via such technologies as retinal scanning as consumers wander through a shopping area, enabling a firm to beam individually customized holographic advertisements directly into the consumer's immediate vicinity.[61] In this imagined future, consumers pass down an aisle at their local grocery store as packages call out to them. Brands that have been previously selected ask whether the consumer was satisfied with the prior purchase and recommend the new and improved version, while competing brands suggest how they could offer greater satisfaction at a more interesting price. Parents selecting a package of breakfast cereal with high sugar content upon the urgings of their children are confronted in the store by a holographic celebrity dentist suggesting that they should also purchase some extra dental care products if they intend to include that type of food in their children's diet.

These somewhat frightening prospects, based on presumed applications of technological advances that to some extent are already being developed, raise ethical concerns linked to privacy, confidentiality, and coercion. Although technology is envisioned as central to reaching individual consumers with personalized messages, such views of the future hardly portray a marketing approach that puts the consumer first. In Fitchett's view, the technologies may change the way marketers seek to communicate, but the basic marketing principles that are being applied are familiar ones:

> The principles of sales promotion, consumer behavior, and direct marketing are consistent with those that have been applied for decades. The efficiency and effectiveness of contemporary marketing techniques may improve with future technological advances such as these, assuming that it becomes feasible to realize them, but they would only be expected to be effective so long as consumer behavior norms and communication expectations remained largely unchanged. The scenario only determines the impact of a specific technology and fails to account for other possible changes.[62]

Among the potential changes that Fitchett had in mind is the possibility that retail formats such as shopping malls and self-service hypermarkets, themselves a relatively recent historical phenomenon, might eventually be replaced by more interactive, automated purchasing methods. As another example, consider the fact that manufacturers have begun to devise new product launches in the snack and convenience market that can compensate for the deterioration of in-home family meals. So while it may be possible to envision a future in which breakfast cereal packages call out to children in the supermarket, it may well be that waning consumer demand for packaged cereals will ultimately lead to their disappearance from the market before we ever get to the point of talking packages.

The environment and sustainable marketing

Since the 1990s, momentum has been building for product designers, manufacturers, and marketers to give more serious attention to their ethical responsibilities toward the welfare of consumers and the survival of the planet.[63] This is a function of increasing awareness of the Earth's finite resources, an exponentially growing world population, and a rise in consumers' desire to be informed about the nature of products and their impact on the health of the planet and the well-being of its inhabitants. In terms of product design, the question of how to strike a balance between fashion and timelessness has become a prominent focus of debate, as designers are being pressured to respond to consumer demands for products that look good, but more importantly, are durable, long-lasting, and unlikely to become quickly obsolescent (see Chapter 3). As expressed by designer Hugh Aldersey-Williams: "A primary goal for designers now has to be to bring an object's material existence and practical utility into harmony."[64] In their 2008 book *Cradle to Cradle: Remaking the Way We Make Things*, chemist Michael Braungart and architect William McDonough argue that most products today are the result of a modern manufacturing system that is based on a one-way "cradle-to-grave" model:

> Resources are extracted, shaped into products, sold, and eventually disposed of in a "grave" of some kind, usually a landfill or incinerator. You are probably familiar with the end of this process because you, the customer, are responsible for dealing with its detritus. Think about it: you may be referred to as a consumer, but there is very little that you actually consume—some food, some liquids. Everything else is designed for you to throw away when you are finished with it. But where is "away"? Of course, "away" does not really exist. "Away" has gone away.[65]

Braungart and McDonough cite estimates that in the US more than 90% of materials used to make durable goods almost immediately become waste, with a majority of the products themselves quickly following suit, in large part because of a built-in obsolescence that requires that they be replaced after a certain period. As a radical alternative, the authors propose a "cradle-to-cradle" model, which argues for an approach to industrial manufacturing that mimics processes of nature through the use of either *technical nutrients* (non-harmful synthetic materials that have no negative effects on the natural environment and can be repeatedly reused in continuous cycles as the same product without any loss in quality) or *biological nutrients* (organic materials that can be disposed of in any natural environment after use, where they safely decompose into the soil and nurture small life forms). In Braungart and McDonough's vision of a cradle-to-cradle future, running shoes will release nutrients into the earth, garbage bags will be edible, buildings will generate oxygen like trees, appliances will be leased and returned to manufacturers, where they will be entirely recycled, and people will be encouraged to toss packaging on the ground in response to "Please litter!" signs.

With sustainability in mind, product life cycles are now the focus of research oriented toward developing means to eliminate inefficiencies and avoid harmful processes that pose dangers to the environment (see Box 6.6). In recent years, results are apparent in the development of products that are manufactured with lighter and energy-efficient substances and simpler, recyclable packaging designs that avoid the use of several layers of protective materials. Novel marketing campaigns increasingly encourage the reuse of products after their initial purpose has been fulfilled and discourage unnecessary waste and disposal. In the latter case, Coca-Cola launched a campaign in Asia to encourage reuse of its iconic plastic soda bottle, in part by distributing thousands of new caps for free that convert the bottle so that it can function as a toy water gun, pencil sharpener, soap lotion or condiment dispenser, and so on.[66] The French supermarket chain Intermarché, citing statistics revealing that more than 300 million tons of fruits and vegetables are thrown away uneaten each year, launched its "Les Fruits et Legumes Moche" ("inglorious fruits and vegetables") initiative to "rehabilitate the noncalibrated and imperfect fruits and vegetables" that are typically disposed of by growers before they ever get to the market. Intermarché offered to purchase those products from its growers and then put them on sale in the supermarkets in separate displays at a 30% price reduction. To promote this initiative, Intermarché launched a multimedia campaign poking fun at misshapen and deformed fruits and vegetables, featuring the "grotesque apple," "the ridiculous potato," and "the disfigured eggplant," and also designed and distributed in stores free soups and fruit juices made from the ugly fruits and vegetables. The program met with great success, with average sales of 1.2 tons sold per store during the first two days, a 24% increase in overall store traffic, and greater increased consumer awareness about food waste.[67]

BOX 6.6 SELF IDENTITY, PEER PRESSURE, AND ENVIRONMENTALLY FRIENDLY BEHAVIOR

Although efforts to encourage consumers to engage in environmentally friendly (or "green") behaviors have ranged from persuasive public service advertising

(Continued)

(Continued)

campaigns to the provision of monetary incentives, research reveals that individuals often engage in such behaviors even when there is nothing of value to
gain. The results of a 2010 study involving American consumers revealed that
only 10% admitted to not being green at all, whereas the other 90% claimed
to be green in their daily routine at least to some extent.[68] The largest percentage of respondents admitted to doing a few things that were green, but that
they had a long way to go (43.9%); followed by those who tried to be as green
as possible, but not 100% (37.3%), and those who were completely green in
how they lived their lives (8.8%).

More recently, the results of a series of Dutch studies found that persuasive campaigns that remind people of the environmentally friendly behaviors
they already perform can serve to motivate them to engage in additional
actions of this type.[69] This is particularly the case for persons whose self-
identity is consistent with being pro-environmental—that is, they strongly
perceive themselves as individuals who engage in green behaviors. Campaigns that remind such individuals of the environmental actions they
frequently perform can strengthen their self-identity as environmentally
friendly people, thereby increasing their likelihood of following recommended
pro-environment actions.

Social pressure also appears to play a role in consumer decisions to engage
in pro-environmental behavior. One recent investigation focused on the
factors that influence the cooperation of hotel guests in reducing the number of towels they use during their stays, which cuts costs and benefits the
environment by reducing the use of water, energy, and washing detergent.
Researcher Noah Goldstein and his colleagues manipulated the hotel room
sign that asks guests to reuse the towels in a mid-sized, mid-priced chain hotel
in the United States. For some guests, the sign in their room read that "75
percent of the guests who stayed in this room (room 313)" had reused their
towels, whereas other signs prompted guests to join their fellow "citizens"
or "men and women" by engaging in more environmentally friendly behavior.[70] The signs that cited the guests' room numbers resulted in a significantly
higher towel reuse rate (49.3%) than when a standard, more generic sign
was used (37.2%), suggesting the efficacy in persuading people with narrowly
directed appeals as opposed to more general characteristics like gender ("men
or women"). More recently, these findings were replicated in a similar research
project conducted at two hotels in Swiss and Austrian ski resorts.[71]

"Sustainability" has become something of a buzzword in recent years, yet clarity as to what the term denotes in the marketing context is often lacking,
in part due to a failure by marketers to anchor the concept to meaningful

action in the marketplace.[72] Marketing theorists Hélène de Burgh-Woodman and Dylan King have argued that confusion about the meaning of the terms "sustainability" and "sustainable consumption" can also be understood as a consequence of symbolic discourse. That is, they believe that meaning can best be derived by focusing on the existing connection between humans and nature, as opposed to the more common forward-looking approach that projects future environmental risks:

> One answer to the question what does sustainability speak to is that we, as humans, already enjoy a historically embedded relationship with nature in either its literal or metaphoric sense, which has the effect of rendering nature a passive constant—that is to say it is hard to imagine it gone. Rather than moved by the risk of future catastrophic outcomes, we suggest the greater resonance for sustainability as an idea among consumers resides in our historical and social recognition of nature as an imminent element and therefore constitutes something that is *just there*.[73]

In their view, sustainability is an idea that is embedded in the past, rather than the future, which may in part explain why it resonates symbolically with consumers without having, at least to date, much of a mainstream practical effect on production and consumption behaviors.

Despite the merits of de Burgh-Woodman and King's arguments, in the future, the reality of the planet's limited resources is likely to become more salient to consumers when they increasingly come to experience restrictions in the use of water as droughts become more frequent, purchase more "green" products as the alternatives fade from the marketplace, and so on. Whether it is too late to reverse the environmental damage remains to be seen. Businesses and consumers are increasingly modifying their behaviors to respond to growing concerns about the survival of the Earth's environment, yet they still have a long way to go. According to the results of my modest survey on millennial consumers' preferences and demands discussed in Chapter 3, "ethical (i.e., the product is associated with economic, political, or social virtues)" and "ecological/green (i.e., the product is not harmful to the environment and may in fact provide environmental benefits)" scored dead last in terms of their degree of importance and likelihood to influence a purchase decision (see Table 3.1).

Returning to the question of definition, a starting point for defining "sustainability" is the straightforward statement offered by the US Environmental Protection Agency (EPA), a federal agency that enforces regulations to protect human health and the environment based on laws passed by the US Congress:

> Sustainability is based on a simple principle: Everything that we need for our survival and well-being depends, either directly or indirectly, on our

natural environment. Sustainability creates and maintains the conditions under which humans and nature can exist in productive harmony, that permit fulfilling the social, economic and other requirements of present and future generations. Sustainability is important to making sure that we have and will continue to have, the water, materials, and resources to protect human health and our environment.[74]

Sustainability is similarly delineated in the academic literature. Economics professor Paul Ekins defined the term as "the capacity for continuance more or less indefinitely into the future,"[75] and marketing professor William Kilbourne characterized sustainability as "meeting the needs of the current generation without compromising the ability of future generations to meet their needs."[76] Together, these definitions imply that sustainability entails an obligation to future generations and distributional equity, in the sense of the sharing of well-being from one generation to the next.

Drawing on these conceptions of sustainability, *sustainable marketing* can be viewed as a systemic rethinking of conventional marketing—which encourages continuously increasing consumption leading to rising business profits—in favor of a new approach to marketing that is oriented toward the promotion of sustainable consumer behavior and the offer of suitable products that have economic, social, and environmental benefits.[77] In their textbook *Sustainable Marketing: A Global Perspective*, business professors Frank-Martin Belz and Ken Peattie elaborate on the nature of this emerging type of marketing:

> Sustainable marketing accepts the limitations of a market orientation and acknowledges the necessity of regulatory alterations to the market mechanism. Instead of avoiding regulations, sustainable marketing fosters corporate and collective commitment to necessary alterations of institutional settings and price signals in favor of sustainable development. From this perspective, sustainable marketing is a macro-marketing concept. It embraces the idea of sustainable development, which requires a change in the behaviour of virtually everyone, including both producers and consumers. In addition to the macro-marketing perspective, sustainable marketing emphasizes the triple bottom line of ecological, social and economic issues, unlike green marketing, which tends to focus on environmental problems and the reduction of the environmental burden.[78]

It should be apparent that sustainable marketing is a more encompassing endeavor than "environmental" or "green" marketing, in that it encourages a mindset that recognizes the more general responsibilities of a business beyond simply taking steps to reduce pollution or produce more energy-efficient products. In this sense, sustainable marketing is consistent with *corporate social responsibility* (CSR), a process of corporate self-regulation that involves taking responsibility for a company's actions so that they have a positive impact on consumers, the environment, employees, communities, and other stakeholders.[79] The transition to becoming a company that embraces sustainability in both philosophy and practice cannot be accomplished overnight, but requires a series of incremental steps and a long-term commitment. Marketing professors Eric Arnould and Melea Press outlined ten steps a firm can take toward achieving the goal of becoming a truly sustainable marketing organization:

1. develop a sustainability policy as a core goal;
2. build a long-term commitment to a sustainability ethic;
3. identify and support sustainability champions within the firm and across functional areas;
4. take concrete measures to educate employees about the benefits of sustainability (e.g., in driving down costs and adding value to product-service offerings) and perhaps including a personal sustainability commitment as an element of the employee performance review process;
5. initiate and sustain a dialogue with sustainability interest groups about best practices and government regulations;
6. develop an assertive sustainability action program integrated into the strategic planning process;
7. have the firm's functional areas or departments work together with leadership to develop flexible solutions for emerging sustainability challenges, and reward real engagement in the sustainability commitment to enhance creative problem solving;
8. back the sustainability commitment with financial support for research and development, marketing communications, and sales to implement sustainable action programs;
9. communicate to customers what the firm is doing about sustainability, bearing in mind consumer skepticism regarding sustainability initiatives; and
10. monitor customers' response to sustainability initiatives through an active market research program.[80]

There are a number of companies that personify the ideals and practices of sustainability marketing, including the apparel retailers Patagonia and Levi Strauss,[81] the consumer goods company Procter & Gamble,[82] the bakery-café chain Panera Bread, and, perhaps surprisingly given its sometimes contentious relationship with its employees and some consumer communities, the discount retailer Walmart.[83] Panera Bread, for example, has a long history of pursuing sustainability in its product offerings and relationships with stakeholders.[84] Originally known for its all-natural breads made from fresh dough, Panera eventually expanded its food offerings, working in collaboration with its farmers and chefs to make "food you can trust" by refusing to purchase chickens fed on a diet of antibiotics and only using meats from animals raised in reduced-stress environments. Panera's commitment to sustainability extends beyond its healthy food goals. In one ongoing initiative, the company works with the community to help feed people in need by donating all of its bakery-cafés' leftover baked goods every night at closing time to local hunger relief agencies and charities. Panera has long participated in other anti-hunger campaigns, which are detailed on the company's website.[85] Appropriately, one of the company's slogans reads: "live consciously, eat deliciously."

Designing services and experiences: The end of products?

Although the focus of this book has been placed squarely on products, it would be remiss to neglect the importance of services and the customer service experience in the lives of consumers. Granted, products and services are intricately related, in that consumers often interact with services through products, or so-called "touchpoints," but in such cases the products typically serve as a means to an end, rather than an end in and of themselves.[86] In marketing, the term *services* refers to a variety of "activities, benefits, or satisfactions that are offered for sale that are essentially intangible and do not result in the ownership of anything," with examples including banking, hotel, tax preparation, and home repairs.[87]

The intangibility of services represents a key way they differ from products. Services lack physical qualities that permit the buyer to evaluate them prior to purchase—they cannot be tasted, touched, smelled, listened to, or directly interacted with in any other way. Unlike tangible goods, which provide customers with personal access for an unlimited period, customers have access to a service for only a limited time. That is, products like cars and computers can provide functional or emotional utility for consumers as long as they continue to be owned. By contrast, services are characterized by a lack of ownership—they are ephemeral, lasting only so long as they are paid for and renewed (as in the case of an insurance policy), or experienced and enjoyed (as in the case of a holiday vacation). Services also are inseparable from their human or machine providers because they are produced and consumed simultaneously. Another key distinguishing characteristic of services is that there is a high degree of variability in their quality, which is dependent on who provides them, how, and under what circumstances. Moreover, services are perishable, in the sense that they cannot be stored for future use or sale, which poses a particular problem when their demand fluctuates.[88]

Because of their lack of tangibility, there is no vestige of services having been consumed and, for that reason, they are unlikely to be capable of conferring status on the user, at least in the same ways that physical products can. It is perhaps for this reason that materialistic consumers tend to place a greater value on materialistic possessions than on service experiences (see Chapter 1). Nonetheless, as material objects such as calculators, agendas, watches, music CDs, encyclopedias, maps, books, and the like disappear into virtual space, products are increasingly becoming embedded in services that are rented, subscribed to, or shared. As discussed earlier in this book, this is all well and good from the perspective of sustainability, storage, maintaining, and upgrading, but what are likely to be lost in the process are the physical, emotional, and psychological connections consumers form with the physical objects they own and use. As we move into the future, a key challenge for marketers and designers will be to develop means for personalizing the consumer/service connection, while acknowledging the fledgling role of "service envy," a concept suggested by Tim Parsons:

> while, if funds allow, we have the option to buy a new car every few years, alternatively, we can decide to keep it, look after it, perhaps personalise it with accessories and develop a long-term relationship with it. After a few years, the car loses the generic "enviability" of being a new car and its value becomes more personal. If a car is provided as part of a service, it is highly likely that "service envy" would be engendered by ensuring all of the cars remained new, therefore stopping the possibility of this personal connection developing. Services need to find ways of allowing people to express their values in highly personal ways, which may have less to do with conspicuous consumption and more to do with responsible and emotional desires.[89]

In virtual space, personalization has become possible with the creation of avatars and online identities, which proliferate throughout social networks as well as company websites and blogs. If customization of products is now becoming a more common, convenient reality, in the future firms will likely find ways to customize their services to fulfill the preferences, identities, and status needs of their customers. But most importantly, as Parsons suggests, service providers must find means for developing connections with their customers in their efforts to create long-lasting, mutually rewarding relationships with them.

Designing services

Given the distinguishing characteristics of services summarized above, it is understandable that service providers and designers are faced with significant challenges in their efforts to design services so that they resonate with customers. The intangibility of services adds to consumer uncertainty; as a result, businesses must be attentive to conveying proper signals (or evidence) of service quality in terms of the place of business, the employees who interact with customers, the equipment that is observable by customers, the company's communication materials, and in the setting of prices. As an example provided by marketing expert Philip Kotler and his colleagues, if a bank strives to be perceived by customers primarily as a business that provides fast and efficient service, these characteristics must become "tangibilized" through the proper utilization of various marketing tools. In designing the bank, both the interior and exterior of the physical setting should convey speed and efficiency. This could be accomplished with a streamlined architecture, well-planned internal traffic flow, and waiting lines that appear short. Employees should appear busy, well-dressed, and organized, and should be especially careful not to keep customers waiting. The equipment and office furniture should look modern, organized, and logically positioned. Communication materials—posters, brochures, customer forms, and so on—should be composed of clean and simple designs, with photos and words consistent with the efficiency image.

As banking and other services increasingly shift to the online environment, efforts to make a service appear more tangible to customers promise to become even more challenging. Careful design of the company's website should become a key focus, with attention paid to each of the following questions:

- What audience do we want to attract to our site, and what action do we want them to take when they visit?
- Is our existing website attracting the audiences we desire? Do visitors contact us for more information?
- Is our site easily navigable, with clear and obvious links, as well as search capabilities for visitors to find answers to their questions?
- Does our website have a fresh design, and is the content up to date?
- Does our website clearly indicate security certificates, awards, and special discounts for groups like seniors?
- How many people visit our site each month? Of those visitors, how many contact the firm or individual service representatives for more information?

In short, in order to facilitate a symbiotic relationship between a firm's online presence and customers, websites need to be easy to read, with information presented in a format that is concise and simple to scan; each of the firm's specialties and offers should be showcased; and attention should be paid to the overall site organization, as well as individual page layouts, so that visitors can readily search for and locate exactly what they need no matter where they are in the website.

Communicating customer experiences

Closely related to service design, creating positive customer experiences is pivotal for companies operating in any industry, as value is set in the experience of the customer rather than embedded in goods or services.[90] The role of customer experiences—the internal and subjective interpretations of any contact with a company or its offering—is likely to increase in the marketing context in coming years. New technologies that enable people to connect with each other through social media and other emerging channels provide a range of unique and promising opportunities for marketing managers, who can utilize strategies to harness customer experiences to achieve profitable commercial outcomes. However, this development also poses a challenge to firms in today's marketplace that are progressively losing control over the experiences they can provide, as customers become actively involved in co-creating the firm's value proposition and shaping other customers' expectations and experiences of it. This is another reason why firms must strive to leverage the consumer conversation by taking steps to engage in two-way communication with consumers and by providing opportunities to make the conversation actionable (see Chapter 5).

In a chapter I co-authored with Elina Jaakkola and Leena Aarikka-Stenroos, we identified several platforms for the communication and sharing of customer experiences, which differ in terms of who is sending and controlling the message, credibility of the message, and its influence on customers.[91] Some of the more common types of customer experience communication are word of mouth (online and offline), referrals and recommendations, customer references, and testimonials. Among the most effective business actions that earn a customer's favorable communication is delivering better products and services and providing a great customer experience.[92] Beyond that, careful listening on the part of the service provider is essential for appropriate steps to be taken to improve its service. Managers have access to many of the same communication networks as consumers, which allows them to gauge what consumers are saying about their experiences with the firm and their reactions to the firm's products and brands. Google and blog search engines such as Technorati,[93] Google Blog Search,[94] and BlogSearchEngine.org[95] are useful resources for monitoring and tracking online conversations, and other services, such as those offered by Quantcast,[96] provide an in-depth breakdown of the characteristics and numbers of people visiting social networking sites. Companies can then reinforce positive and supportive comments posted on social networks and online forums, and address negative ones by explaining why the customer's unsatisfactory experience may have occurred and what the company is doing to improve future service. Such openness and willingness to acknowledge customers' complaints can prove effective in building a trusting relationship with a company's stakeholders.

It is important to add that the value emerging from an experience is not only determined by the current service encounter, but is also affected by experiences prior to, and subsequent to, the service consumption. Customers instinctively compare each new experience, positive or otherwise, with previous ones, and judge it accordingly.[97] Also, past and future customer experiences are modified not only by the experiences of the individual, but also by experiences shared by others. For example, a customer on a first-time visit to Disneyland might have learned from friends that long queues and waiting times are to be expected, and being prepared diminishes the influence such an inconvenience might otherwise have on the experience.

A new logic for twenty-first-century marketing

In their ground-breaking 2004 article "Evolving to a New Dominant Logic for Marketing," marketing professors Stephen Vargo and Robert Lusch stated their case that the marketing exchange had begun to shift from a dominant logic based on "tangible resources, embedded value, and transactions" to a revised service-dominant logic (SDL) that emphasizes "intangible resources, the co-creation of value, and relationships."[98] In other words, within the marketing context, value is not conceptualized as embedded within products through design, but co-created by customers through usage. This shift in perspective, they argue, is not attributed to the evolution of marketing so much as it is the result of a more general evolution of society and technology, which together are affecting the way companies are doing business. Although I have addressed the nature of these changes throughout this book, according to Vargo and Lusch, what stands out as a central theme is the shift in the business context from manufacturing economies to service economies. In their view, *services* are defined as "the application of specialized competences (knowledge and skills) through deeds, processes, and performances for the benefit of another entity or the entity itself."[99] In this sense, services are not viewed as residuals of tangible goods, something offered to enhance a good, or synonymous with services industries such as health care, but rather as a "fundamental function of all business enterprises."[100] This conceptualization of services is consistent with services marketing expert Evert Gummesson's earlier observations:

> Customers do not buy goods or services: [T]hey buy offerings which render services which create value. . . . The traditional division between goods and services is long outdated. It is not a matter of redefining services and seeing them from a customer perspective; activities render services, things render services. The shift in focus to services is a shift from the means and the producer perspective to the utilization and the customer perspective.[101]

Thus, service is something that is always exchanged in a business relationship, in the sense of doing something that is beneficial for some entity. Goods are supportive gadgets or tools that are useful alternatives to the provision of service, the latter of which operates as the common denominator of the exchange process. Moreover, unlike a goods-dominated logic, which is based on a separation between the firm and the customer, with the latter viewed as a passive recipient who is encouraged to purchase and consume output offered by a business, service-dominated logic envisions collaborative value-creation as being at the heart of the consumer/firm relationship.[102] This collaborative, co-creation perspective is likely to be a guiding force in twenty-first-century marketing and is consistent with much of what I have written about in this book, with its emphasis on putting the consumer front and center within the marketing, product, and design processes.

Conclusion

As I was writing this chapter, I was reminded of a familiar joke: "The past, present, and future walk into a bar—it was tense." Change is typically never easy, and it is likely that an untold number of product and brand managers are facing the technological and marketplace developments that now are unraveling at lightning speed with more than a little trepidation. Yet these are exciting times for marketers, and the fundamental changes that are transpiring in the contemporary marketplace should be viewed with hope and inspiration rather than despair. Predicting what the future holds is a tricky business, something pioneering communications theorist Marshall McLuhan and designer Quentin Fiore recognized nearly half a century ago when they observed:

> When faced with a totally new situation, we tend always to attach ourselves to the objects and to the flavor of the most recent past. We look at the present through a rearview mirror. We march backwards into the future.[103]

Nonetheless, there are forward-thinking marketers, new-product developers, and designers who are marching full speed ahead into a future in which sustainability, ethicality, practicality, connectivity, interactivity, virtuality, usability, and service are likely to be prominent features.

Despite the various opportunities offered by new technologies and lifestyles, there are also prices to pay for progress, as reflected in the following comments by information technology pioneer Theodor Holm Nelson:

> On the one hand, we are getting bread and circuses, vast freebies unimaginable scant years ago—free email, phone calls and maps, acres of picture space. On the other hand, somebody or something is reading your mail, and that same somebody or something is looking for new ways to control your future. Some things are more and more fabulous, some things are more threatening and oppressive, except we don't all agree on which is which. Are Facebook and Google marvelous ways of communicating, or a threat to our privacy? Yes![104]

To date, researchers tell us that consumers are willing to forego their anonymity and endure a loss of privacy so long as they still have access to the "bread and circuses" to which Nelson refers. Whether there is a point at which that trade-off will no longer be tolerable is something that should eventually become apparent.

Business author Patrick Dixon once suggested that the word "future" can be viewed as an acronym for "Fast, Urban, Tribal, Universal, Radical, and Ethical."[105] It is likely that what lies ahead will be all these things, but beyond that, there is no certainty as to what form these elements will take in the marketplace of consumer products and product design. As I worked to complete this chapter, several new product developments were announced on technology websites, including a smartwatch that projects notifications directly onto the wearer's skin, a handheld projector that turns any flat surface into an interactive screen, a digital camera that enables users to modify the focus of photographs after they have been snapped, and an application that uses Google Glass and a brain activity monitoring device to take photos by reading the user's mind. In the few months it has taken this book to go to print, any number of other new products have likely arrived on the scene, further transforming the marketplace of things in ways that would have been unimaginable only a short time ago.

In what proved to be an interesting exercise, *The International Herald Tribune* approached some noted personalities to obtain their insights into the question, "What might lie in store over the next 125 years?"[106] Their answers revealed some interesting possibilities. For example, speculating on the future of food, chef René Redzepi imagines a "conflict between proponents of human- and robot-controlled restaurants," which began "when a chef robot won the popular television cooking competition MasterChef Worldwide. Protesters strenuously insisted that the main objective of cooking—deliciousness—had been lost and that cold mechanized precision was replacing intuition."

Automotive writer Ezra Dyer foresees a future in which:

> driving is an esoteric, archaic pursuit that enjoys popularity roughly on par with equestrianism. The pastime is . . . enjoying a renaissance among disaffected young urbanites, many of whom drive purely as an ironic commentary on driving. The rest of us are zipping around in cars that largely drive themselves. In 2137, children can get solo passenger licenses at age 6 but can't activate emergency manual control until age 12.

Architect Zaha Hadid envisions advances in design technology that:

> will have enabled architects to radically rethink form and space, using construction methods and materials that are yet to be developed—like sophisticated architectural skins that can be twisted, stretched, bent and folded in whichever way imaginable. These materials will be transparent or opaque, structurally self-supporting and will be able to take any surface quality or color one can think of . . . . With the architecture itself responding to daily usage patterns and changing environmental parameters, all buildings will contribute to a completely sustainable society—a solution to the urgent ecological challenge that is a defining question of our own era.

Imagining the future of literature, novelist Martin Amis predicts that "the publishing industry will work out an equitable modus vivendi with the digital sector, and the life of what we helplessly call 'the literary novelist' will not be much affected." Poignantly, Amis adds: "as for the far future, I have no idea—and neither does anyone else."

It is patently absurd to suggest that the changes we are currently undergoing will mark the end of tangible objects in the lives of consumers, as I suggested as a lead-in to the section earlier on services, or that their design will no longer be relevant. We will always need products to satisfy our basic needs (hunger, thirst, warmth, etc.), and it is unlikely that intangible resources will be sufficient to fulfill all of our emotional and psychological requirements and desires. As we move closer to a more fully realized integration between technology and biology, it is likely that our relationship with products will become more intimate and symbiotic. It is not so much that the future will herald the end of products, but the end of consumers regarding products as "things" to be acquired, used, and disposed of. Rather, objects are likely to be increasingly regarded as "partners" in living and being, to be interacted with, not acted upon, in the processes of consumption.

Further reading

Alvin Toffler's *Future Shock* (Bantam Books, 1970) is a prescient examination of how the present era was imagined nearly half a century ago. A much earlier book, H. G. Wells' *The World Set Free* (E. P. Dutton, 1914), represents the famous author's visionary attempt to forecast the future of the twentieth century, couched in the framework of a fictional story.

Marshall McLuhan: You Know Nothing of My Work! (Atlas & Co., 2010) is novelist Douglas Coupland's fascinating biography of the self-professed prophet of the digital age Marshall McLuhan, whose famous aphorism, "the medium is the message," still resonates with communication theorists and sociologists. McLuhan forecast the trajectory of society and communication in the wake of the emergence of electronic media.

Michael Braungart and William McDonough's best-seller *Cradle to Cradle: Remaking the Way We Make Things* (Vintage, 2009) provides a cogent and innovative set of design recommendations for environmental sustainability. The book itself literally puts into practice the principles within by having been printed on a synthetic, waterproof material, rather than standard paper produced from trees.

Highly recommended for a comprehensive overview of recent research on environmental sustainability is a 2008 special issue of the *Journal of Macromarketing*, edited by William E. Kilbourne with a series of papers pertaining to the topic of "Facing the Challenge of Sustainability in a Changing World." The journal is planning to publish a follow-up special issue on the theme "Sustainability as Megatrend" in 2016.

Notes

1   Fitchett, J. (2005). The twenty-first-century consumer society. In A. J. Kimmel (Ed.), *Marketing communication: New approaches, technologies, and styles* (pp. 42–62). Oxford, UK: Oxford University Press.
2   Fitchett, J. (2005), p. 42.
3   Arosteguy, S. (2013, June 21). 10 things I learned: *Things to Come. The Criterion Collection.* http://www.criterion.com/current/posts/2811-10-things-i-learned-things-to-come.
4   Johnson, W. (1972). Journey into science fiction. In W. Johnson (Ed.), *Focus on the science fiction film* (pp. 1–16). Englewood Cliffs, NJ: Prentice Hall.
5   Parsons, T. (2009). *Thinking: Objects—contemporary approaches to product design.* Worthing, West Sussex, UK: AVA, p. 68.
6   Kitchens of the future. (2008, February 6). *YouTube.* Available: https://www.youtube.com/watch?v=TiACOLuYlJ4.
7   The future kitchen in the 1950s. (2013, January 14). *YouTube.* Available: https://www.youtube.com/watch?v=0q5bH5hn1tg.

8 Novak, M. (2007 April 29). 1999 A.D. (1967). *Paleofuture Blog*. Available: http://www.paleofuture.com/blog/2007/4/29/1999-ad-1967.html.
9 Kurzweil, R. (2006). *The singularity is near*. New York: Penguin.
10 Person, L. (1998). Notes toward a cyberpunk manifesto. *Slashdot*. Available: http://beta.slashdot.org/story/7711.
11 Schwartz, J. (2011, December 5). Out of a writer's imagination came an interactive world. *The New York Times*. Available: http://www.nytimes.com/2011/12/06/science/out-of-neal-stephensons-imagination-came-a-new-online-world.html.
12 Stephenson, N. (1992). *Snow Crash*. New York: Bantam, p. 4.
13 Kolata, G. (2010, November 8). Glimpsing a scientific future as fields heat up. *The New York Times*. Available: http://www.nytimes.com/2010/11/09/health/09stem.html.
14 Kolata, G. (2010, November 8).
15 Lin, T. & Huang, J. (2011, December 13). Imagining 2076: Connect your brain to the Internet. *The New York Times*. Available: http://www.nytimes.com/2011/12/13/science/imagining-2076-connect-your-brain-to-the-internet.html.
16 Endy, D. (2011, December 5). Taking faster and smarter to new physical frontiers. *The New York Times*, p. D3.
17 Patterson, D. (2011, December 5). Computer scientists may have what it takes to help cure cancer. *The New York Times*, p. D11.
18 Smarr, L. (2011, December 5). An evolution toward a programmable universe. *The New York Times*. Available: http://www.nytimes.com/2011/12/06/science/larry-smarr-an-evolution-toward-a-programmable-world.html.
19 Fankhauser, D. (2012, November 21). Can't find a parking space? This app can help. *Mashable*. Available: http://mashable.com/2012/11/21/streetline-parking-innovation/.
20 Thrun, S. (2011, December 5). Leave the driving to the car, and reap benefits in safety and mobility. *The New York Times*. Available: http://www.nytimes.com/2011/12/06/science/sebastian-thrun-self-driving-cars-can-save-lives-and-parking-spaces.html.
21 http://freecarmedia.com/.
22 Schwartz, A. (2009, September 11). Sign of the times: Abandoned phone booths transformed into EV charging stations. *Fast Company*. Available: http://www.fastcompany.com/1354091/sign-times-abandoned-phone-booths-transformed-ev-charging-stations.
23 Butterman, E. (2012, January). Car designing: Past and present. *ASME* Available: https://www.asme.org/engineering-topics/articles/automotive-design/car-designing-past-and-present.
24 Car design history—a brief overview. (2014). *Diseno-Art*. Available: http://www.diseno-art.com/car_design_history.html.
25 Car design history—a brief overview. (2014).
26 Murph, D. (2009). Ultra-tough bulkypapers could build planes, trains and automobiles. *Engadget*. Available: http://www.engadget.com/2008/10/19/ultra-tough-buckypapers-could-build-planes-trains-and-automobil/.
27 Butterman, E. (2012, January). Car designing: Past and present. *ASME*. Available: https://www.asme.org/engineering-topics/articles/automotive-design/car-designing-past-and-present.
28 Rawsthorn, A. (2012, October 15). Transformation of the car light. *International Herald Tribune*, p. 13.
29 Rawsthorn, A. (2012, October 15).
30 Wortham, J. (2014, January 19). Building toward the home of tomorrow. *The New York Times*. Available: http://www.nytimes.com/2014/01/20/technology/building-toward-the-home-of-tomorrow.html.
31 Atluri, V., Rao, S., & Varanasi, S. (2014, April). New trends in smart devices. *McKinsey & Company*. Available: http://www.mckinseyonmarketingandsales.com/new-trends-in-smart-devices.
32 Wortham, J. (2014, January 19).
33 Bilton, N. (2014, June 2). Intruders for the plugged-in home, coming in through the Internet. *The New York Times*. Available: http://bits.blogs.nytimes.com/2014/06/01/dark-side-to-internet-of-things-hacked-homes-and-invasive-ads/.

34 Roberts, P. (2014, May 15). Pew: IoT will take off by 2015, despite security woes. *The Security Ledger*. Available: https://securityledger.com/2014/05/pew-iot-will-take-off-by-2025-despite-security-woes/.

35 Staff writer. (2014, August 22). Internet of Things grows on consumers. *ITWeb*. Available: http://www.itweb.co.za/?id=137092:Internet-of-things-grows-on-consumers.

36 http://www.fitbit.com.

37 https://jawbone.com.

38 Nunes, P. & Downes, L. (2014, January 10). The five most disruptive innovations at CES 2014. *Forbes*. Available: http://www.forbes.com/sites/bigbangdisruption/2014/01/10/the-five-most-disruptive-innovations-at-ces-2014/.

39 Ulanoff, L. (2014, July 16). Google inks a deal with Novartis to make smart contact lenses. *Mashable*. Available: http://mashable.com/2014/07/15/google-novartis-contact-lenses/.

40 Schmid, J. (2002, March 14). Bend me, shape me: The future of CDs. *The New York Times*. Available: http://www.nytimes.com/2002/03/14/news/14iht-disks_ed3_.html.

41 Pachal, P. (2014, July 11). LG builds flexible, transparent TV you can roll up. *Mashable*. Available: http://mashable.com/2014/07/11/lg-display-rollable-tv/.

42 Bilton, N. (2014, April 13). Bend it, charge it, dunk it: Graphene, the material of tomorrow. *The New York Times*. Available: http://bits.blogs.nytimes.com/2014/04/13/bend-it-charge-it-dunk-it-graphene-the-material-of-tomorrow/.

43 Kimmel, A. J. (2006). Marketing et éthique (Marketing and ethics). In C. Michon (Ed.), *Le Marketeur*, 2nd ed. (pp. 491–505). Paris: Pearson.

44 Handricks, I. (2014). Pricing fundamentals. *Ian Handricks*. Available: http://www.ianhandricks.com/88/pricing-fundamentals/.

45 Parsons, T. (2009).

46 Coulter, K. S. & Coulter, R. A. (2007). Distortion of price discount perceptions: The right digit effect. *Journal of Consumer Research*, *34*, 162–173.

47 Thomas, M., Desai, K. K., & Seenivasan, S. (2011). How credit card payments increase unhealthy food purchases: Visceral regulation of vices. *Journal of Consumer Research*, *38*, 126–139.

48 Kotler, P. (2003). *Marketing Management*, 11th ed. Upper Saddle River, NJ: Prentice Hall.

49 Bosman, J. (2014, March 25). Literary city, bookstore desert. *The New York Times*. Available: http://www.nytimes.com/2014/03/26/business/media/bookstores-forsake-manhattan-as-rents-surge.html.

50 Parsons, T. (2009).

51 Hadid, Z. Aqua Table for Established and Sons. *archello*. http://www.archello.com/en/product/aqua-table-established-and-sons.

52 Parsons, T. (2009).

53 Parsons, T. (2009), p. 32.

54 Kimmel, A. J. (2013). Beliefs about word of mouth among business students and practitioners. *Journal of Customer Behaviour*, *12*, 291–313. East, R., Hammond, K., Lomax, W., & Robinson, H. (2005). What is the effect of a recommendation? *The Marketing Review*, *5*, 145–157.

55 Vanhamme, J. & Lindgreen, A. (2001). Gotcha! Findings from an exploratory investigation on the dangers of using deceptive practices in the mail-order business. *Psychology & Marketing*, *18*, 785–810.

56 Klass, G. (2012). Meaning, purpose, and cause in the law of deception. *The Georgetown Law Journal*, *100*, 449–496.

57 Leinwand, D. (2002, April 29). Parents warned about 24-proof gelatin "Zippers." *USA Today*. Available: http://www.usatoday.com/news/nation/2002/04/29/2002-04-29-zippers.htm.

58 Ayinoglu, N., & Krishna, A. (2010). Guiltless gluttony: The asymmetric effect of size labels on size perceptions and consumption. *Journal of Consumer Research*, *37*, 1,095–1,112.

59 Winestock, G. (2000, October 27). Soft-selling cigarettes. *The Wall Street Journal*, pp. 23, 26.

60 Richtel, M. (2014, March 21). Selling a poison by the barrel: Liquid nicotine for e-cigarettes. *The New York Times*. Available: http://www.nytimes.com/2014/03/24/business/selling-a-poison-by-the-barrel-liquid-nicotine-for-e-cigarettes.htm.

61 Fitchett, J. (2005).

62 Fitchett, J. (2005), p. 47.

63 Kilbourne, W. E. & Beckmann, S. C. (1998). Review and critical assessment of research on marketing and the environment. *Journal of Marketing Management*, *14*, 513–532.

64 Aldersey-Williams, H. (2008). Applied curiosity. In P. Antonelli (Ed.), *Design and the elastic mind* (pp. 46–57). New York: The Museum of Modern Art.

65 Braungart, M. & McDonough, W. 2008). *Cradle to cradle: Remaking the way we make things*. London: Vintage, p. 27.

66 Beltrone, G. (2014, June 5). Coca-Cola invents 16 bottle caps to give second lives to empty bottles. *Adweek*. Available: http://www.adweek.com/adfreak/coca-cola-invents-16-crazy-caps-turn-empty-bottles-useful-objects-158136.

67 Claire D. (2014, April). Un peu d'amour pour les fruits et légumes moches, avec Intermarché. *La Réclame*. Available: http://lareclame.fr/101419-legumes-moches-intermarche.

68 MarketingCharts staff. (2010, January 21). 9 in 10 Consumers put "green" in daily routine. *MarketingCharts*. Available: http://bit.ly/7DFtFd.

69 Van der Werff, E., Steg, L., & Keizer, K. (2013). It is a moral issue: The relationship between environmental self-identity, obligation-based intrinsic motivation and pro-environmental behaviour. *Global Environmental Change*, *23*, 1,258–1,265. Reese, G., Loew, K., & Steffgen, G. (2014). A towel less: Social norms enhance pro-environmental behavior in hotels. *Journal of Social Psychology*, *154*, 97–100.

70 Goldstein, N. J., Cialdini, R. B., & Griskevicius, V. (2008). A room with a viewpoint: Using social norms to motivate environmental conservation in hotels. *Journal of Consumer Research*, *35*, 472–482.

71 Reese, G., Loew, K., & Steffgen, G. (2014).

72 De Burgh-Woodman, H. & King, D. (2013). Sustainability and the human/nature connection: A critical discourse analysis of being "symbolically" sustainable. *Consumption Markets & Culture*, *16*, 145–168. Kilbourne, W. E. (2010). Facing the challenge of sustainability in a changing world. *Journal of Macromarketing*, *30*, 109–111.

73 De Burgh-Woodman, H. & King, D. (2013), p. 146.

74 What is sustainability? | What is EPA doing? | How can I help? *United States Environmental Protection Agency*. Available: http://www.epa.gov/sustainability/basicinfo.htm.

75 Ekins, P. (2000). *Economic growth and environmental sustainability*. New York: Routledge, p. 70.

76 Kilbourne, W. E. (2008). Special issue on environmental sustainability. *Journal of Macromarketing*, *28*, 308.

77 Sheth, J. N. & Parvatiyar, A. (1995). Ecological imperatives and the role of marketing. In M. J. Polonsky & A. T. Mintu-Wimsatt (Eds.), *Environmental marketing: Strategies, practice, theory, and research* (pp. 3–20). New York: Hawarth Press.

78 Belz, F.-M. & Peattie, K. (2012). *Sustainability marketing: A global perspective*. Chichester, West Sussex, UK: John Wiley & Sons, p. 28.

79 McWilliams, A. & Siegel, D. (2001). Corporate social responsibility: A theory of the firm perspective. *Academy of Management Review*, *26*, 117–127.

80 Arnould, E. J. & Press, M. (2011). Sustainable marketing and marketing sustainability. In J. C. Hershauer, G. Basile, & S. G. McNall (Eds.), *The business of sustainability* (pp. 197–220). Santa Barbara, CA: Praeger.

81 Elks, J. (2013, October 1). Patagonia launches "responsible economy" campaign. *Sustainable Brands*. Available: http://www.sustainablebrands.com/news_and_views/communications/patagonia-launches-responsible-economy-campaign Boynton, J. (2013, January 30). How Patagonia, Levi Strauss connect with consumers through sustainability. *TriplePundit*. Available: http://www.triplepundit.com/2013/01/patagonia-levi-strauss-customer-engagemen-sustainability-initiatives/.

82 Sustainability. *P&G*. http://www.pg.com/en_US/sustainability/index.shtml.

83 Arnould, E. J. & Press, M. (2011). Sustainable marketing and marketing sustainability. In J. C. Hershauer, G. Basile, & S. G. McNall (Eds.), *The business of sustainability* (pp. 197–220). Santa Barbara, CA: ABC-CLIO.

84 Hanson, E. (2014, June 9). Panera bread makes a clean break toward sustainability. *24/7 Wall St.* Available: http://247wallst.com/general/2014/06/09/panera-bread-makes-a-clean-break-towards-sustainability/.

85 https://www.panerabread.com.

86 Parsons, T. (2009).

87 Kotler, P., Armstrong, G., Saunders, J., & Wong, V. (2002). *Principles of marketing*, 3rd European ed. London: Prentice Hall, p. 460.

88 Kotler, P., Armstrong, G., Saunders, J., & Wong, V. (2002).

89 Parsons, T. (2009), p. 141.

90 Prahalad, C. K. & Ramaswamy, V. (2004). Co-creation experiences: The next practice in value creation. *Journal of Interactive Marketing, 18*, 5–14.

91 Jaakkola, E., Aarikka-Stenroos, L. (2014). Leveraging customer experience communication. In J. Kandampully (Ed.), *Customer experience management: Enhancing experience and value through service management* (pp. 45–72). Dubuque, IA: Kendal Hunt Publishing.

92 Sernovitz, A. (2007, July 25). Dealing with negative word of mouth. *Andy Sernovitz's Damn, I Wish I'd Thought of That!* Available: http://www.damniwish.com/dealing-with-ne/.

93 www.technorati.com.

94 www.google.com/blogsearch.

95 http://www.blogsearchengine.org/.

96 www.quantcast.com.

97 Meyer, C. & Schwager, A. (2007). Understanding customer experience. *Harvard Business Review, 85*, 117–127.

98 Vargo, S. L. & Lusch, R. F. (2004). Evolving to a new dominant logic for marketing. *The Journal of Marketing, 68*, 1–17.

99 Vargo, S. L. & Lusch, R. F. (2004), p. 2.

100 Vargo, S. L. & Lusch, R. F. (2004), p. 2.

101 Gummesson, E. (1995). Relationship marketing: Its role in the service economy. In W. J. Glynn & J. G. Barnes (Eds.), *Understanding services management* (pp. 244–268). New York: John Wiley & Sons, pp. 250–251.

102 Lusch, R. F. & Vargo, S. L. (2009). Service-dominant logic—a guiding framework for inbound marketing. *Marketing Review St. Gallen, 26*, 6–10.

103 McLuhan, M. & Fiore, Q. (1967). *The medium is the massage: An inventory of effects.* New York: Random House, pp. 74–75.

104 Holm Nelson, T. (2011, December 5). Full speed ahead, without a map, into new realms of possibility. *The New York Times*. Available: http://www.nytimes.com/2011/12/06/science/theodor-holm-nelson-on-the-information-superhighway-destination-unknown.html.

105 Dixon, P. (1998). *Futurewise: The six faces of global change.* London: Profile Books.

106 The Big Question. (2012, October 3). *International Herald Tribune*. Available: http://rendezvous.blogs.nytimes.com/2012/10/03/the-big-question/.

INDEX

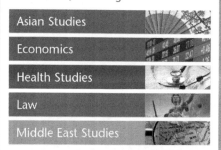

An environmentally friendly book printed and bound in England by www.printondemand-worldwide.com

PEFC Certified

This product is
from sustainably
managed forests
and controlled
sources

www.pefc.org

PEFC/16-33-415

MIX
Paper from
responsible sources
FSC® C004959

www.fsc.org

This book is made entirely of sustainable materials; FSC paper for the cover and PEFC paper for the text pages.

#0065 - 170815 - C0 - 229/152/17 [19] - CB - 9781138812246